Praise for *Tableau Certified Data Analyst Study Guide*

Packed with practical tips and advice, this guide prepares analysts for
the Tableau exam format, structure, and topics—while offering
value to any Desktop user looking to sharpen their skills.

—*Maureen Henry, Tableau Certified Data Analyst,*
Senior Business Intelligence Platform Administrator, The Ohio State University

A fantastic resource for anyone preparing for the Tableau Certified Data Analyst exam.
Chris offers a comprehensive overview of Tableau along with practical insights, all
delivered in a conversational tone that simplifies complex concepts. This guide
isn't just about passing the exam, it's about truly learning to use Tableau.

—*Kevin Riegle, Senior Director of Integrated Data Services,*
University of Michigan

Christopher has managed to capture all the essential information you'll need for the
certification in a very concise and accessible way. He has brought his real-world
knowledge to life and made it far more memorable. This book isn't just for the
certification, but for creating a strong working knowledge of Tableau.

—*Carl Allchin, Tableau Zen Master,*
Global Head Coach at The Data School UK,
and author of Data Curious, Communicating with Data, *and more*

As a server administrator, this guide helped me better understand what the user
needs, bridging the gap between technical management and user-centric data
visualization. It equips you with essential insights into Tableau's security
structures and publishing processes.

—*Brian Saltzman, Server Administrator, University of Michigan*

Full of clear and concise material on all the core concepts of Tableau, this book is great for anyone who wants to study for the exam or fill in knowledge gaps! Presented in a variety of formats, the information here will help you pass the exam and prepare you for work in Tableau.

—*Patrick Franklin, Application Programming Manager,*
Web & Application Development Services, University of Michigan

Tableau Certified Data Analyst
Study Guide

Learn the Core Concepts and Techniques
Necessary to Ace the Exam

Christopher Gardner

O'REILLY®

Tableau Certified Data Analyst Study Guide

by Christopher Gardner

Published by O'Reilly Media, Inc., 1005 Gravenstein Highway North, Sebastopol, CA 95472.

O'Reilly books may be purchased for educational, business, or sales promotional use. Online editions are also available for most titles (*https://oreilly.com*). For more information, contact our corporate/institutional sales department: 800-998-9938 or *corporate@oreilly.com*.

Acquisitions Editor: Michelle Smith	**Indexer:** Judith McConville
Development Editor: Sarah Grey	**Interior Designer:** David Futato
Production Editor: Gregory Hyman	**Cover Designer:** Karen Montgomery
Copyeditor: nSight, Inc.	**Illustrator:** Kate Dullea
Proofreader: Helena Stirling	

May 2025:   First Edition

Revision History for the First Edition

2025-05-14:   First Release

See *http://oreilly.com/catalog/errata.csp?isbn=9781098175078* for release details.

978-1-098-17507-8

[LSI]

Table of Contents

Preface

Data visualizations are all around us. They are in the news, in our classrooms, at our jobs, and part of our lives. They can be simple, like the speedometer on your car, or complex, like the analysis of voting patterns in a presidential election. Visualizations rely on our ability to group like items, follow trends, and identify outliers to deliver us information from the noise of complex data. This information is imperative for effective decision making.

Businesses rely on carefully calculated decisions to achieve success, but to get this information, they rely on analysts to gather, interpret, and visualize data. Information derived from data reveals insights on customer behaviors, periodicity, outliers, and more. The analyst must understand the nuances behind gathering, organizing, visualizing, and interpreting data. They need to understand the subject matter of their charts and apply context to the information they display. They must also present their analysis in a meaningful and understandable way to business decision makers.

Executive leadership needs information to make effective decisions to drive the direction of the business; however, the benefits of data analysis are not limited to leadership. Any area of a business benefits from analyzing data, including HR, finance, production line, purchasing and beyond. In addition, technologies such as artificial intelligence, machine learning, and natural language processing are opening new avenues for analyzing large, complex data sets. It's no wonder that a skill set in a data visualization tool like Tableau is in such high demand.

Since you're reading this book, you probably understand the benefits of visualizing data, but why is this book beneficial to you? When I first became an analyst and started my journey with Tableau, I received a very basic introductory course on how to use the software to analyze data. After that, however, my experience in Tableau was simply what I discovered on my own as I worked with the tool for my job. After using it for a couple of years, I learned about the certification process and decided this would be a great way to compare my knowledge to that of others in the industry.

In preparation for my first exam, I went online and searched for example questions, study guides, and other resources. To my dismay, I found nothing specifically oriented toward studying for the exam. I did find some information on what to study, along with some sample questions on the Tableau site, but I knew that these few questions were not representative of the overall exam. I ended up paying for a study course with a sample exam at the end, which I passed with reasonable ease. I took my first exam and passed with a 93%.

From that point on, every two years, I prepared to refresh my certification. At the same time, I renewed my search for study guides and sample exam questions online. Each time I looked, the results were the same: I could find a few sample exam questions and some video training, but nothing that truly served as an effective study guide. Most of the sample questions I *did* find were littered with trick questions or not realistically something you would find on the exam. Without any reliable resource to study from, I simply had to rely on my own knowledge to review and prepare for the exam.

That's where I hope this book comes in for you. My goal is to provide you with a guide to review and study from as you prepare for your Tableau Certified Data Analyst exam. My goal is not to dive into the deep details and explain everything to you; rather, I want to give you a quick synopsis of what you need to remember before you take the exam. More importantly, I want to provide you with *example questions*! I've scattered example questions throughout the book and provided a complete example exam at the end. You can use these to test your knowledge, identify weaknesses to study, and give you confidence when taking the exam.

Why Tableau?

Data visualization provides a powerful way to dig into data, and Tableau is one of the leading software titles in the field. Tableau Desktop can measure and segment data in a variety of visual formats, allowing you to see patterns and outliers quickly. It hosts powerful tools that allow you to filter, sort, and organize data easily. It also provides a variety of data source connection types, both stored locally and hosted online. This means that you can combine data between multiple systems that otherwise would not talk to each other, further enhancing your analytic opportunities.

In addition, Tableau Prep Builder was developed to supplement the Tableau visualization tool. This data preparation tool further simplifies the data pulling process via an interactive visual interface. It lets you easily clean, aggregate, and combine data sources; preview the data; and identify data mismatches, typos, and other common data errors. Used together, Tableau Prep Builder and Tableau Desktop allow you to investigate and understand complex data sets and relationships.

Certification

Tableau offers five different certifications, which are listed in Table P-1.

Table P-1. Available Tableau certifications for Tableau Desktop and Tableau Server as of early 2025.

Tableau Desktop and Tableau Prep Builder	Tableau Server and Tableau Cloud
Tableau Desktop Specialist	Tableau Server Associate
Tableau Data Analyst	Tableau Architect
Tableau Consultant	

This guide book is focused on certifications related to Tableau Desktop and Tableau Prep Builder. While it includes questions related to publishing and securing content on Tableau Server and Tableau Cloud, it will not contain questions about building or maintaining that server. It focuses specifically on the Tableau Data Analyst certification exam, but contains material relevant to many of the other exams. The list in Table P-2 breaks down what each of the three non-server-focused exams cover, how each exam is structured, how long it takes to complete, and how much it costs in comparison to the others, in order of increasing difficulty.

Table P-2. Comparison of Tableau certification exams.

Exam	Designed for	Structure	Focus	Length	Notes
Tableau Desktop Specialist	Tableau beginners	45 multiple-choice questions with options for selecting one or more answers	Building basic visualizations and utilizing the Tableau Desktop interface	60 minutes	Less expensive and shorter than the other Tableau Desktop exams
Tableau Data Analyst	More advanced Tableau users	40 multiple-choice and multiple-selection questions	Beyond the basics of Tableau Desktop; includes data transformations, Tableau Prep Builder, and sharing and securing your workbook	120 minutes	The primary focus of this book; more expensive than the Tableau Desktop Specialist exam
Tableau Consultant	Professional-level Tableau users	40 multiple-choice and multiple-selection questions	All of the above, plus analyzing a client, determining reporting gaps, and integrating Tableau into existing reporting structures; questions from a consulting perspective cover cloud migrations, requirements gathering, data storage, and data transformation	120 minutes	Same price as Tableau Data Analyst

Here are some specifics:

Tableau Desktop Specialist
> This exam is designed for individuals who are just starting out in Tableau. It is less expensive and shorter than the other Tableau Desktop exams, but focused on building basic visualizations and utilizing the Tableau Desktop interface. It consists of 45 multiple-choice questions with options for selecting one or more answers over the course of 60 minutes.

Tableau Data Analyst
> This exam is the primary focus of this book. The analyst exam goes beyond the basics of Tableau Desktop, pulling in questions about data transformations, Tableau Prep Builder, and sharing and securing your workbook. It is more expensive than the Tableau Desktop Specialist exam and provides you with an additional hour, for a total of 120 minutes. It has 40 multiple-choice questions. See the "Exam Structure" section for more information on the question types.

Tableau Consultant
> This exam has the same in structure and price as the Data Analyst Exam, but goes beyond data preparation and data visualization. The multiple-choice and multiple-selection questions focus instead on analyzing a client, determining reporting gaps, and integrating Tableau into existing reporting structures. The exam also poses questions from a consulting perspective related to cloud migrations, requirements gathering, data storage, and data transformation.

As this guide is designed with the Tableau Data Analyst exam in mind, the content within will be focused on pulling data, transforming it, analyzing it, and utilizing Tableau Server or Tableau Cloud to share it with others. That being said, the content in this guide will also prove useful if you are preparing for the Desktop Specialist or Consultant role, but may fall short of covering the detailed aspects of data analytic consulting.

Exam Structure

As of October 2024, the exam consists entirely of multiple-choice and multiple-selection questions. This new format removes the performance aspect of the exam to focus entirely on your knowledge of the tool. The questions are designed to test your skill in bringing in, transforming, and analyzing data using Tableau or Tableau Prep Builder. There are also questions about dashboard design and server security.

The exam consists of 40 questions and may contain several question formats:

Single-select multiple-choice
> You are asked about something and provided with four to five possible answers, only one of which is correct.

Multi-select multiple-choice
> This type of question asks you to identify multiple correct answers and typically tells you how many you need to select.

Sorting
> This question provides a list of correct answers and prompts you to arrange them in the correct order. An example of this would be sorting a series of filter types by the order in which they are applied.

Fill in the blank
> This question gives you an incomplete form and asks you to place the appropriate fields into the blank sections. Most often, this type of question is related to structuring calculations correctly.

The exam has options to mark questions if you wish to revisit them before submission. Throughout the exam, there are also spaces where you can leave feedback if you feel a question is ambiguous or impossible to answer. These comment sections are reviewed at the end of exams, but usually do not affect the final score.

Exam Format

Tableau is very focused on ensuring that exams are completed fairly. There are three primary ways you can take a Tableau certification exam: online with a proctor, at a certified testing center, or as part of your Tableau Conference experience. Which one you choose will determine what your exam experience will be like. All exams include options for those with disabilities. If you have a disability that requires you to take additional time for the exam, be sure to inquire ahead of time.

Taking an Exam at Tableau Conference

If you plan to dive into Tableau fully, then you will probably want to attend the annual Tableau Conference. This multiday event is great for learning, socializing, and honing your skills. It's also a great place to register for and take your certification exam. Blocks of conference time are available specifically for taking the exam. You register for the exam and simply work it into your conference schedule.

When the time comes, you arrive at the designated location and provide your credentials to enter the exam room. Inside, you and many other test takers will be seated at a personal laptop station to take the exam. Tableau takes steps to ensure these crowded test rooms are protected from cheating. The room is usually mixed with individuals taking any of the listed certification exams. Additionally, your questions can differ in content and sequence from those given to the other users around you. This means that even if your neighbor is taking the same exam as you, their questions may be in a different order or come from a different question set altogether!

During the exam, you'll be provided with a pencil and a piece of paper to make notes. Proctors patrol the room and are available to answer questions related to taking the exam, but not questions related to the topics within. Once you complete the exam, you simply close out of the session and quietly exit the room.

Taking an Exam at a Certified Testing Center

Tableau works collaboratively with Pearson VUE to administer certification exams, and they provide a collection of testing centers. A full list of testing centers is available on the Pearson VUE website (*https://oreil.ly/XoB7S*). The experience is similar to taking an exam at Tableau Conference. On the day of the exam, you will need to arrive at your scheduled time and provide an ID. A computer is provided and steps are taken to avoid cheating.

Taking the Exam Online

Not all of us can afford to attend Tableau Conference; fortunately, online exam sessions are also available. The cost to take an online exam is the same as taking it at Tableau Conference or through a testing center. If you choose to take your exam online, you will need a device with a functioning webcam and microphone. You will also need to clear your workspace of any communication devices, reference materials, and anything else that is not necessary to the exam. There is also a series of pre-exam checks that you will be asked to perform prior to your exam.

During the exam, a proctor will connect with you using a virtual meeting to ensure that you take the exam fairly and without assistance. To start, the proctor will ask that you take your camera and pan around the room. They want to ensure that you have no reference materials available to you nearby or on the desk, that you are not recording or communicating with others via electronics, and that no one else is in the room with you.

They will also connect remotely to your computer to ensure that there is nothing open on your machine that may assist you with taking the exam. You will be asked to close any open applications, browser windows, and other potential sources of information (the only exceptions that may be allowed are special provisions for those with adaptive hearing or visual needs). Last, the proctor will provide you instructions to follow during the test, such as refraining from talking.

While the exam is taking place, the proctor is available for assistance with taking the exam, but not with the question content. They will be connected during the *entire* exam. This ensures that the exam was completed fairly without assistance. If for some reason the exam disconnects during the process, instructions will be provided on how to reconnect. In some cases, a disconnect may invalidate your results. This is a good reason to ensure that wherever you take the exam, your internet connection is solid.

Getting Your Results

Once your exam is complete, the next step is to wait. Typically, the results are available within a few hours. Sometimes it may take longer, depending on the volume of exams and if the results are on the border of passing. The results, sent via email, show if you passed or failed. If you pass, congratulations! You can now proudly share your new title! If you fail, you will need to wait some time before signing up to take the exam again. The time between exams increases with each failure.

Tableau will send a follow-up email shortly after providing your pass/fail results. This email gives you instructions on how to connect to the testing service to get your actual percentage score. If you pass, it will also tell you how to share a digital badge of your accomplishment, add you to a talent directory, and grant you access to exclusive merchandise in the online store. These tools are all available to make yourself known in the community, connect with other Tableau users, and share your certification with potential employers looking for your skills.

What Is Covered

Now that you understand what the exam session will be like, let's get into the important part. What do you need to study to ensure you receive a passing grade? Tableau provides some basic information about the subject areas on the exam (*https://oreil.ly/ OsIgf*). The content is split into four key domains. A full breakdown of the subject areas and their relative portion of the exam is available in Figure P-1.

The first domain is connecting to and transforming data. This comprises approximately 24% of the exam subject matter. In these questions, you will be prompted to demonstrate your knowledge of choosing, connecting to, cleaning, and combining data sources. For this reason, many of these questions relate to using the features of Tableau Prep Builder and the Tableau Desktop data connection window. These subjects will be covered in more detail with example questions in Chapter 1.

The second domain is exploring and analyzing data. This is the meat of Tableau's functionality, accounting for 41% of the questions. These questions test your understanding of calculated fields, table calculations, dates, filters, structuring data, interactivity, and utilizing the built-in Tableau Analytics pane. This domain also forms a large portion of this book and is covered in detail in Chapters 2 through 4.

Question Topic (Approximate)

24%
Connecting to and Transforming Data

41%
Explore & Analyze Data

26%
Create Content

9%
Publish & Manage
Content

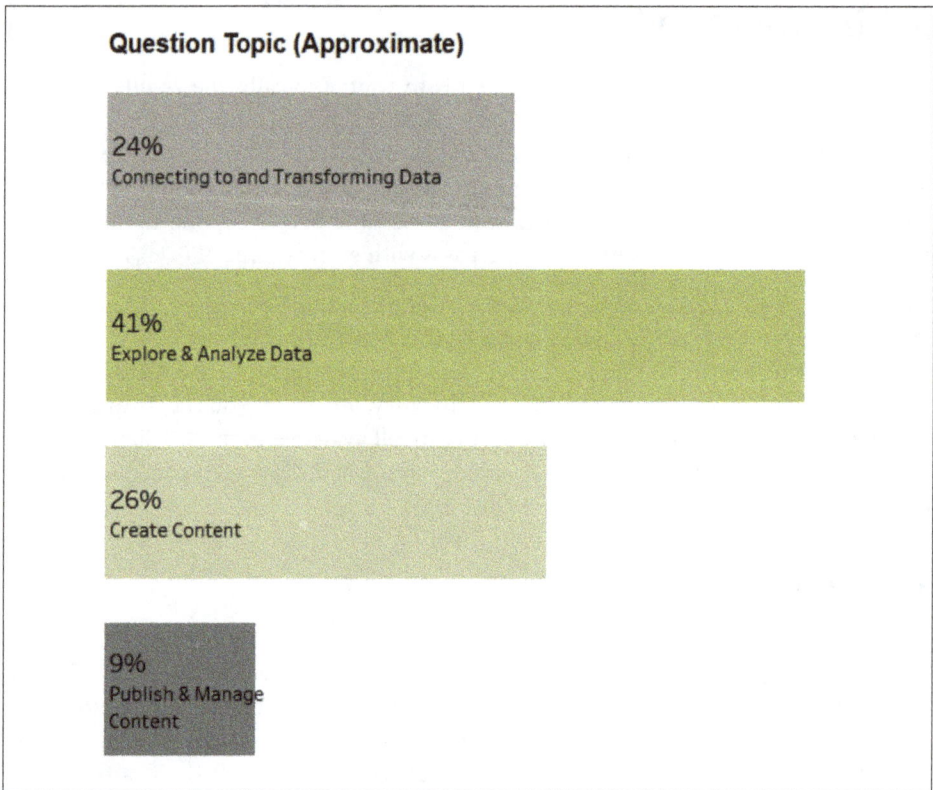

Figure P-1. The Tableau exam covers four subject areas, with a focus on exploring and analyzing data.

The third domain, which overlaps with the topics in the second domain, is creating content. While smaller than the analytics portion, this section is still substantial, containing 26% of the exam questions. In these questions, you will demonstrate building charts from the available chart types. You will be tested on utilizing chart features such as reference lines, mark labels, dual axis, sorting, and formatting. You will also be asked to demonstrate knowledge of basic dashboard construction. These topics are covered in Chapters 4 and 5 of this book.

The final domain is relatively small, at only 9% of the questions; however, it is still extremely important. It covers what happens once the data visualizations and dashboards are created. How do you publish to a Tableau server or Tableau Cloud? How do you ensure that the workbooks are secure and are refreshing regularly? These topics and a few additional items are covered in Chapter 6.

Studying for the Exam

To help you study for the exam, I've placed multiple example questions throughout the chapters and at the end of each chapter, as well as a full exam's worth of questions at the end of the book. If you can answer the questions without referencing this book or reviewing online, then you are probably going to do well on the exam. If you can't answer the questions on a topic without assistance, you should review that topic further.

The best way to prepare for the exam outside this book is simply to work in both Tableau Prep Builder and Tableau Desktop. Connect to a range of different data sources or use the provided sample data sources to manipulate data, experiment with identifying trends, isolate outliers, and just explore. As you encounter visualizations in the real world, think about how you might recreate them in Tableau. Try exploring new ways to visualize data and experiment with new chart types and features, such as reference lines, box plots, and more.

To facilitate your studying, explore the O'Reilly Learning Platform. It provides a wide variety of online recorded training courses, books, and helpful articles designed to help you broaden your experience in Tableau. These offerings may cover things you already know, but also tips and techniques that you might not have been aware of. Some also give examples that you can test your knowledge against in preparation for the exam.

Finally, the exam can be intimidating, so take a deep breath and relax. As you work through the sample questions in this book, imagine yourself taking the exam. Work through the problems by identifying a correct answer and then verifying that the remaining answers are incorrect. Sometimes you will find what you think is the best answer, only to find an even better option in the list!

Final Thoughts

This book is a resource for you to review from and a rough estimate of what to expect, *not* a perfect recreation of the exam. It provides a *very* high-level description of the topics that may appear on the exam. Use it to help you identify strong and weak points in your knowledge. As you try the sample exam, make note of any challenging questions, so that you can review the topic in more detail later. Use the book as a tool to refresh your knowledge, but also feel free to utilize other resources to supplement your understanding.

Visually analyzing data is an extremely valuable skill, and I encourage you to keep working with Tableau. This exam is simply a way to validate your experience and skill with the software. Keep that in mind when you take the exam. Remember that 75% is a passing score; be confident in your skills. Don't let tricky questions discourage you! Do your best to answer them and move on to questions you can answer more confidently. With this mindset and the tools provided in this book, I am confident that you will do well on your exam.

Conventions Used in This Book

The following typographical conventions are used in this book:

Italic
> Indicates new terms, URLs, email addresses, filenames, and file extensions.

`Constant width`
> Used for program listings, as well as within paragraphs to refer to program elements such as variable or function names, databases, data types, environment variables, statements, and keywords.

> This element signifies a general note.

O'Reilly Online Learning

For more than 40 years, O'Reilly Media has provided technology and business training, knowledge, and insight to help companies succeed.

Our unique network of experts and innovators share their knowledge and expertise through books, articles, and our online learning platform. O'Reilly's online learning platform gives you on-demand access to live training courses, in-depth learning paths, interactive coding environments, and a vast collection of text and video from O'Reilly and 200+ other publishers. For more information, visit *https://oreilly.com*.

How to Contact Us

Please address comments and questions concerning this book to the publisher:

O'Reilly Media, Inc.
1005 Gravenstein Highway North
Sebastopol, CA 95472
800-889-8969 (in the United States or Canada)
707-827-7019 (international or local)
707-829-0104 (fax)
support@oreilly.com
https://www.oreilly.com/about/contact.html

We have a web page for this book, where we list errata, examples, and any additional information. You can access this page at *https://oreil.ly/tcda-study-guide*.

For news and information about our books and courses, visit *https://oreilly.com*.

Find us on LinkedIn: *https://linkedin.com/company/oreilly-media*

Watch us on YouTube: *https://youtube.com/oreillymedia*

Acknowledgments

You need to make sacrifices to write a book. It takes way more time and effort than you can possibly imagine. It takes weekends in front of your computer, missed social events, and occasional time off from work. I did not realize the sacrifices that this book would require when I started it, and so I want to thank some people who made these sacrifices with me.

First, I would like to thank my family for the love and support they provided as I toiled away at my computer instead of spending time with them. I love you both, Heather and Ian. Next, I want to thank my coworkers, who provided me encouragement and dealt with my additional stress. Patrick Franklin, Matthew Pickus, Leticia Valdez, Mandie Chapman, Brian Saltzman, and Lisa Johnston—your friendship, encouragement, and words of support were always appreciated. I'd like to thank the O'Reilly team that enabled me to write this book. Special thanks to Sarah Grey, Michelle Smith, Greg Hyman, and the host of other editors, illustrators, and more that worked together to make this book a reality. Finally, I'd like to thank my technical reviewers—Matthew Pickus, Kevin Riegle, and Karl Allchin—who dug through my writing to uncover the typos, inaccuracies, and details I missed throughout the book.

There are a host of other people who also deserve recognition for supporting me both at work and at home as I gained and continued to improve my expertise using Tableau. To all of you who made this book possible, thank you for all of your love and support.

CHAPTER 1

Connect to and Transform Data

I've worked in Tableau for over 10 years. During that time, I've come to realize that a majority of my work isn't in building charts, designing dashboards, or analyzing data—it's in connecting to, cleaning, and structuring the data before I even get started. I now understand that building meaningful visualizations depends on well-structured and properly combined data sets. Most errors I find during my analysis appear due to mistakes that happened during the original data pull. Getting the data into Tableau correctly and efficiently is absolutely essential to generating accurate, responsive, and actionable insights.

Tableau Desktop and Tableau Prep Builder (or Tableau Prep) work directly with data from a variety of sources. They can connect locally to file types such as Excel, comma-separated values (CSV), or JSON, or to hosted database tables such as those in Oracle, Microsoft SQL, or Postgres. With such a large variety of data source options, Tableau wants to ensure that its users understand what makes a good data table and what does not. More importantly, they want to ensure that users connecting to data sources know what to do to make poor-quality data sources accessible and usable within Tableau. For this reason, around 24% of the exam questions focus on connecting to and manipulating data.

In this chapter, I will dig into the steps of data preparation. I want to provide you with an understanding of how to pull data from multiple sources, combine them together, and manipulate them to answer your organization's questions. My hope is that the topics I cover combined with the example questions throughout will give you a foundation of knowledge for you to utilize when you tackle the Tableau Data Analyst Exam.

Choosing a Data Source

Before your data even enters a Tableau application, it needs to be structured in a way that facilitates reporting. The exam contains very few, if any, questions about specific data connections or data structuring; however, you should understand these topics when developing in Tableau.

When deciding on what data to use in your workbook, you should ask some basic questions about your data and your workbook. These questions will help you determine what steps you should take prior to building a visualization. They will also lead to some of the data preparation and joining questions that compose a large portion of the exam:

- What data do you need to answer the questions being posed to your dashboard and visualizations? Your work will be useless if the data you pull is unable to answer your customer's questions.

- Will your data be coming from the same source or will it be from separate data types and connections? This will determine if you are connecting to one data type or multiple and will impact how you connect the data together.

- Is the data clean or are there errors that could potentially impact your results? If your data has typos, split fields, separated dates, or other potential issues, you may need to run your data through a data flow to clean and prepare it.

- What data is valuable and what can be filtered? Pulling all the data from a table may seem like the best way to ensure you have all the information; however, the more data you pull, the slower your workbook or extracts may run.

- Is the data structured correctly? To extract information from the data, it needs to be structured correctly with dimensions and measures distributed accordingly and at the right granularity.

> Exploring data is a huge part of an analyst's job, so there will be questions on the exam relating to how to connect to data, how to join data together, and how to clean data. How you choose to do these steps will depend on if you are using Tableau Prep Builder, Tableau Desktop, or external methods to do so. There are benefits and drawbacks to each, and you will need to know what options are available within each method.

Connecting to Data

Tableau can connect to local files such as Excel or delimited files or to relational databases such as Oracle or Microsoft SQL. You can use Tableau Prep Builder to connect and join these data sources or pull them directly into Tableau Desktop. Let's dig deeper into each connection type to examine the available functionalities.

Local Files

Local files can be anything stored locally on your computer or hosted on a network storage space. These files can be simple, like a CSV, or more complex, like an Access database. The functionality for these files varies depending on what you are connecting to and which tool you are using to do so (Tableau Desktop or Tableau Prep Builder). Understanding what is possible with each data type is not as important as understanding some of the capabilities built into Tableau for working with these files.

The first such tool is the Data Interpreter built into Tableau Desktop and Tableau Prep, which works with Excel, CSV, PDF, and Google Sheets data sources. The Data Interpreter is designed to take data designed for nonreporting purposes and translate it to something more appropriately organized for Tableau. It examines the data source and makes educated guesses on what is likely a column header, what is likely a value, what is contained in merged cells, and what may need to be excluded. It does its best to clean up your tables and present the data in a structured format that can be used in Tableau. Once the process is complete, Tableau provides you with an option to review the results. Doing so will provide you with information on what changed to make the data file more usable in Tableau.

The second tool also works with the same data types. This is the Pivot feature. *Pivots* convert data in a crosstab format into a columnar format, as seen in Figure 1-1. Pulling in your measures and their names as fields allows you to manipulate them with filters and calculations, unlike the existing Measure Names and Measure Values fields in Tableau. A question about which manipulation to perform will likely appear in the exam. Tableau Desktop allows you to complete one pivot on your data, while Tableau Prep provides options for multiple pivots.

Dimension	A	B	C	D		Dimension	Letter	Value
Red	4	6	2	1		Red	A	4
Blue	7	5	4	3		Red	B	6
Yellow	9	2	8	7		Red	C	2
Green	3	9	4	8		Red	D	1
Orange	8	6	7	5		Blue	A	7
Purple	3	0	9	2		Blue	B	5
White	2	2	1	2		...	...	...

Figure 1-1. Pivoting data into a more usable format.

Relational Databases

Unlike local files, *relational databases* are hosted structures of tables that can be pulled from a hosted server. There are many types of relational database connections built into Tableau and Tableau Prep Builder for pulling this type of data. While the exam won't dive deeply into any specific database type, it will prompt you with some basic questions about how to pull data from these types of connections.

The main feature of most relational databases is the ability to code SQL to query the data held within them in Tableau Desktop. Using SQL enables you to manipulate and refine the data before it is pulled into Tableau. The Tableau SQL editor is located in the Data connection pane below the listed schema and tables, as seen in Figure 1-2. Custom SQL can be used to pivot data, change a data type, or simply limit the amount of rows pulled from the table. There is also a feature to utilize an existing parameter to modify your SQL query. There are no questions about how to write specific SQL code in the exam, but there may be questions about when to use and what it might be used for.

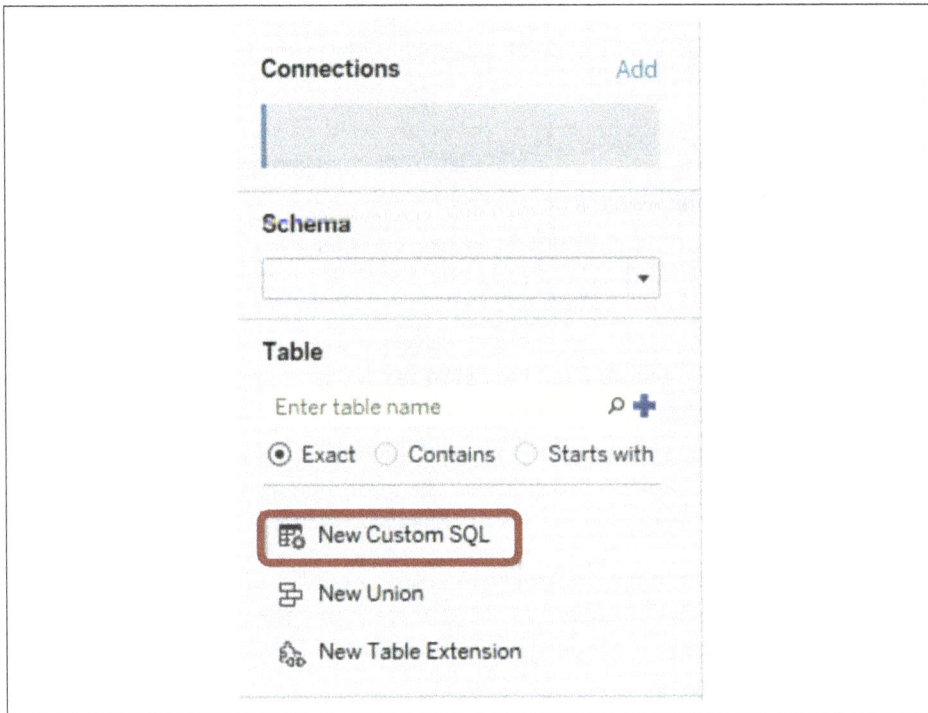

Figure 1-2. Location of the New Custom SQL tool in Tableau Desktop. This can be dragged to the data area (marked "Drag tables here") to bring up a custom SQL window where code can be applied to the data pull.

Published Data Sources

The Tableau exam doesn't always ask about published data sources, but it is a potential topic. For this reason, we should dive in and take a look at what published data sources can and cannot do.

To start with, let's look at what published data sources can do. A *published data source* is any type of data connection in Tableau Desktop or Tableau Prep Builder published to Tableau Server or Tableau Cloud. The main difference between it and a regular data source is that it is published up to the Server or Cloud rather than being embedded with the corresponding data visualization workbook. This published format makes the data available to other users with access to it on the server.

Publishing data to Tableau Server or Cloud provides some key benefits:

- First, published data sources allow analysts with expertise in the business area to generate an easier-to-use version of the data with all the necessary joins, relationships, filters, and calculations already built in. Other users within the organization can then use this streamlined data source to build their own visualizations without needing to understand the underlying data structures.

- Maintenance tasks become much easier with published data sources. Changes in business processes that impact the data only need to be updated in one place. Once the published data source is updated, the workbook views relying on that data will update to include the new information.

- Aggregated data can be published and made available to those without the credentials needed to access the primary data source. This means that aggregated data can be used to derive insights without the need to grant access and train multiple users on how to pull the data directly. Additionally, aggregation can be used to keep information at a lower granular level, meaning that users can see broad information rather than the potentially more secure details.

- Instead of multiple data connections reaching out to an external data source to refresh, only one connection is needed. The published data source does the connection and refreshes the data instead of the individual workbooks.

Unfortunately, there are some drawbacks to utilizing published data sources, and the Tableau exam may contain a question about these limitations. For this reason, let's look at what obstacles a published data source may create:

- You cannot join or create a relationship on a published data source in Tableau Desktop.[1] Tableau Prep does allow physical relationships such as joins and unions with published data sources. Blends are the only way to combine published data sources to other data sources in Tableau Desktop. Otherwise, published data sources are restricted to what was included in the original data pull.

- Everything is taken from a data source when it is published, including calculations and parameters. While some calculations may be helpful, they cannot be edited. Only the resulting field is visible to the end user, and adjusting the calculation requires duplicating the field and modifying the duplicate.

- Modifications on a data source can negatively impact the connected workbooks if the change is not communicated clearly and thoroughly to the workbook owners. For example, if a dashboard connected to the data source relies on one of the fields in a visualization, and that field is removed, the visualization may no longer render.

I've covered the different types of connections to data available in Tableau Desktop and Tableau Prep Builder. Once you have connected to data, your next important step is to decide if your connection should be live or extracted.

---

1 At Tableau Conference 2024, it was announced that improvements are being made to remove these restrictions.

Live Versus Extracted Data

Once you've connected to data, you need to decide how often to refresh. This decision comes with multiple factors to consider, such as how often the source data updates and the volume of data being pulled. These details will lead you to decide on whether your dashboard will have live data or a regularly updated extract. The certification exam is going to test you in some way about live versus extracted data. It will typically question your knowledge of which to choose as well as what options are available within each.

Live Data

Live data is exactly what it sounds like: the data is pulled directly from the source on demand, meaning there are few options available. The main consideration is whether or not to embed credentials into the connection to provide an additional layer of security. That is, does the user need access and credentials to the data source to view the information in your workbook, or will you embed your own and let them just utilize the workbook?

Alternatively, you can embed a service account's credentials. Service accounts are generic accounts with access to a data set not tied to a specific user. They provide the benefit of not storing personal credentials on Tableau Server or Cloud. They also are generic, so if the workbook author ever leaves the organization, the service account remains active and enables the data connection to keep functioning.

There are some drawbacks to using live data. Live connections reach out to the data source to pull down data with every action you make as you build the visualizations. So, as you add a field to a column or row, add a filter, add a color, or make any other change to a visualization, Tableau Desktop is querying the data source and repulling the data down before generating the visualization. For smaller data sets with fast connections, live connections are no big deal; however, larger data sets and network latency will generate delays pulling down the data while you build visualizations. The larger the data set or latency, the longer this delay could be. So, for many of your data sets, you will probably rely on *extracts*.

Extract Data Features and Options

The alternative to live data sources is *extracts*. Extracts pull data from the source at scheduled intervals. They also provide benefits such as improved performance and additional calculation functionality. These can be beneficial to developers and improve the visualization-building experience as well. Before we get into the benefits, though, let's review what an extract is and how to configure it.

Extracts are copies of the data stored locally on the machine. The Tableau Desktop application queries the data source and grabs the data you identified. It then translates the data into a format that is faster for Tableau to employ and stores it in your Tableau Repository. This can eliminate any potential delays with pulling data over the network and allows you to build visualizations more quickly. One of the biggest benefits of generating an extract is that once it is created, you no longer need to be online to continue building visualizations with the data. When you generate an extract, you are provided a window with several options, as shown in Figure 1-3.

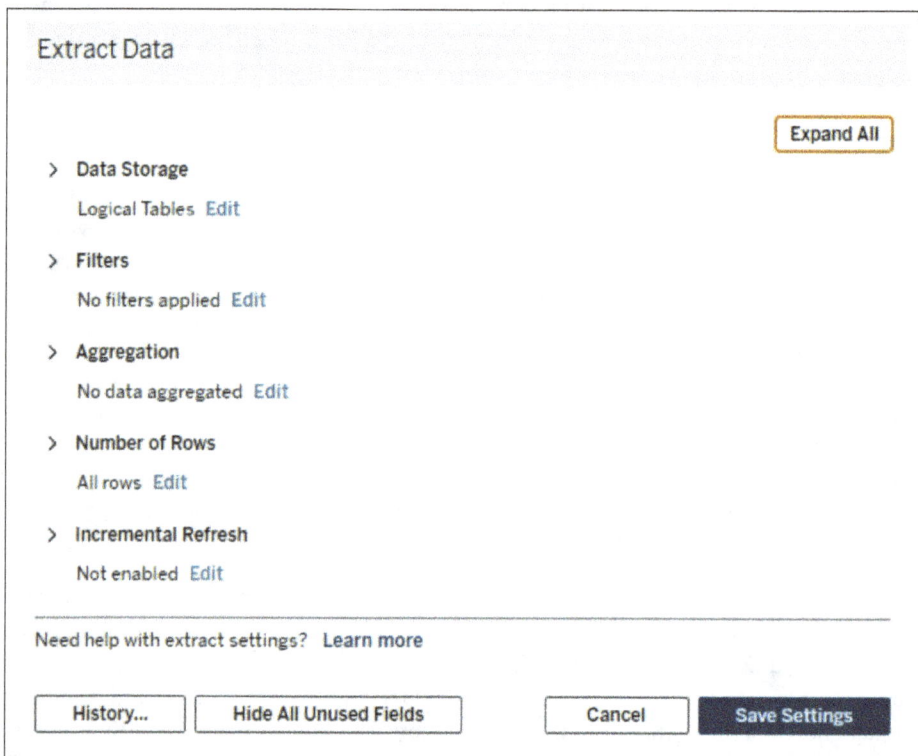

Figure 1-3. *The extract window offered by Tableau Desktop when generating an extract of your data. Tableau changed the appearance of this window in a 2024 release, and the latest version is provided for reference. Several options in this window are potential candidates for questions in the exam.*

First, you have the option to save the extract as logical tables or physical tables. *Physical tables* store the data in its original table structure as the most granular row level. Tableau recommends physical table extractions when joining tables as they can potentially improve performance and reduce the size of the extract. Conversely, *logical table extracts* complete any joins you have in the physical layer and combine the result into one large table. This allows you to perform logic-based actions on the data as well, such as including aggregation, adding filters, and hiding unnecessary fields.

Next, you can apply extract filters to the data. This is the highest level of filters in Tableau's filter hierarchy, and something we will cover in more detail in the section on manipulating data when we discuss order of operations. Extract filters remove rows of data *prior* to the data being added to the extract. The result is that filtering data will generate smaller extracts and reduce the number of rows pulled into the workbook.

The Aggregation option is another way to simplify extracts. Aggregation will roll up the data to the field level you indicate. For example, if you are pulling sales data for the stores in your business, but you will be reporting the results state by state, then you can use this option to aggregate the individual store sales to the level of states. This can significantly reduce the size of your data pull and improve performance once the data is in Tableau.

The "Number of Rows" pulled has multiple choices, but the thing to remember is that this happens *after* the data is filtered and aggregated. So, once you limit the data pulled with filters and aggregation, you can tell Tableau to pull all of the resulting rows, the top number of rows based on a field, a sample selection of *N* rows from the data set, or only the rows that have updated. You must pull all rows to use an incremental refresh, and you need to use a field to identify new rows.

The final options on the extract window are History and Hide All Unused Fields. History shows a history of when the data was extracted. This can be helpful when working in Tableau Desktop, as you can quickly identify how fresh the extracted data is and if you might be missing newer values. Hide All Unused Fields tells Tableau to pull all the data but to hide the fields that are not currently used in a visualization. This cleans up the Data pane when building visualizations and makes the data easier to work with. Hidden fields can easily be restored using the Data pane or data connection window if required.

Once you've configured the settings as desired, click the OK button (or other button in different versions of Tableau). Tableau Desktop will then generate the extract files locally and return you to your workbook. The icon on the data pull will change from a single cylinder (live data pull) to a double cylinder (extract), as shown in Figure 1-4. At this point, your workbook will use the extracted file to generate the results as you build your visualizations. It's important to know what this file looks like and how to identify it.

🗄 Sales Commission	🗄 Sales Commission

Figure 1-4. The image on the left is a live data connection, while the image on the right is extracted.

File Types

You've gone through the steps to build an extract, but what does that extract file look like on your local drive? It is very likely that the Tableau exam will question you in some way about the file types Tableau uses when saving files, extracts, or flows. The goal of these questions is to ensure you can identify these files in your repository when you need to return to them in the future. Table 1-1 contains a list of Tableau file types, what program generates them, and what they contain.

Table 1-1. The most common Tableau software file extensions and what they are used for.

File extension	Source	What it contains
.tfl	Tableau Prep Builder	A Tableau Prep Builder flow containing the step-by-step changes made to a data set in preparation for use.
.tflx	Tableau Prep Builder	A Tableau Prep Builder flow, packaged with a copy of local data, allowing it to be shared with others.
.twb	Tableau Desktop	The standard Tableau workbook save file containing views and dashboards.
.twbx	Tableau Desktop	A Tableau workbook packaged together with a copy of any local data or an extract, allowing it to be shared with others.
.tds	Tableau Desktop	A file containing information about a data source, providing what is necessary to quickly reconnect and reapply any modification.
.tdsx	Tableau Desktop	A file containing a copy of the .tds file as well as any .hyper or other local data source. This extension as well as .twbx are technically .zip files and can be renamed with that extension to allow for exploration and extraction of the subparts.
.tde	Tableau Desktop	An older version of a Tableau data extract file, containing a local copy of the data used in a workbook. This file extension was discontinued in early 2023 in favor of .hyper files.
.hyper	Tableau Desktop and Tableau Prep Builder	An extract of a subset or entirety of data used in a Tableau workbook (post-2018 version).

> Knowing Tableau file extensions is important not only for the exam, but also for sharing data and files with others. As mentioned in Table 1-1, some of the file formats contain copies of the data (including .hyper file extracts of relational databases). If you are working with secure information, then you will want to make sure that the user you are sharing with has the correct access level to view that data. This may mean that your save file switches from a .twbx to a .twb (or a .tds versus a .tdsx if you are sharing a data file). Alternatively, including the data within a file means that the user doesn't have to provide credentials to access the data unless they need to refresh it.

Working with Extracts

The exam may ask questions about creating an extract or about what to do once you have extracted data in your workbook. This section covers how to change, update, or remove an extract. I'll also briefly discuss some of the Tableau Desktop features that are only available once data is extracted. This section does not dive deeply into all the details about extracted data but focuses on the highlights that may be sources for potential exam questions.

First, you will want to understand how to work with extracts once they are in your workbook. To access the Extract menu, right-click on the data source with the extract and hover over the Extract submenu to display the options:

Refresh

Unlike live data, which refreshes constantly, extracted data is a static snapshot of the data at the time it was extracted. To refresh, you need to right-click on the data source, hover over the Extract menu option, and choose Refresh. The normal data refresh option in the base of the pull-down menu does not work on extracts.

Use Extract

Within the Extract menu is an option to use the extract. Unchecking the box will revert the workbook to live data, but retain the extract file in case you wish to return to using it. Once unchecked, it can be rechecked to return to using the extract.

Remove

> This option also removes the extract from the workbook, but unlike the previous option, this selection will prompt you to keep or remove the extract file.

Next, there are a couple of calculations that have varying availability based on the data type and whether you're using an extract or a live connection. One example of this is the MAKEDATE() calculation. Only extracts and a few other select data sources can use the MAKEDATE() calculation. It is fed a numerical year, month, and day to generate the date. A similar version of this calculation is DATE(), and it requires recognizable string, numerical, or date-formatted versions of the year, month, and day to function properly. Here are examples of both for May 23, 2024:

```
MAKEDATE(2024,5,23)
DATE("May 23, 2024")
DATE("5/23/2024")
```

As an aside, the MAKEDATE() function will automatically correct invalid numbers. So, for example, if you use: MAKEDATE(2024,4,31), the output will automatically adjust to May 1, 2024 (since April 31 does not exist). For additional information on date functions, see Chapter 3.

Other examples of functions that only work with certain data sources or extracts include PROPER() and COUNTD().

Combining Data

Combining data will likely be the topic of two or three questions on the exam, as this is a common task performed by data analysts. Let's review the methods for combining data, the differences between them, and the situation for which each method is best suited. I'll also investigate the differences between how Tableau Prep Builder and Tableau Desktop combine data.

Joins

Tableau will test your knowledge of combining data in different ways. At least one question will ask you about joins. The easiest way to think about joins is to consider them as ways to widen your data: that is, to add additional columns of information to your existing table. For example, consider the Superstore data set built into Tableau Desktop. It has information about orders made by customers in one table and returns data in another. Joining them creates a table with information about both.

You will want to be able to identify the types of joins and what they return. You will also want to know about joins that are specific to Tableau Prep Builder and how to manipulate the data to enable otherwise impossible joins. The types of joins available in both Tableau Prep Builder and Tableau Desktop include:

Left join

Every row from the left table and any row from the right table with a matching value in the join field

Right join

Same as a left join only in reverse (everything from right table)

Inner join

Only rows from both tables where there is a matching value in the join field

Full Outer join

All rows from both tables

Tableau Prep Builder also contains three extra join types:

Left Only

Pulls all the data from the left table, but excludes any rows where a matching value is found in the right table.

Right Only

Pulls data from the right table, but exclude any rows where a matching value is found in the left table.

Not Inner

Returns only rows from both tables where there is no matching join field value between them.

Both Tableau Desktop and Tableau Prep Builder also offer additional ways to overcome difficult joins. In Tableau Prep Builder, there are data cleanup tools that can be used to correct typos and capitalization for join fields with potentially dirty data. This allows these fields to be used as joins when otherwise there would not be a match. Tableau Prep Builder also enables you to see which fields are being used for the join, what the join type is, and what is being included or excluded from each table.

Tableau Desktop and Tableau Prep allow you to do join calculations within the Data pane. With a join calculation, you can change the join to make it work differently. For example, you can do UPPER() on a field to make the values all capitalized, or change the relationship to an inequality to create unique join types. An example of this would be pulling data from the left table where a value is less than or greater than a value on the right. These calculations can also happen in Tableau Prep Builder, but the calculation occurs in a filtering node prior to the join occurring.

Relationships

Relationships are another way to combine tables in Tableau, but how they differ from joins can be confusing to some people. Table 1-2 highlights some of the key differences.

Table 1-2. Comparing joins to relationships in Tableau.

Joins	Relationships
Physically combines the two tables into one	Logically combines the tables, allowing the connection to flex based on what is needed
Created by double-clicking a table in the Data pane to enter the logical layer	Created by simply adding another table to the Data pane
Represented by a Venn diagram	Represented by a "noodle" (a curvy line) connecting the tables

A better way to think of relationships is to consider them *dynamic joins.* The query that pulls the data into your visualization is contextual, based on where you place the fields in the visualization build.

An example data set might help clarify this idea. If you want to see how many returns each of your customers made using a join, you need to build a specific data source with the customer table left-joined through the order table to the return table, as in

Figure 1-5. This join method may be great for this particular question, but it may make it challenging to answer different questions in the future.

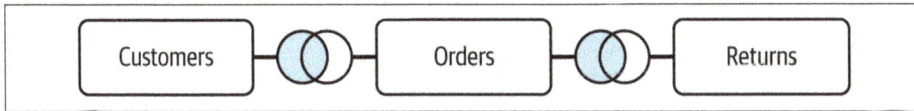

Figure 1-5. Joined tables pulling all customers, then pulling the orders those customers made, and then identifying the returned orders from that group.

A *relationship* dynamically combines the tables based on what happens in the visualization. In short, you would pull all the customers, making the customer table into a dimensional table and the returns table into a measure table, as in Figure 1-6. Later in the same workbook, Tableau would completely change that relationship if you wanted to count how many customers created a return.

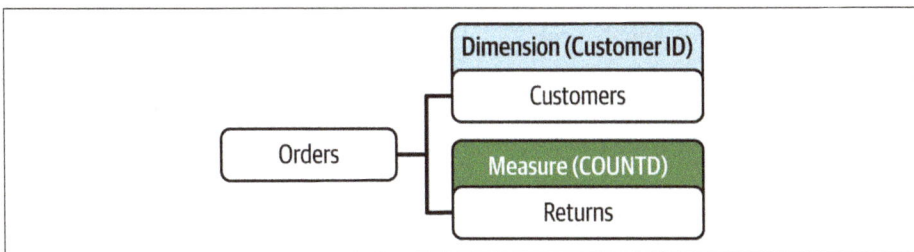

Figure 1-6. A relationship built between customers, orders, and returns. The customers are a dimensional list, and the thing being measured is the count of orders that had a return.

One of the key features of relationships is that dimensional values will display based on what is in the visualization, but measures always return. To continue the same example, if you bring in both the returned Order ID and the Customer ID as dimensions, Tableau will only bring back rows from each table that match the customers who made a return. However, if you bring in customers and then *measure* returns (such as by counting the number of returns), it will bring in all customers, showing "0" for the customers who did not make a return.

Measures in a relationship will always render at their native level of detail; that is, the granularity of what they were designed to measure. If the visualization gets more granular than that level, the measure will still act at the level for which it was designed. Continuing on our example, if the visualization contains information on returns, and returns are measured at the level of the order, then adding product information to the visualization will not alter the number of orders being returned. To clarify further, suppose Heather returned three orders. If you are showing customer names and measuring returned orders, adding the product names to the visualization will not change the number of returns, even if each returned order contained hundreds of items.

Example Question

You have two different tables you wish to join together. One contains information about your company's orders and the other contains information about returns. You only want to pull information on the orders that were not returned. What type of join should you use?

A. Orders Left join Returns

B. Returns Left join Orders

C. Orders Inner join Returns

D. Orders Left Only join Returns

E. Orders Full Outer join Returns

Answer: D—Left Only joins include everything from the left table less the rows that have a matching value in the right table.

Blends

Sometimes you want to have separate data sources in your workbook for reporting, but for certain visualizations, you need a way to relate them together. This single-sheet combination is called a *blend* in Tableau Desktop. Unlike the other combinations discussed thus far, blends are performed after the data is pulled. Data blending is dependent on a primary and secondary data source. The two are connected via one or more linked fields indicated on the Data pane with a chain-like symbol (🔗).

Data blending is effectively a sheet-specific left join. Instead of joining both data sets in the data pane, you are effectively joining them on a per-sheet basis. The relationship can be defined more clearly using the Edit Blend Relationships option in the Data menu in Tableau Desktop.

There are some caveats to using blends. The first is that blends can sometimes create results that appear as a series of asterisks. In short, if you blend on a field that appears multiple times in the primary data set, Tableau cannot determine which row blends to the other table. For example, pretend you are blending the customers table to the orders table based on the Customer ID field. If you then try to display region from the orders table and a customer has purchased items from multiple locations, Tableau doesn't know which region to show, and thus shows an "*".

Likewise, blends can sometimes result in NULL values. Left joins return everything from the left table and only the rows with matching field values in the right table. If you are displaying dimensions from the left table and measures from the right table, you will get a null if there are no values for a particular dimension. For example, imagine you have customers on the left and returns on the right. If you are showing sales value from the returns table and a customer didn't make a return, you get a NULL value.

The questions about blends on the exam revolve less around how to create them than when to utilize them. The key things to take away from this section are:

- Blends are specific to a particular sheet in your workbook. Once you navigate away from that sheet to another location in your workbook, you no longer retain the blend.

- Tableau blends based on fields with matching names. If you need to edit a blend, you should do so from the Edit Blend Relationships option in the Data menu.

- In Tableau Desktop, blends are currently the only way to combine published data sources with other data sources.

Unions

Until now, you have been expanding your data horizontally. That is, you have been adding information to each row in your data set. There are situations that arise where you don't want to add more columns, but rather more rows. This is where unions come into play. A *union* is used to append additional rows to an existing table. The most common example happens when you have a table from one year and a table from another. If the data is structured the same way, you can append one to the other using a union.

Data structure is key to a union. The order and data type of the fields must match from table to table. If anything differs in structure between the two tables, you must provide Tableau guidance on what to do with the mismatch (for example, when a yearly data table has an extra column). This can sometimes make unions difficult to complete.

To make a union in Tableau Prep Builder, you connect to the two tables, then drag one table to the other. The software provides a Union option to combine the two tables. You can add more tables by clicking and dragging them to the existing unioned tables and choosing Add. Tableau Prep Builder has a limit of 10 tables that can be unioned in this way. If you need additional unions, perform them in the data-input stage (when you bring the tables into Tableau Prep Builder).

Tableau Prep also allows you to union files based on structure. These are called *wild-card unions*. In a wildcard union, you identify the files to union together based on the structure of the file name. For example, if your datasets are named `2022sales.csv`, `2023sales.csv`, and `2024sales.csv`, you can program Tableau Prep to find files that have a pattern of `*sales.csv`.

Tableau Desktop performs unions in a similar fashion to Tableau Prep Builder. Dragging one table to another will present an option to union the tables. Once combined, you can click on the union and edit it to define which fields align with which and ensure that the combination works successfully. Tableau Prep Builder and Tableau Desktop provide union options for data files stored in the same location, allowing you to union all files from a specific directory on your computer.

> The exam will likely touch on unions in one way or another. Types of questions about unions might include the requirements for data structure or when to use a union when you also want to join. Most likely, you will see *union* as an answer choice when a question provides a scenario for combining tables together. Knowing the basics of a union, what it does, why you would use it, and how to make one in Tableau Prep and Tableau Desktop will be beneficial when you take the exam.

Example Question

Last year, you built a dashboard based on your company's sales data pulled from an Excel file. Today, your sales team provided you with this year's data in a separate Excel file. The fields are all the same, but the data is specific to this year. They've asked you to combine it with last year's data to allow them to see trends. What method should you use to join last year's data to this year's data?

A. Custom SQL to the tables.

B. Union the tables.

C. Left join last year's data to this year's data.

D. Create a relationship between the tables.

E. Create a blend on all the fields except year.

Answer: B—A union is used to combine data vertically when the fields align and contain the same types of data.

Manipulating Data

Bringing data in is only part of making the data ready for visualization. Most data requires some level of transformation to make it functional for analysis. There are many types of data transformation, including renaming, aliasing, filtering, and more. This section is dedicated to understanding the key ways to manipulate data.

Cleaning Data in Tableau Prep Builder

Tableau Prep Builder is designed to manipulate data and structure it for ease in reporting. It also makes these steps more visible and easily repeatable. You can use Tableau Prep Builder to perform a wide variety of data alterations while displaying sample data for you to review. This way, you can see the impact of the change and determine if the step is functioning correctly before continuing on.

The exam will likely give situational examples and ask which of the functions from Tableau Prep Builder would best resolve them. Let's look at some of the capabilities of the software:

Input data
> The most important step of any data flow is to pull in the data. This can be any type of data from a wide variety of sources.

Join data
> Joins are available to combine tables. As a reminder, there are seven types of joins in Tableau Prep Builder: Left join, Right join, Inner join, Outer join, Left Only join, Right Only join, and Not Inner join.

Union data
> Unioning data was also covered earlier. This stacks tables together rather than adding dimensional information.

Aggregate
> Aggregation takes the row-level values within a table and aggregates them up to a higher level. This may be necessary when trying to combine tables at different aggregation levels.

Pivot
> Mentioned earlier in the chapter, pivoting tables takes columns and converts them to rows or converts rows to columns. This eliminates multiple columns in favor of a single column containing multiple dimensions or measures.

Script
> You can write R or Python scripts to manipulate the data.

New rows

Sometimes data is incomplete (maybe the business was closed on a holiday). While Tableau has a missing values feature, Tableau Prep Builder can fill in the blanks and create rows for that missing data. This creates something for Tableau to display rather than generating a void of dataless space.

Clean data

This is the bread and butter of Tableau Prep Builder. Within clean data, there are options to filter, rename, and do calculations against the data. The goal of these types of steps is to eliminate duplicates and correct data mismatches based on a variety of criteria.

Output

This is the end result of a flow. In this step, you choose a method to produce the resulting data set of all the previous steps. There are two options—produce an output file or publish the resulting data to a Tableau server or Tableau Cloud. Output files are stored as a Hyper file, Excel file, or CSV, and you will be prompted to provide a location to save the output file. When publishing the output to a server or Tableau Cloud, you will be prompted for a server name, a site, and a project location to place the data source.

Insert Flow

This allows you to insert an existing flow into your current flow file.

Clean data deserves additional attention, as there are subfeatures that could appear in a Tableau exam. Typically these features revolve around making a particular table better align with another, but they can also be used to change data types, correct typos, or change field names. Let's look at some example uses for the clean functions:

Combine or separate fields

Perhaps your data comes with separate fields for first name and last name. You could combine them into one using a calculation. You could also do the reverse.

Alias fields

If one of your tables gives state names while a different table uses abbreviations, you can easily go through and rename either one to match the other.

Change data types

If an employee number is coming through as an integer field, you can convert it to a string to retain leading 0s.

Catch typos

You can group together values in a field that are similar in nature. You can do this by pronunciation, common characters, spelling, or manually. If someone types *Saint Louis* instead of *St. Louis*, Tableau Prep Builder can identify them as the same thing and update either one to the format you wish to use.

As mentioned before, Tableau Prep Builder is designed to perform a series of repeatable steps called a *flow*. The idea is that any new data brought into the tables should also be subjected to the steps of the flow. For this reason, Tableau Prep Builder has a server counterpart designed to rerun these flows on a scheduled interval to ensure that future data is cleaned and correctly joined. Information about publishing, server security, and scheduled refreshes is available in Chapter 6.

> Exam questions about Tableau Prep Builder could be about changing data in a table to enable it to be combined with another table. You might also see questions about combining related field values with a table. Playing with the example data sets that come with Tableau Prep Builder is another excellent way to better understand the software.

Example Question

Your sales team provides you with annual data for sales by state. Unfortunately, in this year's data, they've used abbreviations instead of full state names. They also broke the most current year's data down to the county level. Which choice shows the order of the steps you could use in Tableau Prep Builder to combine the tables?

A. Union, Clean, Aggregate

B. Clean, Union, Aggregate

C. Clean, Aggregate, Join

D. Clean, Aggregate, Union

E. Join, Clean, Aggregate

Answer: D—The state abbreviations need to be cleaned up and then the data aggregated to the state level. Once this is done, the two files share the same structure and field types, allowing them to be unioned.

Cleaning Data in Tableau Desktop

If you don't have Tableau Prep Builder, there are still ways to manipulate data in Tableau Desktop. As mentioned earlier in the chapter, some local data sources offer options to pivot data or utilize the data interpreter. For relational databases, you can write custom SQL to modify data pulls to your needs.

Once you've brought in and joined data in Tableau Desktop, you can modify the data fields in multiple ways. The data preview pane available when editing data sources offers several options on the field pulldown menu. Figure 1-7 illustrates the field preview and pull-down menu in Tableau Desktop, which describe each option and what it does.

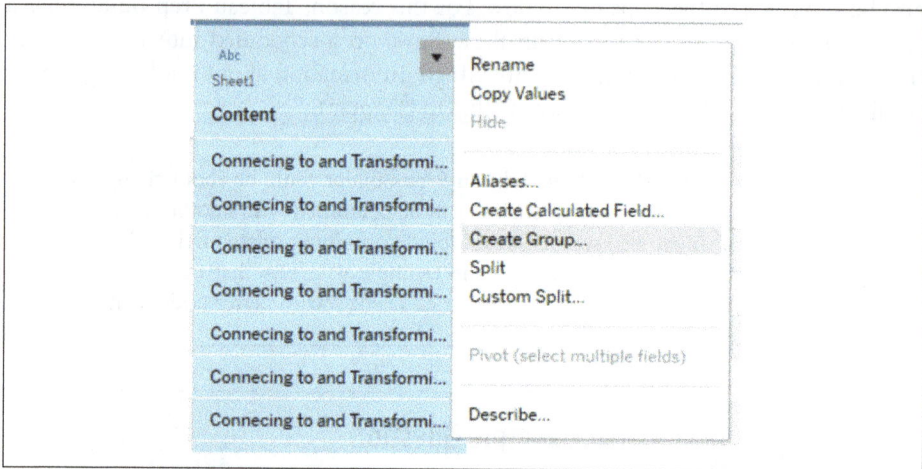

Figure 1-7. Data in the preview pane in the Tableau Desktop data tab. The menu options are described in detail in the data manipulation menu description list.

The data manipulation menu list is as follows:

Rename
Any field brought into Tableau can be renamed.

Aliases
This option allows you to rename the values within the field.

Create Calculated Field
This allows you to write a calculation to create another field in the data.

Create Group
This option will allow you to group similar items manually and give them another name (more information about groups is located in Chapter 3).

Split/Custom Split
These take a field with multiple values and split it based on a delimiter, for example, a full name can be split into first and last name fields.

Hide
This option hides a field from view once you are building visualizations in Tableau, and is primarily used to keep things cleaner and easier to use.

In addition to manipulating the names of fields and field values, Tableau desktop also incorporates an icon in the upper left of each field indicating data type, such as string, integer, float value, or date. This allows you to quickly alter the type of data each field contains, which can be useful for tasks such as changing a date/time field to just a date or switching an ID number to a string to maintain leading zeros.

> The Tableau exam could have questions about data manipulation in Tableau Desktop, for instance, about how to split a name field or change the default data type of a date field. Many of the types of actions that can be taken on the Data tab can also be performed later, once you're in Tableau Desktop building visualizations. To practice, pull a sample data set into Tableau Desktop and experiment with the pull-down menu for several of the fields. This is also a great place to experiment with extracts and filters.

Extract Filters and Data Source Filters

There are multiple ways to filter data in Tableau, and the first few filter types are valuable parts of the data-pulling process. Extract filters and data source filters narrow data down before you use it to build a visualization, as shown in Figure 1-8. Since Tableau Prep Builder transforms data and outputs it into a usable format, filters within the software are also applied before entering the visualization stage.

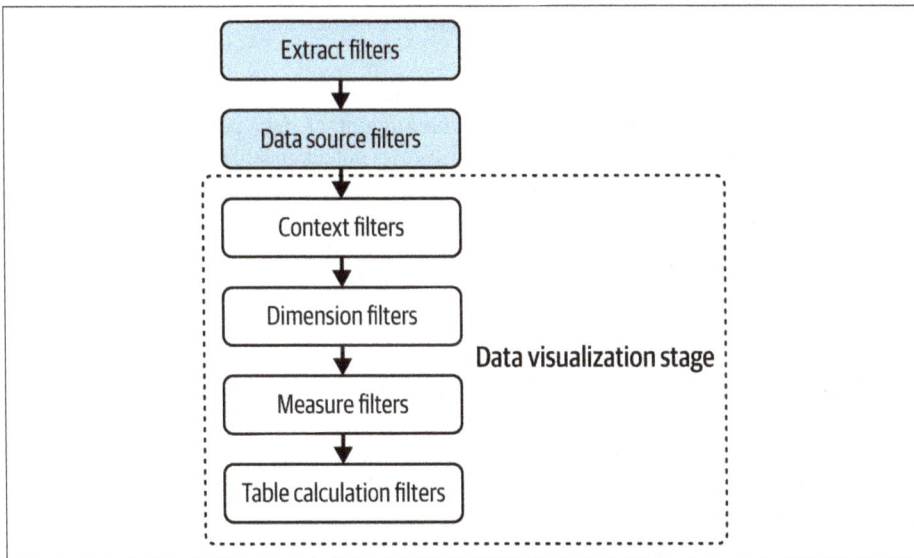

Figure 1-8. Extract filters and data filters are applied before the data is available for visualization.

The difference between extract filters and data source filters can be confusing, so let's start by comparing the two. *Extract filters* are applied during data extraction, as the data is pulled from the source location, to limit the amount of data brought in. They are located within the extract window. So, when you have built your data source and select the option to create an extract, the window that appears offers options for filtering the data. The important thing to remember is that extract filters are applied *before* the data is brought into Tableau.

Data source filters behave the same way, with one notable exception. Like extract filters, they filter out data prior to visualization, but they *do not* filter the data before you bring it into Tableau. As Figure 1-9 shows, *all* of the data is pulled as part of the extraction process, but the data available for visualization is filtered. This means that data extracts with extract filters will have significantly smaller file sizes than those with only data source filters. Data source filters are available on the Data tab in Tableau Desktop.

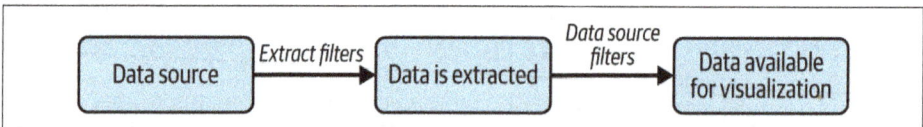

Figure 1-9. Location of extract filters and data source filters during the data pull timeline.

Extract filters and data source filters behave similarly to filters within Tableau Desktop's data visualization (covered in more detail in Chapter 2).

> For the exam, you should understand that extract filters are used when you want to decrease the amount of data pulled into an extract. They limit the number of rows pulled, making your extract smaller and more performant. In comparison, data filters remove data after it has been pulled but before it enters the visualization stage. This allows you to reduce the amount of data being used to generate the visualizations, but it does not decrease the file size of the underlying extract.

Working with Existing Data Sources

When you develop visualizations in Tableau Desktop, you will inevitably need to modify an existing data source for one reason or another. Perhaps you need to pull more dimensional data from another source, or perhaps the database server is being replaced, and you need to redirect your extract to pull from another location. Whatever the case, the Tableau exam will question you on how to make changes to your data sources.

Replacing Data Sources

It's not often that you encounter a reason to completely replace a data source, but it does happen. Let's say you've been working on sample data in the development database. Now, the data is verified and pushed to a production environment. You need to update your data source to point to this new production system. You have two choices for how to proceed with this change.

Your first option is to modify the data source on the Data tab. For relational databases, this should be as simple as replacing the server with the new connection. For local files, you will need to change which file the data source is pointing to. Changing the data source this way shouldn't impact your workbook, as Tableau is still pulling data from an identical source table.

The alternative to modifying the data source manually is to replace it completely within the Data pane. To use this method, follow these steps:

1. Connect to the new data source.

2. Right click on the old data source (or use the Data menu).

3. In the menu that appears, choose Replace Data Source.

4. In the subsequent window, select which data source is the current one and which is the new one to replace it (see Figure 1-10).

5. The Replace Data Source window also allows you to change only the data source for the current sheet, while leaving all other worksheets intact.

6. Once the data is pointing to the new source, you can close the old source.

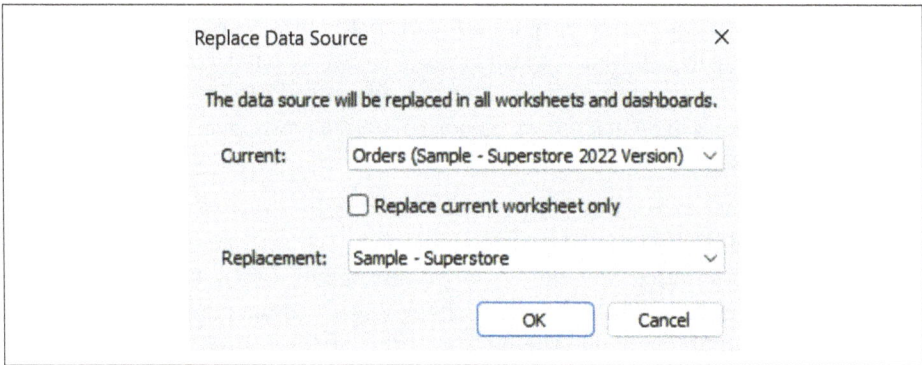

Figure 1-10. The Replace Data Source window.

Replacing the data source is easy, but sometimes it causes issues. This is true when fields are named differently, change data types, or disappear altogether when the data sources switch. For these situations, you will need to identify solutions to repair the workbook based on the changed data. Tableau has an option in the field menu called Replace References that will make this change for you. The following example demonstrates how this works.

In this situation, you are switching from a nonproduction data source to a productionalized version. You follow the list of steps to replace the data source, but discover that in the migration from nonprod to production, the field name for Ship Date changed to Shipping Date. As a result, Tableau now indicates that the Ship Date field is no longer valid by tagging it with an "!". The missing field is causing many of your well-crafted visualizations not to render. You need to replace any occurrence of Ship Date with Shipping Date. To do so:

1. Right click on the old field, Ship Date, in the Data pane.
2. In the menu that appears, select Replace References.
3. Tableau will provide you with a list of fields to replace it with.
4. Select the Shipping Date field to replace the Ship Date field.

> Swapping out data sources and repairing mismatched fields is a potential question on the exam. Review these steps and try swapping a few data sources. Tableau may also ask you how to deal with fields that are no longer available or have changed. How to replace fields is another great thing to look over.

Modifying Published Data Sources

Published data sources can be easy or difficult to change, depending on how they were built. When you publish a data source to Tableau Server, it asks you what to do with the workbook it is sourced from. You can choose to keep the data source local within the workbook or switch the workbook to use the newly published data source. Both options have advantages and disadvantages.

If you keep the data source local, any content within the workbook will still be pointed at the original data source. This allows you to change anything just as you would with any other data source; however, if you publish the workbook itself to the server, it will not be using the published source. Changes made to the published source will not impact the workbook at all. The benefit of this method is that you can create a workbook entirely devoted to creating the data source, allowing you to make changes, updates, and more.

Alternatively, you can publish the data source to the server and convert the workbook to use that published data as its source. The workbook would use the published data source and show up-to-date information from the last time the source refreshed on the server. The drawback to this method is that if you want to make a change to the source data, you need to right-click on the published data source within the workbook and choose Create a Local Copy. Once that copy exists, you will have to swap the published data source for the local one using the replacement method described in the previous section.

Example Question

You have a published data source that is being used in an existing workbook. Unfortunately, changes in the structure of the data require you to update the data source with new information. What steps should you take to make this update?

A. Open the workbook, then right-click and edit the published data source.

B. Open the workbook, right-click the published data source and create a local copy, edit the local copy, then republish the workbook.

C. Open the workbook, right-click the published data source and create a local copy, replace the published data source with the local copy, edit the local copy, then republish the data source.

D. Open the workbook, right-click the published data and choose Replace References, and replace it with the updated data source.

E. Open the workbook, connect to the updated data source, right-click the published data source and choose Replace to replace it with the updated source, and republish the workbook.

Answer: C—The published data source must be made local to update data changes. Once the changes are made, the data source can be published again. You would also want to make sure that all connected workbooks function correctly after the change.

Conclusion

You need data to create visualizations in Tableau. The exam will quiz you on many data-related tasks to see if you understand how to connect to data, manipulate data, and work with existing data connections. As a reminder, these topics comprise approximately 24% of all the questions in the exam. Before we step into exploring data and working with the Tableau Desktop interface, take a moment to review these sample exam questions to ensure that you have a strong grasp of the Chapter 1 topics.

CHAPTER 2

Exploring Data: Getting Familiar with the Tableau Desktop Interface

Tableau's exam outline (*https://oreil.ly/OsIgf*) indicates that over 65% of the material is about creating content and exploring and analyzing data. As a result, when I prepare for the exam, this is where I spend most of my time. I will use this chapter to ensure that you are equally comfortable with exploring data and utilizing key features of the software interface.

Building data visualizations in Tableau Desktop is as much an art as it is a science. It takes time and practice to become familiar with building and modifying visualizations, applying filters and sorts, and quickly finding data exploration tools within the interface. In this chapter, I will start with a brief tour of the interface's key features before diving into the tools for building basic visualizations. From there, I will briefly explore filtering data before diving into how to control the visual aspects of your chart. Also, for simplicity, I will start referring to Tableau Desktop as just Tableau.

A Tour of the Interface

If you've used Tableau for any amount of time, you'll know that there are menus and submenus hidden everywhere. While I may touch on some of these briefly, this section will primarily focus on the main components of the interface: data, visualization, marks, and filters, as shown in Figure 2-1. The goal will be to build or refresh your fluency in where the main visualization-building components reside. I want to ensure that you have a strong grasp of navigating the interface quickly to explore your data.

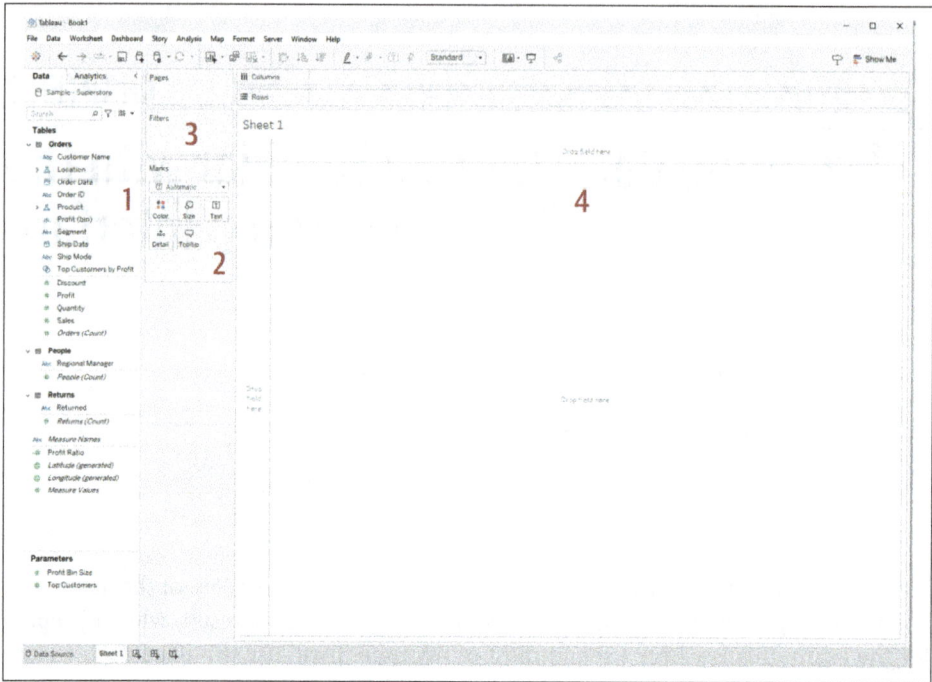

Figure 2-1. The main areas of the Tableau Desktop interface: the Data pane (1), the Marks card (2), the Filter pane (3), and the visualization area (4).

The Data Pane

When you connected to your data source, you told Tableau which fields from which tables you wanted to use to build a visualization. These tables and their associated fields are now located to the far left of the interface. In Figure 2-1, you can quickly identify the main tables: Orders, People, and Returns. Within each table are the associated fields. Tableau indicates several key pieces of information about these fields by their location, their icon, and the icon's color:

Location

> The fields within each table are divided into subsections based on if they are a dimension (above the line) or a measure (below the line). *Dimensions* are how the data can be split, while *measures* are what is being assessed. Measures must be aggregated before being displayed.

Icon

> Next to each field is an icon indicating the type of data in that field. There are many data types, but the most common are numbers, strings, and dates.

Color

The color of the icon indicates if the field is continuous or discrete. Blue indicates that the field is *discrete*: that is, it can be split into discernable chunks or buckets. A green icon indicates that the field is *continuous*, meaning it can have any value within a scale. An easier way to remember this is that discrete fields lend themselves to forming bar charts (each bar is a bucket), while continuous fields are better represented by line and area charts (where each value is possible, with other possible values in between).

Tableau breaks down some data types even further. Numerical data can be whole numbers or decimals, for example. Dates can be shown at many different granularities, including dates with timestamps. Tableau also gives the field a globe icon if it can be used to represent geographic locations.

In addition to the fields that reside in your data source, Tableau provides several built-in fields. These are identified in the Data pane by their italicized names:

Measure Names

This field displays the names of every measure in your data set. In Figure 2-1, the Measure Names field would show Discount, Profit, Quantity, and so on.

Measure Values

Combined with Measure Names, Measure Values shows the numerical value of the corresponding measure. So, if the Measure Name was Sales, the Measure Value would be the numerical value of the Sales.

(Count)

Every data table will have a field that contains *(Count)* after the field name. This is effectively Tableau's way of counting the rows in the table. In Figure 2-1, you can find the number of rows in the Orders table using the Orders *(Count)* field.

Longitude/Latitude

When Tableau detects geographic fields in a data set, it automatically generates Latitude and Longitude for those locations. It uses these fields to create maps to display the geographic location visually.

The Data pane also contains any field types you create. These can include calculations, sets, groups, histograms, parameters, and hierarchies. Chapter 3 will explain in further detail.

While the Data pane's main purpose is to provide access to the fields associated with your data, it has other important capabilities. For instance, it allows you to continue to modify your data fields and their properties. Most of these features reside under a menu associated with each field. You can find it by hovering over the field and clicking the menu icon or by right-clicking.

Within the menu for each field is a plethora of options that allow you to change various aspects of your data fields, including:

Duplicate
This option creates a duplicate of the field. The duplicate field is technically a calculation containing only the original field.

Rename
This option renames the field, but does not impact the values within the field.

Hide
Hiding the field makes it unavailable in the Data pane for use in visualization building. Using Hide cleans the Data pane, making it easier to find the fields you *do* want.

Aliases
If you wish to change a value within a dimension, you can give it an alias using this tool. This is available for discrete dimensions, but not for measures: you should be able to change the name of a division of the data, but not the names of the numerical data values themselves.

Create
From the Create submenu, you can create calculations, groups, sets, and more. These will be covered in detail in Chapter 3.

Transform
The Split and Custom Split options mentioned in Chapter 1 are also contained within this menu item.

Convert
Sometimes Tableau misinterprets fields. For example, it might mistakenly interpret employee ID numbers as measures instead of dimensions. Use Convert to change dimensions to measures or vice versa.

Change Data Type
Tableau sometimes also interprets data types incorrectly, or you may need to change data from one type to another, such as converting a date/time to a date. This option can convert data types without the need for a calculation.

Default Properties

A field's default properties include things such as color, shape, and sort order. You can change any field's default properties by using this menu option. Default properties exist across the entire workbook, meaning that any changes you apply here will appear in every view. Properties applied to a field within a specific view will override any default properties you set using this menu item.

Geographic Role

You can use fields with information about countries, states, counties, zip codes, and more to populate maps in Tableau. Geographic Role allows you to indicate when a field is related to geographic space and identify what type of location information it contains.

Image Role

This field is used for data sets with URL paths to images. Switching this menu to URL will instruct Tableau to render the image hosted at the URL location instead of the URL text.

Group By

You can switch between grouping fields in folders or by their source table, to make the Data pane easier to use. This is *not* the same as creating a group for the field.

Hierarchy

Sometimes data falls into natural hierarchies. This option allows you to nest one field beneath another, providing drill-down capabilities for your visualizations. Hierarchies will be covered in detail in Chapter 3.

Replace References

The Replace References option was covered in Chapter 1. As a reminder, this option finds all instances of a selected field (such as the Data pane, visualization, or calculations) and replaces them with another field of your choosing.

Describe

This option is probably one of the most vital tools available in the Data pane. Describe will provide you detailed information about a field, including its role, type, table column name, if it contains null values, sort order, and more. It will even provide a quick preview of the fields in the data.

Example Question

You have pulled in a data set to build visualizations about the sales your company has made over the past five years. Most of your charts show sales rounded to the nearest dollar, but for this specific view, you would like the chart to show decimals. What is the best method to use to adjust this formatting without changing it in every other view?

A. Right-click the field in the Data pane and adjust the default properties for formatting.

B. Right-click the field in the visualization area and adjust the default properties for formatting.

C. Right-click the field in the Data pane and choose Format.

D. Right-click the field in the visualization and choose Format.

E. Click the Format menu at the top and choose Text.

Answer: D—To adjust formatting for a single visualization, you need to right-click and choose Format on the field within the visualization. Default formatting is only available in the Data pane, but it applies to all visualizations.

Get familiar with the many options nested within the Data pane before taking the exam. Be sure you understand the different data types, the difference between measures and dimensions, and how discrete values differ from continuous.

The Visualization Area

The main area of the Tableau interface is called the *visualization* or *view* (I will use these terms interchangeably). Using the rows, the columns, and the components of the Marks card to efficiently build views to explore your data is the major functionality of Tableau, so understanding these areas is vital.

The main visualization area revolves around the Columns and Rows panes. Dimensions appear across the top of the visualization when placed on Columns and down the left side when placed on Rows. Measures you add to Columns will show the extent of the values horizontally, while adding measures to Rows will make them appear vertically. Figure 2-2 shows both options.

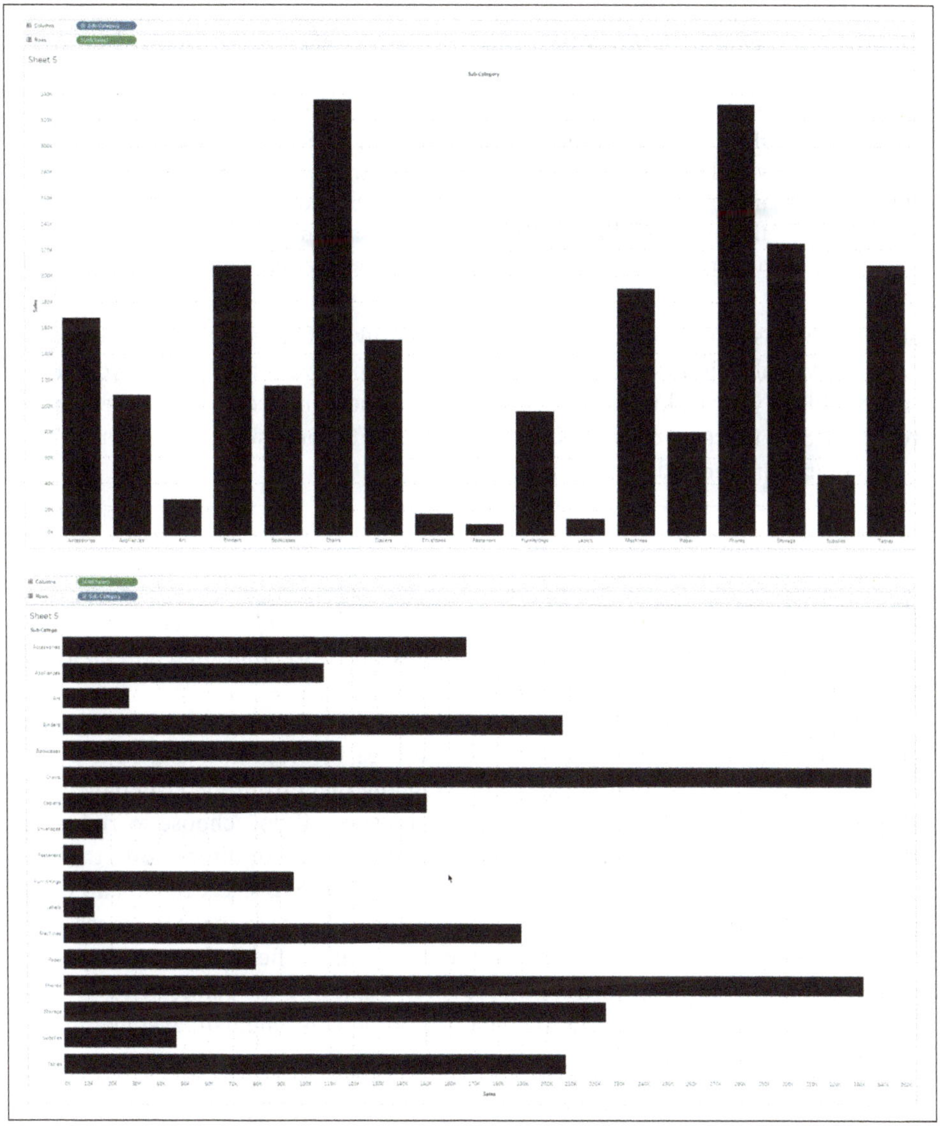

Figure 2-2. Charts showing a dimension on Columns and a measure on Rows (top) and a dimension on Rows with a measure on Columns (bottom).

Most visualizations go beyond just one dimension and one measure, but knowing where to place fields in your visualization to achieve the desired view is a vital skill. Keep in mind that dimensions divide your data up by the values in a field, while measures are what you are examining via this divide. The more dimensions you add, the more granular your information will be. Tableau refers to this granularity as *detail*, which will come up again as I dig into the Marks card later in this chapter.

Most people who have used Tableau understand how to build a basic visualization. The exam will ask you the steps to replicate or build a visualization based on provided specifications in a virtual environment. You will not have access to Tableau Desktop during the exam! To practice for the exam, try predetermining a type of visualization you want to build. Then try to complete it without moving any of the fields you've already placed. You can also practice replicating existing charts using the same data. Can you rebuild a chart quickly without having to move fields around the interface?

Tableau contains three icons at the top of the window that are extremely helpful when building a visualization (see Figure 2-3). The first icon swaps the fields in your Rows for the fields in your Columns. The other two sort them in ascending and descending order. The Sort function only guesses at how you want the visualization sorted. I will discuss more complicated sorting in Chapter 3.

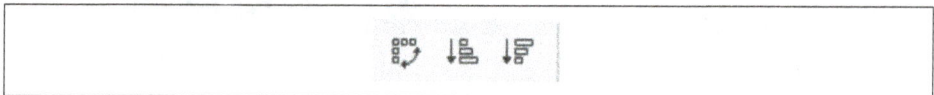

Figure 2-3. Tableau's quick-action icons, available near the top of the screen. These icons—from left to right—Swap Rows and Columns, Sort Ascending, and Sort Descending. Use them to adjust your visualization on the fly.

Another important feature of the visualization area involves how a field is added. You'll mostly add fields by left-clicking and dragging them from the Data pane to the visualization area, the Rows, or the Columns; however, if you choose to right-click and drag a field, you are prompted with additional options. For dimensions, the main choice will be to display the field as is, but you can choose to select the maximum or minimum value based on its default sort. You can also choose to make it a measure by counting the value or by counting the distinct values in the fields. Date fields provide granularity options (discrete and continuous) for displaying the values. Measures will prompt you for how to aggregate the data, including sum, median, average, max or min values, and more.

At the bottom of the visualization area are tabs for each sheet and dashboard within the workbook. The right-click menu on these tabs contain multiple items, but I'll focus on three key options:

Duplicate
    The Duplicate option on the tab right-click menu creates an exact replica of the existing chart. This means that you can make alterations without having to worry about damaging the original chart.

Duplicate as Crosstab

This option is invaluable to validating data within a visualization. It creates a crosstab using the fields within your visualization, allowing you to validate the data and results.

Color

This option applies a colored line to the bottom of the tab. They provide a way for you to quickly identify charts or sets of charts using color.

One final tool available in the visualization area is the Show Me menu, which identifies the field types in a visualization and suggests chart types to visualize them. For instance, if your visualization contains geographic data fields, maps will be available as options. The Show Me menu is provided to assist you in understanding where to place fields to build your desired visualizations. If you are ever unsure about how to build a pie chart, cross tab, or any other visualization type, the Show Me menu will take the fields in your visualization and rearrange them appropriately.

Example Question

How would you build a horizontal bar chart of sales split horizontally by Order Date years vertically by each Category?

A. Order Date and Sales on Columns; Category on Rows

B. Order Date on Columns; Category and Sales on Rows

C. Order Date and Sales on Rows; Category on Columns

D. Order Date and Category on Rows; Sales on Columns

E. Sales on Rows; Order Date and Category on Columns

Answer: A—To display a horizontal bar chart, the measure (Sales) must be on Columns. Splitting items horizontally means that the order date is also on Columns. Splitting things vertically means that the Category is on Rows.

When studying for the exam, practice rebuilding existing charts. Try experimenting with chart types to better understand how to place each field to get the result you want. Review the Filters and Marks sections that follow. Finally, while the Show Me toolbar is accessible, I highly recommend not using it. You can easily build many types of visualizations without relying on this tool.

Marks, Filters, and Pages

Nestled between the Data pane and your visualization is a pane with multiple sections that are referred to as *cards*. The cards include Pages, Filters, and Marks (Figure 2-4). They control what is included in your visualization, how your visualization appears, and how the data populates it. Because this part of the chapter is simply an overview of the layout, I won't go into much detail about what each card can do. Rather, I will give you some insight on the capabilities of each card to prepare you for when I dig in deeper later in the chapter.

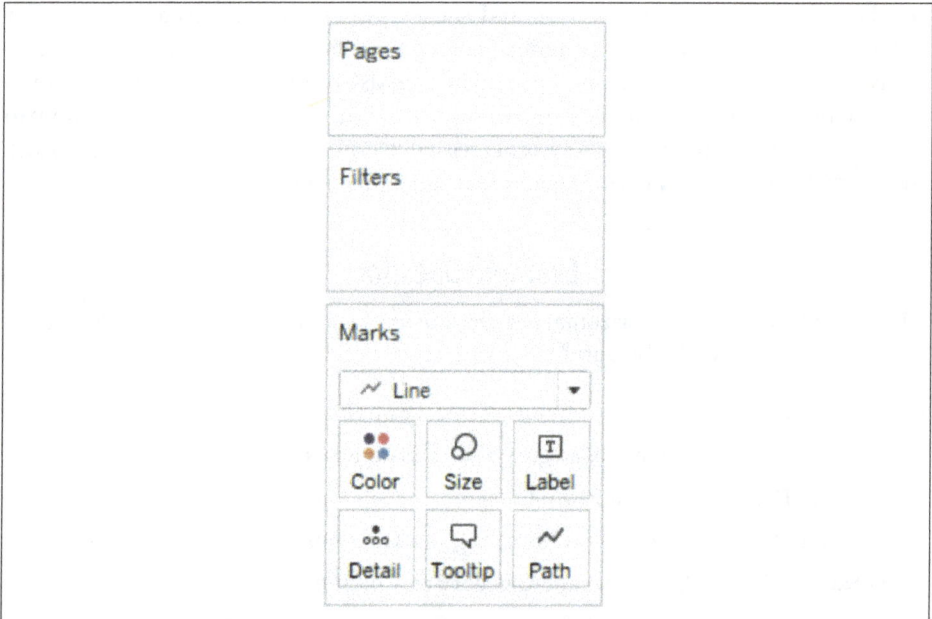

Figure 2-4. The Pages, Filters, and Marks cards are positioned between the Data pane and the visualization area in Tableau Desktop.

The first card in this area is the Pages card, which makes snapshots of a chart. For example, let's say you build a bar chart containing dates and sales. If you then add the dates field to the Pages card, Tableau will provide an interface allowing you to navigate date-by-date through the discrete dates (see Figure 2-5) as you would through a slideshow. You have the option to show history or play through the data automatically, forward or backward, at three different speeds. This is very beneficial when you're looking through your data using specific dimensional points.

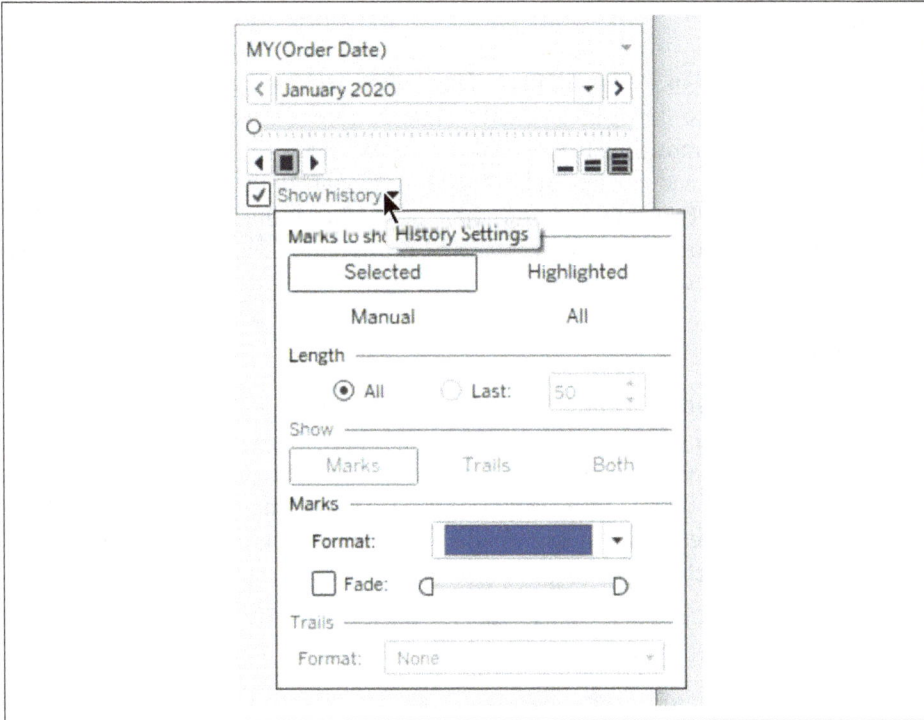

Figure 2-5. The Pages playback control menu allows you to page through dates at various speeds and provides an option for showing your history.

The Filters card provides options for limiting the data in your visualizations. There are many types of filters, many ways to apply them, and many ways to render them to your users. Some fields, such as dates, have even more ways to filter. The Filters card holds the fields by which the visualization is filtered. If you're limiting your chart by years, for example, then you likely have a date field somewhere in your Filters card. Later in this chapter, I'll detail the types of filters and how they interact.

The last card I will examine is the Marks card. You can build most basic charts just by adding fields to Rows and Columns; however, you probably want to add additional details via color, text, and more. This is where the Marks card comes into play. While Columns and Rows determine the structure of the chart, the Marks card controls how the chart *looks*. It contains multiple options, each of which can be used in multiple ways. The next two sections of this chapter cover the Filters and Marks cards in more detail.

Filters Card

Filters are invaluable to exploring data. They allow you to dig deeper into specific aspects of your data to find patterns, outliers, and more. Tableau comes with a wide arrangement of filters for dimensions and measures, makes them dependent on each other, and provides a wide variety of layouts to make your filters available to your end users. In this section, I will dig deep into the types of filters, the priority in which they are applied, and demonstrate how each can be configured. I will also provide sample questions to illustrate what might appear on the exam.

Filters Overview

First, I want to examine how filters work overall. This is important because order of operations plays an important role in understanding where the filtering will take place. In Chapter 1, we looked at the order of operations, discussing Extract and data filters. Now, we are building visualizations, and we're starting to look at context filters, dimensional filters, and measure filters, as seen in Figure 2-6. These happen once the data is extracted and being used, and their order is important.

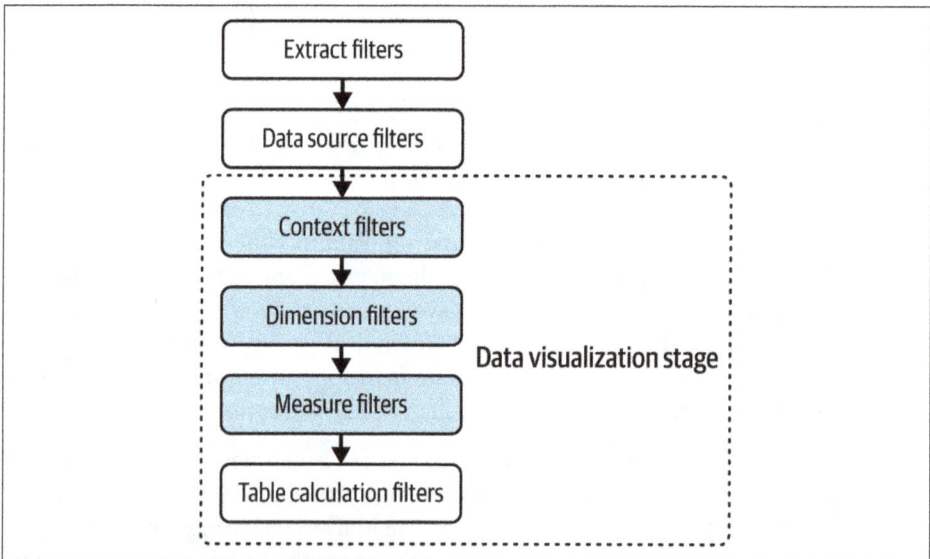

Figure 2-6. Once we are in the visualization building and data exploration stage, we can start using context, dimension, and measure filters.

Filters can be added by dragging any field from the Data pane to the filter card or by right-clicking on any field added to a visualization and choosing Filter from the menu. The resulting window that appears depends on what type of field is being filtered. For this reason, I will break out this chapter by dimension filters, measure filters, and date filters. This way, you can compare and contrast the filter types to help you understand how they work. Fields added to the filter card are executed in order from top to bottom. Additionally, most filters come with the option to include or exclude the values identified.

In Figure 2-6, you can see that the first filters applied in the visualization stage are context filters. A context filter can be a dimension, a measure, or a date filter. A filter can get added to context by right-clicking the field in the filter card and selecting "Add to Context." This will ensure that the filter happens before anything else. It narrows down the data before other filters are applied.

Context filters are special because they create a temporary subset table of your data, eliminating the filtered rows. This means that the remainder of the chart is reliant on a smaller data set, which improves performance. For this reason, context filters are often not provided as a changeable filter to the end user. Context filters are great for narrowing down data to the specific rows you are interested in, especially with dates or regions for example.

Dimension and measure filters come next in the order of operations, but they are a bit more complicated and deserve their own section of this chapter for discussion. That being said, the basic order of operation for these filters is dimension first and then measure. If you have multiple of either kind, the filters will be additive. This is important to remember, because earlier applied filters may impact the options available to those that appear later.

Date filters have many options, and as a result, they have a special window provided when applying them. For this reason, I have called out date filters and will examine them in more detail later in this chapter. Additionally, table calculations, sets, level of detail calculations, and more happen in between some of these filter steps. We will cover these functions and identify when they occur in Chapter 3.

Filters can also only be applied once unless one of those occurrences is added to context or the granularity of the field is different. For example, if you added states to the Filters card and then attempted to drag it in again, it would bring up the existing state filter window. However, if you dragged in a date field at the year level and then dragged it in again at the month level, Tableau will interpret it as two separate filters.

A final note about filters is that they can be shared across visualizations. If you right-click on any filter, one of the options that appears in the menu is "Apply to Worksheets." This allows you to take any filter and apply it to manually selected visualizations, all visualizations using the same data set, or any visualization using similar data sets. This is extremely useful when developing dashboards for your end users. One filter will change the results of all charts on a dashboard rather than having the separate copies of the same filter for each visualization.

Dimension Filters

Filters applied to dimensions happen next in the order of operations Tableau uses to process filters. Discrete dimensions offer you four distinct ways to filter your data. Each method has its own use, and the types of filtering offered are important to review. The available options are listed as tabs at the top of the filter window, as seen in Figure 2-7.

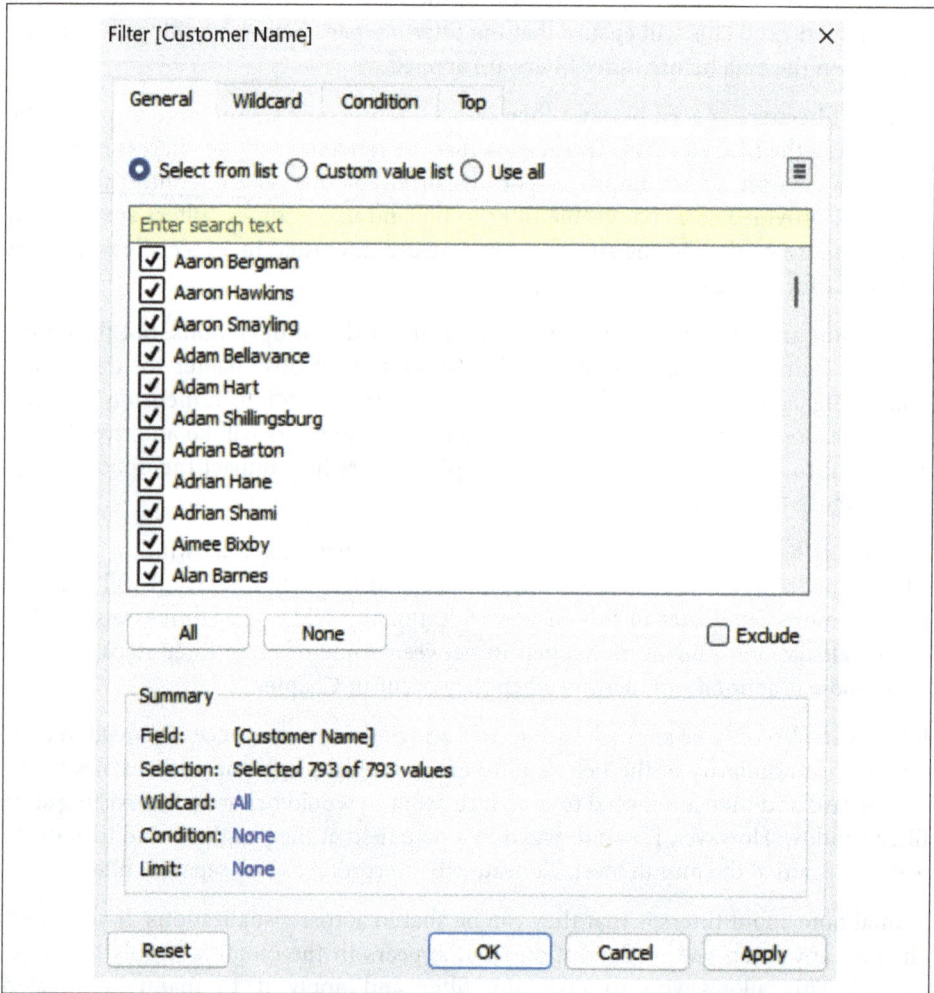

Figure 2-7. The Dimension filter window, offering four methods for filtering data: General, Wildcard, Condition, and Top.

The tabs to choose from are:

General

The most basic way to filter data is to select the options you wish to see or exclude. The General filter window provides you a checkbox list of the dimension values for you to select and deselect to filter your data.

Wildcard

The Wildcard tab provides options for selecting data based on the string value of the dimension. You can tell Tableau to keep values that contain, start with, end with, or exactly match the syntax you provide. For example, maybe you only want to look at data rows for states that begin with the letter "M." Wildcard filters are also case-sensitive.

Condition

The Condition tab allows you to limit the rows returned for this dimension based on the numerical value of another field. For example, you could use the Condition tab to filter state date to only those with a certain amount of sales. The window provides options to be above or below a value, within a range of values, or meet the criteria defined within a custom formula.

Top

Similar to condition filtering, Top filters rely on the value from another field. Within the top window, you can choose to filter to the top or bottom *n* field values based on what is being measured. For example, you may want to filter states to the top 10 by sales.

The most important aspect of Dimension filters is the fact that all of these tabs *work in cooperation*. What does this mean? If you use the General tab to filter down to 10 states and then use the Top tab to select the top 5 states by sales, the resulting rows returned will be the top 5 states by sales selected from the 10 you manually chose in the General tab. Thus, if you wish to only use one of the tabs in the Filter menu to narrow your data, you must be sure to undo any changes you make on the other tabs or risk limiting the data further than you intended.

As mentioned before, same-type filters in the Filters card are additive. If you filter by one thing and then by another, the end result will not contain anything excluded in those two filters. So, if you filter by field A and then do a Top 5 filter on field B, the result may only be two values. Filter B may be asking to show five values, but Filter A removed three of them. If you want to see the top five of the *remaining* values once Filter A is applied, then you will need to add Filter A to Context.

Example Question

You have a visualization showing sales by state. Your director would like to know what the sales were for the top five states in the East region. Which methods would successfully calculate this result?

A. Place the State field on the Filters card and limit it to only the states in the East region, then drag it to filters again to limit the states to the top 5 by sales.

B. Place the Region field on the Filters card and limit it to East, then add the State field to the Filters card and set it to top 5 by sales.

C. Place the Region field on the Filters card, limit it to East, add it to Context, then add the State field to the Filters card and set it to top 5 by sales.

D. Place the Region field on Columns and then place State on the Filters card, restricting it to the top 5 by sales.

E. Place the State field on the Filters card, set it to top 5 by a custom calculation that only returns sales values for the East region.

Answers: C (also E)—C is correct because adding Region to Context will create a subset of data only containing data from the East region. The Top 5 filter will then apply to that remaining data. E can also be used, but requires a calculation that will be covered later in Chapter 3: SUM(IF [Region] = "East" THEN [Sales] END).

Measure Filters

Dimensions are usually discrete and values can be individually selected, but for measures, filters work very differently. The reasons are that measures are usually continuous and they require some form of aggregation before they can be filtered. As a result, when you add a measure filter, you will be prompted with two windows: one to identify the aggregation and one to define the filter.

The aggregation window asks you how to compile the measures from your data together before filtering them. In short, do you want to add them, average them, count them, or use the maximum or minimum value as a filter? Your selection in this window will determine what the filter is being applied to. An example of the aggregation window is shown in Figure 2-8. The same window will appear if a measure is right-clicked and dragged into a visualization.

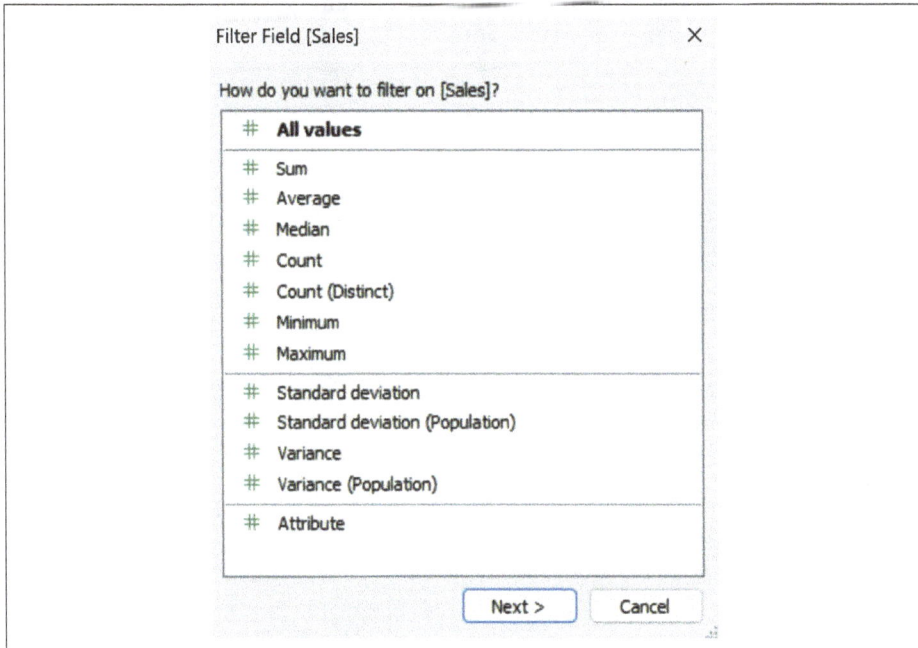

Figure 2-8. The aggregation window prompt that appears prior to filtering a measure. If you right-click and drag a measure to the visualization window, you will be prompted with the same window.

Once you select the aggregation of the measure, you will arrive at the Filter window. Similar to the dimension filter, you will be offered four options. However, instead of tabs, you will be provided icons to select from, as shown in Figure 2-9. It's important to understand that the granularity of the chart will determine how the values are filtered. For example, if you filter sales to values between $1 and $100, you may not see anything in the visualization showing data at the state level. However, if you build a visualization based on the specific items being sold, any item that has sales between $1 and $100 will appear in your visualization.

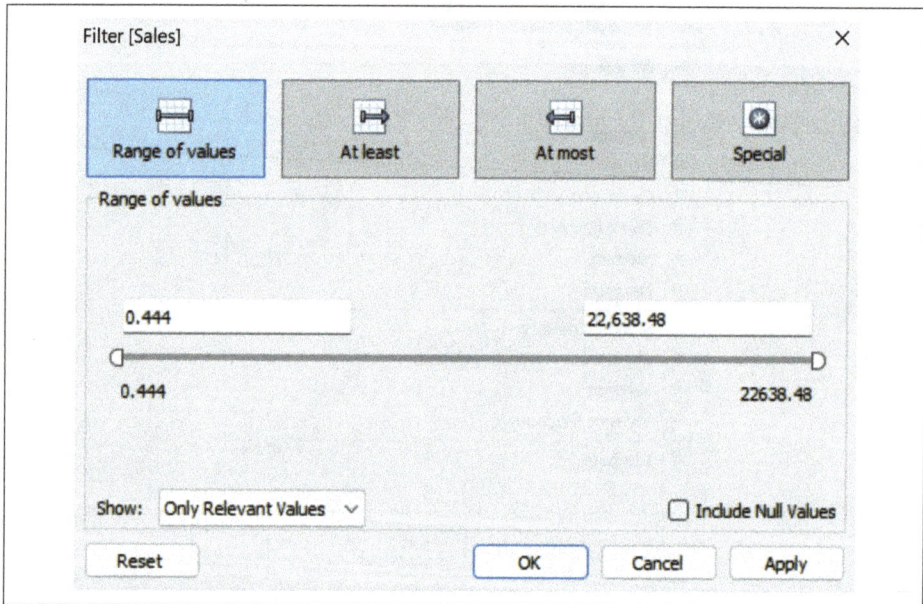

Figure 2-9. The measure Filter window contains icons instead of tabs, but gives you control of what to show in your visualization based on the level of granularity.

"Range of values" filters the visualization to only show dimensions where the value of the measure falls between the values specified. "At least" and "At most" set lower and upper bounds on the measure value respectively. Special contains options for showing null values only, non-null values only, or all values.

Within each filter is a menu option called Show Filter, which is used to show all or only relevant values in the filter. I will touch on relevant values more when I discuss making filters available to users, but effectively, the Only Relevant Values option will limit what is available in this filter based on previous filters. For example, if your visualization contains a date filter limiting the data to the previous five years, and this filter follows it, selecting to show Only Relevant Values will restrict this measure filter to only values that happened in the past five years.

Example Question

You have a visualization showing sales that is divided by several dimensions. You apply a measure filter to limit the data to only show when the sum of sales is greater than $500,000. You're pretty certain your company has done millions in sales and there are no other filters. Unfortunately, your chart still goes blank once the filter is applied. Which of the following is likely the cause?

A. Your company hasn't truly made over $500,000 in sales.

B. The data is out of date and needs to be refreshed.

C. You are filtering by a measure when you should be filtering the dimension based on the value of the measure.

D. Your chart is too granular. The combination of all the dimensions in the visualization mean that no end result exceeds $500,000 in sales.

E. You set the filter to be a "Range of values" instead of an "At most" filter.

Answer: D—Sales in your visualization is being split up by each dimension you include. The more dimensions you add, the more the total sales are split up. Eventually, the sales are split enough that no resulting value exceeds $500,000. To get the chart to appear again, adjust the value of the filter or make the chart less detailed by removing some dimensions.

Date Filters

Dates are unique when it comes to filtering. Since dates can be discrete or continuous, the controls for filtering a date need to be different. When you drag a date field to the Filters card, you are prompted with a window asking you to identify which level of granularity you wish to filter your date, as shown in Figure 2-10.

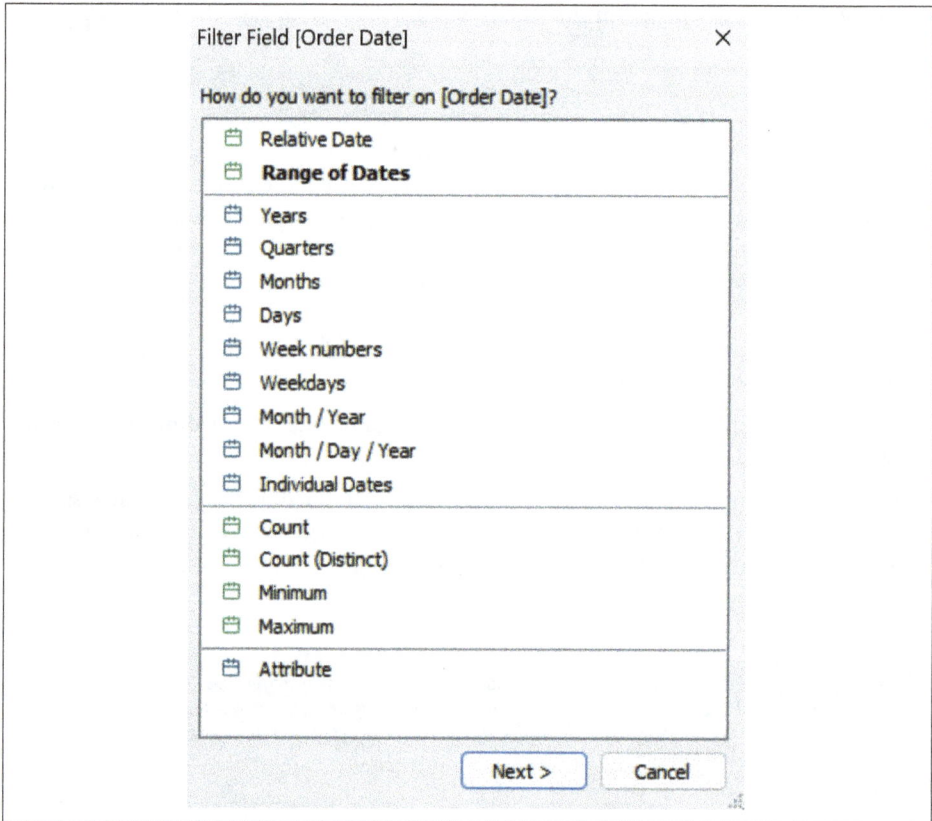

Figure 2-10. The date filter window gives you multiple options for how to filter the date.

The menu in Figure 2-10 becomes available to you if you right-click and drag a date to any other location in the visualization building interface, allowing you to choose between discrete and continuous at any granularity. The right-click-drag method works for all fields and is a quick way to change aggregation on measures or add aggregation to dimensions; it's a valuable tool to use for quickly building visualizations.

Your decision on this window will determine what type of filter will be conducted. Looking at Figure 2-10, you can see that the window is divided into four sections.

Each section does something different. The middle two sections relate to discrete dates and date measures. As a result, selecting anything in these two areas will prompt you with a discrete or continuous filter, as described above. The Attribute option will likely result in an "*" result, and is not regularly used. I will explain attributes in detail when I discuss calculations in Chapter 3.

The top options in the date filter window are unique to dates. Choosing either option will provide you with a special window prompting you with options for filtering the dates based on provided parameters (Figure 2-11).

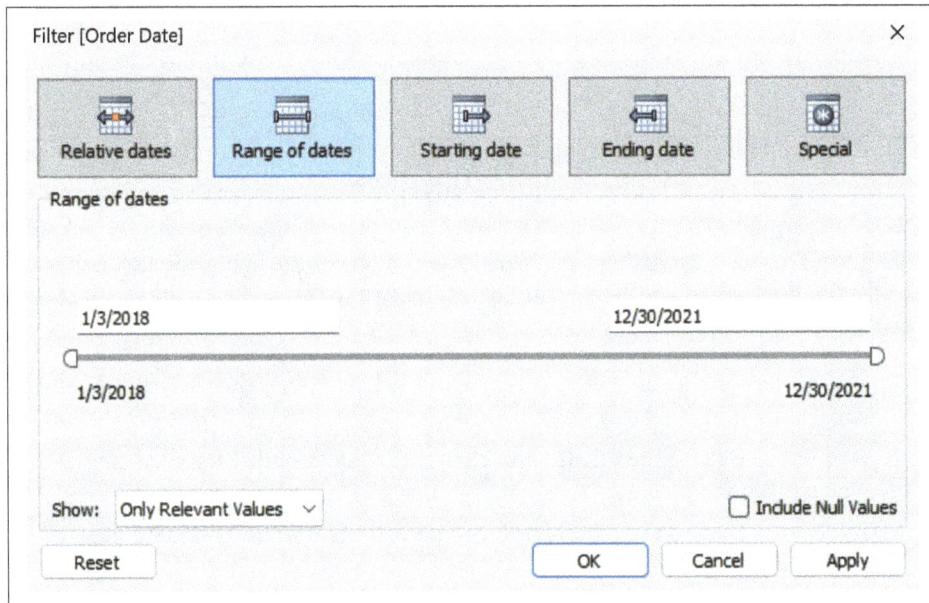

Figure 2-11. Dynamic date filter window showing all the options for dynamically filtering a date.

The Filter window shown in Figure 2-11 shows the five ways to filter a date:

Relative dates
> This filter is unique because it can be dynamic. Relative date filters are based on the date that the workbook is viewed. They provide options to show previous or future dates based on a certain number of years, quarters, months, weeks, or days (or hours and minutes for date/time fields). Because the filter is based on the date the workbook is viewed, the data shown dynamically changes over the course of time. The checkbox in the lower left corner will remove the dynamic aspect of the filter, instead anchoring it to a specific date. Just below the special button is some display text that details what dates are being shown based on your selection.

Range of dates

This filter will restrict the data to dates that fall between a minimum and maximum date. This option is static, and the dates will not change as time goes on.

Starting date/Ending date

Similar to "Range of dates," "Starting date" and "Ending date" filters set begin and end dates respectively. Choosing either will include all data before or after the specified date. This is especially important for "Starting date," as any future data added to the data set will dynamically be shown.

Special

Similar to filtering measures, the Special section allows you to filter to null only, non-null only, or all date values.

Example Question

Your boss would like to see what happened with sales values for orders in the six months following a marketing campaign. Assuming the campaign started on January 1 of 2023, how would you filter your data to show only those six months? Select all that apply.

A. Add Order Date to the Filters card, choose Relative Date, choose last 6 months, and anchor it to January 1, 2023.

B. Add Order Date to the Filters card, choose discrete Month, and manually select January through June.

C. Add Order Date to the Filters card, choose discrete Month / Year and manually select January 2023 through June 2023.

D. Add Order Date to the Filters card, choose Relative Date, choose next 6 months, and anchor it to January 1, 2023.

E. Add Order Date to the Filters card, choose discrete Year, choose 2023, then add the Order Date field to the Filters card again, choose discrete Month, and select January through June.

Answers: C, D, and E—Any of these three methods would work to limit the data to January through June of 2023. Option D is probably the most efficient.

Date functions, format, and filters are very common questions on the exam. Explore by adding dates and filtering dates in sample Tableau workbooks to help you study. Try changing the type of date field and see how it impacts the display and your filters.

Marks Card

If Columns and Rows hold the structure of a visualization, the Marks card holds the design. Understanding and designing visualization building in Tableau requires you to understand the components and actions available through the Marks card. Each icon within the Marks card controls an aspect of the visualization from labels to colors, and each has multiple facets that can be used to change the appearance and design of your chart. Tableau refers to these icons as shelves, and I will use this terminology as well. The components of the Marks card relate to preattentive attributes (key components that draw attention without conscious thought), which are key to extracting information from data. In this section, I will drill into each of the components of the card to examine what they can be used for and what features you should be aware of as you prepare for the exam.

Chart Pull-Down Menu

The first portion of the Marks card is a pull-down menu containing a variety of mark formats to display your data in, as seen in Figure 2-12. Changing the menu allows you to convert your chart from bar to scatter to text or any of many other formats. The menu defaults to the format that Tableau determines works best for the data brought into the visualization. You should note that just because the format menu contains a chart type, does not mean that visualization type will represent the data clearly for analysis. Changing a one dimension and one measure chart into a map for example, will likely not return the results you desire.

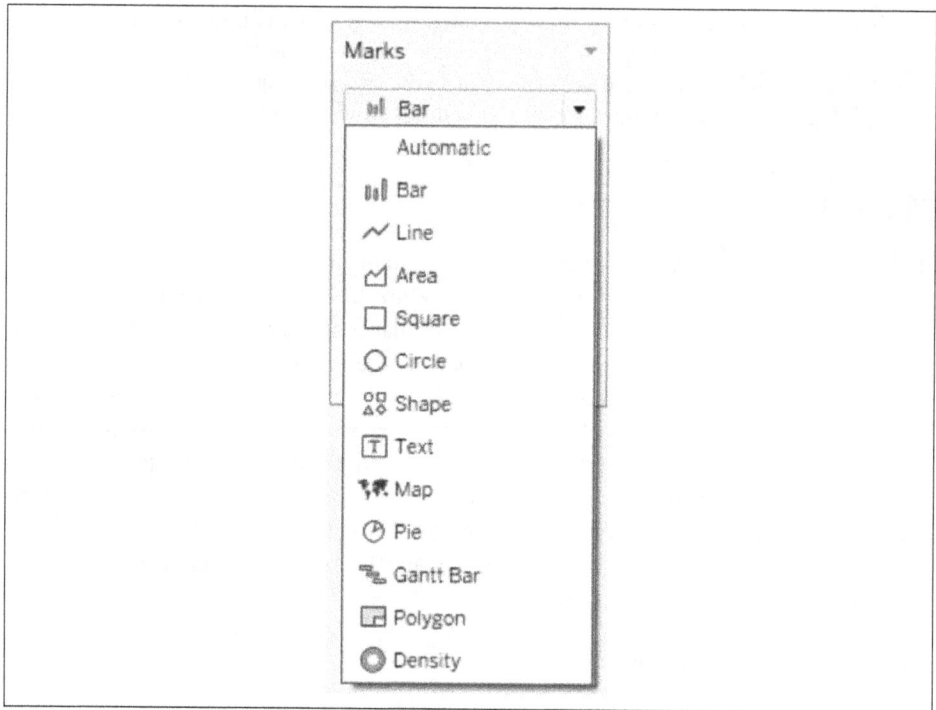

Figure 2-12. The chart pull-down menu on the Marks card.

The chart type pull-down menu has 13 chart types to select from, and they are important to understand:

Automatic
This is the default; Tableau will recommend a chart type based on the dimensions and measures added to the visualization area.

Bar
Bar charts can be vertical or horizontal and are typically of one measure and one or more discrete dimensions.

Line
Line charts are typically built from a continuous dimension and a measure. It differs from an area chart in that the space below the line is not filled.

Area
An area chart is the same as a line chart with the space below the line filled in.

Square

Square, Circle, and Shape charts are scatter plots or other charts with shapes representing the marks. Square charts can also be used to generate highlight tables and treemaps.

Circle

The circle chart can be used to make a basic scatter plot. They are usually made when comparing two measures—one on the horizontal axis and one on the vertical. Circle charts can also be used to make bubble charts.

Shape

Similar to circle and square charts, shape charts are most commonly used to make scatter plots. The shape chart allows you to change the type of mark used in the scatter plot.

Text

Crosstabs are invaluable when validating data in visualizations, and they are the most common type of text visualization.

Map

Map charts are geographic representations of data. They can be choropleth (filled maps) or symbol maps.

Pie

Pie charts illustrate composition and are usually composed of a dimension dividing the pie and a measure determining the size of the slices.

Gantt Bar

Gantt charts are used to illustrate events and duration in a visualization. The beginning of the bar illustrates the start of the event and the length of the bar illustrates its duration. They can also be used in waterfall charts to show increases and decreases in values. Gantt charts contain at least a date field and a dimension.

Polygon

Polygon charts are unique in that they follow a path to draw a shape. As a result, a new mark appears called "path" when a polygon chart is selected. Polygons can be used to draw unique maps of nongeographic areas, such as a building or even a body. A polygon chart can also be used to make more complex visualizations such as Sankey charts.

Density

Similar to maps, density plots mark points on a chart, but with a fading radius around the point. This is used to illustrate the density of value. The darker the shade, the higher concentration of data points or values in an area. This gives the effect of creating areas of frequency or heatmaps.

Color

The first control on the Marks card is Color. As expected, this shelf manages the color of your chart. It can be used without a field applied to it or it can be combined with a dimension or measure to provide granularity or detail to your visualization. Because the color field can be used in so many ways, it is important to discuss all its different uses.

The first way to interact with color is to use it without a field applied to it. With any visualization, you can click on the Color shelf to interact with it. Doing so reveals a menu of colors, allowing you to quickly change the color of the marks in your visualization. In addition, there are options to change opacity and add borders to the marks, as seen in Figure 2-13.

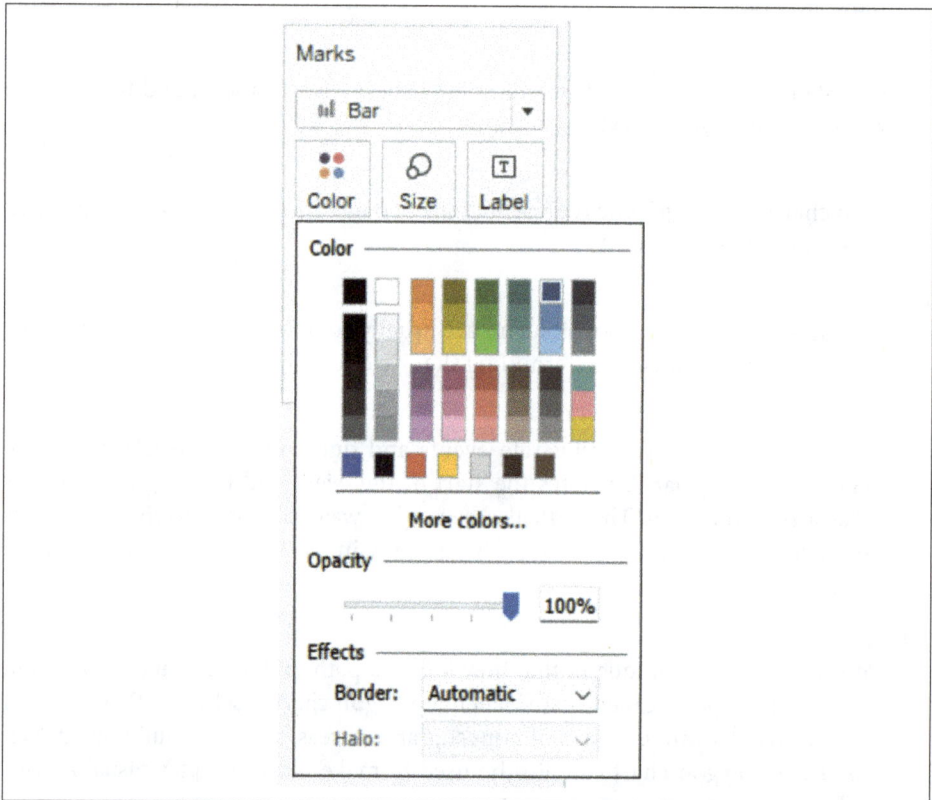

Figure 2-13. The color menu with no fields applied to the shelf.

Like most shelves in the Marks card, the color shelf can also be populated with a field from your data set. If you drag a field from your Data pane onto the Color shelf, the menus and options within change completely. The results are different for discrete values and continuous values as well. First, I will examine the options available to discrete values on the Color shelf.

When you drag a field to the Color shelf, the chart will automatically color by the values of the field. For example, if you add a State field to Color, your chart will have a different hue for every state in the data (except if a color repeats). Tableau will automatically apply a default color palette to the chart, but you can change this by clicking on the Color shelf once the field is added. The menu that appears is different from the menu for the single color select, as seen in Figure 2-14.

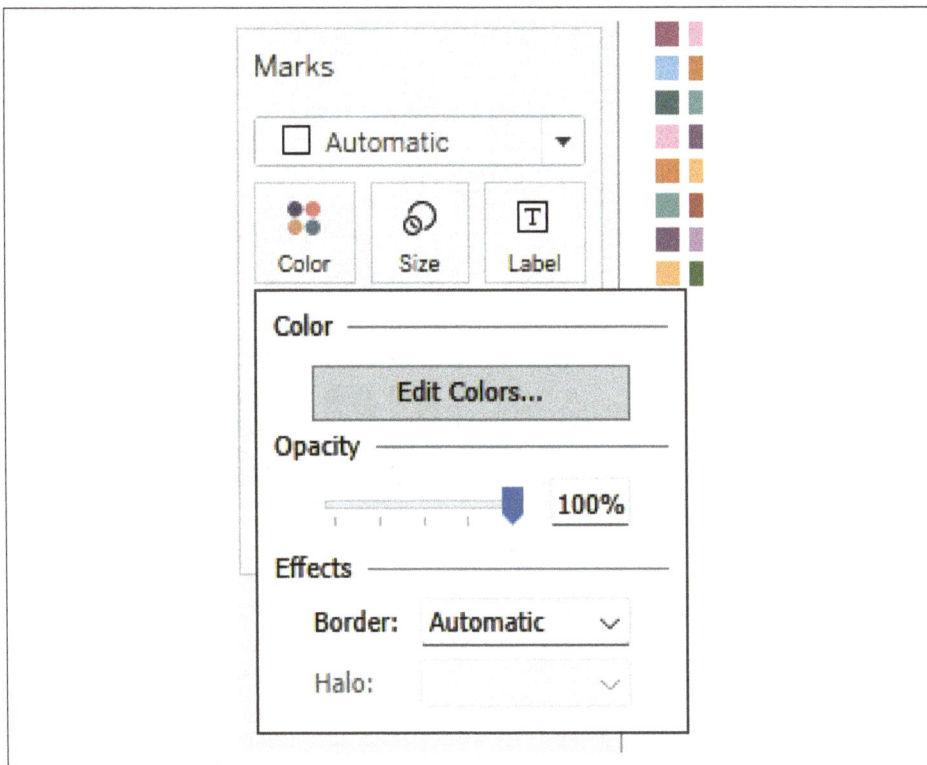

Figure 2-14. A different color menu appears when a field is added to the Color shelf and the shelf symbol is clicked.

The menu changes because now there is a field dividing the data into multiple sections or into a range of colors, meaning that more than one color is required. As a result, instead of selecting a single color in this menu, you are given the option to Edit Colors.

When you click Edit Colors, you will get one of two windows. The first Edit Colors window appears if you've selected a discrete field and added it to the Color shelf. Because discrete values divide the data into chunks, the color window provides options to color each field item independently, as shown in Figure 2-15. You can choose colors from the default palette or any of a large selection of palette options provided by Tableau. You can also import your own color palettes using a preferences file.

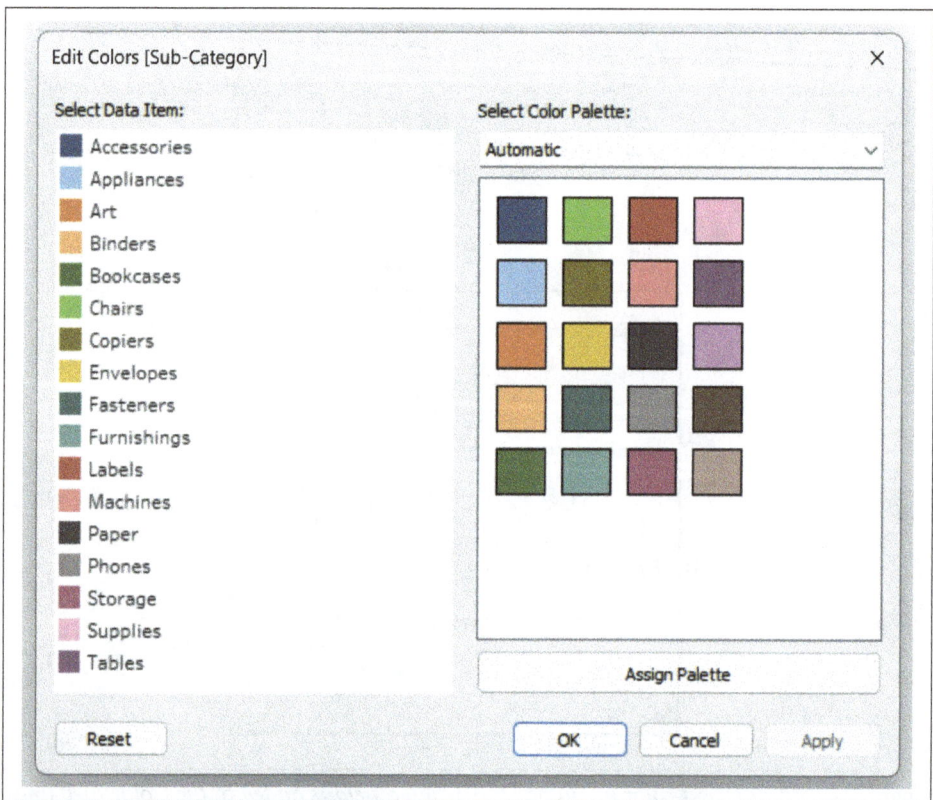

Figure 2-15. The discrete color window offers separate colors for each value in the field.

Continuous values added to the Color shelf behave differently. There are no discrete values to apply individual colors to. Instead, continuous fields have a range of values to which color can be applied. As a result, the Edit Colors window provides an option to add a gradient of colors, as shown in Figure 2-16. Similar to the discrete version of the window, the continuous Edit Colors window provides options for selecting a palette and applying the colors.

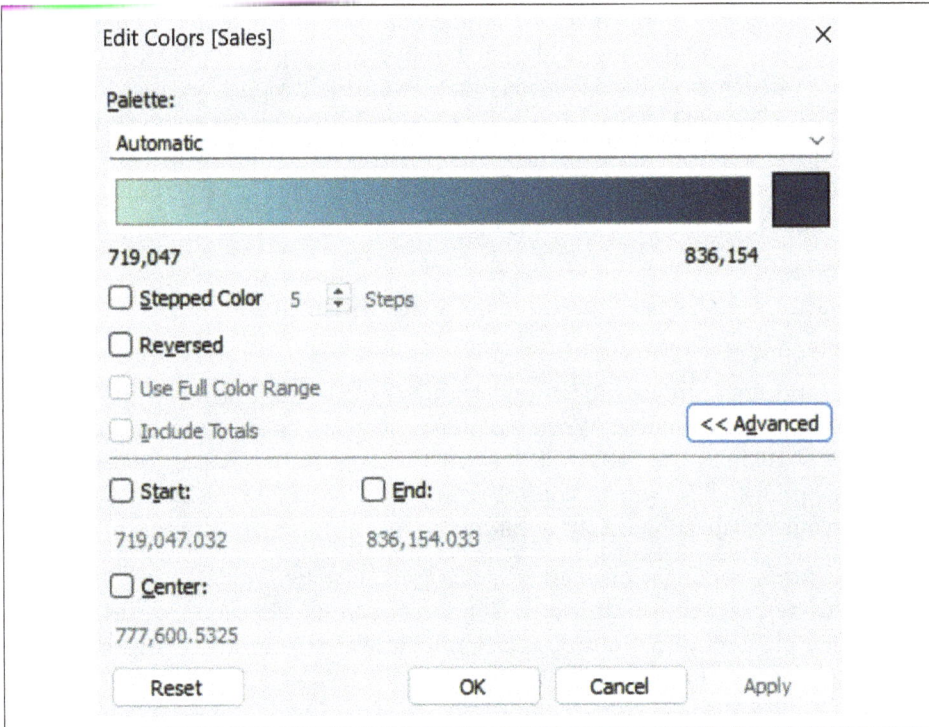

Figure 2-16. The continuous Edit Colors window displays a gradient to represent the values in the field. In this screenshot, the Advanced menu is expanded.

Unlike the discrete Edit Colors window, the gradient version provides a wider variety of options that you should know:

Stepped Color
> The Stepped Color option effectively divides your continuous range into discrete steps. You can set how many steps by adjusting the associated menu next to the Stepped Color option.

Reversed

> This option swaps the order of the gradient applied to the continuous value. For example, in Figure 2-16, the Reverse option would change the gradient to go from dark on the left to light on the right.

Use Full Color Range

> Within the color palette options are solid colors like those in Figure 2-16 or diverging colors—colors that have a midpoint with different colors on each side. If you have a continuous field with positive and negative values, a diverging palette will center at 0. This means that if your field values are heavily skewed positive or negative, those colors will be much richer than the opposite side. This option will ensure that the richness is equivalent on both sides of the midpoint. So, if your data values go from –10 to 100, the –10 will be as rich in the negative color as the 100 is in the positive color.

Include Totals

> This will assign the palette colors to the totals as well.

Start/End/Center

> These three options are hidden underneath the Advanced menu on the continuous Edit Colors window. When assigning the color palette to your continuous range, sometimes you need to shift where the range starts, ends, or centers. These three options allow you to control where the color range resides regardless of how your visualization is split or filtered.

Color is a key component of many visualizations. It draws attention and illustrates patterns using preattentive attributes. For these reasons, Tableau provides a Color shelf with a plethora of options designed specifically for your chart, regardless of it being a solid color or assigned a value based on the field assigned to it. Understanding how to utilize color in visualizations is key to exploring data and extracting information from it.

> When studying for the exam, practice assigning color to your visualizations and using colors to divide your charts by dimensions or identify highs and lows of a measure. Pay special attention to the additional options in the continuous Edit Colors window and experiment using them to highlight key values in your visualizations.

Your managers know that there are many states making large amounts of profit for your company, but there are some that are still losing profit. They'd like you to help highlight these states and how much they are gaining or losing. You know a map colored by profit would accomplish this. How should your Color shelf be configured to accomplish your goal?

A. Add the State field to Color, choose Color By in the window that appears, and select Profit as the field to color by.

B. Simply add color to the Profit menu

C. Add Profit to the Color shelf, but check the box for Use Full Color Range to ensure that the low profit states are brightly colored.

D. Add Profit to the Color shelf, but change the center to 0.

E. Add the State field to Profit and sort state by profit.

Answer: C—Adding Profit to the Color shelf will automatically select a diverging (multicolored) palette. If you do not select Use Full Color Range, the states losing profit will not be as vividly colored since some of the other states have profits that are very high.

Size

After color, size is the next way to adjust your visualizations. Similar to the previous shelf, the Size shelf has multiple ways to interact with it. It adds a level of detail to the visualization. It also plays a pivotal role in multiple types of visualizations.

To begin with, you can interact with the Size shelf by simply clicking it, as shown in Figure 2-17. The slider that appears will adjust the size of objects depending on the visualization type. For bar charts, it changes the width of the bar, for line charts it adjusts the width of the line, and for scatter plots, it adjusts the size of the dot or shape used in the visualization. It can also be used with crosstabs to adjust the size of the text! The slider provides hash marks along the line indicating key points that can or should be used when adjusting the size of the mark.

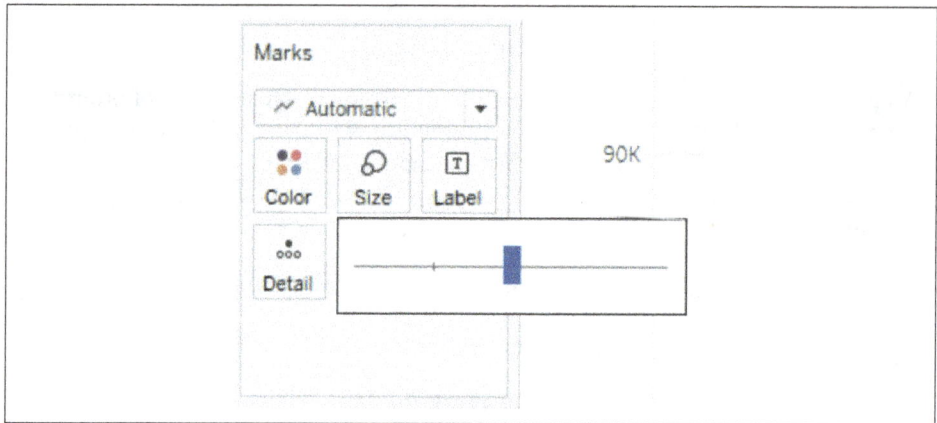

Figure 2-17. For any chart type, the size slider will adjust the size of the mark, be it bar, line, dot, or other type.

As with color, the Size shelf can also have fields applied to it. Discrete fields, when applied, adjust the size of the marks in the visualization by the field applied. For example, if you have a scatter plot chart and apply a category field to Size, the size of the dots on the scatter plot will be adjusted based on the category they represent. The field on the Size shelf doesn't change the underlying menu much. If you click the Size shelf, you will still see the slider option shown in Figure 2-17 with potentially more hash marks based on the visualization. Continuous fields added to the Size shelf are binned into ranges, and each bin is assigned a different size.

Both continuous and discrete fields on the Size shelf have additional controls associated with them. After applying a field to the Size shelf, Tableau will automatically generate a legend for the sizes. Clicking on the menu for the legend gives you an option to edit sizes, as shown in Figure 2-18. This option is the same for both types of fields (continuous and discrete), but the resulting window is slightly different.

The window that appears allows you to adjust some of the settings for the Sizes menu. Both continuous and discrete windows allow you to adjust the size of the smallest and largest marks in your visualization. They both also provide an option to reverse the order of the sizes. For continuous fields, the window also provides options to adjust how the sizes vary and the numerical values in your data where the sizes start and end, as shown in Figure 2-19. The "Sizes vary" menu gives options to adjust the sizes of the marks by the values in the field or force them to start at 0.

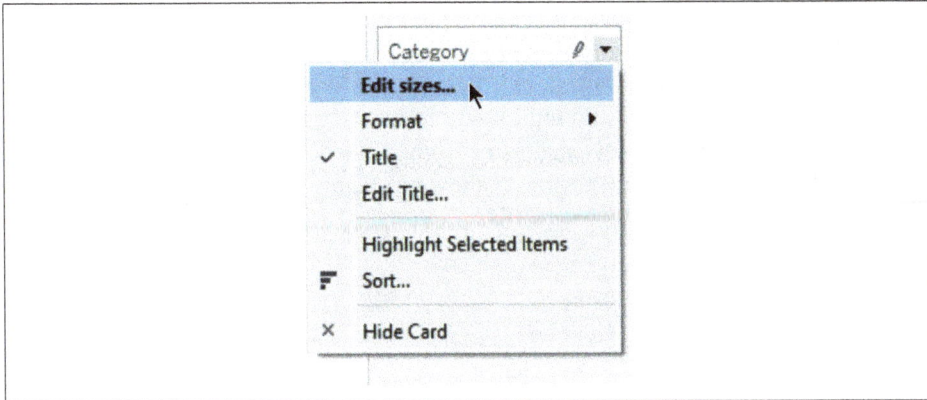

Figure 2-18. The menu on the Size legend contains an option to edit sizes, which will open a size control window when selected.

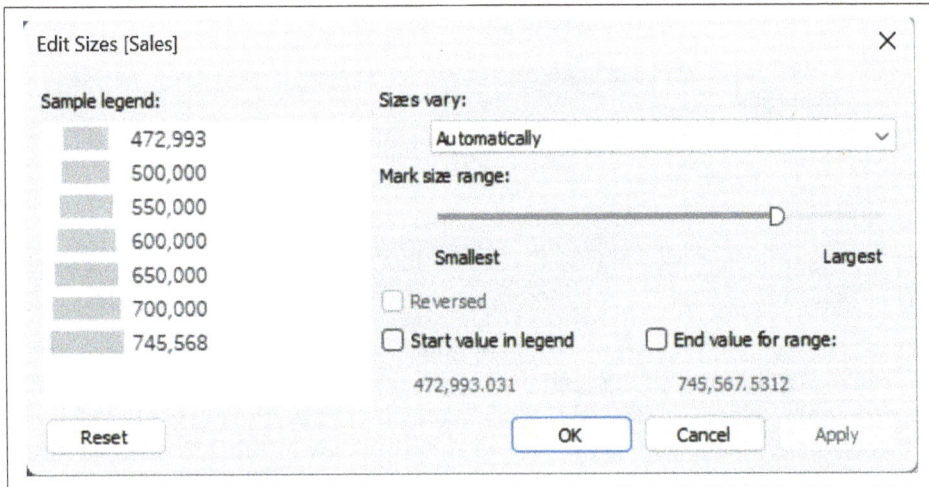

Figure 2-19. The Edit Sizes window for a continuous field, illustrating the multiple ways to control how the sizes are applied.

Label/Text

Tableau provides the ⊤ icon above the visualization area to enable and disable labels on a visualization. This option is great for quickly labeling your visualizations, but it lacks control on how the values appear. The better way to control text on your visualization is the Label or Text shelf on the Marks card. The name of the shelf and the options within change based on the type of visualization. To understand each possibility, I will examine them one at a time.

The shelf is labeled "Text" when the visualization is a crosstab. Crosstabs are made by adding dimensions to Rows and Columns while placing a measure on the Text shelf. As a result, crosstabs will always have a field on the shelf (unlike shelves like Color and Size). This means there is no logical way to interact with the Text shelf without a field on it. With a field, the Text shelf controls how the font aligns within the areas of the crosstab and how the text appears, as shown in Figure 2-20.

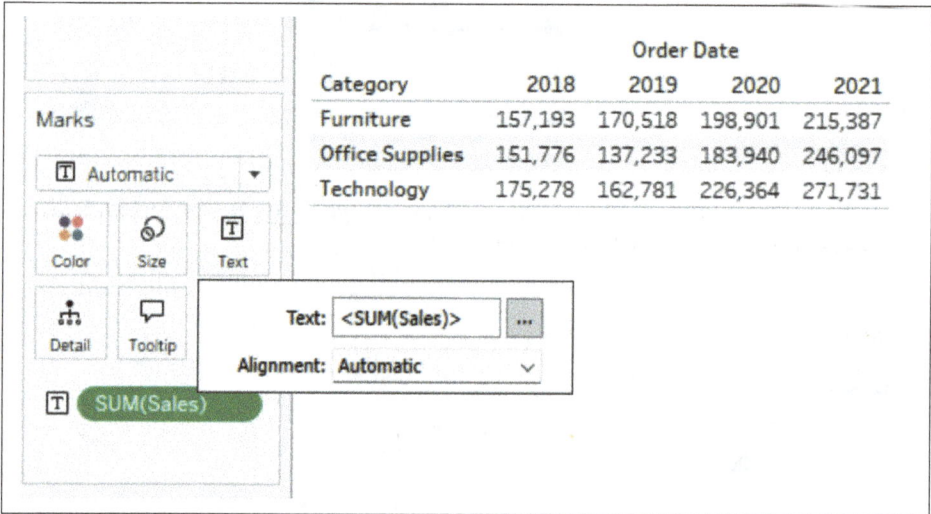

Figure 2-20. The Text shelf window that appears when clicking the Text shelf for a crosstab.

The ellipsis menu next to Text provides options for font and more; I will cover those in detail toward the end of this section. The Alignment menu controls where the text appears in the cell of the crosstab both horizontally and vertically. Additionally, you can control the orientation of the text, rotating it in any of the four cardinal directions. Finally, there is an option to control wrap, which controls how larger values of text traverse to the next line when they reach the end of a cell. Without wrap, long sections of text can get cut off or even revert to hash marks if they do not fit entirely in the cell of the crosstab.

For other types of visualizations, the shelf changes its title to "Label." Labels can be applied without a field added to the shelf, similar to how Color and Size work without fields. When you click on the Label shelf without a field, the menu that appears gives options to turn labels on and off, change the font and alignment, and adjust which of the marks on the visualization to label, as shown in Figure 2-21. There is also an option to allow labels to overlap, which forces Tableau to label all the marks in a visualization even if they overlap other marks, labels, etc.

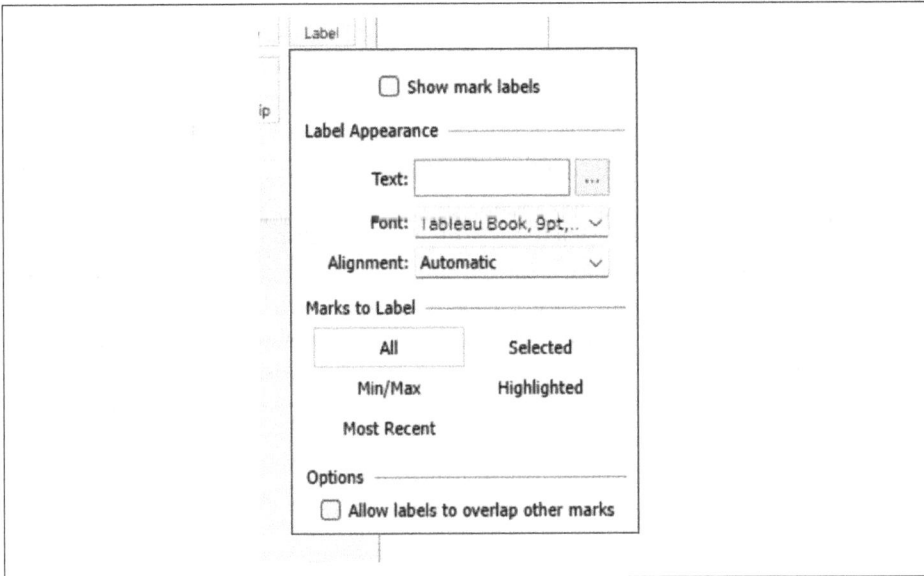

Figure 2-21. The Label shelf menu holds options to control how and where labels appear in a visualization. Without a field on the shelf, the ellipsis next to the Text field is grayed out.

The "Marks to Label" option needs to be explained in a bit more detail. By default, the option is set to label all marks in the visualization, but it can be changed to any of the other options. The available choices depends on the type of visualization and the fields within:

Min/Max
Selecting this option will expand the menu. The expanded area will include scope—do you want the maximum and minimum of the whole visualization or each subsection within? It will let you choose which field to use to calculate the minimum and maximum, and then provide you options to show minimum, maximum, or both.

Line Ends
Selecting this option will label the ends of a line chart.

Selected
This option will disable labels until the user clicks on one of the marks in the visualization. Clicking the mark will enable its label.

Highlighted
Similar to selecting, highlighting a mark will make the label visible.

Most Recent

Only available in charts with dates in the visualization, this option only labels the most recent mark in the data.

When you add a field to the Label shelf, the field gets added to the label. In addition, in the shelf menu, you will find that the Text ellipsis is no longer grayed out. Adding a field to the label allows you to have direct control over the text in the label itself. This control is extremely beneficial when designing labels with multiple fields or controlling fonts and text modifications. Clicking the ellipsis will open the Edit Label window, prepopulated with the field on the shelf, as shown in Figure 2-22. From here, you can change attributes of the font such as the type, color, size, alignment, and formatting. You can also directly enter text in this window as desired.

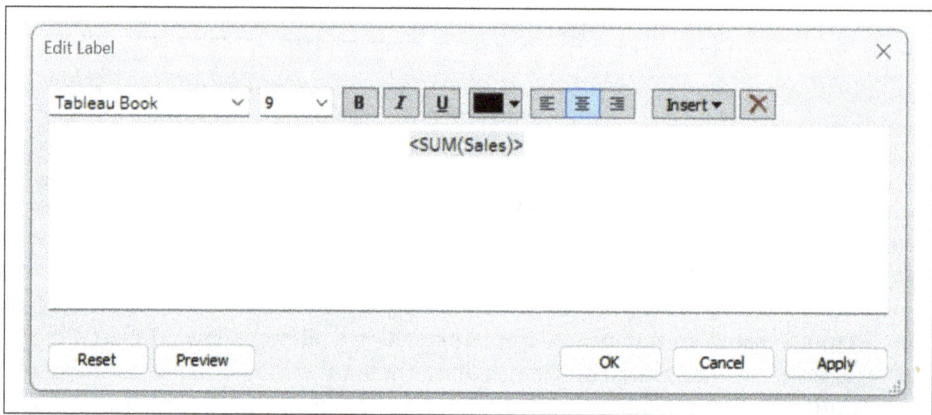

Figure 2-22. The Edit Label window provides you with options to modify what text the label contains.

The Label and Text shelves allow you to add multiple fields. These fields are then available in the Edit Label window. As mentioned before, you can also type freely in the window, allowing you to create more informative labels. For example, if you added the Product field and Sales field to the label, you could type the following:

```
Product Name:       <Product Name>
Amount of Sales:    <SUM(Sales)>
```

to get a label that shows not only what the value of the mark is, but also what product it represents, as shown in Figure 2-23.

Sheet 1

Product Name: Cisco Unified IP Phone 7945G VoIP phone
Sales: 6,751.6

Product Name: Hon Every-Day Series Multi-Task Chairs
Sales: 6,748.5

Product Name: ClearOne CHATAttach 160 - speaker phone
Sales: 6,695.9

Product Name: Standard Rollaway File with Lock
Sales: 6,595.0

Product Name: Hon Multipurpose Stacking Arm Chairs
Sales: 6,584.6

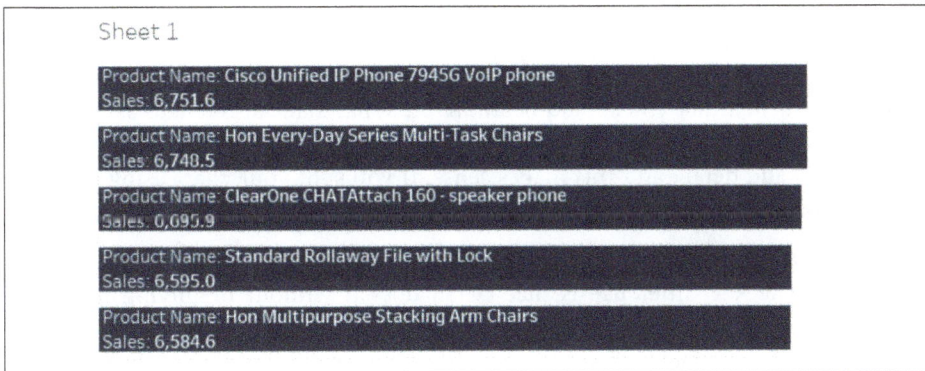

Figure 2-23. Combining multiple fields to make a more useful label.

> When studying for the exam, experiment with adding fields to labels. Try recreating labels already existing in charts on Tableau Public or within your own dashboards. Pay special attention to the Marks to Label option and explore how it reacts as you change selections.

Example Question

You created a beautiful bar chart showing sales for your company by year for the past five years. If you wanted to show only the value for the most recent year, which option would you use in the label menu?

A. Most Recent

B. Selected

C. Highlighted

D. Line Ends

E. All

Answer: A—Most Recent is the only answer that works. Min/Max could work here as well, but only if Max was checked and the field set to your date field. Min/Max applied to another field, such as Sales, would show your maximum sales instead. Line Ends is only an option when the chart is a line chart, not a bar chart.

Detail

This particular shelf is abstract, but also very important. There are several key uses for the Detail shelf that you should be aware of. What Tableau refers to as *detail* can also be thought of as granularity. In the previous sections, I mentioned that both color and size also add detail, and this makes sense. If you split your chart using colors or sizes, you are adding granularity to the visualization.

Detail does the same thing as Color and Size—it splits the chart up by some other dimension. The key difference is that Detail does it without modifying the visual appearance of the chart as significantly. Detail is also the only shelf that requires a field to be on it to impact the visualization. Clicking the shelf itself does nothing at all. Also, Detail requires the field added to be discrete to impact the chart. Since this shelf adds granularity to a chart via a field, it makes sense that the field applied be a discrete value.

The best way to understand detail is to create a bar chart such as sales by discrete year. If you were then to add a dimension such as product category to the Detail shelf, the bars would split into sections based on the category. Nothing else would indicate that anything changed on the chart. It's effectively the same thing as adding a discrete dimension to the Color shelf except that the chart doesn't get colored.

Detail can be used for other tasks as well. For map visualizations, the Detail shelf holds the granular field that will divide up the sections of map, such as state or country. For scatter plots, the Detail shelf divides up the points on the plot, as shown in Figure 2-24. The Detail shelf can also be used to hold continuous values that you wish to use elsewhere in the visualization, such as titles.

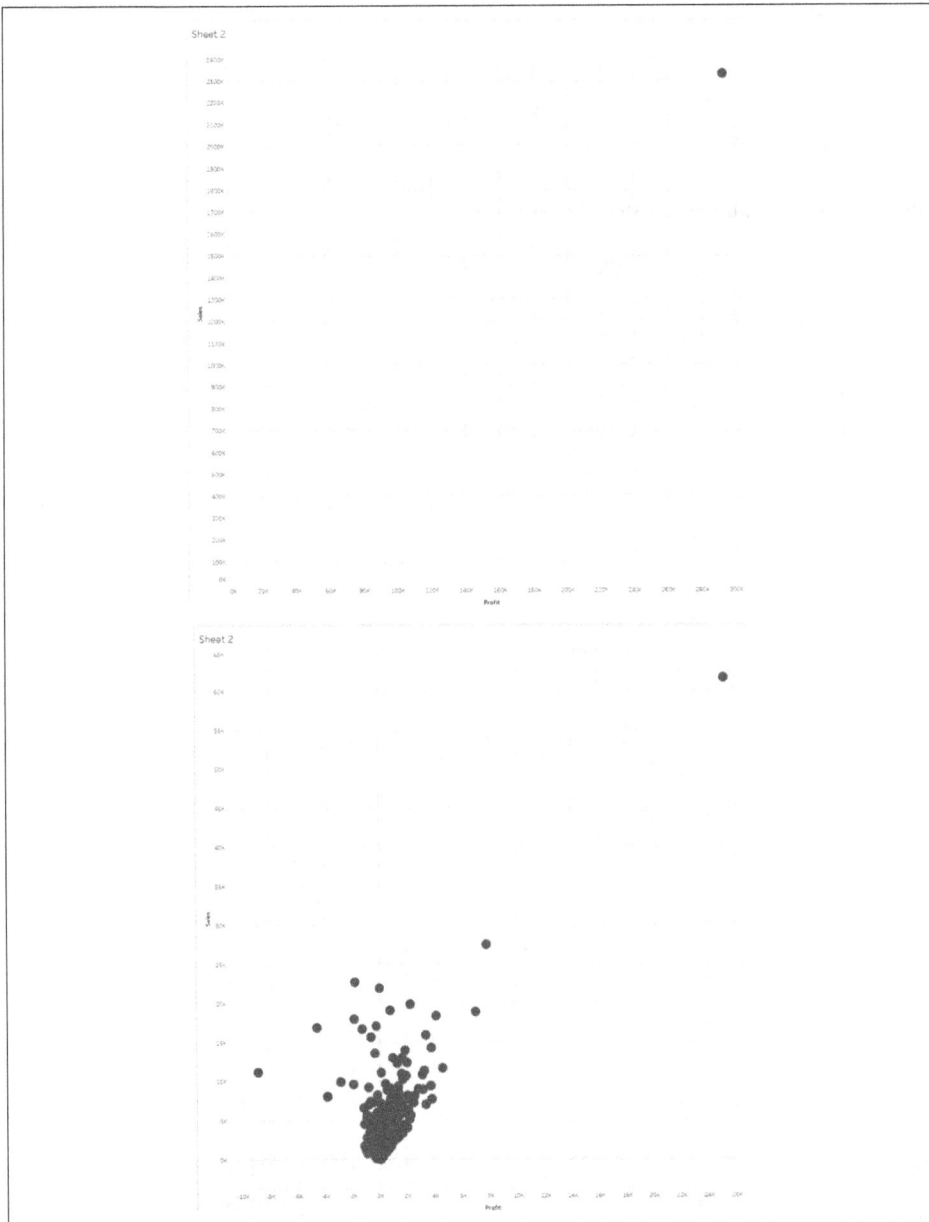

Figure 2-24. The Detail shelf divides up scatter plots by the field they hold. The chart on the top has no detail and shows a single point illustrating the total sales by the total profit for the entire data set. The chart on the bottom shows the sales and profit at the detail, or granularity, of each product (the Product field is placed on the Detail shelf).

Tooltip

Tooltips are generated automatically when you build a visualization. Tableau populates them with the dimensions and measures added to the view. Similar to labels, you can modify tooltip appearance and content. You can also drag fields to the tooltip to provide information as necessary. There are also several options and features within the tooltip that you should be familiar with.

Tooltips populate automatically. When you click on the Tooltip shelf, you will be provided the Edit Tooltip window prepopulated with the fields in the visualization, as seen in Figure 2-25. If nothing is in the visualization, the window will be blank. The buttons at the top control options about the tooltip, such as font, color, formatting, and alignment. Similar to labels, there is also a pull-down menu that provides options for adding additional information. I'll dig into this menu shortly.

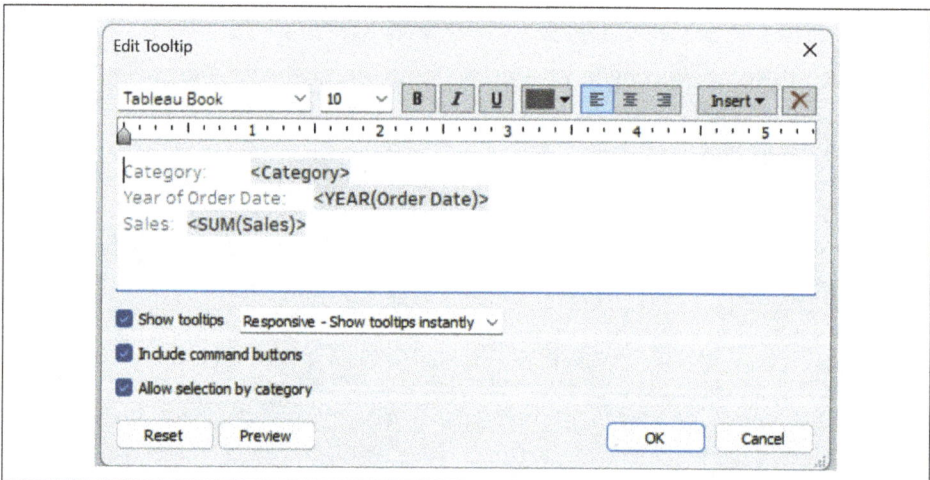

Figure 2-25. A Tooltip window for a chart containing sales by the year of the order date and category.

The idea behind tooltips is to provide additional specific details about the mark being hovered over. If you assume the chart associated with Figure 2-25 is a bar chart, then the tooltip will display the associated sales, product category, and year information for the bar that you hover over. The panel is completely editable, which allows you to adjust the syntax and formatting of the tooltip. You could make the tooltip sound more like natural language by changing it to say:

```
In <YEAR(Order Date)>, for the <Category> category,
the total sales were <SUM(Sales)>.
```

If you then hover over the 2021 bar for Office Supplies, the resulting tooltip pop-up would contain the sentence, "In 2021, for the Office Supplies category, the total sales were $137,670."

At the bottom of the Tooltip window are three checkbox options. Each checkbox is selected by default and controls how the workbook displays tooltips:

Show tooltips

This checkbox enables and disables tooltips. The pull-down menu to the right controls tooltip menus. The Responsive selection (currently selected in Figure 2-25) will show the tooltip with no menus or options for a brief period. If the user hovers over the mark for an extended period of time or clicks on the mark, the command buttons will appear. The On Hover selection will show the tooltip with these command buttons visible immediately.

Include command buttons

The command buttons are a menu of options that appear at the top of the Tooltip window. This option allows you to control whether these buttons are available. The command buttons allow the user to include or exclude (filter) the selected item within the visualization. They also allow the user to create groups and sets of marks on the fly by clicking and highlighting multiple marks at a time. Doing so will update the tooltip values to create a summary of what is selected. Depending on the option selected in the "Show tooltips" menu, these buttons will appear automatically, after a brief delay, or when the mark is clicked on by the user.

Allow selection by category

If the view has multiple marks, this option will allow the user to click and drag a selection box around multiple marks. Doing so will update the tooltip and show the user an aggregate summary of the marks selected.

The remaining buttons within the Edit Tooltip window are self-explanatory. They reset the tooltip to its default view (Reset) and provide a sample preview of the tooltip using data from the view (Preview).

The Insert menu at the top deserves additional attention, as it provides functionality that is not immediately apparent. Options for inserting objects into the tooltip are broken out by their function within the menu, as seen in Figure 2-26.

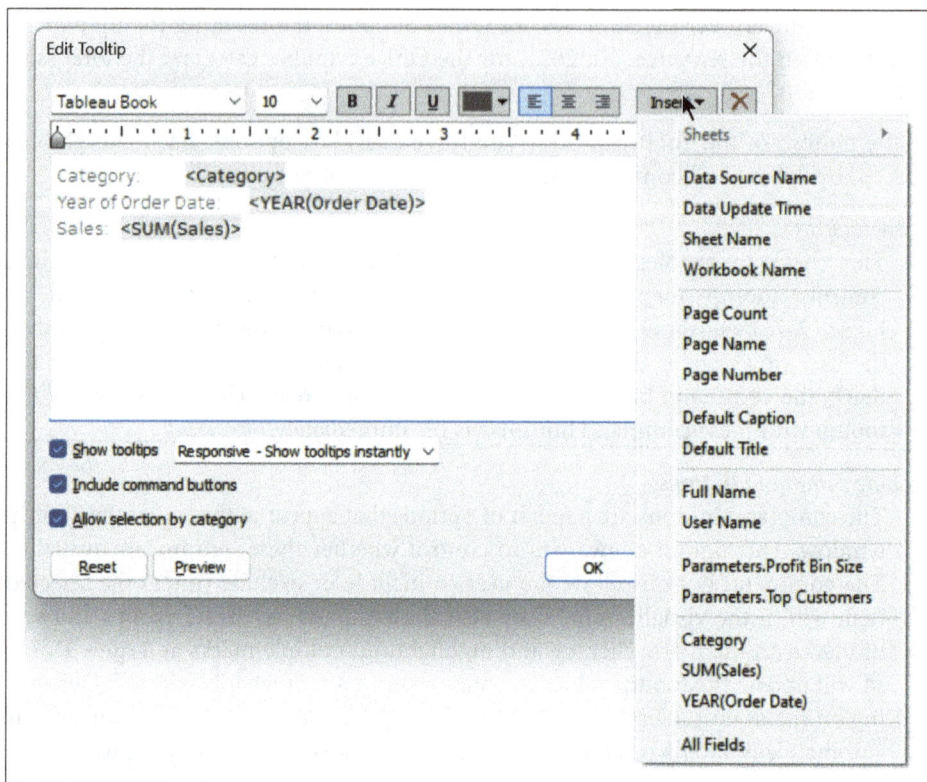

Figure 2-26. The Insert menu within the Edit Tooltip window provides additional items to add to your tooltip.

At the very top is an option to include sheets in the tooltip. If your workbook contains multiple visualizations, you can insert one as a tooltip for another. For example, if you build a map showing profit across the United States, you could include a state-specific chart in the tooltip, detailing profit profits by city for that state. When you click the Sheet option, it shows you a selection list of all other available charts in the workbook. When you select one, it populates the tooltip with a modifiable chunk of code similar to this:

```
<Sheet name="Cities" maxwidth="300" maxheight="300" filter="<All Fields>">
```

This code tells Tableau to generate the inserted view (Sheet name), applies a limit for the height and width (`maxwidth`, `maxheight`), and then filters the tooltip visualization based on what is being hovered over in the main visualization (filter). You can then use these fields to make the tooltip visualization larger or smaller and control what fields are being used to filter the tooltip chart. The result is a tooltip that displays additional information based on what is hovered over in the main visualization. The inserted sheet also does not need to be alone, and it's entirely possible to add other fields and values from the main view in addition to the nested tooltip visualization, as seen in Figure 2-27.

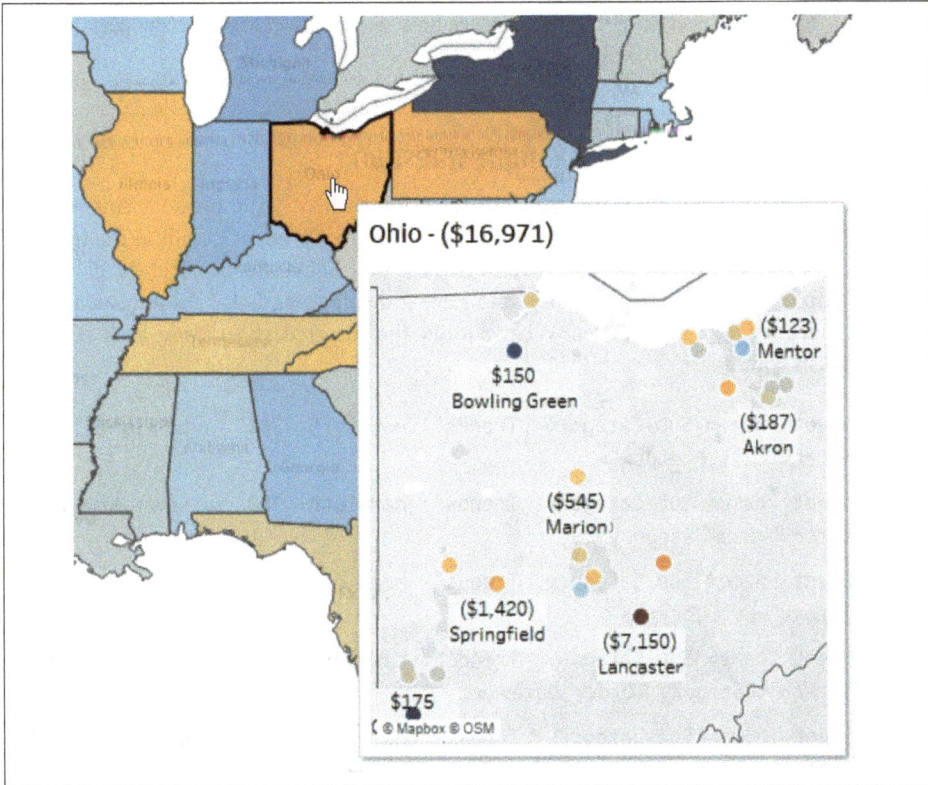

Figure 2-27. A visualization within a tooltip. The state name and total profit for the state are populated by fields in the main (national) visualization, while the city names and values are contained in a separate chart. The separate chart in the tooltip populates based on what state is hovered over within the main visualization.

In addition to inserting sheets, the pull-down menu also contains options to add worksheet metadata, data source metadata, information about the user, parameter values, and field values from the view. There are also options to complete inserted sheet field values. For example, if you are modifying your insert sheet code and wish to reset the filter code to its default, there is an option in this menu to insert the All Fields designation.

An exam question about views in tooltips is entirely possible. Practice building some of your own and experiment with changing sizes and filter values. Review the command button options by enabling and disabling them to see how the tooltip reacts in visualizations you've built.

Example Question

You create a chart showing the trend of sales for each of your product categories. You've made a similar visualization called "Sub-Category Trends" detailing the trends for each of the subcategories. You wish to include the "Sub-Category Trends" chart in the tooltip of your main visualization and have it display trends for the subcategories of the category you hover over. What should the inserted sheet code look like to accomplish your goal?

A. `<Sheet name="Sub-Category Trends" maxwidth="300" maxheight="300" filter="<All Fields>">`

B. `<Sheet name="Sub-Category Trends" maxwidth="300" maxheight="300" filter="<Sub-Category>">`

C. `<Sheet name="Sub-Category Trends" maxwidth="300" maxheight="300" filter="<Category>">`

D. `<Sheet name="Sub-Category Trends" maxwidth="300" maxheight="300" filter="<Category, Order Date>">`

E. `<Sheet name="Sub-Category Trends" maxwidth="300" maxheight="300" filter="">`

Answer: C—You want to show trends on the tooltip visualization. If you include the date, as in A and D, you will also filter down to the year you've hovered over in the main chart. B is not an option because Sub-Category is not an available field in the main chart. E will show all subcategories in the tooltip, not just the category you hover over.

Shape, Path, or Angle

The final shelf on the Marks card is not always visible. When it is visible, it can take one of three forms—Shape, Path, or Angle. The type of chart you build determines the visibility and shelf type available in this field.

The Shape option appears by default when you develop a visualization that is a scatter plot or a shape map. Similar to other shelves, the Shape icon can be controlled by clicking on it or dragging fields to it. Without a field added to it, the Shape shelf allows you to change all the marks in the visualization to a different shape. Tableau offers a default selection of common shapes and then provides a More Shapes option. Clicking this will send you to the Edit Shape window, as seen in Figure 2-28. The Edit Shape window contains multiple shape palettes with a wide variety of shapes in each. You can add custom shapes as well, as described in the Tableau documentation (*https://oreil.ly/vl5Jt*).

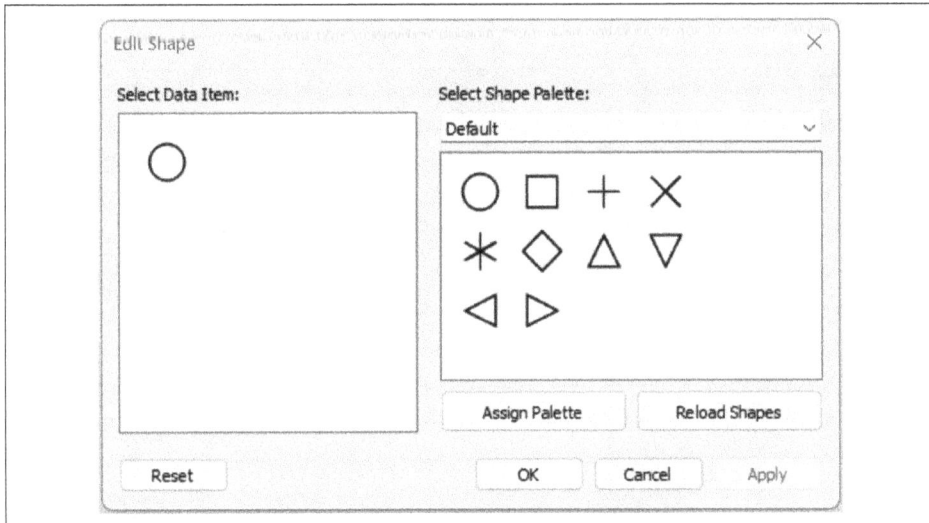

Figure 2-28. The Edit Shape window allows you to change the shape of points in your visualization from a large number of predefined shape palettes.

When a field is added to the Shape shelf, it will change the shapes of the points in the view based on the value of the field you added. Since a mark can only have one shape, anything you add to the Shape shelf will instantly be converted to discrete. With a field added to the Shape shelf, the Edit Shape window changes slightly, giving you a list of the added field's values to associate with the shapes.

The shelf changes to Path when your mark type becomes a polygon. Unlike other shelves, this type of shelf cannot be clicked on. It must have a data field applied to it. Polygon charts map out the shape of an object based on coordinate points and connect the points using the field applied to the Path shelf. In this way, they are very similar to a child's connect-the-dots puzzle. Polygon figures can be used to generate unique types of visualizations, such as Sankey, radar, and coxcomb charts. They can also be used to create a mapping for nongeographic figures.

Angle appears only when building pie charts. Typically speaking, pie charts are divided into sections by a dimension on the color field. The proportion each dimension value takes in the pie chart is then determined by a measure placed on the Angle shelf. Angle only allows measures to be added and does not have a direct interaction associated with it.

For the exam, you will need to recognize chart types and how to assemble them correctly. There will likely be questions asking you where to place fields to recreate a visualization presented to you. Understanding how the Rows, Columns, and Marks interact with each other is vital to doing well, so practice building and rebuilding charts until you are comfortable with how each shelf works.

Conclusion

The exam will test your knowledge of the interface, especially the Marks, Rows, and Columns cards and shelves. These areas are the basis for building any and all types of charts. The exam will likely contain questions challenging you on how to replicate an existing chart. They may also ask questions about where data fields need to be placed to achieve a certain type of view into the data. Other questions may ask you to determine a value by placing fields from a data set into a view. Being able to quickly navigate through the interface to design and develop reliable visualizations is key to addressing these questions successfully.

CHAPTER 3

Analyzing Data in Tableau Desktop

At this point, you should understand the basics of how to utilize your data fields to build data visualizations in Tableau. You should have a strong grasp of how the Columns, Rows, Filters, and Marks cards work together to help you identify trends, relationships, and outliers in your data. Now, I want to dig deeper into what is possible within the software, beyond building simple bar and line charts, and start digging into the data. In this chapter, I will explore some of the built-in functionalities of Tableau: how to manipulate your data with calculations, implement multiple axes, and group and sort your data. More importantly, I will show you a wide array of tools designed to help you more thoroughly analyze your data.

Quickly Building Basic Visualization Types

Chapter 2 demonstrated what happens when you place fields in regions of the Tableau interface. Dimensions placed in rows or columns divide the chart up vertically or horizontally, respectively. Measures in rows or columns add an axis vertically or horizontally (respectively) to quickly gauge the value of that measure. The Filters card controls what is and isn't shown, and the Marks card controls what the chart looks like through the chart type menu, color, size, label, and more. In this section, I want to cover the basic chart types and how to develop them to get your desired results quickly, without wasting time moving fields around or using the Show Me menu.

Bar Charts

There are five main types of charts that use bars: vertical bar charts, horizontal bar charts, histograms, bullet graphs, and Gantt charts. While the first two are pretty simple, the others take a bit more work to build:

Vertical bar charts

    The bread-and-butter chart for most data analysts is the vertical bar chart. It consists of at least one measure on Rows and any number of discrete dimensions on Columns. Without a dimension on Columns, you will get a single bar indicating the value of the measure for the entire data set. Each dimension you add to Columns divides the bar based on the discrete values of the dimension. Vertical bar charts become stacked bar charts if you add additional dimensions to the Color or Detail marks.

Horizontal bar charts

    These charts are exactly the same as vertical bar charts, except that the fields on Columns and Rows are reversed. This move splits the chart on the y-axis and displays the measure values on the x-axis, creating horizontal bars. This type of chart is typically used when you want to add a bar chart to your dashboard, but lack the real estate to fit a vertical bar chart in or when you have categorical data and need headers to be easy to read.

Histograms

    Histograms are statistical bar charts illustrating the frequency of events. I will discuss them in detail later in this chapter, but to build one, you need a bin field and a measure. Typically the bin field is placed on Columns, and the measure is placed on Rows. This will show you the distribution of that measure across the range of values in the binned field. It's possible to build horizontal histograms, but they are traditionally viewed vertically.

Bullet graphs

    Bullet graphs are used to track progress toward a goal or value. Effectively, they consist of two overlapping bars, with one showing the values of one measure and the other showing the second measure overlaid, as in Figure 3-1. In Tableau, bullet charts are usually constructed with a bar chart atop reference bands or lines. The bullet graph is a rare case where using the Show Me menu is the fastest way to develop the chart, since you'll need additional Tableau features (reference lines) to display it properly. To build a bullet graph quickly, add both measures to either axis, then use the Show Me menu to select the bullet graph. You can then add dimensions to divide up the graph.

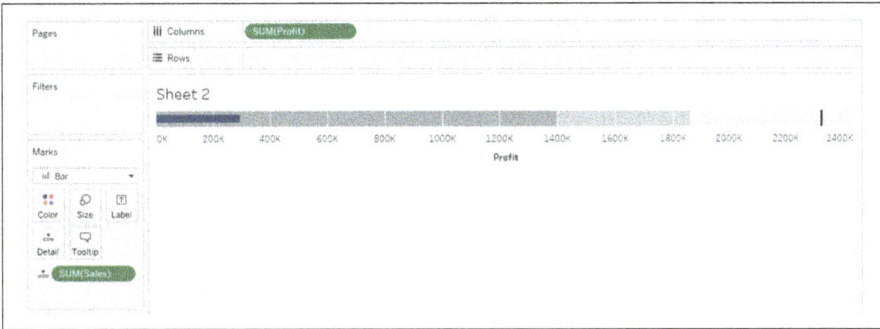

Figure 3-1. A bullet graph overlays two bar charts to illustrate how far one measure reaches in comparison to the other. This bullet graph shows total profit atop total sales. Tableau uses reference zones and lines to build out the underlying measure.

Gantt charts

Gantt charts are used to visualize the duration of events on a timeline. Building one requires a continuous date field on Columns that represents when an event started. It also requires a duration field on the Size mark to tell Tableau how long to make the Gantt bar. This duration field often requires a calculation to measure the difference in time between a starting point and endpoint within the data. Once you've added these fields, you can split the Gantt chart by a dimension to get the desired level of granularity.

For a simple example: you can use the Superstore data built into Tableau to make a Gantt chart. To try it, place the Order Date field on Columns as a continuous date at the level of Day. This plots every order date continuously on the X axis. Then you can write a calculation (covered later in this chapter) to determine the number of days between when an object was ordered and when it shipped. Placing this measure on the Size mark extends the bar from `Order Date` to `Shipped Date` in the visualization. Then just divide the bars at the level of granularity you are interested in (such as `Product Name` or `Order ID`).

Lines and Area Charts

Line charts are used to measure values over a continuous field or ordinal data. Continuous fields do not divide the data into chunks, but rather follow the range of values. The granularity of the continuous field determines how detailed the line chart is at each point. For example, charting sales by continuous order date at a monthly level will have fewer hills and valleys than charting sales by continuous order date at a daily level (Figure 3-2).

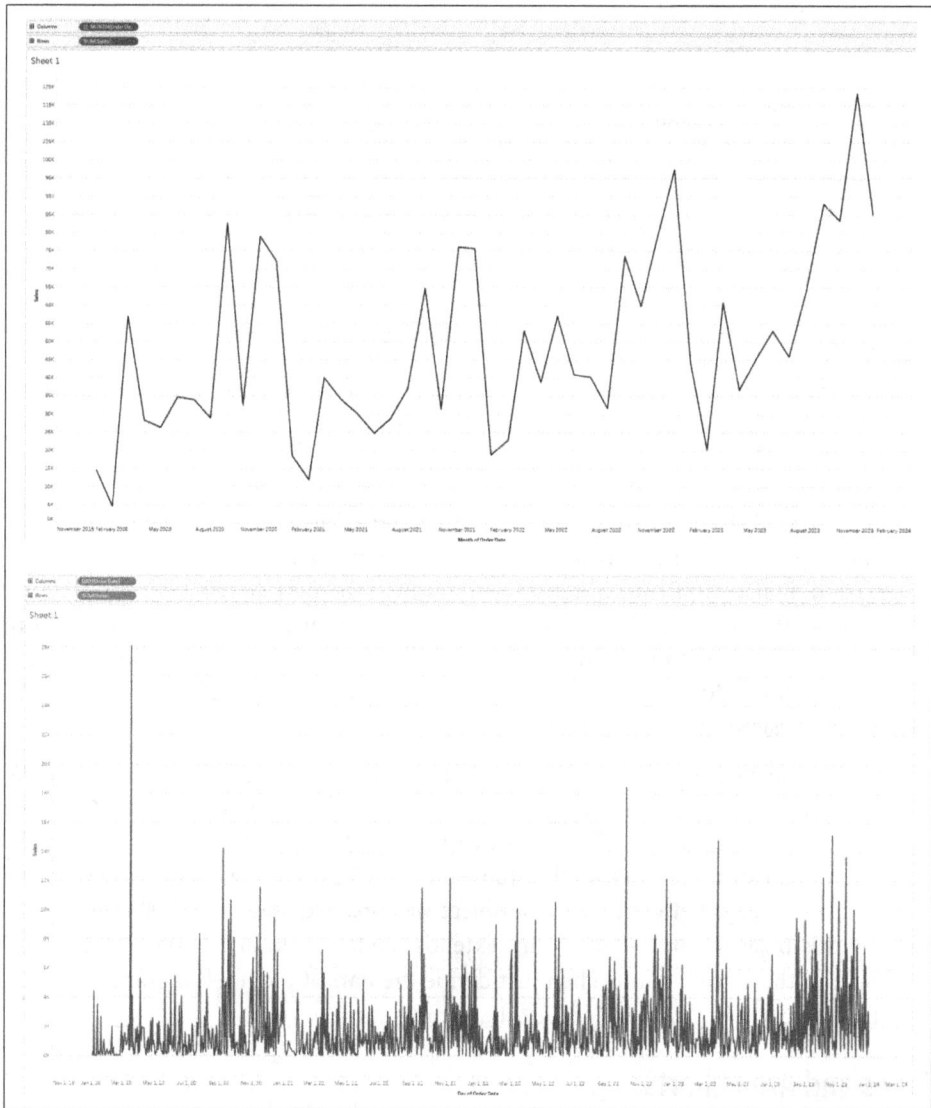

Figure 3-2. The granularity of a continuous dimension will determine how detailed the corresponding chart is. The chart at the top is sales by continuous month of order date; the chart at the bottom is sales by continuous day of order date.

The level of granularity you want is determined by what question you're using the chart to answer:

Line charts

Line charts are used to represent continuous fields because they encourage the eye to follow the flow of data from left to right, whereas bar charts are read chunk by chunk. You can build a line chart quickly by adding a continuous dimension to Columns and a measure to Rows. Tableau also allows you to use a discrete dimension on columns to make a line chart, though these are generally better visualized as a bar chart.

Area charts

Like line charts, area charts map out the flow of values over a continuous dimension, usually time. An area chart is simply a line chart with the space below the line filled in with a solid color. It is built exactly the same way, except for changing the chart type in the Marks card from Line to Area.

Scatter Plots

Scatter plots use the Cartesian plane to display information about your data at the level of granularity you define. The values of the x-axis and y-axis are typically continuous, and the individual points plotted on that plane are based on the intersections of those two values in the data. While technically there is only one type of scatter plot, Tableau offers two ways to build scatter plots and identifies them as different chart types:

Dimensional scatter plots

A dimensional scatter plot uses a dimension to develop the x-axis (Columns) of the coordinate plane. The plotted values are then based on the measure value on the y-axis (Rows). From here, you can divide the chart further by adding dimensions to Color, Size, Shape, or Detail. Doing so will increase the granularity of the data, creating more points and providing additional information. This scatter plot type is called a Circle View in Tableau's Show Me menu.

Measure-based scatter plots

When you see "scatter plot" in the Show Me menu, Tableau means this more traditional type of scatter plot. To build it, you will need a measure on Rows and a measure on Columns. The plotted point will be based on the intersection of these two values. If you have no dimensions on the chart, there will be a singular point at the intersection of the total data set value of the x-axis measure and the total data set value of the y-axis measure.

Both types of scatter plot become more useful and granular as you add dimensions, creating fields on the Marks card (Color, Size, Shape, and Detail).

Text-Based Charts

Visual representations are great, but sometimes it just helps to see the numbers. Tableau offers two main chart types related to text: crosstabs and highlight tables. These charts are designed to display the numerical value of the data, categorized by dimensions on the Rows and Columns. Text-based charts are easier to use and validate and offer direct access to the data values. Their main drawback is fewer visual cues: they can't draw the user's attention to key values like a bar chart, line chart, or scatter plot can. Let's take a close look at both types:

Crosstab

The *crosstab* is the simplest of the text-based visualizations. In short, you add dimensions to the Rows and Columns to split up your data, and add a measure to the Text/Label mark to display numerical values at the Rows and Columns intercepts. This visual data format has been popular for many years because it's a good way to quickly show data values based on the dividing dimensions.

Crosstabs also are unique in that they are easy to create in Tableau from any existing chart. Once you've created a chart, simply right-click on the tab containing that chart and choose "Duplicate as Crosstab." Tableau will translate the dimensions and measures of the chart into a crosstab, allowing you to see the values. This feature is a quick and effective way to validate data values when you're building complex visualizations. It also gives you a way to provide a visualization that is not image-based, making it potentially more accessible to those with visual impairments.

For additional information on how to design workbooks for accessibility, please see "Build Data Views for Accessibility" (*https://oreil.ly/kEtL5*).

Highlight tables

A *highlight table* is simply a crosstab colored by the value of the data in the cells. It is built very similarly to a crosstab, with dimensions on the Rows and Columns and a measure on the Text/Label mark. Once the crosstab is built, you add the same measure to Color and change the chart type to Square. Tableau uses the measure's value to color in the cell behind the text. Adding color gives users a preattentive attribute to use when looking for patterns and outliers in the data.

Maps

Maps are a bit more challenging and varied than the other chart types, with many more options and things to know. In this section, I'll dissect how maps are built, the different types of map visualizations, and how map interactions work within the software.

To build a map, you need a Geographic field within your data. Tableau recognizes fields containing countries, states, provinces, counties, regions, zip codes (in certain countries), cities with a population of greater than 15,000, and many more. It identifies these fields using a globe icon: ⊕. When you place the Geographic field on the Detail mark, Tableau dynamically pulls Longitude and Latitude into Columns and Rows, respectively.

Within Tableau, there are databases of information about geographic areas. When you add a geographic field to Detail, Tableau calls on these databases to plot Longitude and Latitude and build a symbol map with a point indicating the approximate central location in each designated geographic area. By default, the chart type is actually a scatter plot using Longitude and Latitude as the x- and y-axes, overlaid on a map background (see Figure 3-3).

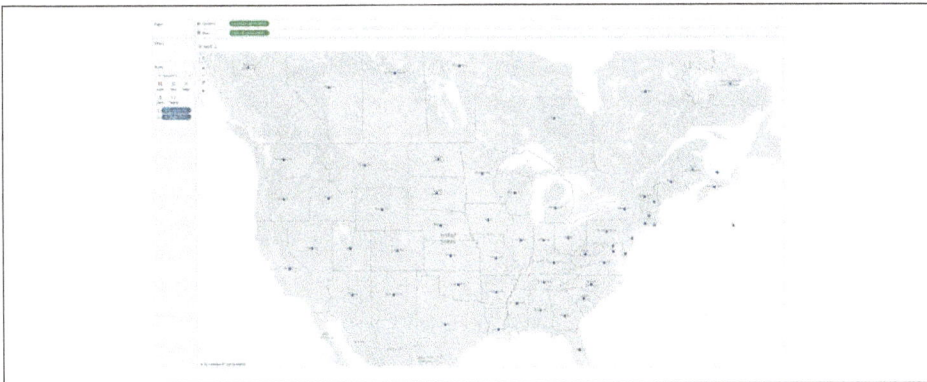

Figure 3-3. The default chart type for a map is a shape plot or scatter plot positioned over a map, with longitude and latitude providing the X and Y axes.

When you change the chart type to Map using the pull-down menu in the Marks card, the chart changes to a choropleth (filled) map. When you make this change, Tableau utilizes a different underlying database, to identify region borders rather than central points. Then it maps out the borders using latitude and longitude and fills them with color (see Figure 3-4).

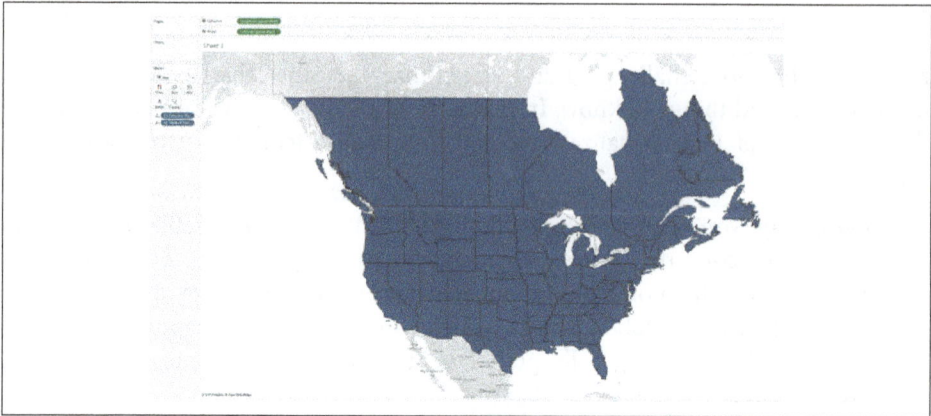

Figure 3-4. A choropleth map fills in each region, allowing you to assign values to geographic areas rather than central points.

Tableau also has one other type of map, a *density map*, which places hazy dots at the geographic locations (see Figure 3-5). Similar to a symbol plot, the density map defaults to identifying the central location of each region; however, instead of a solid dot, the symbol is dark in the center and fades outward into a decreasing color gradient. These plots are ideal when visualizing a number or value of points within an area: for example, crimes in a city. When the hazy dots overlap, the result is a heatmap, with more color in areas with higher values.

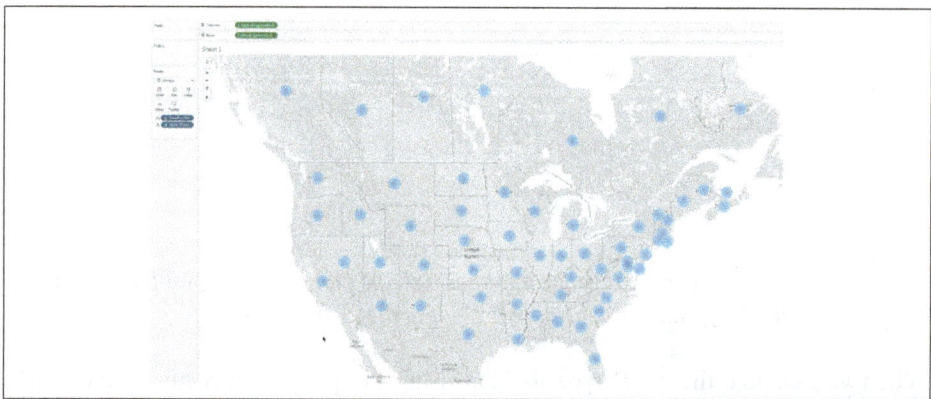

Figure 3-5. The density map defaults to showing a hazy point at the central location of each region, but it can be used to highlight areas based on a measurable value. The overlapping hazy dots create a heatmap with more pronounced color in areas of higher values.

Once you've generated a map, you can add fields to any of the Marks card panels to provide additional details. For example, you can add the Geographic field to the Label mark to provide the name of each region, or add Profit to the Color mark to visually identify if a region is profitable or not.

Each area of the Marks card has an impact on the map, but not all map controls are handled by the Marks card. In fact, Tableau devotes an entire menu at the top of the application specifically to map attributes, with controls to manage the background map image, design, and details. There are also special controls to handle situations where map encoding may be ambiguous. Let's break down the menu features:

Background Maps
> The options in the Background Maps menu (see Figure 3-6) control the appearance of the map behind your data visualization pieces. There are options for light maps (as in Figures 3-3 through 3-5), normal maps (with more detail applied to water and borders), and dark maps (which invert the map to black with white borders). There are options to show a background map with street-level detail or a satellite image. You can also import your own custom background map.

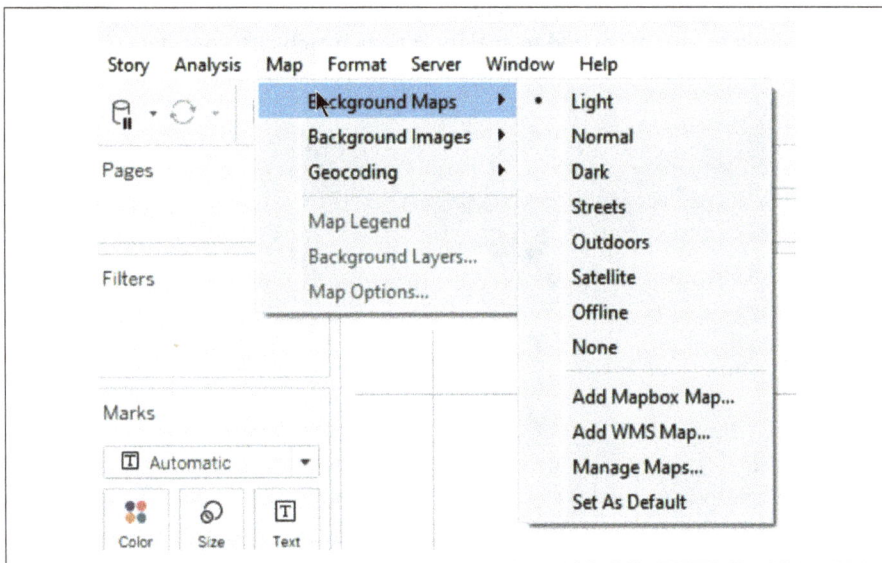

Figure 3-6. The Background Maps options in Tableau.

Background Images

If your background is not a map but an image, this option provides resources to add that image. This is useful for custom mapping applications, such as a map of a building or a campus.

Custom Geocoding

If Tableau doesn't recognize your geographic location data, you can import a custom CSV file with information about geographic properties to use in your workbook.

Edit Locations

Edit Locations is probably the most important item in the menu. The window that appears allows you to designate additional information about your geographic field. For example, if you add a City field to your Tableau view, you'll most likely see an error message near the bottom of your screen indicating that some of your city names are unknown (see Figure 3-7). Clicking the message and choosing Edit Locations will bring you to the Edit Locations window (see Figure 3-8). In most cases, you can tell Tableau to associate the city with a state, province, region, or country field from your data to clear up the ambiguity, but occasionally, you may need to specify exactly which city your data is referring to.

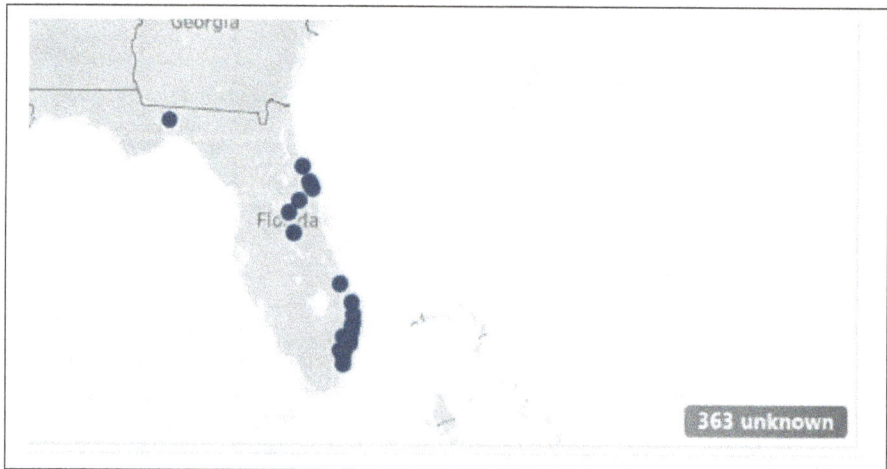

Figure 3-7. A message appears near the bottom right corner of the map indicating that not enough information was provided to map all of the values within the geographic field.

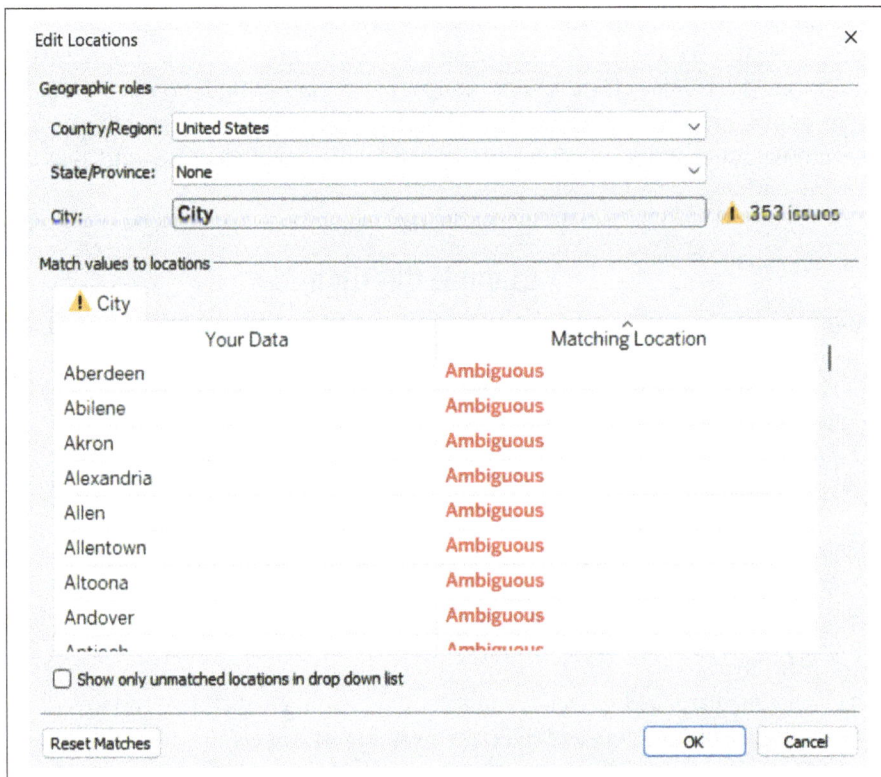

Figure 3-8. Adding only cities to a map visualization in Tableau will likely lead to ambiguity errors, because many cities share the same name. This window will allow you to associate another geographic field with the city data to clarify the ambiguity.

Background Layers

This option controls what is visible on the map, including things like streets, borders, names, cities, points of interest, neighborhoods, subway or train stations, and more. The number of layer options will depend on the type of map background you select.

Map Options

Maps come with a basic controls menu for end users to zoom, pan, and adjust the visual portion of the map. The Map Options item in the Maps menu allows you to dictate which of these features is available.

In summary, maps are an elegant way to display geographic information to your end users. Tableau's backend databases cover a wide degree of map granularity, from country all the way to cities. In addition to basic map design, you can control map backgrounds, details, and layers using the Maps menu at the top of Tableau. Tableau also allows you to utilize custom geographic data to build visualizations that include building outlines, campuses, and other nontraditional map items.

Example Question

You have a data set with city, state, country, and sales amount. You wish to build a map visualization to illustrate sales by city. Where should you drag the City field to build your map, and what additional steps might you need to take to ensure that the cities display correctly?

A. Drag the City field to Detail and Sales to Color. If any cities are ambiguous, use the Edit Locations menu to identify state and country fields in your data.

B. Drag the City field to Labels, Longitude to Columns, Latitude to Rows, and Sales to Color.

C. Drag the City field to Labels, Longitude to Rows, Latitude to Columns, and Sales to Color.

D. Drag the City field to Detail and Sales to Color, then click the "unknown" error message at the bottom and filter out the unknown values.

E. Drag the City field to Rows, then use the Show Me menu to switch the visualization to a map.

Answer: A—Dragging a geographic field to Detail will generate a map. Since the field is a city, you may need to use the Edit Locations window to clarify ambiguous city names by identifying a country and state as well. Option E will work if the data set is preconfigured to have city, state, and country already nested in a hierarchy (such as the Superstore data).

When studying for the exam, get familiar with the types of background maps available in Tableau. Know how to add details using the Background Layers options in the Map menu.

Practice building maps from scratch and see what challenges you may encounter. Can you replicate a map you find online?

Pies, Treemaps, and Bubbles

The remaining chart types I will cover are easy to build in Tableau, and some are quite popular, but they are not as good at delivering information as the other visualization types mentioned already. These charts display information based on area, and unfortunately, human beings are terrible at assessing space in shapes or areas. Still, these charts do provide effective ways to visualize rough relationships between dimensions when exact values are not as important. For that reason, I will cover each briefly:

Pie charts

Pie charts describe *proportionality*: How much of each portion of the data does this value comprise? You can easily build them in Tableau by placing a measure on the Size mark and a dimension on the Color mark. Then, switch the chart type to Pie. You can put the measure and the dimension on the Label field to identify the numerical value of the wedge and what dimension value it represents.

Pies are not very good for comparing values exactly, because humans have difficulty comparing areas—especially if they are curved. When more precise values matter, bar charts are better for displaying information (see Figure 3-9).

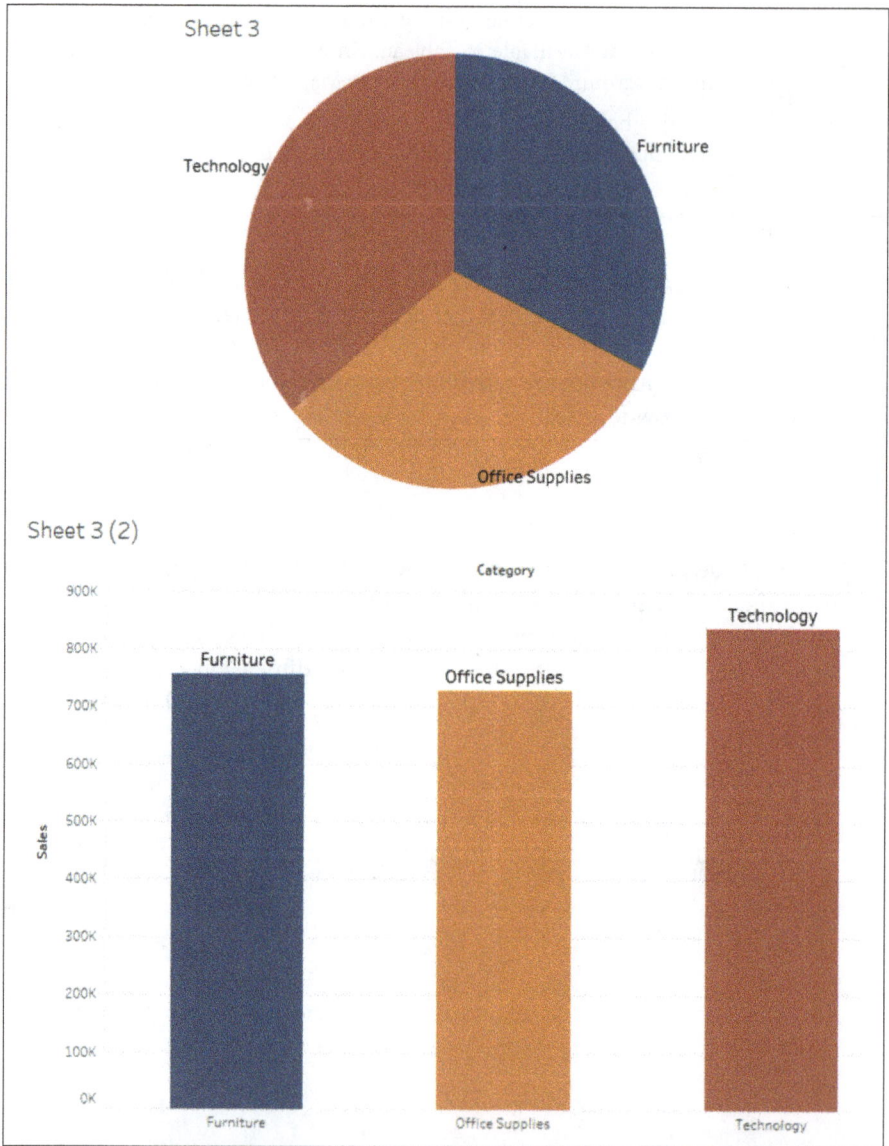

Figure 3-9. Can you tell which category has the most sales from the pie chart? On the bar chart, it is much easier to determine that technology is the largest portion of sales, even without sales value labels.

Treemaps

Treemaps, like pie charts, show proportion (see Figure 3-10, top). They do so with a collection of squares instead of pie slices, and they are built using the exact same steps as a pie chart: add a measure to Size and a dimension to Color. Tableau defaults to treemaps when you add these fields. You don't need to take the additional step of changing the chart type.

While treemaps use squares, which make it easier to estimate size, they still suffer from the same primary challenge as pie charts: it can be difficult to discern size differences without labels.

Bubble charts

Bubble charts (see Figure 3-10, bottom) combine the features of a treemap with the circle shape of a pie chart. They are built exactly the same way as a treemap, only you'll set the chart type to Circle. Bubble charts suffer from the pitfalls of both of the previous charts—it is difficult for the human eye to discern size in circles, and extremely challenging to compare circles of similar size without a label.

> You can build many more chart types in Tableau. If you research the Tableau Public server (*https://oreil.ly/eRvcI*), you will see a wide variety of Sankeys, polar charts, and more. These charts usually require additional complex calculations, reference lines, viz extensions, or specifically structured data. Due to their complexity and time investments, these charts are not as important to study for the certification exam. Focus your study time on being able to quickly and confidently build bar charts, line charts, scatter plots, crosstabs, and basic maps.

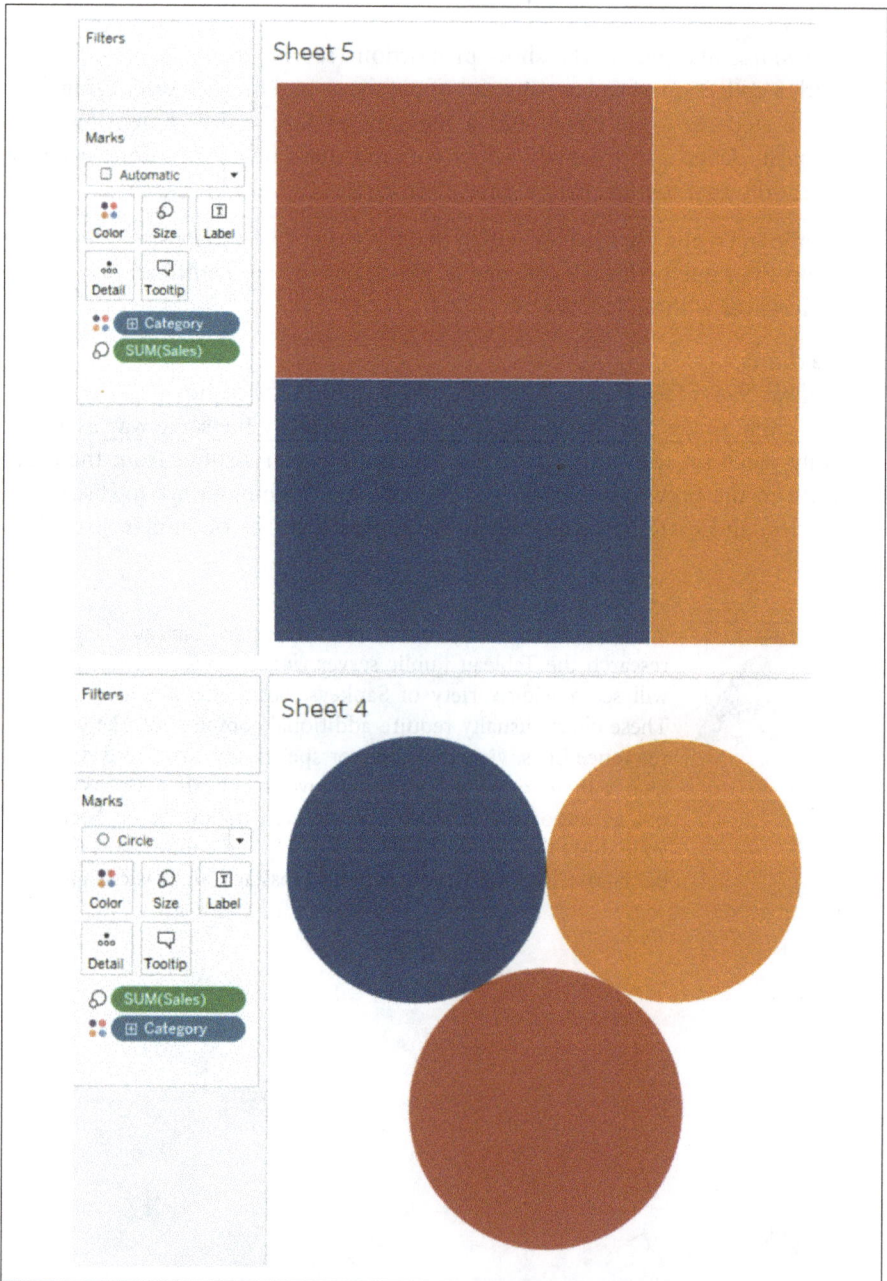

Figure 3-10. Examples of a treemap (top) and a bubble chart (bottom), using the same data values and dimensions as the pie and bar charts in Figure 3-9. Both are troublesome for identifying exact values because the sizes of the shapes are very similar.

Multiple Measure Charts

When you work with data, you probably won't focus on one measure alone. Often, you will want to compare measures, display them together, and use that combination to provide additional information than a single measure chart would provide. In this section, I will focus on the tools and methods Tableau provides to visualize multiple measures at once.

Measure Names and Measure Values

In Chapter 2, I covered how Tableau provides generated fields such as longitude and latitude. Two of these generated fields are called *Measure Names* and *Measure Values*. These two fields work together to pull multiple measures into a visualization. The two fields can be placed on Rows, Columns, or any of the Marks cards. It is valuable to understand how they work.

Measure Names are the field names of the measures in your data set. If you were to pull Measure Names into a visualization and place it on the Rows, you would see a vertical listing of all your measures. Measure Values refers to the numerical value of each of the measures. When you add Measure Values to a visualization with Measure Names, a new pane appears, listing all of the measure fields visible on the chart, as in Figure 3-11.

Adding and removing fields from this pane changes what is visible in the chart. The pane represents the values of Measure Names, and removing something from it filters the Measure Names field. In fact, placing Measure Names on filters ahead of time is a very effective way to limit what is visualized. When you are about to place Measure Values into a visualization, place Measure Names on filters first, and use that filter to dictate which measures you want displayed. For data sets with very large numbers of measures, this can be an incredible time saver. If you ever filter to just one measure, Measure Names and Measure Values will be removed and your visualization will revert to a normal, single-measure visualization.

> Like any dimension or measure, you can use Measure Names and Measure Values just about anywhere in a visualization. Experiment with using these two fields in Rows, Columns, and Marks to prepare for the exam.

There are a couple of time-saving tricks you can do with Measure Values: first, if Measure Values is on the Color mark, you can right-click on it and select Use Separate Legends to have a separate color scale for each measure. Second, if you have a crosstab with a single measure, its name won't appear automatically. You can drag the

Measure Values field onto the crosstab itself (the words "Show Me" will appear) to make the name appear!

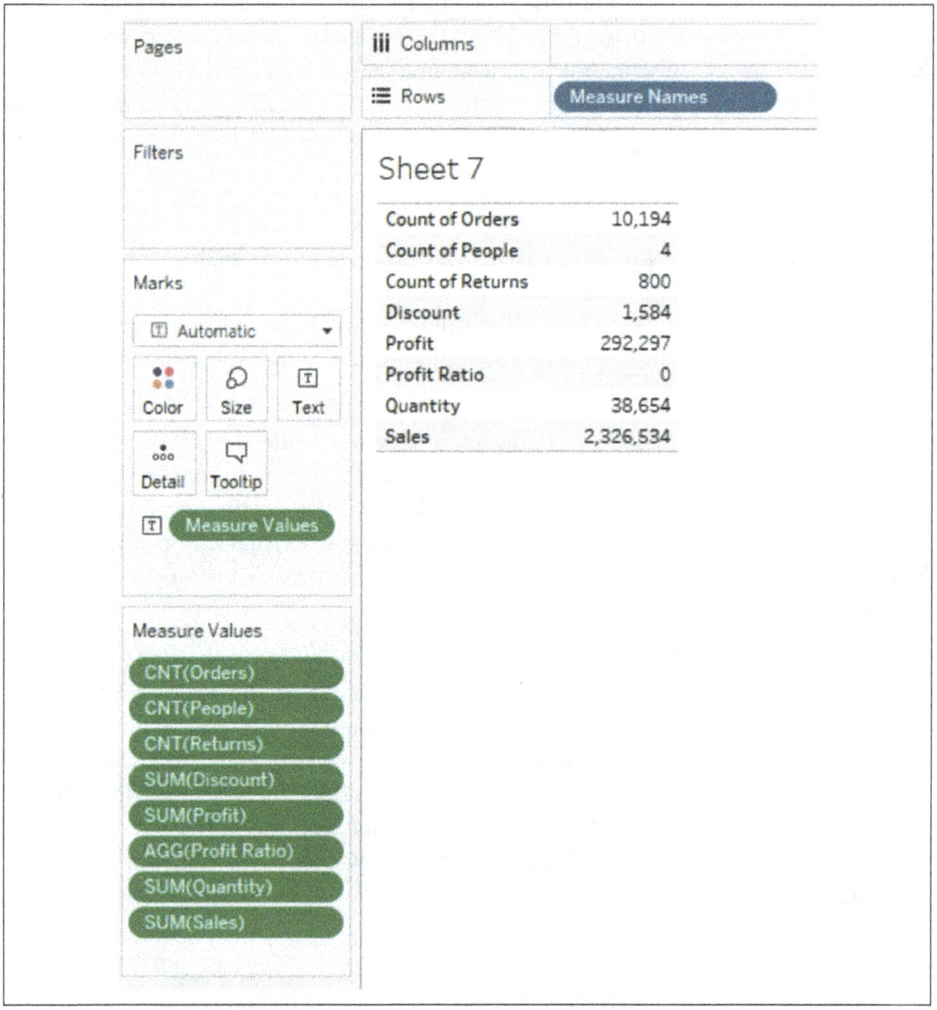

Figure 3-11. Measure Names is a list of the names of every measure in your data set. Measure Values lists the numerical value of each measure. The Measure Values pane indicates which measures are shown. Removing any field from this window creates a filter for Measure Names.

You have a data set with multiple measures for products ordered in the past four years. Your manager would like a simple crosstab displaying sales and profit on the left, with the dates at the top and numerical values within. What fields should you place in each area of the interface to make this happen?

A. Order Date to Columns, Sales and Profit on Rows

B. Order Date to Columns, Sales and Profit to Text/Label

C. Order Date to Columns, Measure Names to Columns, Measure Values to Rows

D. Order Date to Columns, Measure Names to Rows, Measure Values to Text/Label

E. Order Date to Columns, Measure Names to Filters (filtered to Sales and Profit), Measure Names to Rows, and Measure Values to Text/Label

Answer: E—You want to filter Measure Names to only Sales and Profit before placing Measure Values on the visualization. Since you want the values of sales and profit to appear as text in a crosstab, Measure Values should be placed on Text/Label and not on Rows or Columns.

Dual Axis

You can easily add multiple measures to any visualization. Let's pretend you've just built a simple bar chart of sales by order date (by placing the Sales field on Rows and the Order Date field on Columns with a chart type of bar). If you then drag the Profit field to Rows next to Sales, you will get two charts above each other, one showing Sales and one showing Profit (see Figure 3-12). Adding additional measures to the rows of any existing chart will create an additional chart of the same type and style on the same sheet, using the new measure. This is also true if the initial measure is on Columns, except that instead of making more charts vertically, they'll be shown horizontally.

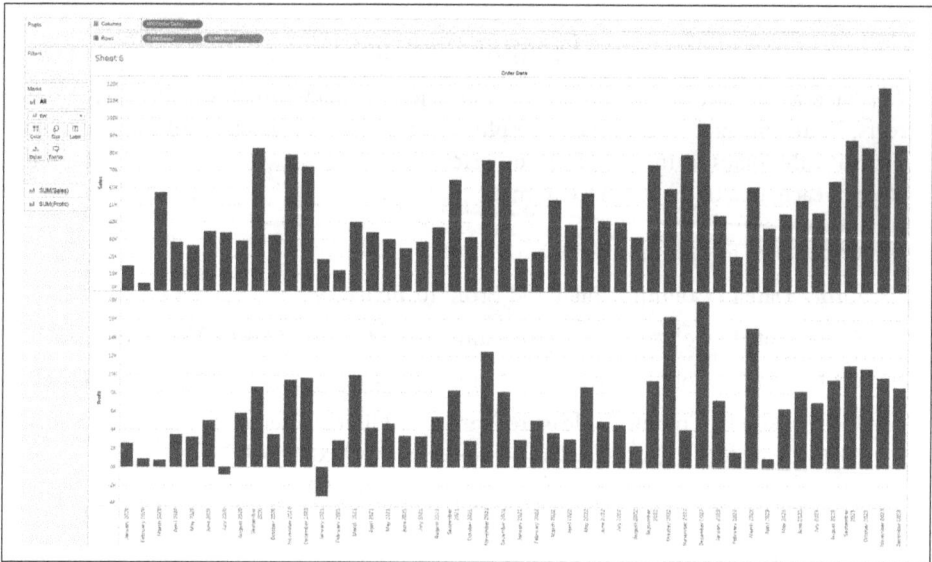

Figure 3-12. Adding another measure to an existing bar chart will split the page into multiple charts.

Besides adding another chart, adding another measure does something else: it splits the Marks card. Instead of a single Marks card, there is now a Marks card for each measure in the view, as well as an overall Marks card called "All" that you can use to globally change all the new charts at once (see Figure 3-13). The global Marks card provides the base mark format of all the charts and is only overridden by measure-specific Mark cards.

The ability to control the mark on each measure independently means you can, for example, make one measure a bar chart while making the other a line chart, and you can color, size, and label each independently. The areas of each Marks card work exactly like they do for a single measure chart. You can adjust the marks or add measures or dimensions to them to modify the appearance of each chart.

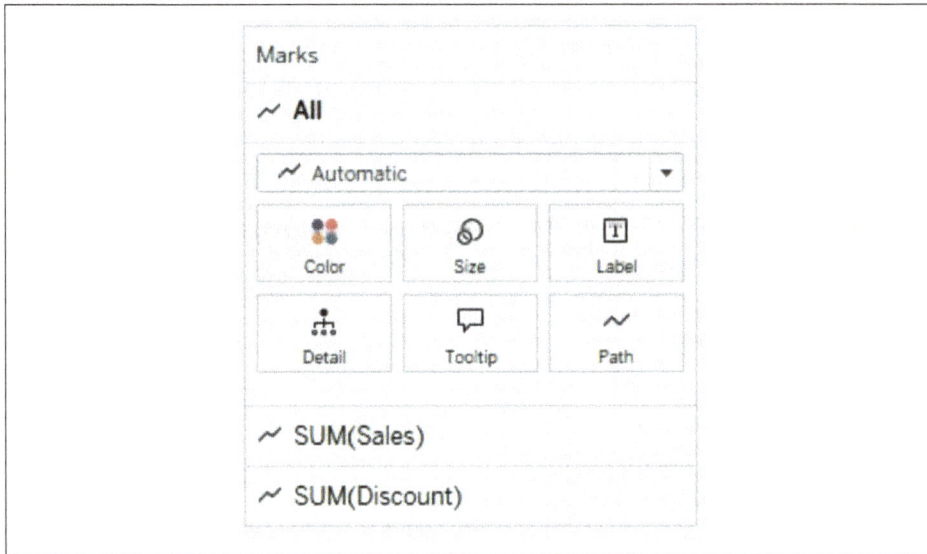

Figure 3-13. Multiple measures on a single view will split the Marks card into an All section and specific sections for each individual measure.

Now that you've seen how to combine multiple measures into a single view, the next step is to make them part of a singular chart. Unfortunately, you can only use Dual Axis with two measures. If you want more than two measures on an axis, you will need to use Measure Names and Measure Values.

To combine two measures into one chart, right-click on the second measure field or the second measure axis and select Dual Axis. This will:

- Combine the two charts into one
- Add Measure Names to the Color mark on all of the Marks cards
- Combine the measure fields into a more unified appearance on the Rows or Columns pane
- Add an axis to the right of the chart for the second measure

You can see each of these things in Figure 3-14.

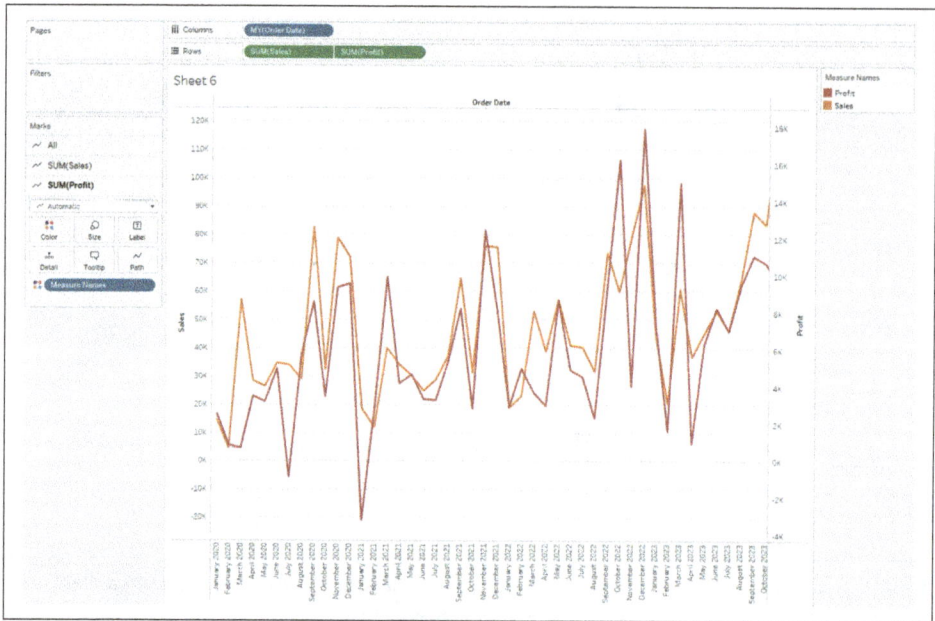

Figure 3-14. When Dual Axis is selected, the charts combine, the Measure Names field appears on each mark color, the measure fields combine together in Rows, and another axis appears to the right.

Once the two charts are combined, the second axis is visible to the right. More often than not, the scale of this second axis is nowhere near that of the first. This leads to a chart that is potentially confusing and misleading. Fortunately, a new option called Synchronize Axis appears if you right-click the second axis. This command will force the scale of the second axis to match that of the first. This should eliminate confusion, since both measures will be mapped against the same scale.

In fact, once the axes are synchronized, you should be able to right-click on the second axis and select Show Header to remove it from the view. Just be sure to update the axis label on the first axis (right-click and choose Edit Axis) to indicate that it now represents *both* measures. (I'll cover formatting axes and labels in more detail in Chapter 4.)

At this point, you have multiple measures on a single axis. You can control how each chart appears using the associated Marks card. For example, you can make one chart a bar and the other a line to easily compare them. You can swap the order of the measure fields in Rows to dictate which appears on top and which is below. You can use the existing Measure Names on the color marks to dictate the colors of each field, or you can remove it and manually color each chart independently by clicking on its associated Color mark.

For the exam, practice adding measures to Rows and Columns to see how multiple measures can change a single chart into a collection of charts within a single view. Once you are comfortable with this, practice combining two measures in a single chart using the Dual Axis command. Interact with the marks for each to see how the visualization changes.

Table Calculations

Reporting on your data directly as it appears can reveal a wide variety of valuable insights. However, sometimes you need to manipulate that data to find insights that otherwise might be difficult to see. This is where Tableau's table calculations come into play. *Table calculations* allow you to take an additional step on any measure, such as Difference From, Percent of Total, or Running Average. They can be simple or incredibly complex, and are often considered one of the more difficult concepts to understand in Tableau. To better explain how table calculations work, I will cover both how to build them and the types of table calculations available for you to use. I will try to work in examples to better explain what the calculation does and how it works.

How to Build a Table Calculation

To build a table calculation, you need to first have a measure in the visualization on Rows, Columns, or the Marks card. On that measure field, right-click and select either Add Table Calculation or Quick Table Calculation. The two fields do the same thing in different ways.

The Quick Table Calculation option will apply the selected option without additional prompting and utilize the available dimensions to apply the calculation. It comes with a majority of the same table calculations as the alternate method, but it performs them automatically. The Add Table Calculation option will create a table calculation as well, but it then opens the Table Calculation window (see Figure 3-15).

The Edit Calculation Window

Regardless of which way you create the calculation, you can return to the Table Calculation window (Figure 3-15) by right-clicking on the field again and choosing Edit Table Calculation. From the Table Calculation window, you can choose which calculation to apply and how to apply it.

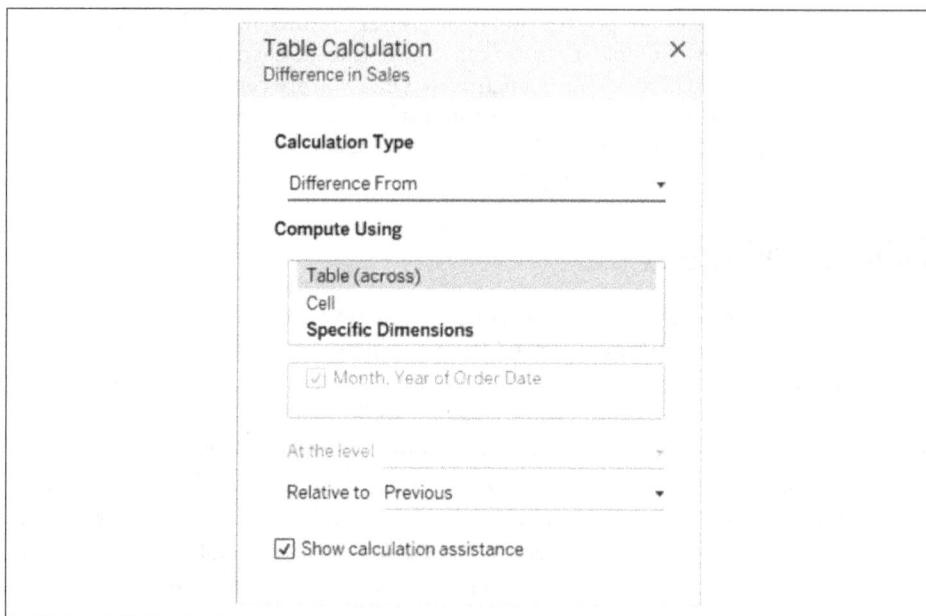

Figure 3-15. The Table Calculation window.

Types of Table Calculations

In Tableau, there are about a dozen different types of table calculations, but don't let that fool you: table calculations are entirely dependent on the structure of the visualization, the dimensions within, how the fields are sorted, and potentially other table calculations! Let's look at some of the basic table calculation types:

Difference From
> This table calculation will compute the difference from one value to the current value. It can be calculated based on any dimension in the visualization, but is usually assigned to time. The current value can be compared to the first value, the previous value, the next value, or the last value. For example, if you make a Difference From table calculation on a sales-by-year visualization, instead of showing the sales value, you can show the difference from a given year to the first, previous year, next year, or last year in the visualization.

Percent Difference From
> This calculation computes the difference from another value and displays it as a percentage of the comparison value. Similar to Difference From, you can use it to compare against the first, previous, next, or last value in the data set. For example, if the current value is 110 and the comparison value is 100, there is a difference of 10. This difference divided by the comparison value is 10/100, or 10%.

Percent From

    While similar to Percent Difference From, the Percent From calculation is a ratio of the current value to the comparison value. It simply divides your current value by the comparison value. Again, assuming your current value is 100 and the comparison value is 110, the Percent From would result in .909 or 91%.

Percent of Total

    This table calculation divides your current value by the total of all the values in the data set. So, if you are looking at sales by product category, Percent of Total would calculate what percent of the total sales each category contributed.

Rank

    The Rank calculation can get tricky very quickly, and it has several options. Effectively, it orders the values in the data set based on the dimensions being shown.

    It has two sections of options. The first section covers how to rank the values: in ascending or descending order. The second asks what to do about ties. There are four options for values that tie, shown in Table 3-1. Continuing on the sales by category example, a Rank table calculation would rank the categories based on the sales values they generated.

Table 3-1. How Tableau addresses ties in Rank table calculations.

Rank type	Explanation	Example
Competition	Tied values share the rank value that is next numerically, skipping the following rank value.	1, 2, 2, 4
Modified competition	Tied values share the rank value but skip a value first before assigning them the rank value.	1, 3, 3, 4
Dense	Tied values share a rank value, but no other rank values are skipped.	1, 2, 2, 3
Unique	Tied values each get a unique value, and the rank assigned to them uses the sort order of the dimension to assign them that value.	1, 2, 3, 4

Percentile

    This sounds like the percent of total table calculation, but it is quite different. The Percentile table calculation assigns a percentage value from 0% to 100%, from the lowest value in the data set to the highest. It then returns the percentile into which the current field falls. This calculation has the option to sort your data in ascending or descending order; descending order would assign 0 to the highest value and 100 to the lowest. Assuming you use an ascending sort, meaning that your lowest value is 0 and your highest value is 500, your percentile value for a value of 335 would be 67%.

Running Total

This calculation shows the aggregation of the data values up to the current point. Unlike some of the other table calculations, how this one is totaled up depends on the sort order of the visualization. There is also an option to define what you are totaling: you can total the sum value of everything prior or calculate the running average, minimum, or maximum. If you have sales by date, you could use this calculation to show the cumulative sales over the year.

Moving Calculation

This calculation is very similar to Running Total, but instead of totaling over the entirety of the chart, you instead can calculate over a defined subset of values. Like Running Total, you can do a moving sum, average, minimum, or maximum. In the Moving Calculation, though, you also get to choose how many of the previous or next values you are calculating over. For example, if you wanted to see how three-month average sales changed in a multiple-year data set, you would add this calculation and choose "Average and Previous 3 Values." The result would be the average sales of the current value and the previous three.

Date Table Calculations

There is a unique subset of table calculations that are based on date. They depend entirely on the data being current, and they calculate values such as year-to-date total, year-over-year growth, and year-to-date growth. Date table calculations will only appear when the dimensional field being calculated over is a date and contains more recent data.

Compute Using

Because table calculations are based on the dimensions within the visualization, they can be simple or extremely complex. In Figure 3-15, you will notice an area called Compute Using. This is Tableau asking you which dimensions you want to use to do the calculation. Tableau defaults this choice to its best guess, based on how the visualization is structured and how the measure is related to the dimension(s). To better understand the various options available to you, let's build the visualization shown in Figure 3-16.

Sales by Order Date, Category, and Sub-Category

Category	Sub-Catego..	Order Date 2018	2019	2020	2021
Furniture	Bookcases	20,037	38,544	26,275	30,024
	Chairs	77,242	71,735	83,919	95,554
	Furnishings	13,826	21,090	27,874	28,915
	Tables	46,088	39,150	60,833	60,894
Office Supplies	Appliances	15,314	23,241	26,050	42,927
	Art	6,058	6,237	5,961	8,863
	Binders	43,488	37,453	49,683	72,788
	Envelopes	3,856	4,512	4,730	3,379
	Fasteners	661	545	960	858
	Labels	2,841	2,956	2,827	3,861
	Paper	14,835	15,288	20,662	27,695
	Storage	50,329	45,048	58,789	69,678
	Supplies	14,394	1,952	14,278	16,049
Technology	Accessories	25,014	40,524	41,896	59,946
	Copiers	10,850	26,179	49,599	62,899
	Machines	62,023	27,764	55,907	43,545
	Phones	77,391	68,314	78,962	105,341

Figure 3-16. A crosstab visualization showing sales by year of order date, product category, and product subcategory.

Example Question

Take a look at Figure 3-16. Which of the options below best describes how the visualization was built?

A. Order Date to Columns, Sales, Category, and Sub-Category to Rows

B. Order Date to Columns, Category and Sub-Category to Rows, Sales to Text/Label

C. Category and Sub-Category to Columns, Order Date to Rows, Sales to Text/Label

D. Category and Sub-Category to Columns, Order Date and Sales to Rows

E. Sales to Columns, Order Date, Category, and Sub-Category to Rows

Answer: B—Dates appear on the top of the chart, so they are on columns. Category and Sub-Category are listed one per row, and the sales is on the text, making a crosstab.

In Figure 3-16, Sales is the measure. You can apply a table calculation to it; however, there are many different ways to calculate the percent of sales. Each one answers a question related to your data. The Compute Using area in the Table Calculation window lists these. For this example, let's assume you want to calculate the percent of total. Here is what each option in the Compute Using menu would do:

Table (across)
> This would calculate the percent of sales as you travel left to right across the table. In our example, it would answer the question, *What percent of sales for a particular subcategory were earned each year?* For Bookcases, 17.37% of sales came in 2021.

Table (down)
> This would calculate the percent of sales down the table. In our example, this would answer the question, *In a particular year, what percent of sales came from each subcategory?* For 2021, Bookcases accounted for 4.06% of the year's sales.

Table
> This would calculate the percent of sales across the entire table, divided up by the dimensions, answering the question, *What percentage of our total sales came from a particular subcategory in a particular year?* In our example, Bookcase sales in 2021 account for 4.06% of all sales for all subcategories across all four years.

Pane (across), Pane (down)
> This would calculate the percent of sales at a lower granularity, but not at the level of the entire table. In our example, you could choose Pane (down), as the rows are divided by Category and Sub-Category. This would answer the question, *What percent of a category's sales came from a certain subcategory in a particular year?* For our example, Bookcases accounted for 12.36% of Furniture sales in 2021.

Pane
> This would calculate the percent of sales across a division of the crosstab. This would answer the question, *What percent of a category's sales came from a particular subcategory in a particular year?* For our example, the pane would consist of a category across all four years. Bookcases in 2021 accounted for 2.65% of all Furniture sales during the four years.

Cell
> This calculates the percent of total for all visible measure values within a given cell. This doesn't really apply to our example, since each cell only contains one number; however, it is possible to have multiple numbers in a cell if you add a dimension to Detail. The detail splits up the measure but is not visible on the chart, causing multiple numbers to appear in each cell. The table calculation in

that case would show a percent of total for each value created by the Detail field. In this example, though, the result would always be 100%.

Specific Dimensions

Everything I've covered thus far is based on the layout of the visualization. Specific Dimensions takes that variable out of the equation, allowing you to directly specify which fields Tableau should use when doing the calculation. In theory, you could replicate each of the other Compute Using options by ordering and selecting the fields in the specific dimensions window. In our example, the fields Category, Sub-Category, and Year of Order Date would be selectable options to compute by.

> The Tableau exam will contain questions involving table calculations. A great way to study table calculations is to create a crosstab similar to that shown in Figure 3-16. Apply a table calculation and test how each Compute Using option changes the values in the chart. Try to replicate each of those values using the Specific Dimensions instead.

Tableau provides helpful highlighting when using table calculations. As you select each option, the chart highlights the cells in the crosstab it will use when performing the calculation. It also provides the ability to specify what level the calculation occurs at. So, in our example, you could calculate at the level of Category, Sub-Category, Year, or whatever level is deepest. This tells Tableau which direction to travel within the chart when doing the calculation and when to stop and restart along the way.

Deeper Levels of Table Calculations

Once you build a table calculation, it is available for use anywhere in the visualization. Table calculations also apply to more than just crosstabs. They can be used in any type of visualization. For example, imagine you were using a rank calculation on sales to find which customers bought the most. You would probably place the Customer field on Rows, add Sales to the Text/Label mark, and do a calculation of rank on the Sales field. You could then right-click on the Rank of Sales field and choose Filter from the menu. This places your Rank of Sales on the Filters menu, where you can quickly limit it to customers who are in the top 10, as in Figure 3-17.

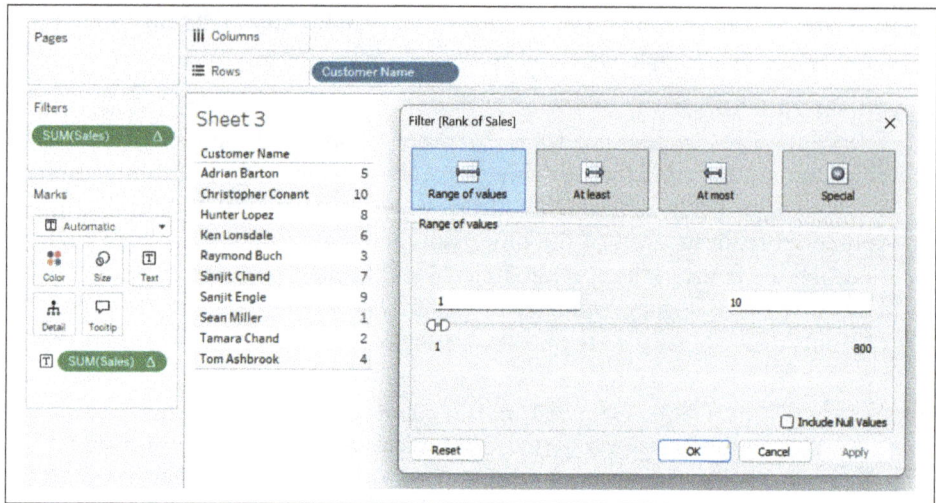

Figure 3-17. You can use table calculations as filters.

You can make table calculation fields in your data by dragging a field from your visualization to the Data pane. Doing so prompts you to name your newly created field. The table calculation then becomes a calculated field, retaining information about the type of table calculation and what dimensions it will use by default when added to a visualization. So, continuing with the example in Figure 3-17, if you drag the Sum(Sales) table calculation to our Data pane, it becomes a calculated field with RANK(Sum([Sales])) as the calculation. The field also indicates how the calculation is computed. In this example, it states: "Results are computed along Table (down)," since our calculation ranks the vertical list of Customer Names. I will cover more about calculated fields later in this chapter.

Table calculations can also be performed on other table calculations. For example, assume you create a calculated field that is a Difference From table calculation measuring the difference between sales from year to year. If you then create another calculated field that ranks the amount of change based on category, you've effectively created a table calculation on another table calculation. If you add the new Rank of Sales Changes calculation to your visualization and edit the table calculation, you will notice that the top pull-down changes: instead of prompting for a type, it is now titled Nested Calculations, and has a pull-down menu for each table calculation involved (see Figure 3-18).

> **Table Calculation** ✕
> Rank of Sales Changes
>
> **Nested Calculations**
> Rank of Sales Changes
>
> Rank of Sales Changes
> C Sales Changes
>
> Table (across)
> Table (down)
> Table (across then down)
> Table (down then across)
> Cell
> **Specific Dimensions**
>
> ☐ Year of Order Date
> ☑ Category
>
> At the level ▾
>
> Restarting every ▾
>
> ☑ Show calculation assistance

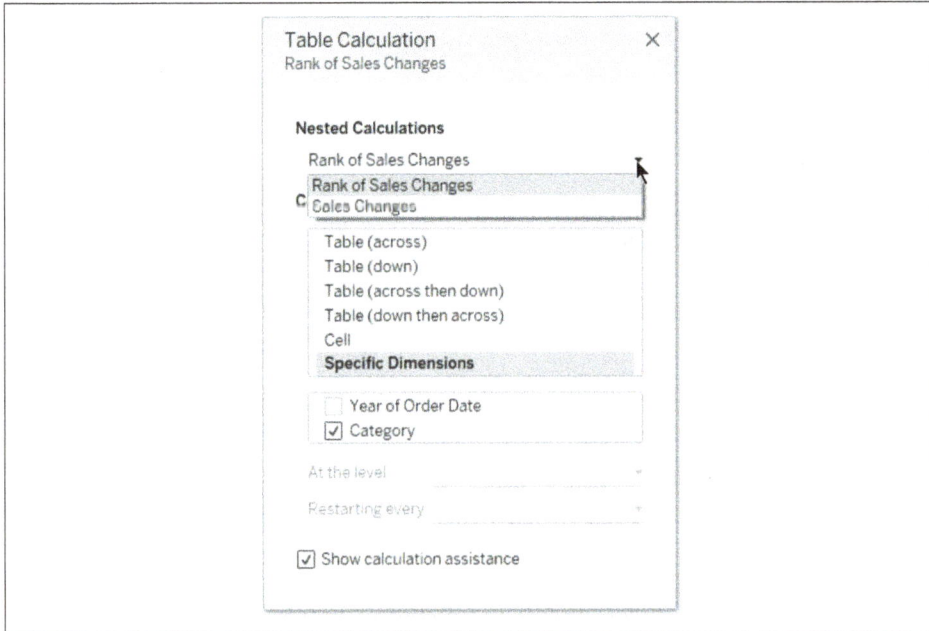

Figure 3-18. Nested table calculations require you to indicate how each table calculation is computed independently. In this example, Sales Changes is calculated over Year while "Rank of Sales Changes" is calculated over Category.

Table calculations can have multiple layers of nesting, each using a different dimension or dimensions to calculate its value. For many table calculations, such as Difference From and Percent Difference From, the sort order of the dimension used is also relevant. You can use table calculation fields as filters, but those calculations happen at the very end, after all other filters have been processed.

> The large number of options available makes table calculations a powerful data analysis tool, but it is also potentially confusing. Experiment with creating table calculations across multiple dimensions. Create calculated fields from them and explore what happens when you build table calculations on top of those created fields. Become comfortable with how Tableau identifies the dimensions being used in the calculation, and make sure you understand how sort order could potentially impact your result.

Example Questions

1. Take a look at Figure 3-16. If the table calculation Difference From was applied to Sales using the dimensions Category and Sub-Category (default sorted), what would the 2023 Sales for Appliances be?

   A. Blank. Using Category and Sub-Category in the calculation will cause the calculation to restart with each new Category.

   B. −15,732

   C. 2,916

   D. 1,150

   E. −34,671

2. Take a look at Figure 3-16. What two methods would calculate the difference in Sales between years for each Sub-Category? Select two.

   A. Table (down)

   B. Table (across)

   C. Specific Dimensions—Year of Order Date and Sub-Category

   D. Specific Dimensions—Sub-Category

   E. Specific Dimensions—Year of Order Date

1. Answer: B—A would be correct if only Sub-Category was selected. C,D, and E are potential values if the table calculation was performed over the other dimensions or in a different order.

2. Answers: B and E—The difference is being calculated between each year, so only the year will return the correct result. Since years are listed across the table, Table (across) would accomplish this as well as the specific dimension Year of Order Date.

Calculated Fields

Table calculations provide multiple ways to expand upon the default aggregation of measures in your data, but they aren't always enough on their own. Sometimes you need to go beyond the table calculation to manipulate or expand the data. In Chapter 1, I discussed how the Data pane allows you to split a field based on a delimiter. Earlier in this chapter, I mentioned that you could create a field from a table calculation. Both of these examples are calculated fields.

Calculated fields are pieces of code that manipulate the fields in your data. They can do simple mathematical calculations or complex logic statements, depending on what you need, and they come with some features that assist with syntax and documentation. Once created, they show up in the Data pane like the other fields in your data, but the data type icon will have an equal sign in front of it (see Figure 3-19).

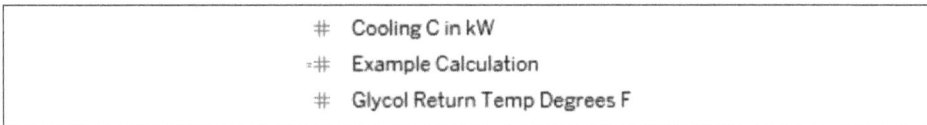

#	Cooling C in kW
=#	Example Calculation
#	Glycol Return Temp Degrees F

Figure 3-19. Calculated fields look like other fields in your data, except that the data type icon has an equal (=) sign before it.

How to Create Calculated Fields

Calculated fields are created in multiple ways. You can make them by taking actions on a field, such as splitting it, or by dragging a table calculation to the Data pane. You can also create them from scratch.

The easiest way to create a calculated field is to use the pull-down menu next to the search field in the Data pane (see Figure 3-20, left). The menu option is Create Calculated Field. This produces a blank calculated field window to begin populating. Alternatively, you can click the pull-down menu on any field (or right-click the field) to find a Create Calculated Field option (see Figure 3-20, right). This method produces a calculated field window and prepopulates it with the field you used to create it.

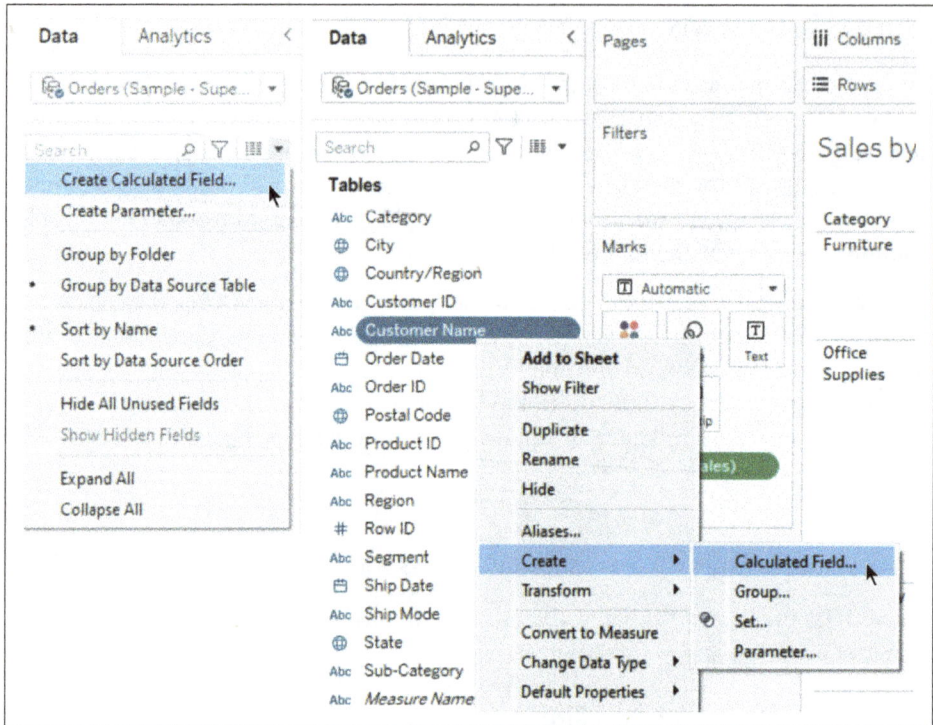

Figure 3-20. You can create a calculated field from scratch in two ways. You can use the menu on the Data pane (left) or navigate under the Create menu by right-clicking on a field in your data (right).

Creating a calculated field opens the calculation window (see Figure 3-21). This window has several key parts that you should be familiar with. The top field is where you name your calculated field. Give it a name that identifies what the calculation is and what it does. Below that is the space where you type your calculation. On the right side of the window is a guide, which can be turned on and off using the triangle on the right-hand side of the calculation area. The guide provides a list of functions that you can filter by type using the pull-down menu above. It gives detailed information on what the function does, as well as an example to demonstrate proper syntax and required fields. In Figure 3-21, it is showing information about the ABS (absolute value) function.

There is another way to create a calculated field: double-clicking on any field in a visualization creates a miniature calculation window within the field, allowing you to add any aggregation or change on the fly. Similar to table calculation, you can then drag the calculated field to your Data pane to make it usable elsewhere. Once you create a calculated field and it appears in your Data pane, you can return to it at any time. Right-click on the calculated field and choose Edit to return to the calculation window.

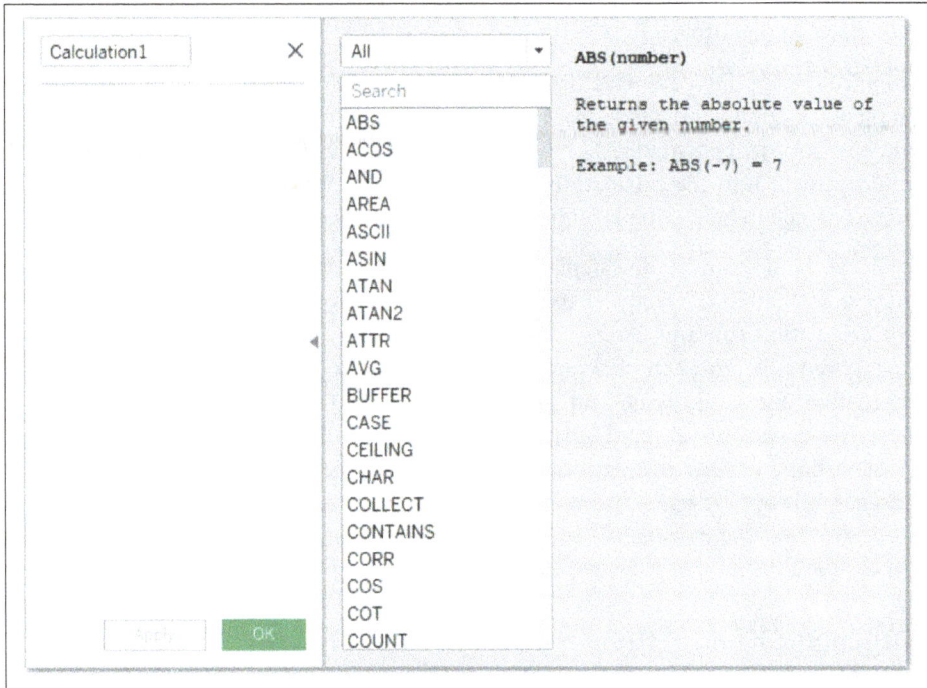

Figure 3-21. The calculation window has a place for the title, a place for code, and a function guide that can be toggled on and off.

Features of Calculated Fields

There are a few features of calculated fields that are important to understand. First, you can add a comment to a calculated field by preceding the comment with two forward slashes (//). This is beneficial not only for documenting what the calculation is doing, but also for troubleshooting complex multiline calculations. You can use the comment feature to disable chunks of code for testing.

Next, calculations ignore line returns and tabs. This means that you can split a calculation onto multiple lines between commands without impacting its functionality. The calculation SUM([Sales]) functions exactly the same as:

```
SUM(
[Sales]
)
```

You can combine this functionality with the comment feature to add and remove lines of calculation code to test and troubleshoot difficult calculations. It also enables you to structure your calculation using line breaks to make it easier to read and understand in the future.

When you're typing your calculated field, Tableau offers options to automatically complete functions and fields from your data. You can finish typing them or select from the options provided. Alternatively, you can drag fields from your Data pane and drop them into the calculation. Tableau indicates the drop location with a small orange triangle to help you place the field appropriately.

Finally, at the bottom of the calculation window, Tableau indicates if your calculation syntax is formatted correctly. If the calculation has an issue, the text will change to "The calculation contains errors," and the problematic area will be underlined with a squiggly red line. You can click on the warning text to get details. Tableau provides information about the issue and how to fix it; however, if you ever reach a point where you do not understand what is wrong in a calculation, use comment symbols to disable parts of your calculation until you identify the error. Additionally, the error messages only appear when the *syntax* of the calculation is incorrect—they won't help you ensure that the calculation is doing what you intended, as I will describe in the next section.

Mathematical Calculations

Tableau provides a wide variety of mathematical operators to use in calculations. You can use the basic mathematical symbols on the keyboard to add, subtract, divide, and multiply. It uses parenthesis, exponents, and modulo (remainder) as well. The Help pane window provides examples of a wide variety of number functions, which can be broken down into several types (see Table 3-2).

Table 3-2. Types of mathematical calculation operators with examples.

Type of function	Examples
Aggregation	MIN, MAX
Rounding	ROUND, CEILING, FLOOR
Exponents	EXP, LOG, LN, POWER
Geometry	SIN, COS, PI, ASIN, ACOS, DEGREES
Statistics	HEXBINX, HEXBINY
Others	ABS, DIV, SIGN

Most mathematical calculations are straightforward, but sometimes they can trip you up. The reason is aggregation. To understand how aggregation causes problems, let's look at an example.

Let's say your manager wants to see the *profit-to-sales ratio* for a given year: that is, the percentage of sales that constitutes profit, calculated by dividing the total profit by the total sales. Unfortunately, if you create a calculated field that simply divides profit by sales, such as [Profit]/[Sales], you will likely get a result that exceeds 100%. That's clearly incorrect. However, Tableau tells you that this calculation is valid (see Figure 3-22). And it is!

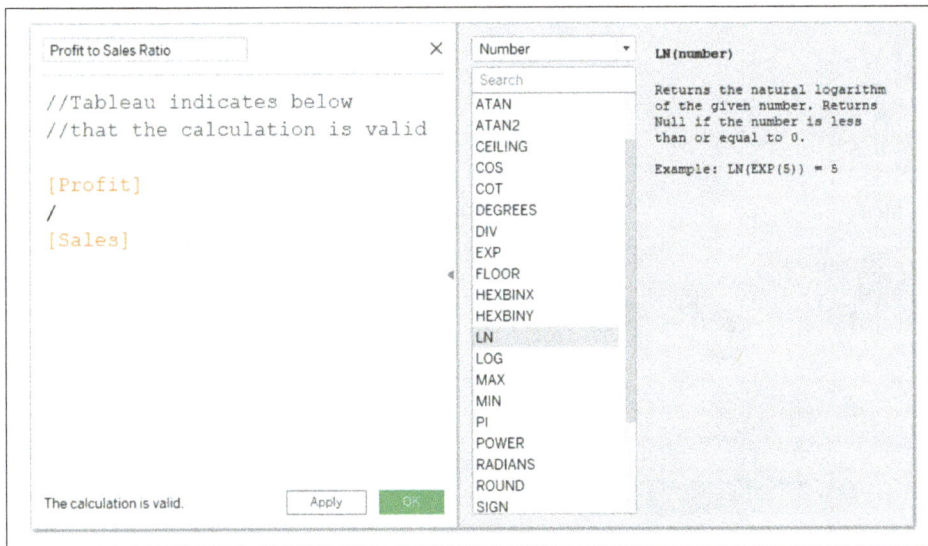

Figure 3-22. The calculation is valid, according to Tableau, but if you insert the field into a visualization, the result will be incorrect.

This is one of the most challenging aspects of Tableau, and it is important to understand what is happening. Tableau is treating this calculation just like all the other measures in your data set. When you add a measure to a visualization, Tableau aggregates it. It takes every row of the data in the data set and adds it up. For example, if you add profit to a visualization, the field will change to SUM[Profit], which sums the profit values of all the rows. It does the *same thing* for the profit-to-sales ratio calculation: for each row in the data, it divides profit by sales and then sums up all those results.

The problem is that you don't want the sum of all the row-level profit ratios. You want the *total profit* of the data set, divided by the *total sales*. That is, you want to *sum* all the rows of profit and all the rows of sales *before* you divide them out. You want to do the aggregation first.

To fix this problem in your calculation, you need to apply aggregation to the Sales and Profit fields: `SUM([Profit]) / SUM([Sales])`. This will sum up all the profit and divide it by the sum of all the sales. When you add the updated calculation to your visualization, it will change to `AGG([Profit to Sales Ratio])` (see Figure 3-23), indicating to you that the aggregation was completed as part of the calculation and the field cannot be aggregated further.

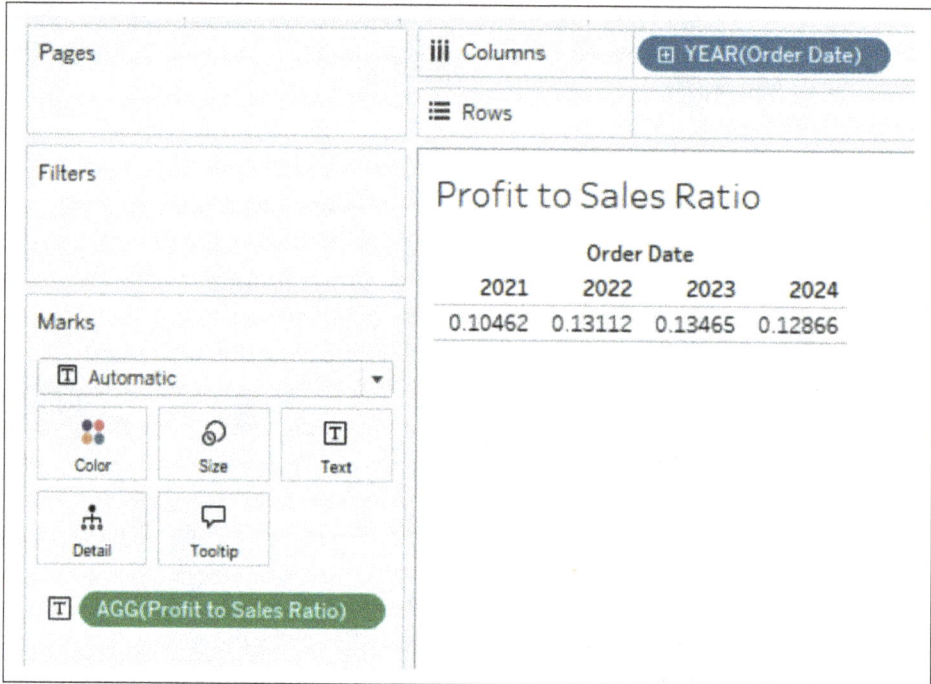

Figure 3-23. When you aggregate the fields within the calculation and then add the resulting field to a visualization, the field will be prefixed with AGG.

Aggregating is necessary to return an accurate result in this example. It's also one of the most common syntax errors you will encounter when writing calculations involving measures. If you aggregate one thing in your calculation, *everything else* must also be aggregated. If you try to work with some fields aggregated and some not, the syntax warning will appear at the bottom of the calculation window and the help text will read: "Cannot mix aggregate and nonaggregate arguments with this function." If you encounter this error, you will need to either remove all aggregation or aggregate all of the fields in your calculation to resolve the issue.

Example Question

Your manager would like to know what the total discounts would have been if each discount provided was increased by $.50. Which calculations would give the correct result? Select all that apply.

A. `[Discount]+.5`

B. `SUM([Discount])+.5`

C. `SUM([Discount]+.5)`

D. `SUM([Discount]) +SUM(.5)`

E. `[Discount] + SUM(.5)`

Answers: A and C—You want to add .5 to every discounted order before you sum them up. A will do this and aggregate the value when it's added to a visualization, while C will aggregate the value as part of the calculation. B and D aggregate the discount and then add .5 to the total discount value of the data set, while E gives a syntax error because part of the calculation is aggregated and part is not.

String-Based Calculations

Number calculations allow you to work with numbers, but sometimes you need to modify string values. While most string calculations are relatively easy, some are very complex. In Chapter 1, I introduced the split functionality, which allows you to split a dimension into separate fields based on a delimiter. This creates calculated fields, using string functions to split the portions of the original field into smaller sections. Like all calculated fields, you can right-click on these fields and choose Edit to review the calculation Tableau uses.

Like mathematical functions, there are several types of string functions (listed in Table 3-3). You learned in Chapter 1 how to use these functions in join calculations. You can also use these functions, alone or in combination, to find, extract, and manipulate string values to meet your data needs.

String calculations can be very useful for combining data sets with join fields that have different cases. For example, if data set A has states listed in all capital letters and data set B has states listed in proper case (title case), you can use a join calculation with a string function (UPPER or PROPER) to adjust the case on one of the state fields to make it match the other.

Table 3-3. Types of string-related functions available in the calculation window. Many of these calculations are used in combination to modify strings.

Type of calculation	Examples
Finding text	FIND, FINDNTH
Case	UPPER, LOWER, PROPER
Shortening text	TRIM, LTRIM, RTRIM
Subsections of text	RIGHT, LEFT, SPLIT
Logic	CONTAINS, STARTSWITH, ENDSWITH
Regular expression	REGEX_EXTRACT, REGEX_EXTRACT_NTH, REGEX_REPLACE
Other	LEN, REPLACE, SPACE

You can combine string functions to accomplish challenging tasks. For example, the split functionality creates the following calculation:

```
TRIM(SPLIT( [Field], ",", 1))
```

This calculation splits the original field on commas and keeps the first item split off. If the field contains "last name, first," it will separate out the last name. It then trims any preceding or following spaces that might cause a problem. The calculation is then saved as `Field - Split 1`. The split calculation to extract the first name is named `Field - Split 2` and has a very similar calculation:

```
TRIM(SPLIT( [Customer Name], " ", 2 ) )
```

You can do similar tasks using functions like `LEFT`, `RIGHT`, and `FIND`. If you want to create a calculation that pulls out the last name (everything before the comma), you can write it as:

```
LEFT([Field], FIND([Field],",")-1)
```

You can see how the equation works by following the steps from inside out. Imagine the person's name is Michael Smith. It is stored as "Smith, Michael" in the data set. The calculation contains two functions:

`FIND(string,substring)`
> This looks through the field to find the numerical location of the comma. It then moves one space back (–1).

`LEFT(string, #)`
> This returns the left portion of the string up to a particular character, based on counting characters from left to right.

In summary, the calculation finds the location of the comma and returns everything to the left.

Regular expressions are also very powerful ways to manipulate string fields and deserve additional discussion. They are more powerful than some of the other string functions because they can combine logic, pattern matching, and more to manipulate strings. For example, you could use regular expressions to find the *n*th combination of a substring of numbers and letters. While an overview of regular expressions is beyond the scope of this book, you can find information and basic examples on Wikipedia's regular expressions page (*https://oreil.ly/iWWnT*) or by referring to other titles such as Michael Fitzgerald's book *Introducing Regular Expressions* (O'Reilly, 2012).

> The Tableau exam might have some questions asking you to interpret a very basic regular expression, but it will not ask you to write or decipher anything complex. However, regular expressions are an extremely valuable tool and should be a part of every Tableau developer's toolbox.

Example Question

Your data has a field that contains your users' email addresses. You want to trim off the "@" symbol and the domain to leave only the first part of the email address. Which calculation would accomplish this task?

A. `LEFT([Email],FIND([Email],'@'))`

B. `LEFT([Email],FIND([Email],'@')-1)`

C. `[Email]-RIGHT([Email],FIND([Email],'@'))`

D. `SPLIT([Email],'@',0)`

E. `SPLIT([Email],'@',1)`

Answer: B—You want to find the "@" symbol and then take one step to the left (–1) to not include it as part of the returned substring.

Data Type Conversion Calculations

Occasionally, you might need to change the data type of a measure or a dimension. For example, let's say you want to display the value of a measure along with some text. Since the measure is a float or an integer (a number) and your text is a string, you will be unable to combine the two with a calculation. If you try it, you'll get an error and Tableau will tell you that you cannot combine a string with an integer or float. In this situation, you need to change the measure value into a string to combine it with your text:

```
STR(SUM([Sales]) + " Sales"
```

Tableau has 11 type-conversion functions that fall into four categories: dates, numbers, strings, and spatial:

Dates

There are five calculations that convert fields to dates: DATE, DATETIME, MAKEDATE, MAKEDATETIME, and MAKETIME. Since there are a huge variety of calculations involving dates, I will cover these calculations in the next section.

Numbers

There are two calculations that convert fields into numbers: INT and FLOAT. INT transforms the field into a numerical value with no fractional part: for instance, INT(3.14) would return 3. FLOAT will convert the field to a number that, by default, will have enough decimal places to make the value contain four digits. For example, while FLOAT(3.14) would return 3.140, FLOAT(333) would return 333.0. Float calculations can have more or fewer decimals if the formatting is changed (more on this in Chapter 4).

Strings

There is only one string calculation: STR. This calculation converts any type of field to a string. For example, if you have user ID numbers in your data, you may need to include leading zeros for the field. STR([UserID]) changes an otherwise numeric field into a string, keeping the leading zeros.

Spatial

Tableau provides several calculations involving converting numbers to spatial fields. They include MAKEPOINT, which will create a point at the given coordinates; MAKELINE, which will draw a line between two coordinates; and INTERSECTS, which will return a Boolean true or false depending on whether the geometric lines or areas intersect.

Date and Time Calculations

Tableau's variety of date and time functions is large enough to necessitate its own section. When you work with dates and time in your data, you often need to translate these fields to accomplish your analysis. You can use date calculations to identify data that falls within a specific range of dates or make year-over-year comparisons within your data. Tableau provides the functions you need to make these adjustments, but knowing which function or functions to use is a skill that takes lots of practice.

There are 20 date functions available in Tableau. These functions do many things and return values of different data types (see Table 3-4). For this section, I will refer to values coded as DATEs or DATETIMEs in the International Organization for Standardization (ISO) format: #YYYY-MM-DD HH:MM:SS#. This notation should indicate to you that the value in question is a date or date with time. Also, if you are practicing with these calculations using copy and paste, be aware that quotes and double quotes often do not copy correctly. It may be best to type these calculations manually when you test them.

Table 3-4. A listing of date functions available for use in calculations in Tableau.

Function(s)	Description	Output value	Example
DATE, DATETIME, MAKEDATE, MAKEDATETIME, MAKETIME	Converts strings or a sequence of integers into a date	Date or date with time	DATE("August 19, 2024") = #2024-08-19#

Function(s)	Description	Output value	Example
DATEADD	Adds any portion of date or time to an existing date	Date or date with time	DATEADD('day',30,#2024-08-19#) = #2024-09-19#
DATEDIFF	Computes the difference between two date fields using the designated date part	Integer	DATEDIFF('day',#2024-08-19#,#2024-12-25#) = 128
DATENAME	Returns the specified date part as a string	String	DATENAME('weekday',#2024-08-19#) = Monday
DATEPARSE	Returns a date based on a specifically formatted string	Date or date with time	DATEPARSE('yyyy-MM-dd',"2024-08-19") = #2024-08-19#
DATEPART	Returns the numerical value of the specified date part	Integer	DATEPART('day',#2024-08-19#) = 19
DAY, WEEK, MONTH, QUARTER, YEAR	Returns the numerical value of the specified date part	Integer	DAY(#2024-08-19#) = 19
DATETRUNC	Rounds the date to the specified date part	Date or date with time	DATETRUNC('Month',#2024-08-19#) = #2024-08-01#
ISDATE	Returns TRUE or FALSE based on if the evaluated field is a date	Boolean	ISDATE("Cat") = False
ISOWEEKDAY, ISOWEEK, ISOQUARTER, ISOYEAR	Returns the integer value of the specified date part; requires an ISO date as input	Integer	ISOWEEKDAY(#2024-08-19#) = 1
MIN, MAX	Returns the maximum or minimum date in the given field or dates	Date or date with time	MAX(#2024-08-19#,#2024-08-20#) = #2024-08-20#
TODAY, NOW	Returns the date or the datetime of the local system	Date or date with time	TODAY() = The date of when you read this book

The functions that convert strings or integers to dates have some differences. DATE and DATETIME return a date (or datetime) given a number, string, or expression in date format. For example, you can use DATE([Order Date]) or DATE(["August 18, 2024"]). MAKEDATE, MAKEDATETIME, and MAKETIME do similar things, but require the input variables in a specific format to function properly:

MAKEDATE
> Use MAKEDATE(YY,MM,DD) where the year, month, and date values are two-digit integers.

MAKEDATETIME
> Use MAKEDATETIME(Date, Time) where the date is a date, datetime, or string and the time is a datetime (HH:MM:SS AM/PM).

MAKETIME
> Use MAKETIME(HH,MM,SS) where the hours, minutes, and seconds values are two-digit integers and hours are listed in 24-hour notation.

There are some functions that only work in certain scenarios. For example, the MAKE DATE, MAKETIME, and MAKEDATETIME functions only work when the data pull is an extract or uses specific types of data connections. If you are trying to use a date function in your calculation and Tableau is returning an error that the function does not exist, check the Tableau website for date functions (*https://oreil.ly/dvg0Z*) to make sure your data set meets the required criteria.

The power of date fields comes from combining functions together. You will need a logical plan to navigate through the date functions to get to the date you need. The way date functions are structured, this usually means starting from the inside and working your way out. For example, imagine your manager wants to see the dynamic sales values for the end of the previous completed month. You'll need to combine date functions to calculate that date. One way to accomplish this would be to truncate today's date to the start of the current month and then subtract a day:

```
DATEADD('day',-1,
DATETRUNC('month',TODAY())
)
```

This calculation uses three common date functions and is most easily interpreted from the inside out. First, DATETRUNC takes the input value TODAY()and truncates it to the month. This returns the first day of the current month. The DATEADD function then subtracts one day from that truncated date. The resulting value returned is the last day of the previous month.

The Tableau exam's questions about date functions often revolve around syntax or choosing the appropriate date function to accomplish a given task. Familiarize yourself with the structures of date functions and pay special attention to converting to or from date fields. Make sure you can differentiate between DATE, MAKEDATE, DATEPART, DATETRUNC, DATENAME, and DATEPARSE, as these are all common subjects for exam questions.

Example Questions

1. Which calculations would dynamically return the date of the last day of the current year? Select all that apply.

  A. `MAKEDATE(YEAR(TODAY()),12,31)`

  B. `DATEADD('day',-1,DATEADD('year',1,DATETRUNC('year',TODAY())))`

  C. `DATEADD('day',365,DATETRUNC('year',TODAY()))`

  D. `DATE('December 31' + ',' +STR(YEAR(TODAY())))`

  E. `DATEADD('year',1,DATEADD('day',-1,DATETRUNC('year',TODAY())))`

2. Which function is properly formatted to determine the number of days between the order date and today?

  A. `DATEDIFF([Order Date],TODAY(),'days')`

  B. `DATEDIFF('days',[Order Date],TODAY())`

  C. `DATEDIFF('day',[Order Date],TODAY())`

  D. `DATEDIFF([Order Date],TODAY(),'day')`

  E. `DATEDIFF(DAY([Order Date]),DAY(TODAY()))`

1. Answers: All of the calculations return the last day of the year, although option C will be a day short during a leap year. Option A is the most efficient.

2. Answer: C—The correct format for a DATEDIFF function for the difference in days between two dates is DATEDIFF('day',Date1,Date2).

On any date or time field, you can right-click and choose Create → Custom Date. This will prompt you with an option to create a calculation of the date at the granularity you desire. For example, you can choose this option on Order Date to create a date calculation at the granularity of the month and year. An example of this feature with a screenshot is available in the section "Levels of Detail" on page 124.

Logical Calculations

Not all calculations involve working with strings, numbers, or dates. Sometimes you need to use logic to manipulate fields in your data set. Logic-based functions revolve around testing a criteria and taking action based on the result. If the logical statement is true, you do one action; if it is false, you do something else or perform another test. This section will break down the two most common logic functions and explore how to use different operators to modify the result.

The simplest logic function is an if/then function. It checks a criterion and returns a true-or-false result. The basic structure of this type of function is as follows:

1. Starts with the IF statement

2. Provides a field to assess

3. Follows with a THEN statement

4. Instructs what to do if the criteria is true

5. Ends with an END statement

For example, IF SUM([Sales]) >5000 THEN "Good" END will look at the sum of sales for the dimensions in your visualization. If that sum ever exceeds $5,000, the value of this calculation will be the word Good. If the sum is less than $5,000, the result will be NULL. All if/then statements are built from this basic structure; you can provide additional criteria logic and result instructions.

To expand the criteria logic to be more rigorous or complex, you can use a feature called *operators*. Operators are logical additions that change the criteria of the function. You can use operators such as AND, OR, and NOT to isolate the values you desire. For example, if you want to see sales values greater than $5,000 but less than $10,000, you can expand the criteria using an AND statement:

```
IF SUM([Sales]) >5000 AND SUM([Sales])<10000 THEN "Good" END.
```

The resulting output can also be expanded. The most common way to change the output is to provide an ELSE statement after the THEN instructions. This tells Tableau what to do when the statement is *not* true, meaning that both outcomes produce a visible result instead of NULL. You can also use ELSEIF to provide an additional outcome to your statement. For example, review the following calculation:

```
IF SUM([Sales])>5000
THEN "Good"
ELSEIF SUM([Sales])>2000
THEN "OK"
ELSE "Not Good"
END
```

This calculation returns the words "Not Good" for sales value less than $2,000, the word "OK" for sales between $2,000 and $5,000 and "Good" for sales values greater than $5,000.

The order of the logic is important here, because the function stops once it hits a TRUE statement. Compare this function:

```
IF SUM([Sales])>2000
THEN "OK"
ELSEIF SUM([Sales])>5000
THEN "Good"
ELSE "Not Good"
END
```

This returns "OK" for everything greater than $2,000. Because the >2000 logic returns a TRUE value, the function never evaluates the ELSEIF statement—even if the value is greater than $5,000.

Tableau provides an alternative to if/then functions, called *case/when*. While structured similarly, *case/when functions* provide a wider array of potential results and outputs. The basic structure of a case/when function is as follows:

1. Starts with a CASE statement
2. Provides a criteria to check
3. Follows with a WHEN statement
4. Provides a value to compare against
5. Follows with a THEN statement
6. Provides an output if the comparison criteria is true
7. Completes with an END statement

The power behind a case/when function comes from steps 3 through 6. These steps can be repeated as many times as you wish, with any criteria you need to meet. For example, assume your business runs in an April-to-March fiscal year. You can create a calculation called "Fiscal Year" and populate it as follows:

```
CASE MONTH([Order Date])
WHEN 1 THEN YEAR([Order Date])
WHEN 2 THEN YEAR([Order Date])
WHEN 3 THEN YEAR([Order Date])
ELSE YEAR(DATEADD('year',1,[Order Date]))
END
```

The case/when statement traverses through the WHEN statements until it finds a criteria that evaluates as true. It then provides the output from the corresponding THEN statement. If no WHEN statement evaluates as true, the function can contain an ELSE statement to return a value. When the calculation is complete, as long as each output value following the THEN statements is the same data type, Tableau will create the field in your Data pane and assign it a data type. All case/when and if/then functions must end with an END statement.

Tableau also has some shortcut functions that do logic (see Table 3-5).

Table 3-5. Additional logic functions available in Tableau.

Function	Description	Example
IFNULL	Provided a field and an output, this function will return the field value when not null and the output when null.	IFNULL([Category], "No Category") will return the category if it is populated and the words "No Category" if the value is null.
IIF	A shortcut version of an if/then statement, and it is populated by the condition, the THEN output, and the ELSE output (an additional statement can be added to address null values).	IIF([Category] = 'Technology', 'Tech', 'Non-Tech', 'Unknown') returns the value "Tech" if the Category is Technology, "Non-Tech" if it is not, and "Unknown" if the value is null.
IN	This looks for a value within a list, a set, or a combined field and returns TRUE if it is found.	[Category] IN ('Technology','Furniture') returns TRUE if the category is furniture or technology and FALSE otherwise.
ISDATE	Returns TRUE if the evaluated string is a date.	ISDATE('2024-08-19') returns TRUE as the enclosed string is a date.
ISNULL	Returns TRUE if the evaluated field is null.	ISNULL([Category]) returns TRUE if the category value is null and FALSE otherwise.
ZN	Translates a null measure value to 0.	ZN([Sales]) returns 0 if the value of sales is null.

You can combine Tableau's many logic functions based on a wide variety of criteria to narrow down results, isolate key values, and further label the data in your data set. You can also combine logic functions with other Tableau features, such as parameters and sets, to improve interactivity for your end users. This will be explained in more detail later in this chapter and in Chapter 4.

> Like with dates, you can study logic functions by focusing on their syntax. While the exam may ask you to correctly populate a logic function, it is much more likely to present one as part of a question, requiring you to understand what it's doing.

Levels of Detail

In Chapter 1, I discussed areas of the interface where you can add dimensions to increase the detail of the visualization. Any dimension added to the Rows, Columns, or several of the marks will increase the level of detail. The measured values get increasingly more granular as you add more dimensions. Sometimes, however, you need to change the granularity of a measure without adding dimensions. For these situations, you need a *Level of Detail* (LoD) calculation.

LoDs change the level of granularity to which a measure is aggregated. For example, they can make a measure more or less granular or apply specific detail, ignoring the existing dimensions in a visualization. There are three functions that alter details on a measure: INCLUDE, EXCLUDE, and FIXED. In this section, I will review each one individually to explain how they work, what they are used for, and provide examples.

The function syntax for all three is structured the same way:

```
{FIXED/INCLUDE/EXCLUDE [Dimension Fields] : <Aggregation>([Measure])}
```

The function syntax has several key components:

Curly brackets
   The entire function needs to be enclosed in curly brackets {}.

The level of detail type
>   The type of level of detail calculation is the first part within the brackets and indicates what type of LoD is being performed.

The dimension(s)
>   This part of the function indicates to Tableau at what level of granularity to display the measure. Multiple dimensions are separated by commas. No dimension is necessary if the measure is calculated at the level of the entire dataset.

A colon
>   A colon divides the dimensions from the measure being modified.

The measure
>   The measure follows the colon and must be aggregated (a sum, an average, or some other aggregation) to correctly display the value based on the dimensional details. While the measure within the function is aggregated, the function *itself* is not, meaning you can aggregate it as part of your visualization. You should also note that ATTR is not an acceptable aggregation for fields in an LoD calculation.

LoD calculations interact with the data at specific points in the visualization-rendering process, so it's important to review the order of operations to see where each LoD falls (see Figure 3-24). FIXED LoDs come first, falling just after context filters but before any dimensional filters. Thus, if you want a filter to affect a FIXED LoD, you need to add that filter to context. INCLUDE and EXCLUDE LoD calculations happen after dimensional filters are applied.

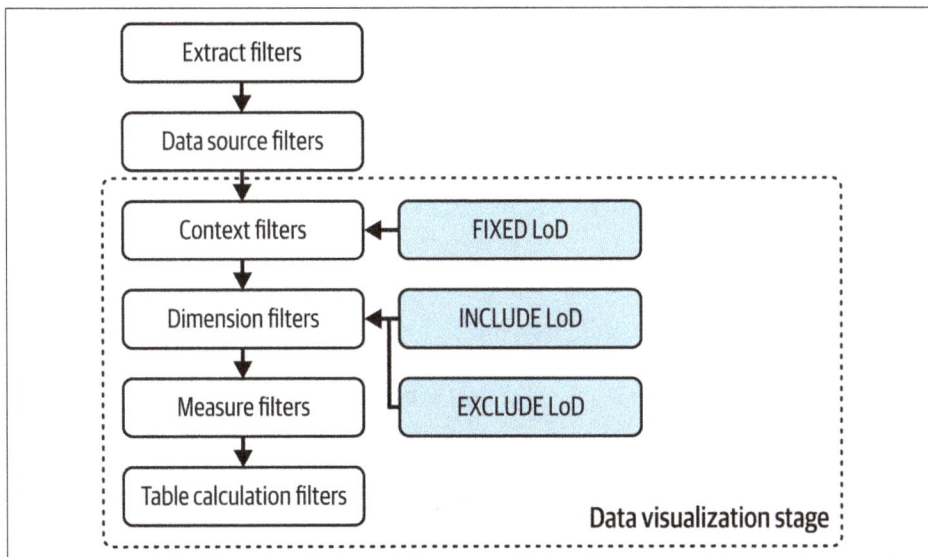

Figure 3-24. Updated order of operations, including LoD calculations.

FIXED Function

The first LoD function is the `FIXED` function. This is the most common and easiest to understand of the three functions. In a `FIXED` LoD, the dimensions you provide lock the detail to the provided values. For example, examine the function:

```
{FIXED YEAR([Order Date]):SUM([Sales])}
```

This LoD locks the sales value and forces it to be calculated at the level of the year of the order date. It doesn't matter if the visualization has categories or any other dimension dividing it up—the resulting value of this calculation will be determined at the level of the year of order date. Importantly, this also includes noncontext filters (see Figure 3-25). You can also use the `FIXED` function without specifying any dimension at all. This locks the value to the entire data set.

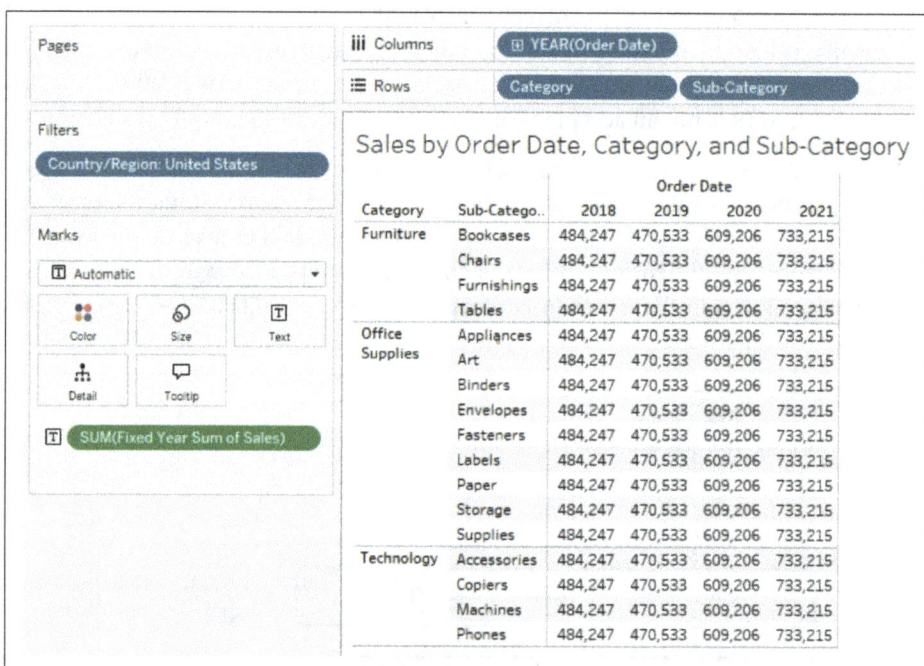

| | | Pages | | | | | | | Columns | | ⊞ YEAR(Order Date) | | |

Figure 3-25. *The measure calculation on the Text mark contains the* FIXED *LoD function, locking the sales to years. The other dimensions on the chart, including the noncontextualized filter, do not alter the value of the measure.*

`FIXED` LoD calculations ignore the dimensions in the view, relying instead on those dictated in the function. They have many uses in Tableau, including:

Comparisons to first or last values

Imagine you work in healthcare. Your management would like information on patients' first and last visit dates. Most patients have multiple visits, and each patient might have a different first or last visit date. To separate the first or last visits out, you use a FIXED function to lock the calculation to the patient, then calculate the minimum or maximum date:

```
{FIXED [Patient ID]:MIN([Visit Date])}
{FIXED [Patient ID]:MAX([Visit Date])}
```

Ratios without table calculations

Say you want to calculate the percent of sales each state contributes to a region. You know you can calculate Percent of Total with a table calculation, but what if you don't want to use a table calculation because of filters or other dimensions on the chart? You can use a FIXED LoD function instead (see Figure 3-26):

```
SUM([Sales]) / SUM({FIXED [Region]:Sum([Sales])})
```

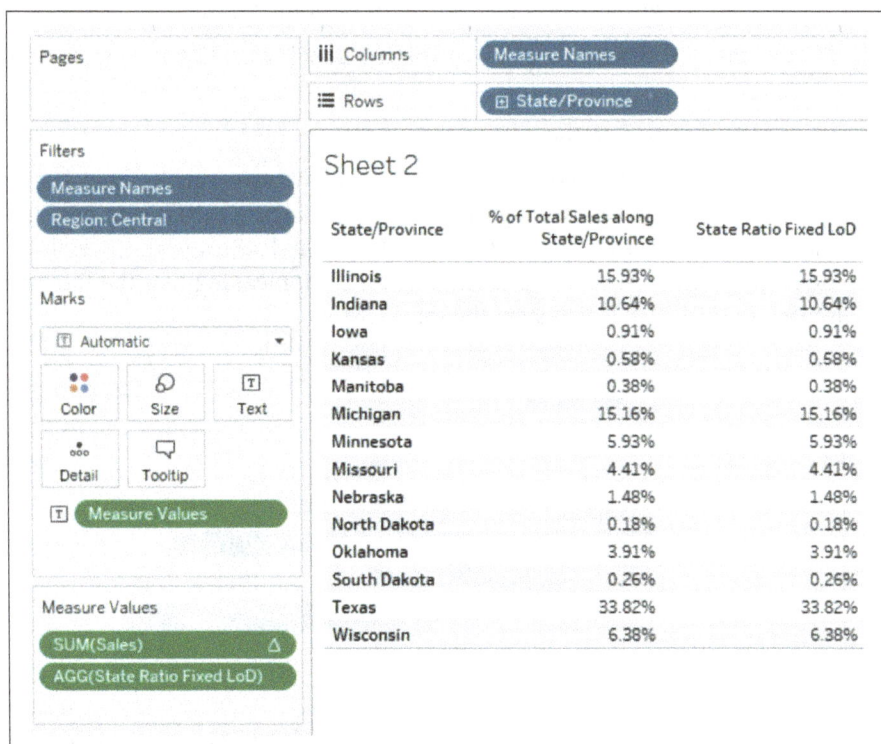

State/Province	% of Total Sales along State/Province	State Ratio Fixed LoD
Illinois	15.93%	15.93%
Indiana	10.64%	10.64%
Iowa	0.91%	0.91%
Kansas	0.58%	0.58%
Manitoba	0.38%	0.38%
Michigan	15.16%	15.16%
Minnesota	5.93%	5.93%
Missouri	4.41%	4.41%
Nebraska	1.48%	1.48%
North Dakota	0.18%	0.18%
Oklahoma	3.91%	3.91%
South Dakota	0.26%	0.26%
Texas	33.82%	33.82%
Wisconsin	6.38%	6.38%

Figure 3-26. A FIXED LoD can accomplish the same thing as a table calculation.

Comparisons to overall

What if you want to compare the sales for a product category in each region to the overall sales in a bar chart? You might be able to accomplish this using sets or groups (discussed later in this chapter), but the colored section of your bar would move. Instead, you can use a FIXED LoD. You can use the built-in data set in Superstore to try this out. First, create an LoD calculation called Regional Sales:

```
{FIXED [Region]:SUM([Sales])}
```

This will calculate the total sales by region. Next, set up the visualization:

1. Place [Region] on Rows.

2. Place SUM([Regional Sales]) on Columns.

3. Place SUM([Sales]) on Columns.

4. Dual-axis the two measures.

5. Synchronize the axis.

6. Convert the visualization to a bar chart for both measures.

7. Use the Size mark to slightly shrink the SUM([Sales]) bar to make it easier to see.

8. Add [Category] to the Filters card.

Assuming you did this correctly, you should have two equally long bar charts overlapping each other (see Figure 3-27). Try changing the filter to only include one or two categories. The SUM([Sales]) bar should adjust to the filter; however, the Region Sales LoD is fixed to the Region field, meaning that the filter has no impact on the value, which stays the same size.

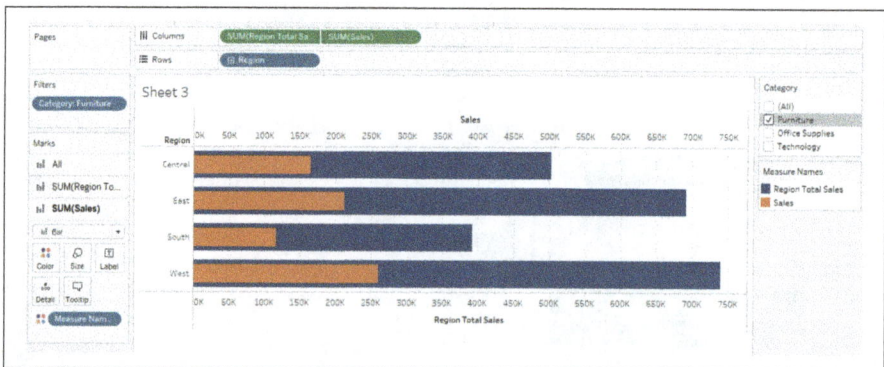

Figure 3-27. The FIXED LoD calculation for Region Total Sales is not affected by the filter. It stays the same size, while the Sales bar shrinks and grows based on what you select.

FIXED LoDs have a wide variety of other uses as well. The important part to remember is that any calculation using one will *only* utilize the fixed dimensions when calculating the measure's value. The only exception to this is context filters, which happen first due to the order of operations. FIXED LoDs also do not need to have a dimension field. A fixed calculation without a field will calculate at the level of the entire data set.

Example Question

You need to determine the sales by category and region regardless of order date. What fields should populate the following FIXED calculation respectively to accomplish this?

    {FIXED <a>,<b>,<c>: SUM(<d>)}

A. a. Category, b. Region, c. Order Date, d. Sales

B. a. Category, b. Region, c. Nothing, d. Sales

C. a. Category, b. Order Date, c. Nothing, d. Sales

D. a. Order Date, b. Region, c. Nothing, d. Sales

E. a. Region, b. Nothing, c. Nothing, d. Sales

Answer: B—The Sales value is calculated based on the dimensions in the FIXED function. Since we want the sales to be based on Category and Region only (ignoring date), these are the two fields that should appear before the colon.

INCLUDE Function

The INCLUDE function is used less frequently than the other LoD functions, but it still has value. This LoD adds dimensions to the detail beyond what is available in the visualization or data source. It makes the measure show results at a different granularity than the detail of the chart. In the previous examples, the aggregation is usually SUM, but the power of the INCLUDE LoD comes when the aggregation is something different. The following examples help clarify where and how to use this function.

Imagine you are looking at a crosstab showing average sales per year (see Figure 3-28). Tableau uses the data's row-level granularity to determine the average sales per year per row (orders). Let's assume that you also want to see the average sales per category per each year. This is where you would use an INCLUDE function.

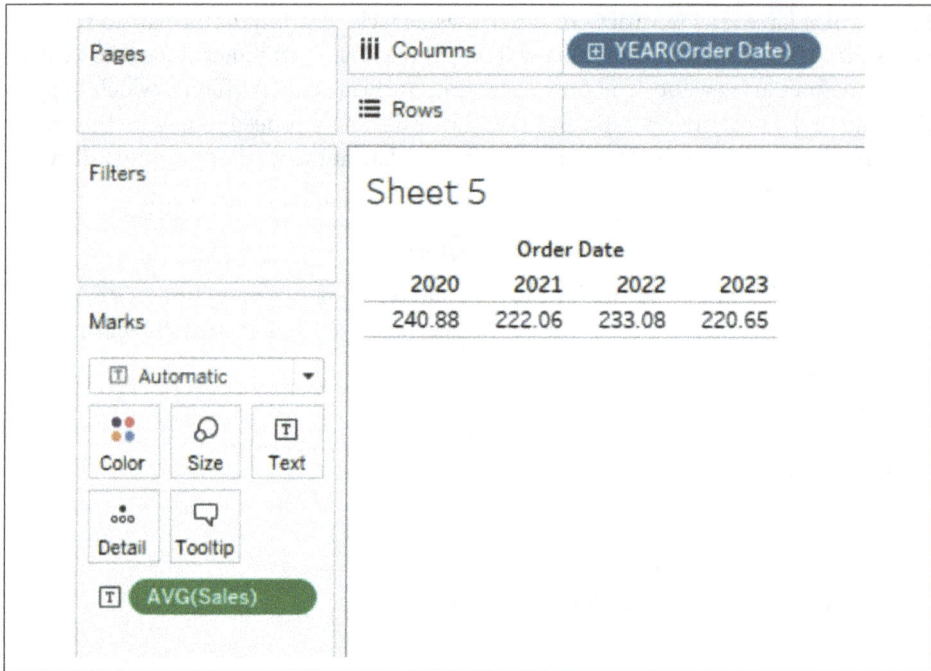

Figure 3-28. A crosstab showing average sales per year. The granularity is at the row level of the data. The average sum of sales per row is shown.

The `INCLUDE` function is structured as follows:

```
{INCLUDE [Category]:SUM([Sales])}
```

When you drag this to the crosstab and change its aggregate to `AVG`, you get a different result (see Figure 3-29). This is because you instructed Tableau to include the category as part of the average calculation. You are no longer calculating the average sum of sales per row per year, but instead the average sum of sales per *category* per year. You have reduced the granularity of the average sum of sales by rolling it up to the category level.

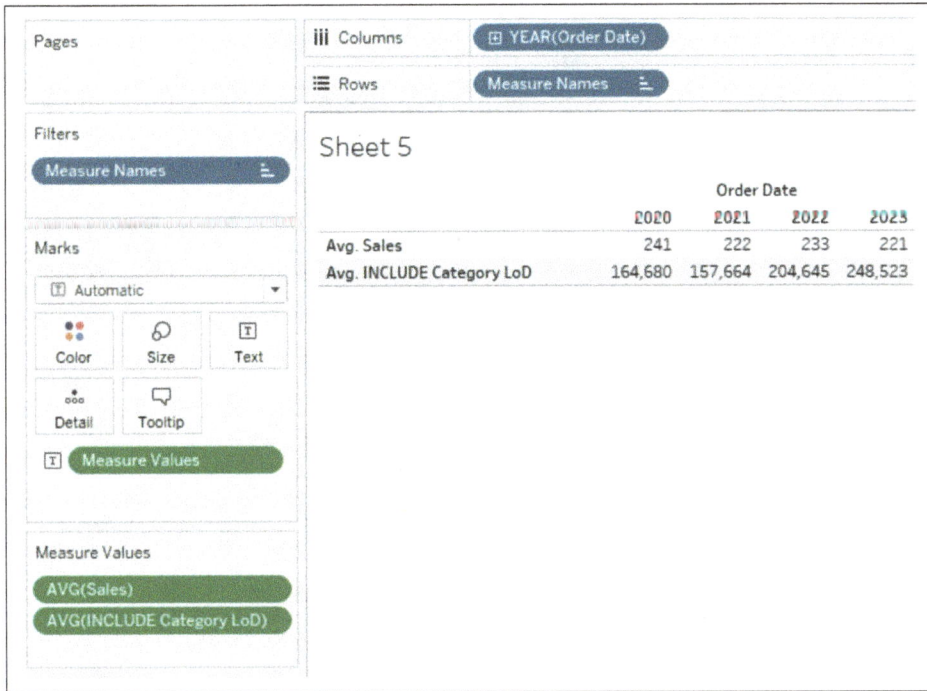

Figure 3-29. The INCLUDE function changes the granularity of the average sum of sales by year by calculating it at the category level.

Now that you have these results, you decide to include subcategory *and* category in an INCLUDE function. What happens to the results? The calculation you use is as follows:

```
{INCLUDE [Category], [Sub-Category]:SUM([Sales])}
```

When you add this new calculated field to the visualization, the results fall between the average sales per row per year and the average sales per category per year (see Figure 3-30). This is because you have added another level of detail to the average sum of sales. You've made it less granular than row level, but more granular than including category alone.

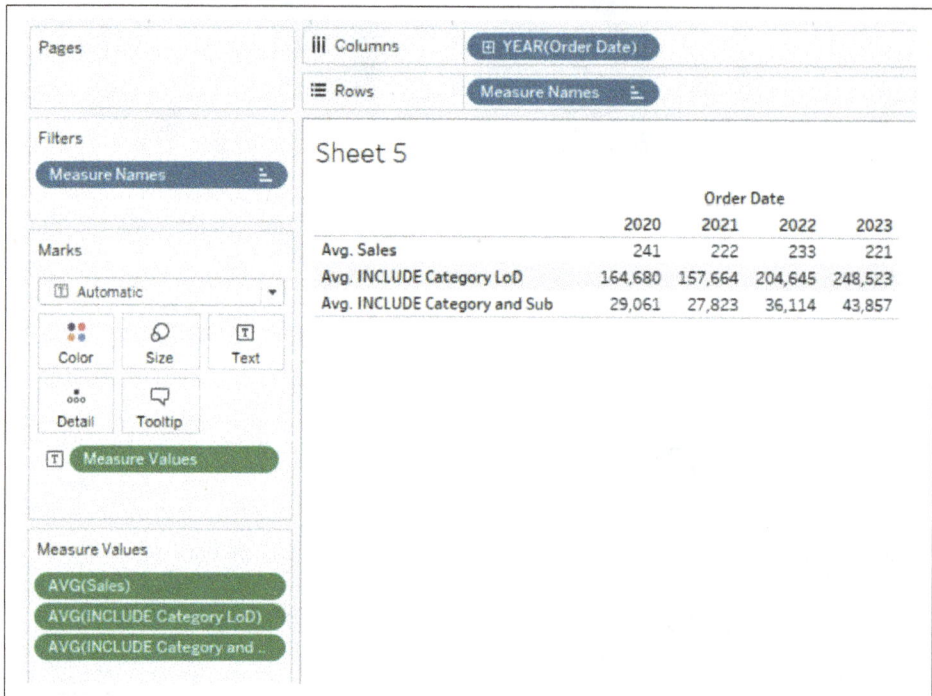

Figure 3-30. The second `INCLUDE` *LoD calculation includes subcategory in the detail, making it less granular than the average sum of sales by year, but more granular than the average sum of sales by year and category.*

When you use `INCLUDE`, you are changing the granularity of the query of the data. The dimension details you add to the calculation determine how the result is calculated. This may increase or decrease the granularity of the results. If you're wondering why the `SUM` aggregation is not used with `INCLUDE`, that's the reason: adding additional dimensions shouldn't change the sum of the measure. For example, if you have the sum of sales by Category and then add Region to the visualization, the sum of sales by Category doesn't change. To put it a different way, even though you split the category up, the underlying sum of its parts is still the same.

EXCLUDE Function

The `EXCLUDE` function does what you might expect: it excludes a dimension within the visualization from being used to calculate the measure. Like the `FIXED` LoD, it's very powerful when calculating Percent of Total or when showing an aggregation of something that is split on the visualization. It allows you to calculate values that otherwise might require a table calculation or other adjustment. The following examples will help you understand how to use `EXCLUDE` LoDs.

For this first example, look at average sales over time for each product category in Figure 3-31. The chart is a line chart that shows a differently colored line for each category (because the category dimension is on the Color mark). It's a simple visualization, but your managers love it. It quickly shows them which category is making higher average sales per order.

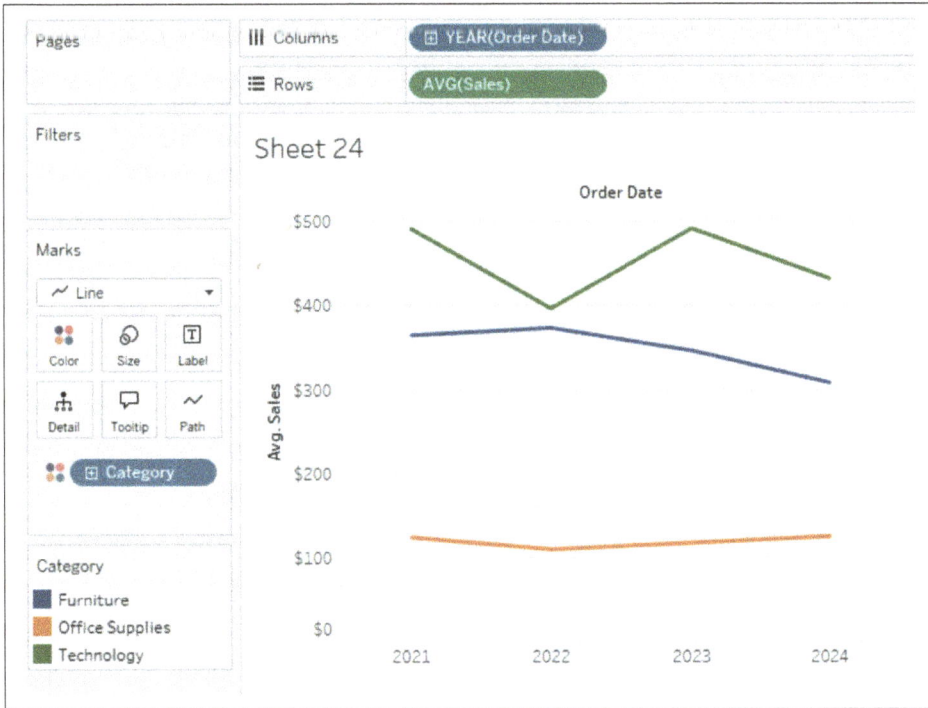

Figure 3-31. This chart shows the average sales per order for each of the categories.

They have one additional request to add to the chart. They want an additional line to compare against, showing the average sales across all four years. This is challenging, because the Category field is on Detail and will split any measure you add to the visualization. This is where you use the EXCLUDE LoD.

The first step is to create a calculated field with the function:

```
{EXCLUDE [Category]:AVG(Sales)}
```

This calculation ignores the Category dimension on the Color mark and instead calculates the average sales per order overall. If you want to display it as part of the original chart, you need to follow the dual-axis steps listed earlier in this chapter:

1. Add the new LoD measure to Rows.

2. Right-click on the added field and choose Dual Axis.

3. Right-click on the axis for the newly added field and choose Synchronize Axis to line it up with the previous chart's axis.

4. Remove the Category dimension from Color on the newly added Field's Marks card.

The result should be the same chart as Figure 3-31, but with an additional line for the average sales regardless of category (see Figure 3-32). This new line may make you pause, since it doesn't naturally fall at the average for each line; however, remember that each category doesn't necessarily have the same number of orders. For example, even though the Office Supplies category has lower average sales per order, it may have more orders in total than the other two categories. Since the LoD line uses *all* orders, it shows the average sales of every row, regardless of category.

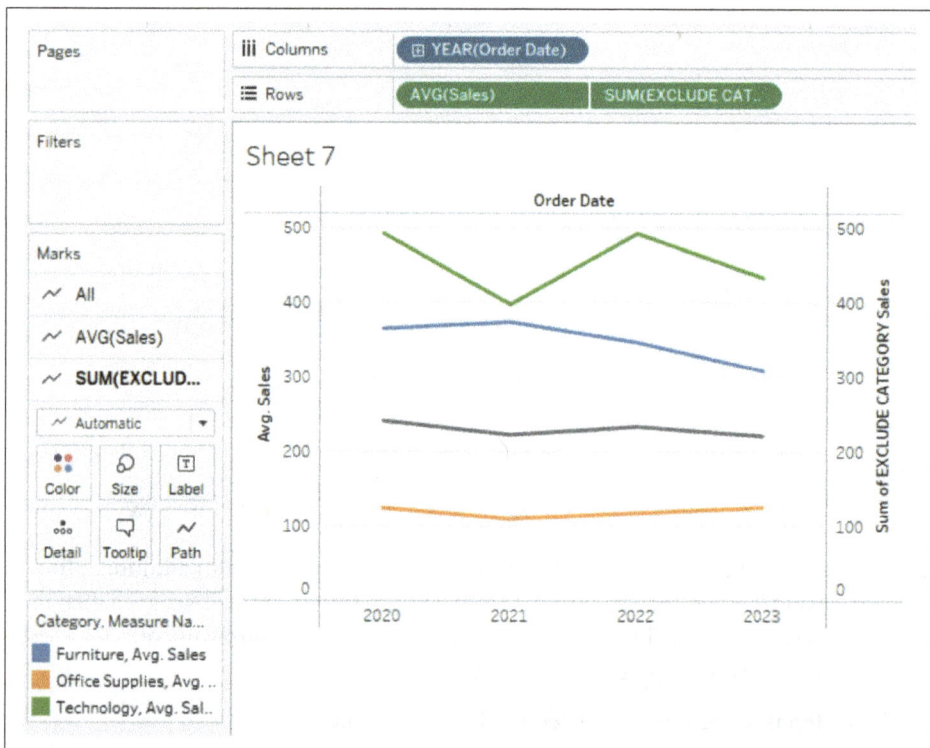

Figure 3-32. The EXCLUDE LoD is used to find the average sales per order regardless of category. Using Dual Axis and synchronizing allows you to see this line in addition to the existing average sales lines for each category.

The previous example placed the LoD on the Rows using a SUM aggregation. The aggregation doesn't matter in this example, because there is only one value: the average sales per order. You can AVG, SUM, MAX, or MIN the measure, and it will return the same result. If you add additional dimensions as details to the chart, you then need to determine which aggregation to use to display the results correctly.

Another place you can use EXCLUDE LoDs is to calculate the Percent of Total. This LoD is a bit trickier to use than FIXED. The FIXED LoD locks the measure's granularity to the listed dimensions, while EXCLUDE only ignores the listed dimensions. If you add more dimensions to the visualization, the results can change.

Let's revisit the example in Figure 3-26 to test how this might work. Figure 3-26 used a FIXED Lod to calculate the Percent of Total each state contributed to the overall sales:

```
SUM([Sales]) / SUM({FIXED [Region]:Sum([Sales])})
```

You can write a calculation using EXCLUDE to do the same thing:

```
SUM([Sales]) / SUM({EXCLUDE [State]:Sum([Sales])})
```

This calculation ignores the state dimension when calculating the sum of sales (see Figure 3-33).

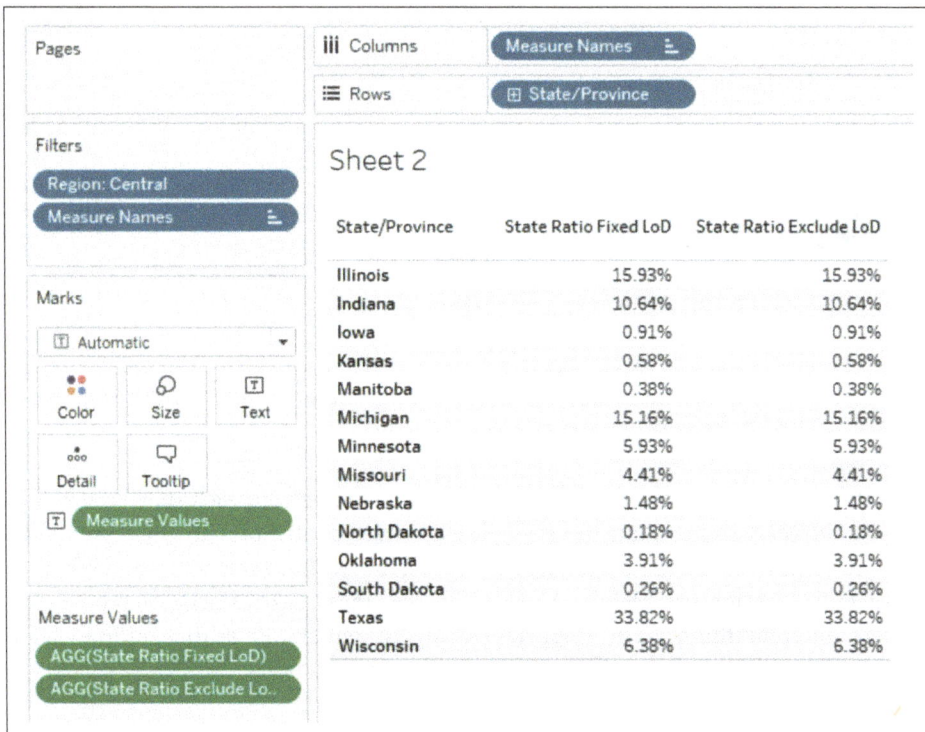

State/Province	State Ratio Fixed LoD	State Ratio Exclude LoD
Illinois	15.93%	15.93%
Indiana	10.64%	10.64%
Iowa	0.91%	0.91%
Kansas	0.58%	0.58%
Manitoba	0.38%	0.38%
Michigan	15.16%	15.16%
Minnesota	5.93%	5.93%
Missouri	4.41%	4.41%
Nebraska	1.48%	1.48%
North Dakota	0.18%	0.18%
Oklahoma	3.91%	3.91%
South Dakota	0.26%	0.26%
Texas	33.82%	33.82%
Wisconsin	6.38%	6.38%

Figure 3-33. EXCLUDE LoD calculations can be used to calculate percent of total just like FIXED LoD calculation.

The difference comes when you add further dimensions to the chart (see Figure 3-34). The new dimension makes the numerators of both calculations much smaller. The denominator in the FIXED calculation continues to ignore the new detail added to the chart, which means that the ratios also get smaller but still sum to 100%. The EXCLUDE denominator *is* impacted by the new detail (since the new dimension is not excluded), and therefore gets split further.

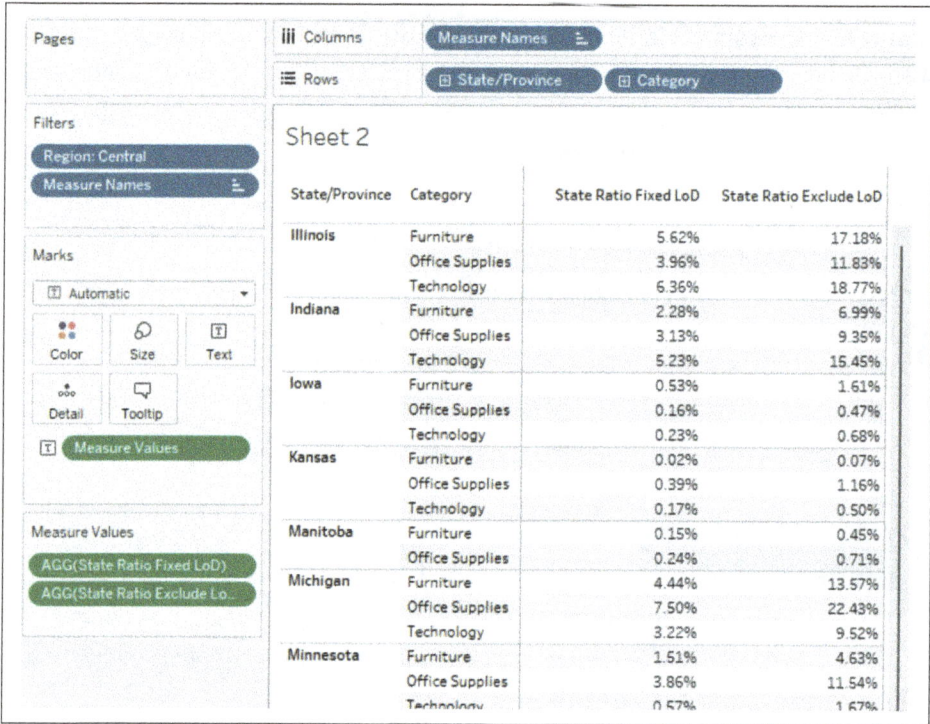

Figure 3-34. Adding detail dimensions increases the granularity of the FIXED ratio, but completely changes what the EXCLUDE ratio is showing.

The ratio calculated in the EXCLUDE function is now the percent each state contributes to each *category*, rather than the percent each state contributes to the *region*. The FIXED ratio now shows the percentage each category within each state contributes to the overall sales for the region. As you can see, these two calculations are doing entirely different things. The important thing to remember is that adding detail dimensions can affect your EXCLUDE functions.

Expanding on Level of Detail Functions

You've seen how to add LoD functions to calculations to compute measures that otherwise would be inaccessible due to the visualization's existing detail dimensions. Now that you understand this, you can take the next step and nest LoD functions within a calculation. This sounds extremely daunting, but breaking it apart helps make it easier to understand. The following example will combine an EXCLUDE function with a FIXED function to calculate the average sales per month. This example will use the built-in Superstore data set if you wish to follow along.

To start, review the custom date feature mentioned at the end of the section "Date and Time Calculations" on page 117. Use it on Order Date to create a custom date field at the detail of Month / Year (see Figure 3-35). This creates the calculated field Order Date (Month / Year).

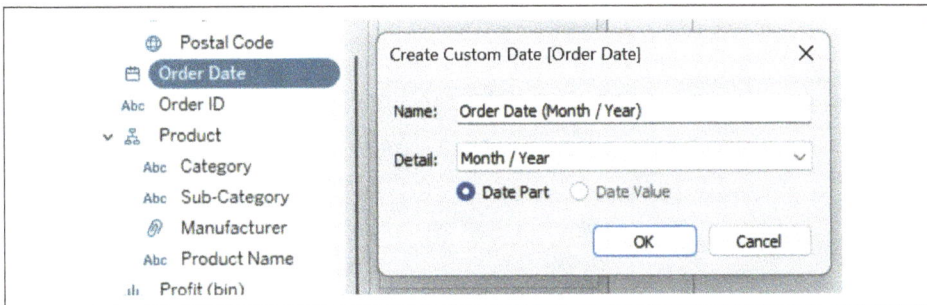

Figure 3-35. The custom date window is available by right-clicking on a date field and then choosing Create → Custom Date.

Next, you want to know what the sum of sales is for each combination of Month and Year. You can do this using a FIXED LoD:

```
{FIXED [Order Date (Month / Year)]:SUM([Sales])}
```

This gives the sum of sales for each month of the year. It's exactly the same as simply dividing up the sum of sales by our date calculation (see Figure 3-36).

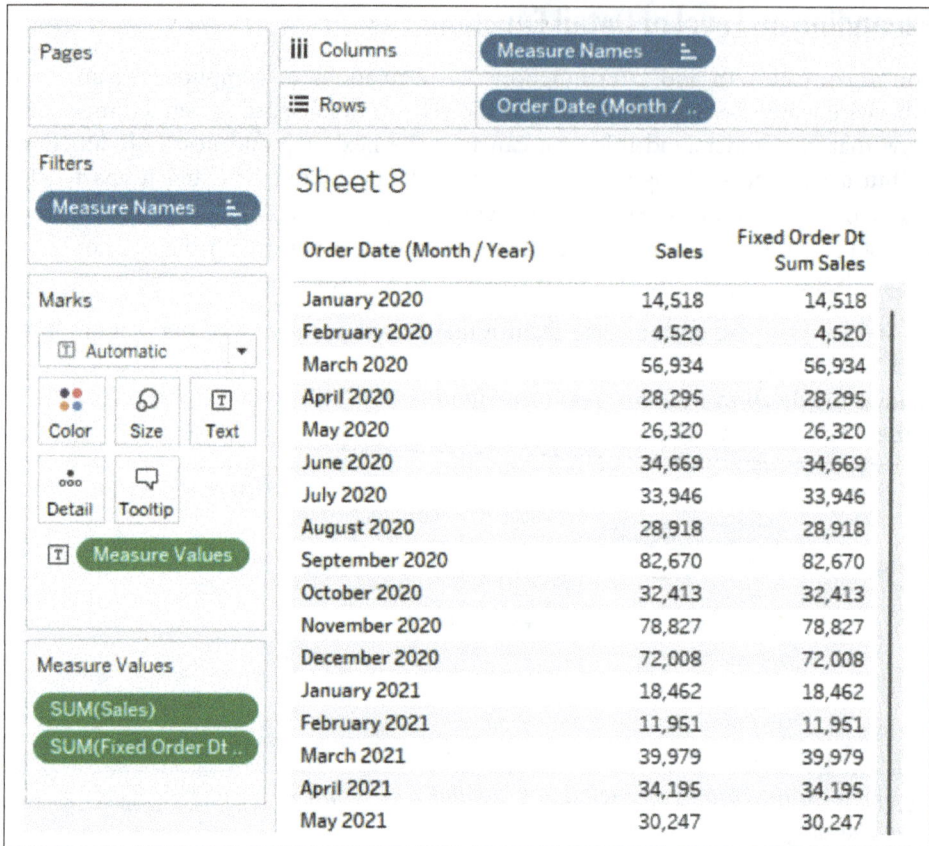

Figure 3-36. The LoD computing the sales fixed to each date is the same as making a chart of sales by date.

If you then want the average sales across *all* the dates, you can't just take an average. The average will continue to be calculated at the Order Date (Month / Year) level. Instead, you have to ignore the Order Date (Month / Year) and then calculate the average. This requires you to exclude the order date you originally fixed:

```
{EXCLUDE [Order Date (Month / Year)] :
AVG({FIXED [Order Date (Month / Year)]:SUM([Sales])})
}
```

When this is added to the visualization, the value is the average sum of sales across all the order dates (see Figure 3-37).

Pages

Columns — Measure Names

Rows — Order Date (Month / ...

Filters

Measure Names

Marks

Automatic

Color | Size | Text
Detail | Tooltip

Measure Values

Measure Values

SUM(Sales)
SUM(Fixed Order Dt ...
ATTR(Exclude Order...

Sheet 8

Order Date (Month / Year)	Sales	Fixed Order Dt Sum Sales	Exclude Order Dt Avg Sum
January 2020	14,518	14,518	48,469
February 2020	4,520	4,520	48,469
March 2020	56,934	56,934	48,469
April 2020	28,295	28,295	48,469
May 2020	26,320	26,320	48,469
June 2020	34,669	34,669	48,469
July 2020	33,946	33,946	48,469
August 2020	28,918	28,918	48,469
September 2020	82,670	82,670	48,469
October 2020	32,413	32,413	48,469
November 2020	78,827	78,827	48,469
December 2020	72,008	72,008	48,469
January 2021	18,462	18,462	48,469
February 2021	11,951	11,951	48,469
March 2021	39,979	39,979	48,469
April 2021	34,195	34,195	48,469
May 2021	30,247	30,247	48,469
June 2021	24,797	24,797	48,469

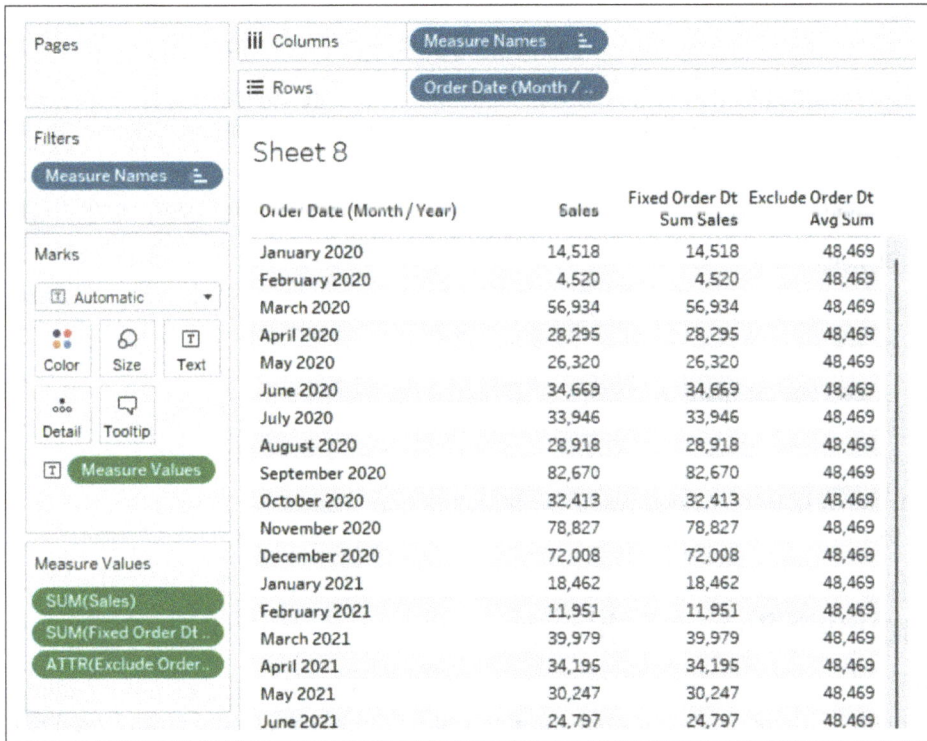

Figure 3-37. The nested LoD calculates the average sum of sales across all the month/year dates listed.

Obviously, this is not the only way to nest LoD functions, but it gives you a good idea of what these functions make possible. LoDs are extremely valuable when a chart's level of detail is different from the value you need to calculate.

> LoD questions *will* appear on the Tableau exam, and they usually involve syntax or deciphering what the LoD is doing. Practice using all three of these functions in different ways. See what happens when you swap out details, both in the calculations and in the visualizations utilizing them. Make sure you commit the proper syntax to memory.

Grouping Data in Tableau

Sometimes the dimensions in your data add detail that is too granular or not granular enough. In these cases, you need a tool to roll up dimensional values into a level that is one step in between. Tableau has two built-in features that allow you to categorize dimensional values. Each has its benefits and drawbacks, but both are extremely useful when analyzing data.

Groups

The first way to categorize dimensional values is called a *group*. A group allows you to manually combine dimensional values together under a new title. For example, you may want to combine the states Michigan, Indiana, and Wisconsin under the heading Midwest. Grouping allows you to do this.

To make a group, right-click on any dimension and choose Create → Group. This opens the Create Group window (see Figure 3-38), which shows you the values of that dimension and provides you with tools to collect and combine them. You can use the shift or control keys on your keyboard to select multiple values and the Group button to group them together. Once you create a group, the Rename and Ungroup buttons become available.

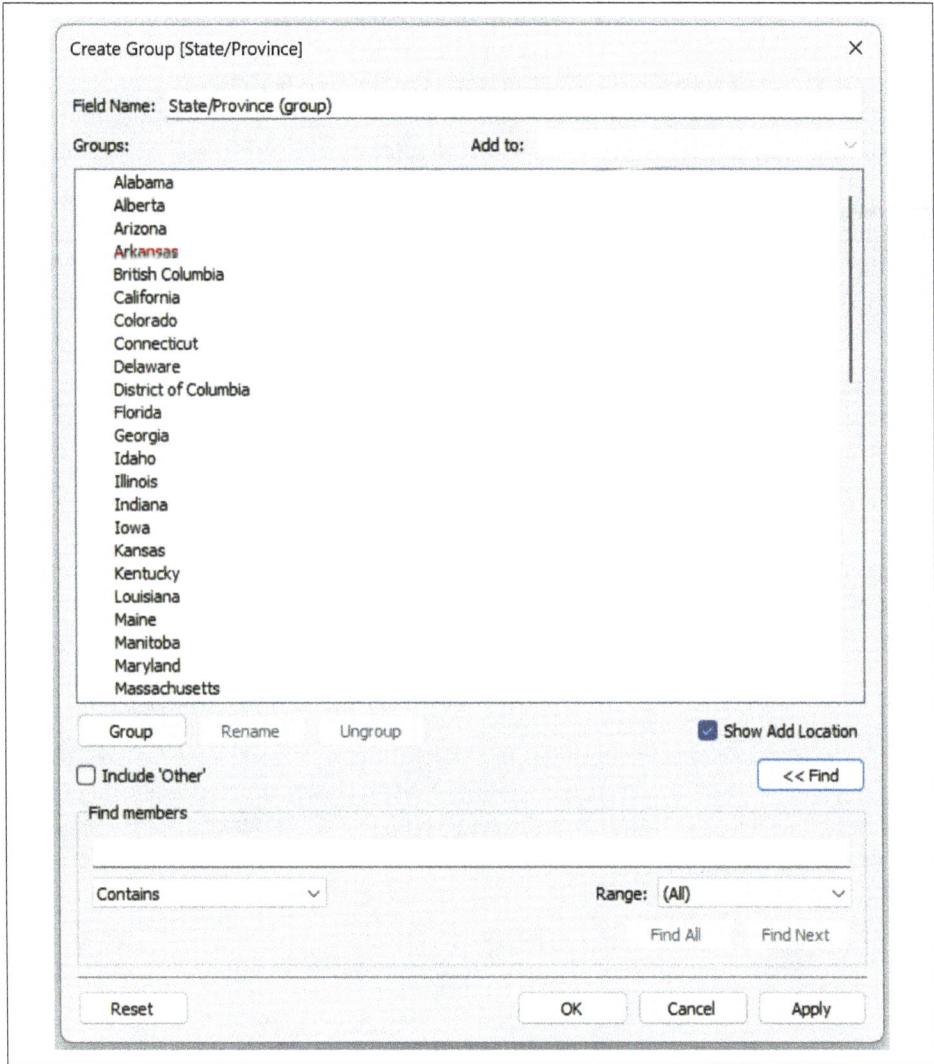

Figure 3-38. The Create Group window for a State/Province dimension.

You can also add other fields to a group quickly by right-clicking on an ungrouped value and choosing "Add to:" to select a group to add the value to. You can also click and drag values to groups. There are no limits to the number of groups you can create. If your dimension is populated by an overwhelming number of values, there is a "Find members" section in the window where you can search through the values.

One caveat: you cannot name a group "Other" in the group window, because the built-in option called Include 'Other' is used to automatically label everything not in a group. When it's toggled on, anything that is not grouped is gathered into the Other group. When it is turned off, ungrouped items maintain their current name and stand alone in addition to the groups you've created.

Another caveat to groups is that they are static. Except for the Include 'Other' option, all values have to be manually added to groups. There are no options to include an object in a group if certain criteria are met. That means that future changes in data may require you to return to the workbook to update your groups.

After a group is created, it is visible as a field in the Data pane. You can identify groups quickly by the paper clip icon, which indicates that the field is composed of grouped values (look ahead to Figure 3-40). Groups can also be useful when creating hierarchies, which I will discuss in further detail in Chapter 4.

Sets

Another way to categorize field values in a dimension is to create a *set*. Unlike groups, sets can be dynamic. The Create Set window contains instructions for defining how a value is included or excluded from the set (see Figure 3-39). Once a set is created, it can easily be identified in the Data pane by the field's Venn diagram icon (see Figure 3-40).

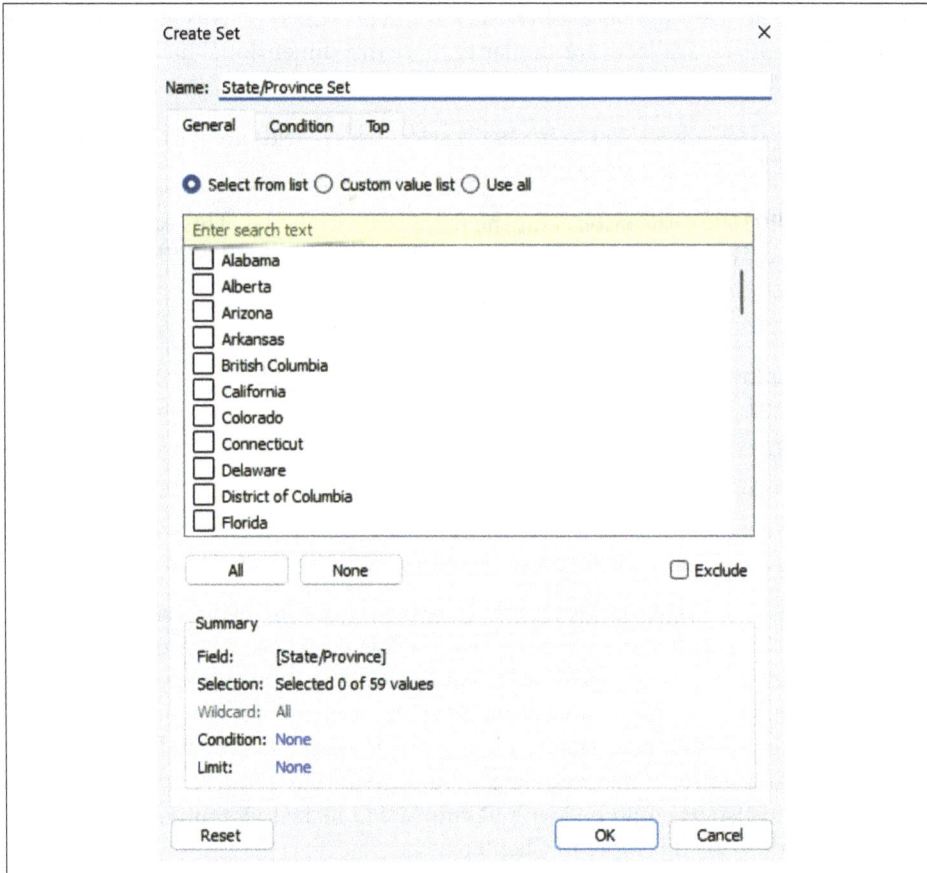

Figure 3-39. *The set creation window.*

Figure 3-40. *Icons for a group, "State/Province (group)" and set, "State/Province Set" in the Tableau Data pane.*

The set can be defined in several different ways, represented by tabs at the top of the window. The options available are similar to those in a dimensional filter:

General
>   The General tab allows you to manually select which fields are part of the set.

Condition
>   The Condition tab sets criteria for the fields to be in the set. This can be based on other values. For example, the state set in Figure 3-39 could be limited to states with a certain value of sales.

Top
>   This tab allows you to select the top or bottom number of values based on another field. In Figure 3-39, for example, you could select the top 10 or bottom 15 states by sales.

Selection on a View
>   If you have a visualization built, you can select one or more marks, right-click, and create a set. The set will be a static representation of the marks you selected.

The biggest caveat to using sets is that they are binary. A dimension value is either in the set or not. Thus, you can only have two possible outcomes when using a set. On the other hand, sets can be dynamic. If your set is based on dynamic values, data changes in the future might cause set members to adjust. For example, if you select the top 10 states by sales, new data may change which states fall in the top 10. The set will automatically adjust to the new data without requiring you to reopen and adjust the file. Sets can also be combined with parameters to make them interactive for your end users. I'll describe this more in Chapter 4.

> For the Tableau exam, it is helpful to know the benefits and drawbacks of sets and groups. You should also be able to identify them in the Data pane by their icons. Take some time to understand their nuances, such as the Other category for groups and the Criteria window for sets.

Bins

Tableau is built around dividing measures by dimensions; however, occasionally, you want to evaluate dimensions based on the measures themselves. In statistics, you often want to see how many fields within a dimension fall within each range of a measure. For example, if you sell thousands of different products, perhaps you want to see how many products bring in certain levels of profit. Dividing measures in this way is called *binning*. A bin takes the values of a measure and divides them based on tiers. You can then use these tiers to divide a dimension's values into those tiers. Typically, you will then count how many dimension values fall in each tier.

In Tableau, you can make any measure into a bin by right-clicking it and selecting Create → Bin. This will provide the Edit Bins window (see Figure 3-41), with options for naming the bin field and determining the size of the bins (tiers). It suggests a bin size based on the values in the measure. If you change the size of the bin, it also provides a button to revert to the suggested size.

The bin window also provides you with information about the measure you are binning, such as the Min, the Max, the Diff (difference; range), and CntD (the number of distinct measure values available). For example, the "Profit (bin)" in Figure 3-41 indicates that the profit field has a min of –6,600 and a maximum of 8,400, which is a range (difference) of 15,000. There are also 7,597 unique profit values in the field.

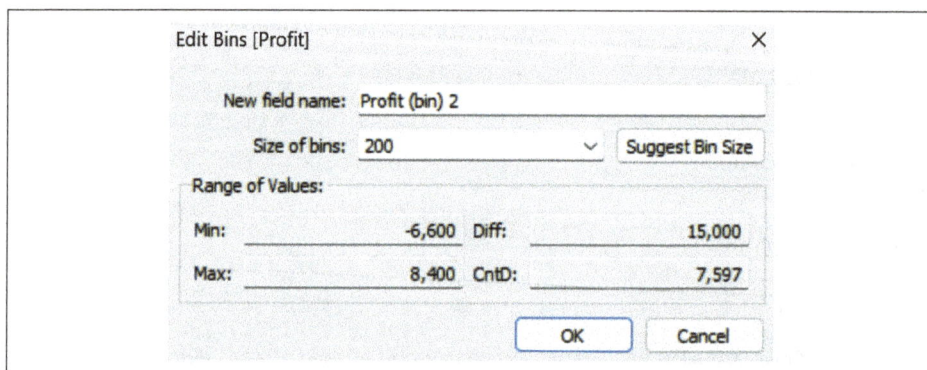

Figure 3-41. A bin window for the Profit field. The names and sizes of the bins are adjustable, and Tableau provides statistics on the measure to help you determine a size to use.

Bins can be used like other fields in a visualization. If you take the bin from Figure 3-41 and use it as an x-axis (that is, place it on Columns), you can count how many products fall within each $200 profit range. To count the products, drag the Product Name field to Rows, then right-click it and choose "Measure - Count Distinct." The result is a histogram showing how many products bring in the amount of profit in each range (see Figure 3-42).

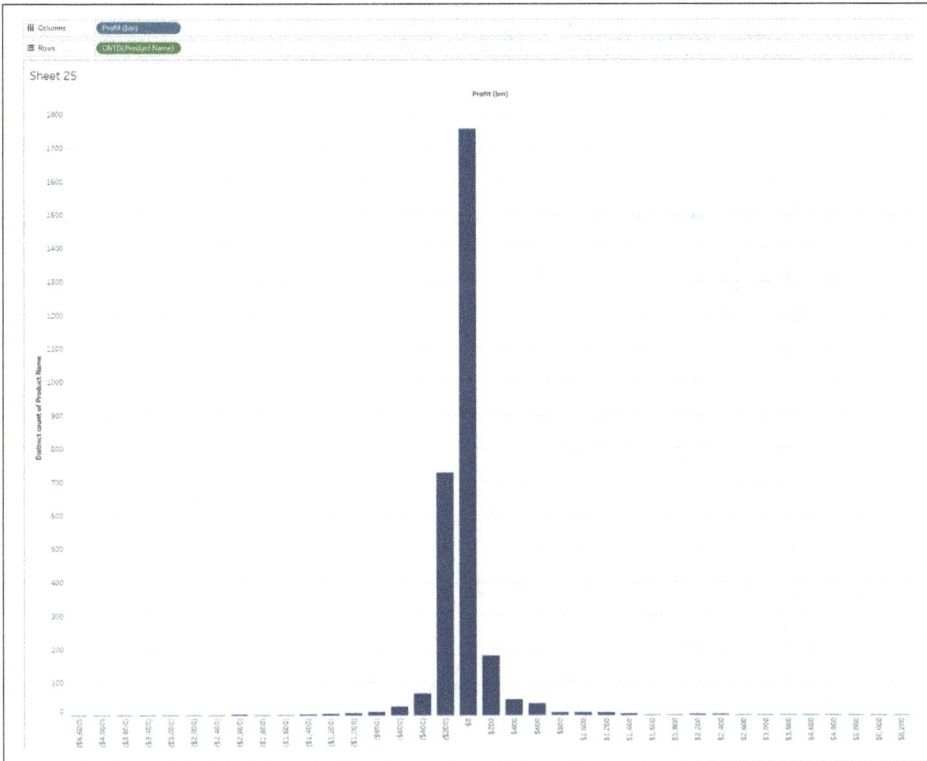

Figure 3-42. A histogram showing the number of products that bring in the amount of profit defined by each $200 range.

You can expand this example further. Instead of counting orders, you could find out the average discount offered for each profit range. That is, for data rows with *x* amount of profit, how much discount does the company typically offer its customers? To do this, simply swap the CNTD([Order ID]) field with the AVG([Discount]) field. This new chart shows that profit-losing orders typically have higher discounts (see Figure 3-43).

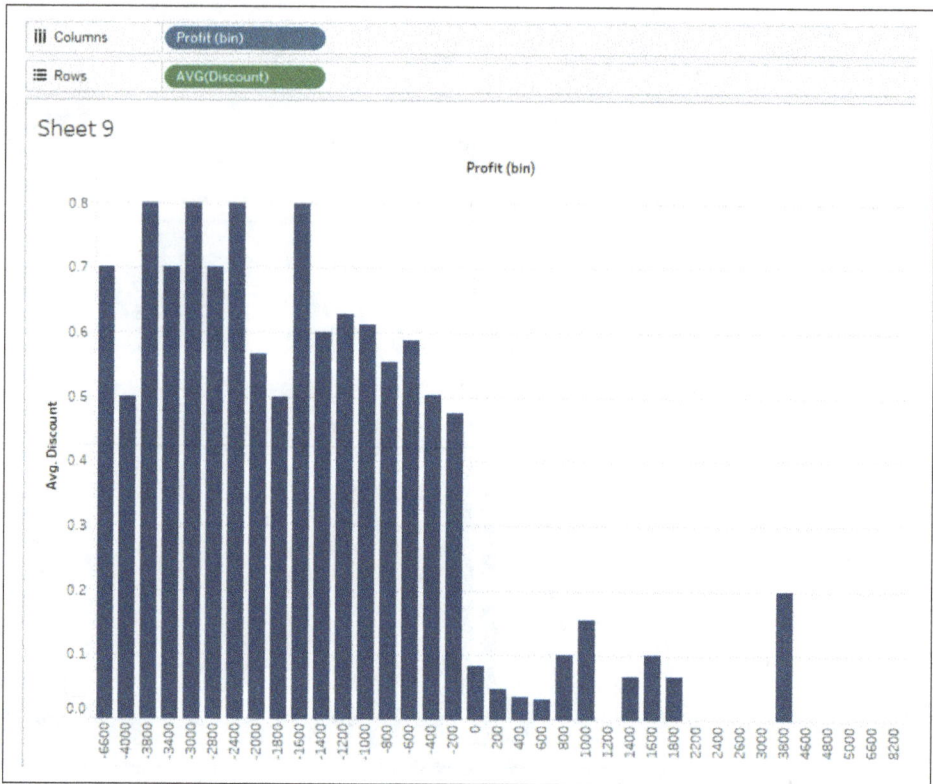

Figure 3-43. Plotting profit ranges against the average discount given. The chart shows that rows of data with higher profit loss usually have higher discounts. This can be misleading, since you also need to know how many orders are made at each profit range. Looking at Figure 3-41 shows that a majority of orders are likely made with –$600 to $600 of profit.

Bins will likely appear once or twice on the exam. Know what they are and what they are used to illustrate. There may also be a question on how to set specific bin sizes or use a bin in a visualization to find a result.

Analytics Pane

Tableau provides some additional analytical tools, accessible via the Analytics tab at the top of the pane (see Figure 3-44). The Analytics pane contains options and shortcuts to analyze, summarize, model, or further detail your visualizations.

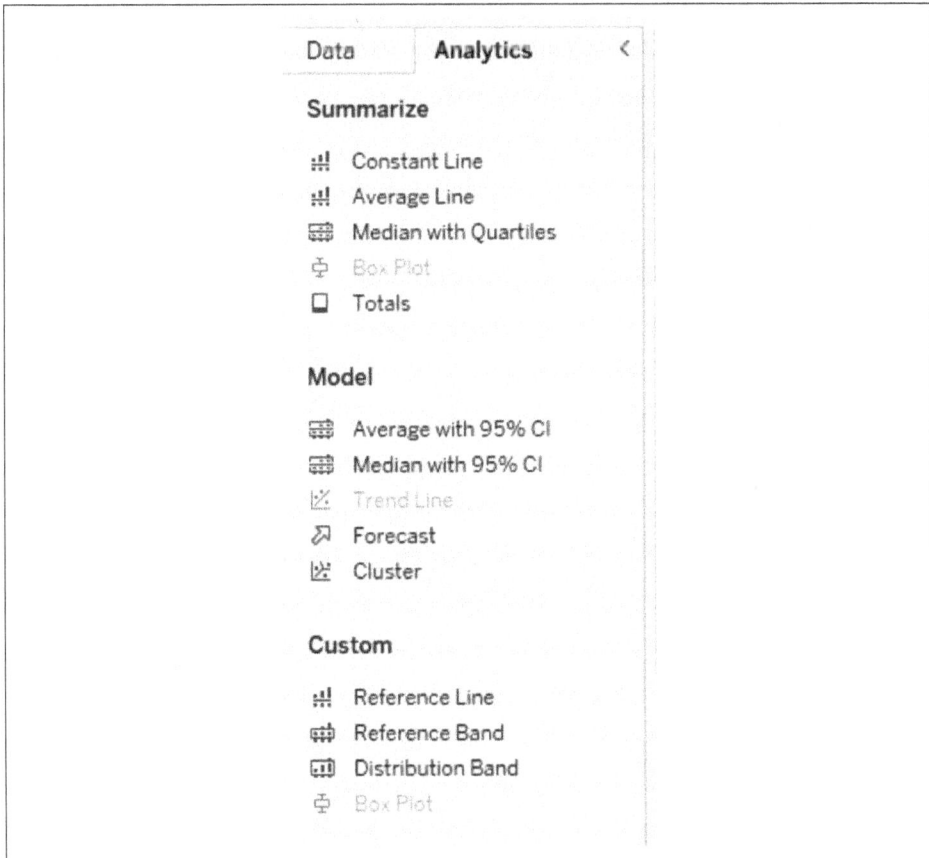

Figure 3-44. The Analytics pane replaces the Data pane when the tab at the top is switched.

The Analytics pane is broken into three sections: tools to summarize, tools to model, and custom tools. Some options will only be available with the right type of visualization. If the option is grayed out, you can hover over it to see what requirement is missing to use the tool.

Summarization Tools

To start, let's examine the summarization tools. *Summarization* tools provide information about the data being visualized in aggregation. Many of these tools are *reference lines*, or lines drawn across a chart or part of a chart based on the required value. I will discuss them in detail, as well as the sections of charts, in Chapter 4. The following list is just for quick reference. The summarization tools are:

Constant Line
> A constant line creates a solid line across the visualization at any value you choose.

Average Line
> An average line draws a line across the table, pane, or cell at the average value of the measure within.

Median with Quartiles
> Similar to the average line, this draws a line at the median for the table, pane, or cell and then overlays it with an interquartile range (a shaded range above 25% and below 75% of the possible values of the measure).

Box Plot
> This type of visualization is also called a *box-and-whisker* plot or a *candlestick* plot, due to its shape. Box plots provide a five-figure summary of the measure in a particular dimension value. These figures include an indicator of 1.5 times the median lower, an indicator of 1.5 times the median higher, the lower quartile, the upper quartile, and median values. You can also create box plots via the Show Me menu.

Totals
> This option adds a total point, row, or bar, depending on the visualization type. It can be used to show totals for Rows, totals for Columns, or, if there are multiple dimensions, subtotals. You can also add totals and subtotals via the Analysis menu.

Modeling Tools

The next set of analytics tools pertains to statistical analysis, predictive analytics, and grouping. While a few of these are types of reference lines, the remainder are unique to this tab and only available here:

Average with 95% CI
> The CI stands for *confidence interval*. That means that using this tool will provide an average line, as well as a shaded band indicating how "good" the estimate is at guessing where a value will fall.

Median with 95% CI
> This does the same thing as Average with 95% CI, only using a median.

Trend Line
> This line can take many shapes depending on the regression you choose (see Figure 3-45). The regression is your guess as to what shape best describes your data. Is it a straight line, slowly curving up, or curvy in general? The regression you choose will be applied to the chart and represent your data as accurately as possible.

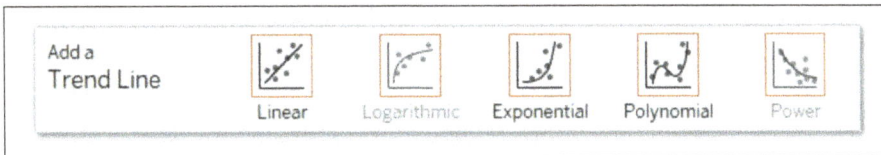

Figure 3-45. Options for modeling a trend line include Linear, Logarithmic, Exponential, Polynomial, or Power.

Once you apply a trend line, you can examine it for accuracy or adjust it to meet your needs. When you hover over the line, it provides the *R-square* and *p*-values, which describe how accurately the line describes the variation of your data and how significant it is. Ideally, you want high R-square and low p-values.

If you right-click on the trend line, the Trend Line Options window appears. Here, you can change the trend line type or, if you choose a polynomial trend line, adjust the polynomial degrees (number of curves). It also provides options to show tooltips, show confidence intervals, show multiple trend lines, and redraw the line based on user interaction (see Figure 3-46).

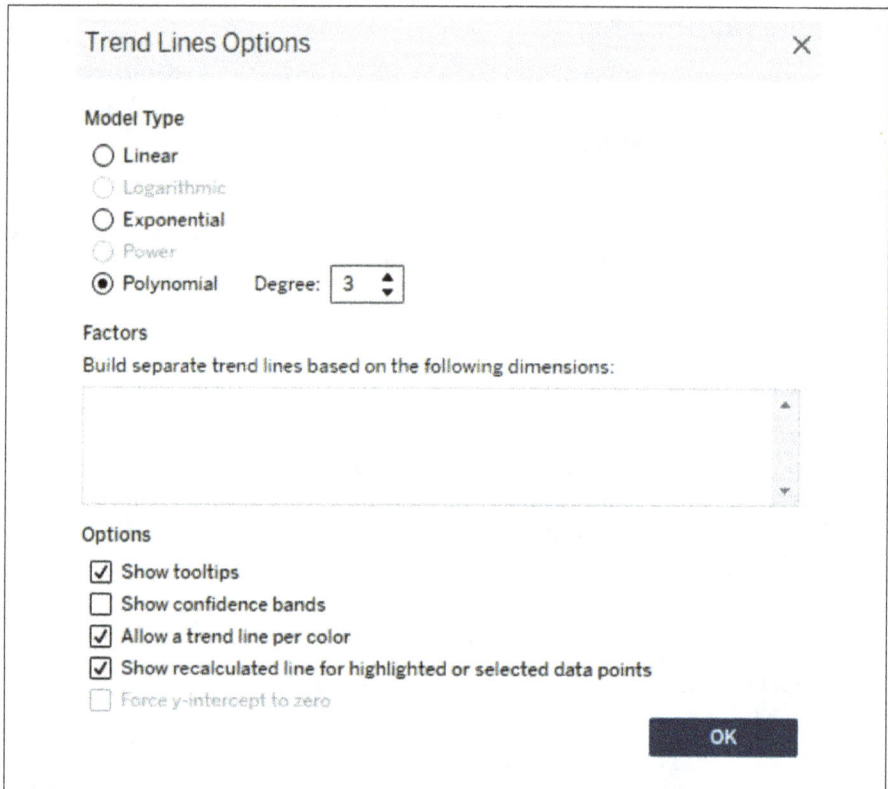

Figure 3-46. The Trend Lines Options window.

Forecast

Forecast is a type of predictive analytic. Tableau uses statistical calculations to model the data and predict where your chart might go if extended into the future. In addition to the predictive values, it also provides a shaded area or a range line to indicate the variance in the predicted value—that is, in what range the next value is likely to fall.

You can right-click on Forecasts to get an Options window with settings for length of time, how to aggregate, how to handle missing values, which model to use, and the confidence interval (see Figure 3-47).

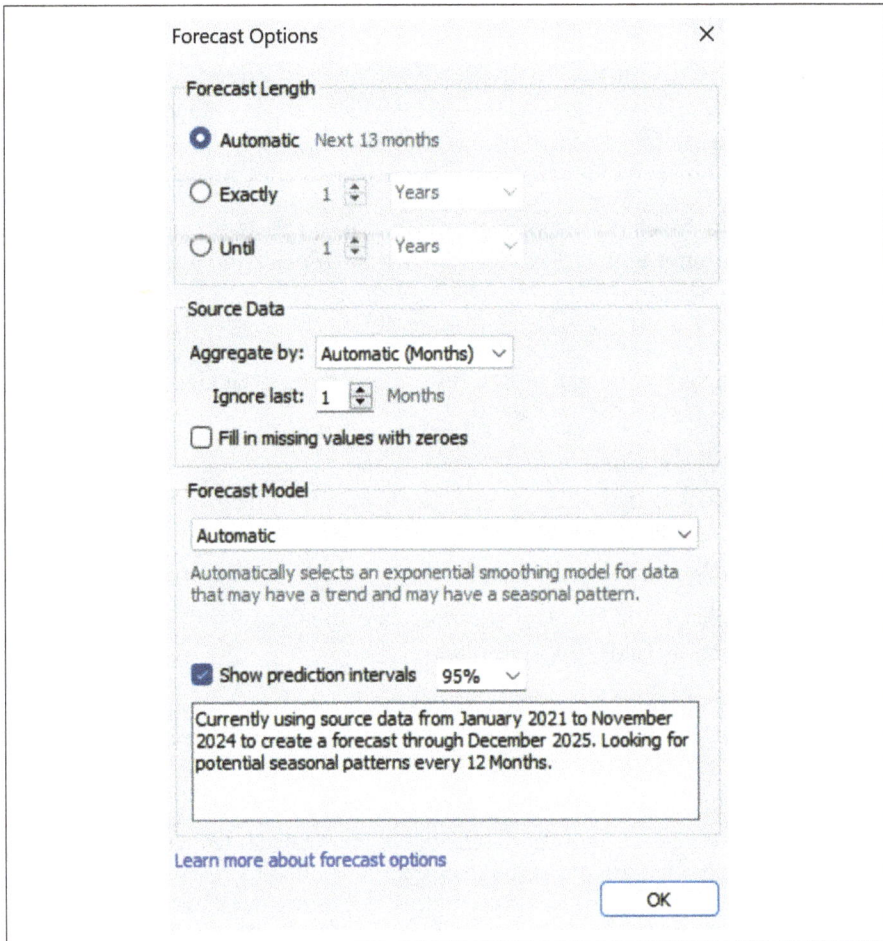

Figure 3-47. The Forecast Options window.

Cluster

When you drag Cluster to your visualization, it prompts you for the number of clusters you want. It then looks through all the measure values in the visualization and groups them into the number of clusters you indicated, based on the values of the measure. For example, if your measure goes from 0 to 100, and you select five clusters, you can assume that the chart will be divided into sections of 0–20, 20–40, 40–60, 60–80, and 80–100. Tableau then redraws the chart, giving each cluster its own color and adds a Cluster field to the Color mark.

Reference Lines

The final set of tools on the Analytics tab are types of reference lines. They can be created in multiple other ways, so the options listed in this tab are simply shortcuts for commonly used lines and defined areas on charts:

Reference Line
> This is a line based on the average, median, or a constant value. Using Reference Line will prompt you with options for where to place the line, what it measures, and how to label it.

Reference Band
> This is just like a reference line, but it produces a shaded area based on the parameters you supply.

Distribution Band
> This will add a statistical band on your chart indicating 60% and 80% of average, although it can also be modified based on parameters you provide.

Box Plot
> This is duplicated in the Analytics tab. (See the "Box Plot" entry in the section "Summarization Tools" on page 150.)

While some of its features are unique, many can be recreated manually. Because many of the features it provides are visual and descriptive, I will focus on this in more detail in Chapter 4.

> While a majority of the features in the Analytics tab can be created in other ways, it is still important to familiarize yourself with how they work. You can expect at least one or two questions about these shortcut tools.

Conclusion

This chapter has focused heavily on exploring and analyzing data in Tableau. This is a major part of what Tableau is designed to do, and this will be reflected in the exam. This chapter is worth spending extra time on. Practice quickly building visualizations and adjusting values with table calculations and calculated fields, and experiment with Tableau-provided analytical tools. Fully familiarize yourself with the tools and capabilities described here to ensure you are confident and prepared when confronted with them on the exam.

CHAPTER 4

Developing User Interactions

Analyzing data is not only a skill; it's also an art. In my job, I use data visualizations to analyze data. When I design these visualizations, my goal is to not just answer the customers' questions, but also attempt to preempt any follow-up questions they may have. To do this, I utilize features built into Tableau to improve accessibility, interaction, and insight into the data. All of these features are extremely valuable for a data analyst to understand, and more importantly, are regularly used in questions on the certification exam.

In this chapter, I will dig into the interactive portions of Tableau. These include things like filters, parameters, and sorts, which allow your users to interact with and manipulate the visualizations. I will also cover features of Tableau that help your end users arrive at an insight, such as reference lines and bands, distributions, box plots, and hierarchies. The chapter will conclude with items that make your charts easier to read and understand. I will discuss formatting, totals, and additional ways to annotate your visualizations.

Filter Controls

Filters provide a method for chart end users to manipulate and explore data visualizations. Chapter 2 discussed how filters are created and controlled, but filters are not just for analysts. This section will discuss how to make your filters accessible to end users, how to format them, and how to contextualize the available options.

End-User Filter Controls

Filters are created via the Filter card in the Tableau interface. This filters the visualization, but doesn't make it accessible to anyone beyond the analyst. To make a filter visible to other users, right-click on the field in the Filter pane and select Show Filter. This will present the filter on the right of the visualization. To avoid confusion, I will refer to this version of the filter as a *filter control*. The data type of the field determines the filter control's default format when it appears. For example, a discrete dimension might show as a multiple-selection list, while a continuous field may appear as a slider bar.

You can easily change the default format of the filter control using the Filter menu located at the upper right (see Figure 4-1), and there are a wide variety of options to select from.

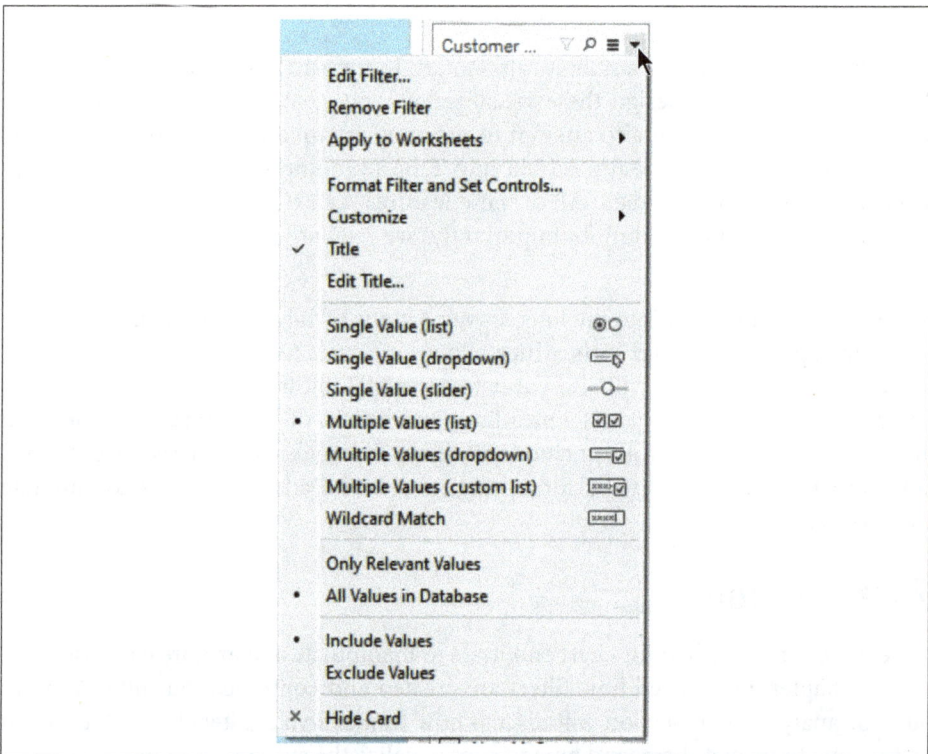

Figure 4-1. Filter control menu showing the multiple different options for displaying the filter control as well as options related to the filter itself. For more information on editing, removing, or applying filters to other worksheets, please see the section "Filters Card" on page 40.

The available formats depend on the filtered field's data type. There are four distinct types of filter controls:

Slider filter control
> Continuous fields can fall anywhere within a range of values, so when a filter control is provided, the options need to include any value within the range. A slider bar is the easiest way to quickly traverse a wide range of values. Tableau offers three types of slider bars to choose from: slide to select value, slide to select starting value, slide to select ending value. You can also use a slider control for dates and single-select discrete values.

Single-select filter control
> When the user can only select one choice from a list of available items, a single-select filter control is used. This type of filter control will deselect any other values when a new value is selected. The only possible way to select more than one value is to select All (assuming it is provided as an option). Single-select filter controls come in three styles: a single-value dropdown list, a radio-button list, or a single-value slider bar.

Multiple-value filter control
> Sometimes, the user will want to select multiple values from a given list. For this type of control, you use a multiple-value filter control. These types of filters let the user select each value from a list, giving them more detailed control over what appears in the visualization. Multiple-value filter controls can be shown in three ways: a checkbox list, a checkbox pull-down menu, or a comma-separated typed field.

Typed-in field filter control
> A user may not want to scan through a list of values to adjust a filter, and typed-in field filter controls give them an alternate option. In these filter controls, the user is presented with a box to enter their filter criteria. The text the user types is then used to match the available values in the field. This type of filter control is also known as a *wildcard match*.

The type of filter controls you present to your end users should be intuitive and accurately reflect the choices available to them. You should provide a single-select filter control when the user should pick only one option and a multiple-value filter control when several options can be selected at once. Only use wildcard filter controls if the data is heavily validated and clean or computer-generated. Since free-entry boxes match strings, it is very easy to type a search term incorrectly or even miss values due to bad data.

Configuring Filter Controls

The type of filter controls is the first step to giving control of visualization filters to your end users; however, there are other ways to improve this interactivity. Filter controls have a nested set of options buried within them (as in Figure 4-1) that provide additional options, limit filterable options, and improve accessibility. They include:

Include/Exclude

This option allows the end user to include or exclude the selected values in the filter from the visualization.

Customize

Nested within the Filter control menu is a submenu called Customize, with several options buried within it (see Figure 4-2). The first option controls whether the user is shown the option to select all values. The remaining options turn on and off features of the filter control that change it from Include to Exclude, allow them to search, and modify the number of options visible at once. The final option in this menu allows the user to select and deselect options in the filter, without applying them, until they press a button.

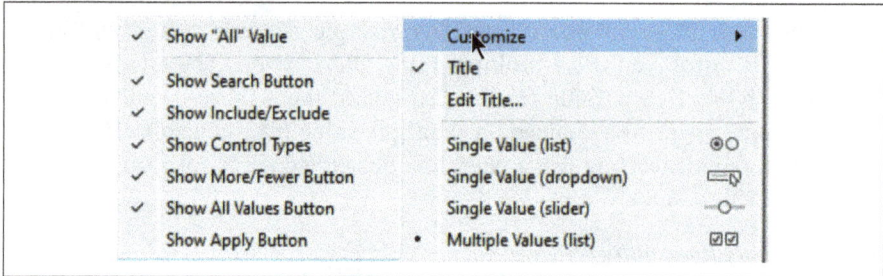

Figure 4-2. The Customize submenu holds options that improve user interactions with the filter.

> The Apply button is invaluable in making charts easier to use once they are published. Without it, the chart would be redrawn each time an option is selected or unselected, causing distracting movement and screen flashes. This way, the visualization isn't redrawn until you press the Apply button.

Title/Edit Title

These two options show or hide the filter control title and give you the option to change the filter title. The default filter title is the name of the filtered field.

Only Relevant Values

This option is extremely useful for simplifying filters for end users. It reduces the available options in the filter-control list to only those that are possible given other filter restrictions. For example, if you were building a workbook for a grocery store, apples and bananas would not be available if a separate filter had already removed produce.

It is very easy to confuse your end users with Only Relevant Values. If you set it on both the primary and secondary filters, it isn't intuitive how to return the filters to their full list. In the grocery example, if your user selects apples and bananas only, they may be confused as to why the meat section is no longer available in the main filter. For this reason, I recommend only using this option on subfilters, not the primary filter for the dashboard.

Hide Card

This last option hides the filter control on the right. The field still appears in the filter and the filter is still applied, but no visual indication or control is offered to end users.

Users need ways to interact with the data in your visualizations. The easiest way to do this is to share access to the filters that control what is shown. Filters allow your end users to limit visualizations to the departments, dates, or other dimensions that pertain most to them.

Example Question

Imagine you are working with a visualization. After filtering a dimension, you no longer have as many values available to choose from in a second filter. What is likely the cause?

A. You did not press the Apply button.

B. The filter was set to Exclude instead of Include.

C. The second filter is based on a table calculation.

D. The second filter is set to show Only Relevant Values.

E. The first filter you changed is set to show Only Relevant Values.

Answer: D—The Only Relevant Values toggle restricts the available options of a filter based on the other filters already applied to the visualization.

Sorts

When you present data to your end users, you want to do so in a logical, easy-to-read way. *How* you present information is just as important as *what* you present. You can change how a chart is presented through how the visualization is organized, including through a sort.

First, it's important to understand how a sort can alter what is shown in a chart. By default, most string dimensions are sorted alphabetically. So, if you design a chart showing "Sales by Sub-Category," the chart will be organized alphabetically by the Sub-Category field (Figure 4-3, top). This chart reveals information about the data, and it shows which Sub-Category has the largest amount of sales, the smallest amount of sales, and everything in between; however, it does not use the sales value in any way to organize the bars. This means the highest and lowest could appear anywhere.

In Tableau, fields can be sorted by other fields. If you change the previous example to sort by sales amounts, it starts to focus on a different story (see Figure 4-3, bottom). Instead of just showing values where they appear, the chart now draws your attention to the higher and lower values. The design of the chart influences the information you present. An unsorted chart just gives information on the sales, while one that is sorted highest to lowest focuses attention on which subcategories did well and which did not.

Tableau provides two buttons in the toolbar that quickly sort a visualization (Figure 4-4). There are also sort icons available on the axis. These buttons use the context of the visualization to determine what field is sorted and what it is sorted by. If you examine the example charts in Figure 4-3, you can quickly swap from the left chart to the right chart using the Sort Descending button.

The visualization continues to use the sort from the buttons once you press them and does not revert if you press the same button again. For example, in Figure 4-3, you can't switch back to the unsorted version through these buttons. Instead, you would have to remove the sort through the right-click menu on the sorted field (Sub-Category). In this menu, you'd select Clear Sort to revert the field back to its default sort method.

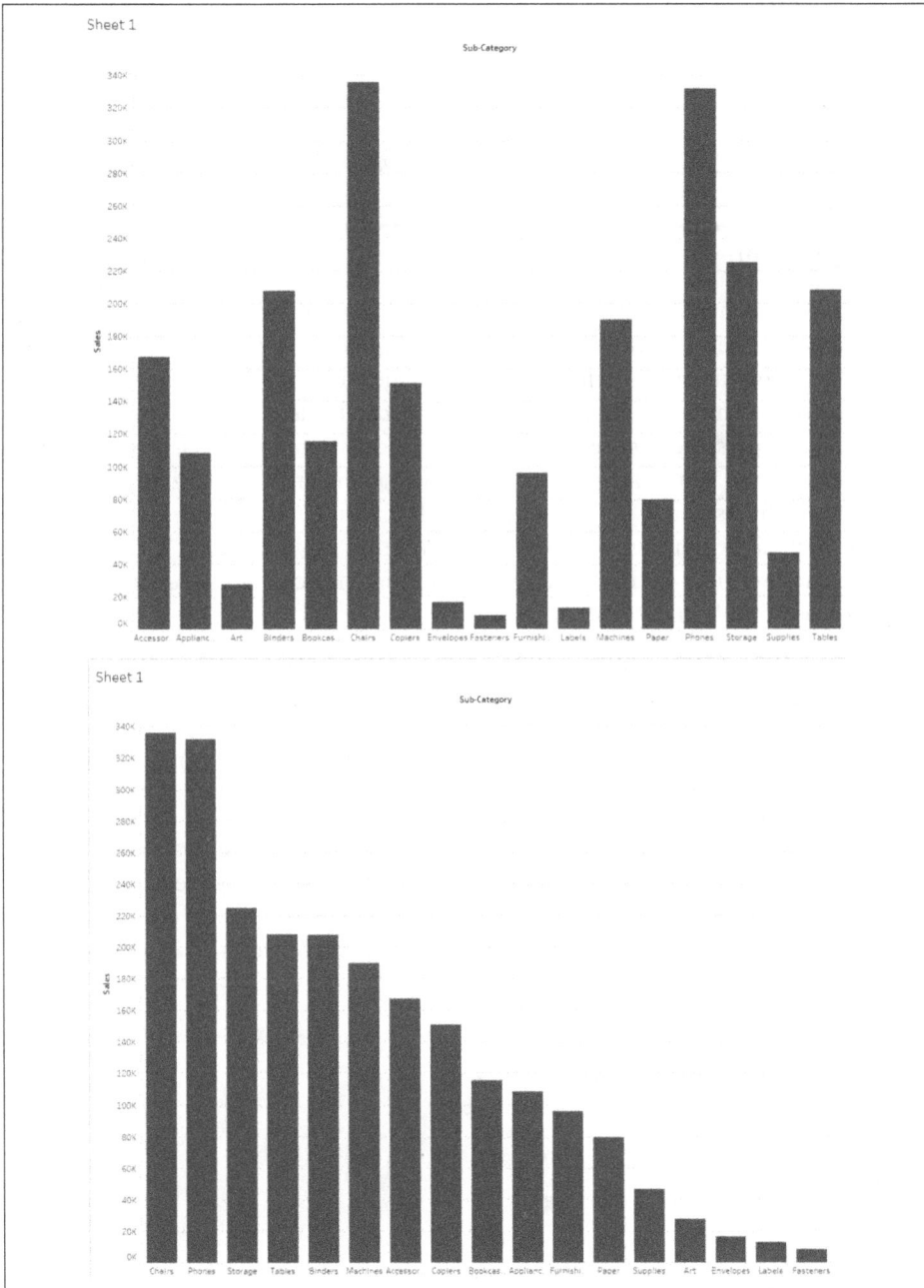

Figure 4-3. The chart on the top is sorted alphabetically by the product subcategory, while the chart on the bottom sorts the subcategories by their sales value. The sort draws attention to what is doing well.

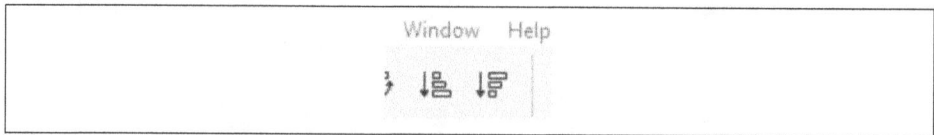

Figure 4-4. The quick-sort buttons sort data ascending (left) and descending (right) based on the available dimensions and measures.

Default Sorting

Every dimension in Tableau has a default sort and most of them are intuitive. Strings, as mentioned earlier, are sorted alphabetically. Numbers are sorted lowest to highest, and dates are sorted earliest to latest. The challenge with sorts is that they can get disrupted as you add more dimensions to view. This can be demonstrated with an example from the Superstore data set, in which the products are organized into categories, subcategories, and manufacturer. The product, alone in a visualization, will sort alphabetically by its name. If you add the Product Name field to Rows, you will see a vertical list of all products shown alphabetically from top to bottom. If you then add the Manufacturer field to the visualization, the sort may change, *depending on where you place the Manufacturer field*.

If you place Manufacturer to the right of the product on the Rows, the sort does not change; the products are still listed alphabetically. If you place the Manufacturer field to the left of the product field, the chart sorts by manufacturer *first* and then by the product. In short, Tableau processes sorting from left to right according to the fields' order in the Rows and Columns.

You can modify the default sort for a dimension field using the Data pane (or the Data Source tab). Right-click on any dimension field in the Data pane and navigate to Default Properties. You will find an option to change the default sort (see Figure 4-5). The default sort applies to the field whenever it is used; however, it is overridden by sorts applied directly to the field within a visualization.

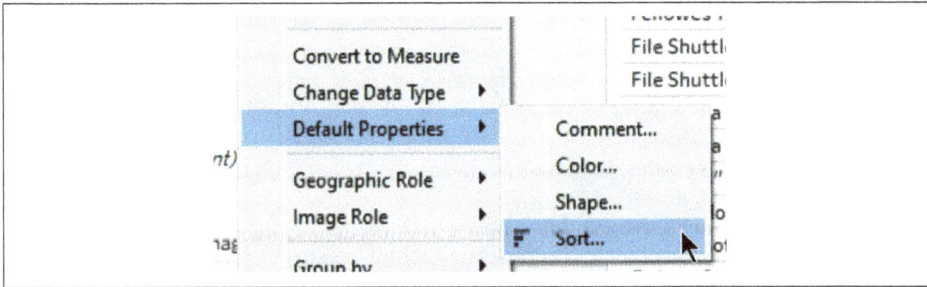

Figure 4-5. The default sort option can be accessed via the right-click menu on a dimension field in the Data pane. The option is nested under Default Properties in the menu.

The Sort Window

The default sort options are not as diverse as those in-visualization. Both sort windows provide an option to select what the field is sorted by and the sort order (see Figure 4-6).

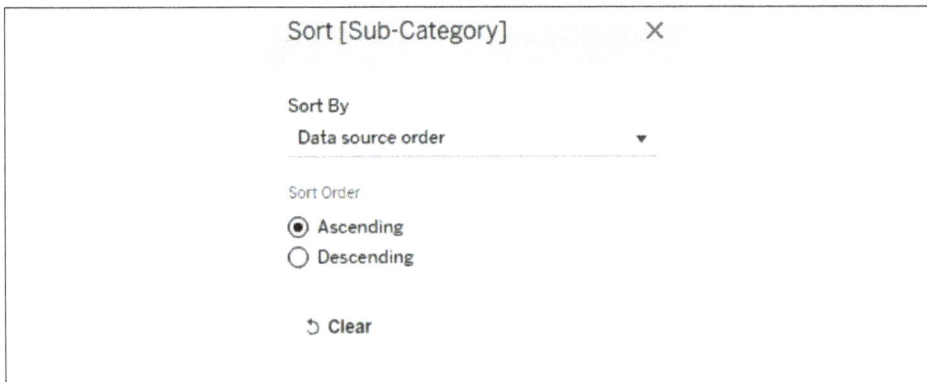

Figure 4-6. The Sort menu provides options to select how the field is to be sorted and which direction to sort it.

The options include:

Data source order
This option simply states that Tableau should use the default sort of the field when displaying it in a chart. If this option is selected, you can choose to sort ascending or descending by default.

Alphabetic
Strings, dates, and numeric dimensions can all be sorted alphabetically, ascending or descending.

Manual
Sometimes certain fields need to be sorted in a specific way, and none of the options available meet your criteria. For these fields, there is a Manual sort option, which lists the values of the field in a window and allows you to organize them by dragging them up and down in a list. This option does *not* allow you to choose ascending or descending.

The in-visualization Sort window adds more options because it uses the measure fields around it to apply different sort orders. These include:

Field
This option provides you the ability to sort based on another field—a *measure*. There is an example of a field sort in Figure 4-3, where the Sub-Category field was sorted by the sales value. If you select this option, you can choose how to aggregate the field you are sorting by: for example, by the minimum, maximum, or average sales instead of by the sum.

Nested
Sometimes the sorts applied to a visualization don't immediately make sense. That's because Tableau uses aggregation to determine the order of the sort. Nested sorts help to clarify this confusion, but are difficult to understand. For this reason, the next section of this chapter is devoted to explaining them.

Understanding Nested Sorts

Pretend you have a bar chart that shows sales by year, broken down by product category. To build this chart, you would place the Order Date and Category fields on the columns and the Sales field on rows (see Figure 4-7).

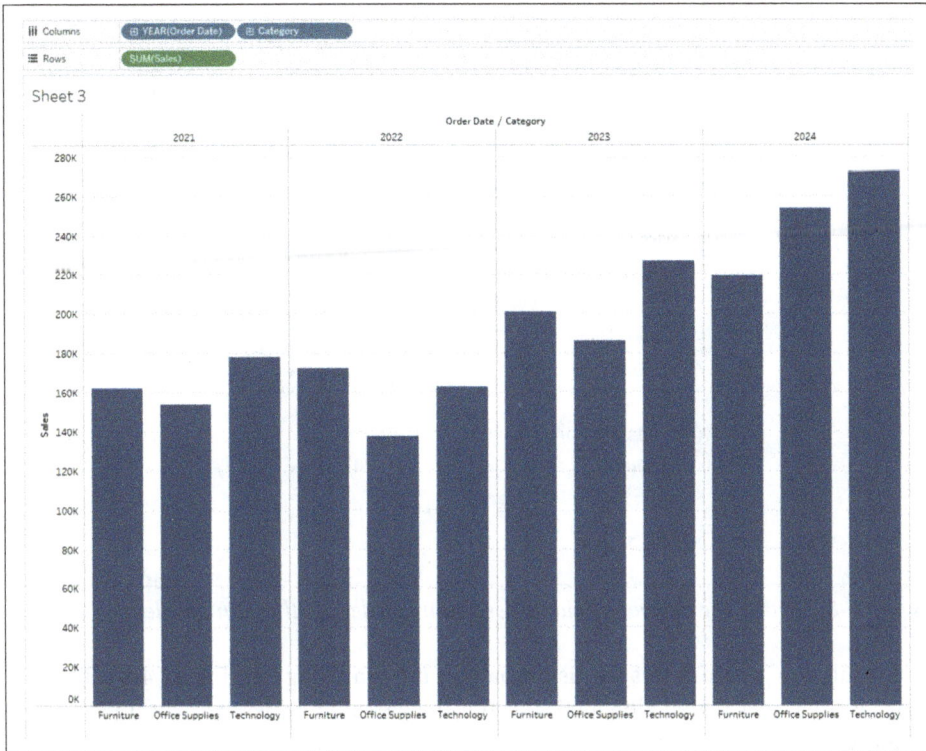

Figure 4-7. Sales by category within each year.

By default, the chart is sorted by year, and within each year, by category alphabetically (Furniture, Office Supplies, Technology, etc.). What happens if you sort the category by sales from highest to lowest (see Figure 4-8)? Let's find out. To do this, you follow these steps:

1. Right-click on the Category field in Columns.
2. Choose Sort.
3. Change Sort By to Field.
4. Set the Sort Order to Descending.
5. Ensure the Field Name is Sales and the Aggregation is Sum.

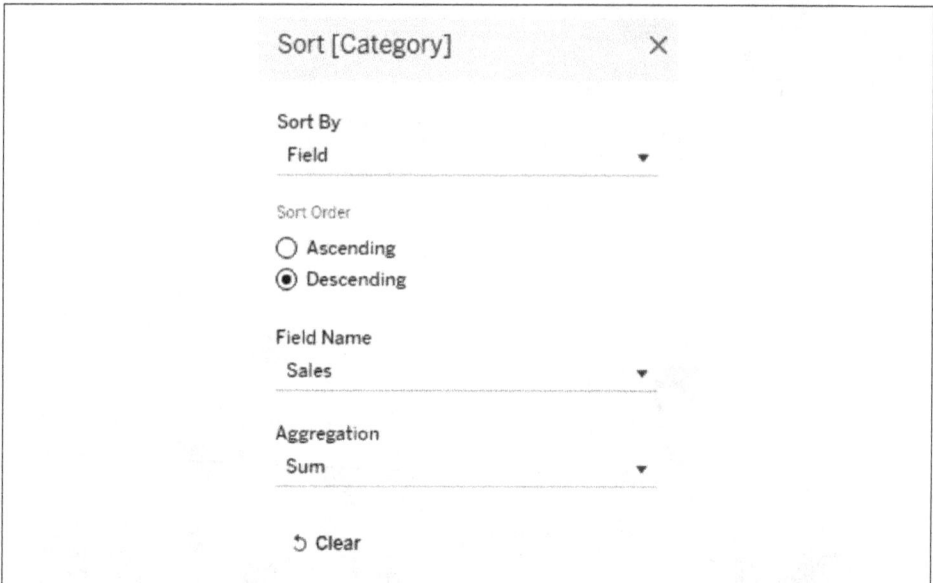

Figure 4-8. Sorting the category field in descending order, by the sum of sales.

The result you get from this sort is probably a bit confusing (see Figure 4-9). The category is no longer sorted alphabetically, but the bars do not descend within each year either; they go up and down in both 2022 and 2024. What is happening?

This sort actually worked perfectly. It sorted the Category field from highest sales to lowest sales *overall* and completely ignored the other field in the visualization (Order Date). In this data set, Technology had the most sales, Furniture was second, and Office Supplies was third. The field was sorted this way *regardless* of whether that sort order changed within a given year. This is where *nested sorts* come into play.

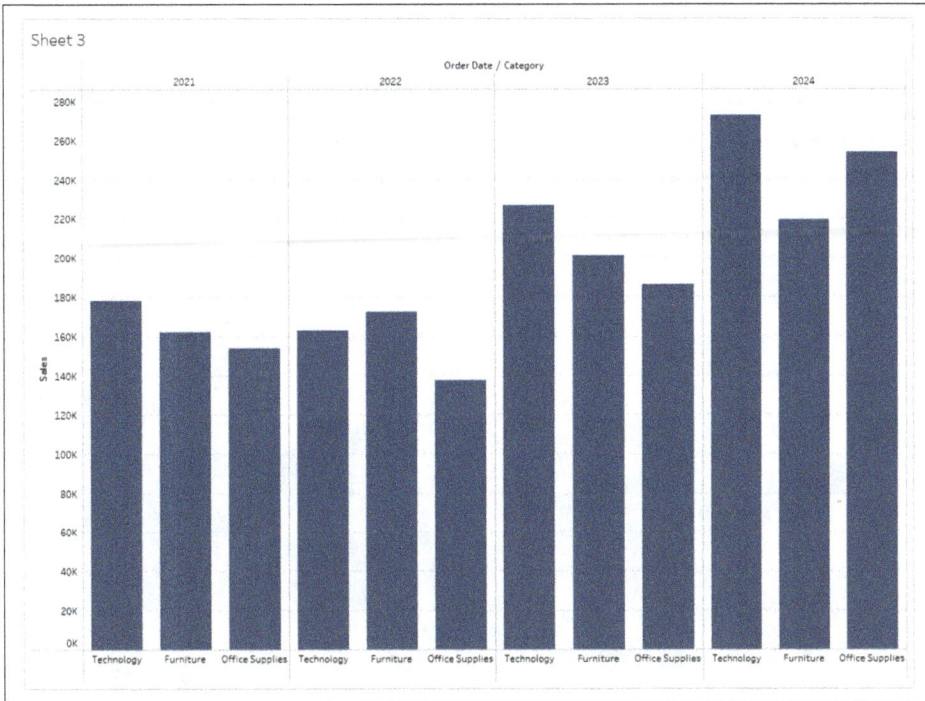

Figure 4-9. Sorting the categories descending by sales doesn't seem to work in 2022 and 2024, as the bars go down and up.

If you return to the Sort menu and change the sort to Nested, Tableau will incorporate the other dimensions in the view as part of the sort:

1. Right-click on the Category field in Columns.
2. Choose Sort.
3. Change the Sort By to Nested.
4. Ensure the Sort Order is Descending.
5. Ensure the Field Name is Sales and the Aggregation is Sum.

The sort now applies within the dimension values of the other field. In this case, it sorts the category based on the sales *within each year*. The bars in the chart are now shown descending within each year (see Figure 4-10).

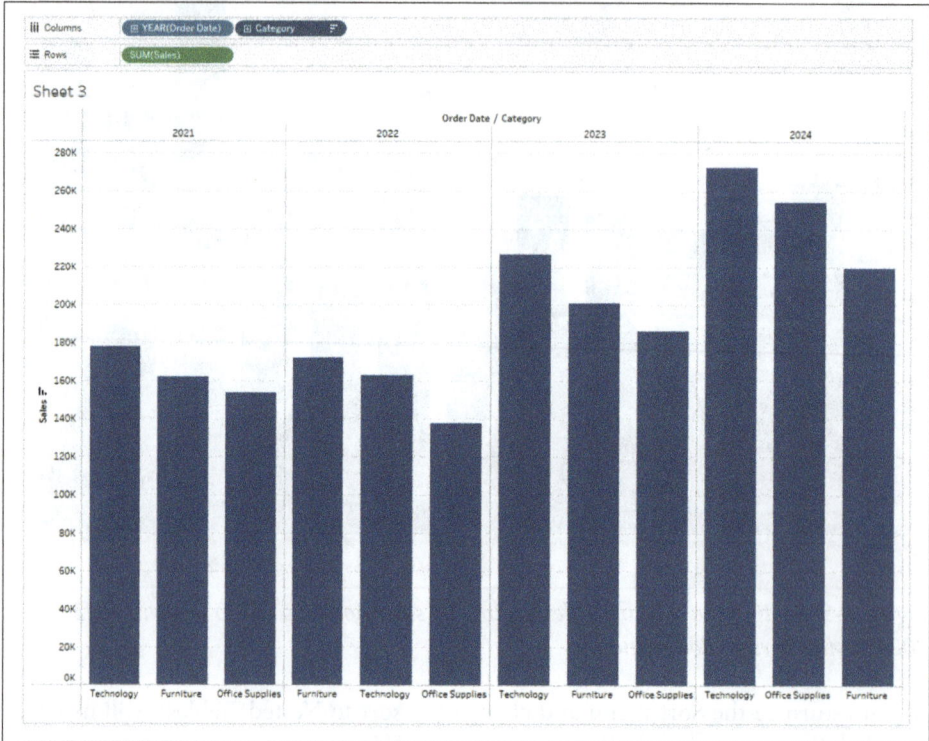

Figure 4-10. Using a nested sort will incorporate other dimensions when sorting by a field.

Nested sorts make the chart appear as you'd expect when you sort by a measure; however, this can be misleading as well. In Figure 4-10, the category is now shifting around from year to year. If the user expects the category to appear in the same place each year, they may misinterpret the results. You could color the chart by the category to help with this, or show the chart in its original state. Avoiding potential confusion as you display data is one of the biggest challenges you will face as a Tableau developer.

Reference Lines, Bands, and Boxes

You might remember from Chapter 3, which discussed the Analytics pane, that many types of analysis were based on adding reference lines. *Reference lines* are lines that supplement a chart based on a value to provide your user with additional information about the chart, such as averages, goals, minimums, maximums, or other key values. You can place them manually or use the methods listed in the Analytics pane.

You create a reference line by right-clicking on a measure axis and choosing Add Reference Line. This opens the "Add Reference Line, Band, or Box" window. The window contains a wide variety of options, depending on what type of line or band you select. The next few sections break down the available options.

Line

The first option is specifically a line (as opposed to a band, distribution, or box plot). This option allows you to draw a line across some or all of a visualization. The formatting options allow you to change where the line appears, how it is labeled, and what it looks like (see Figure 4-11).

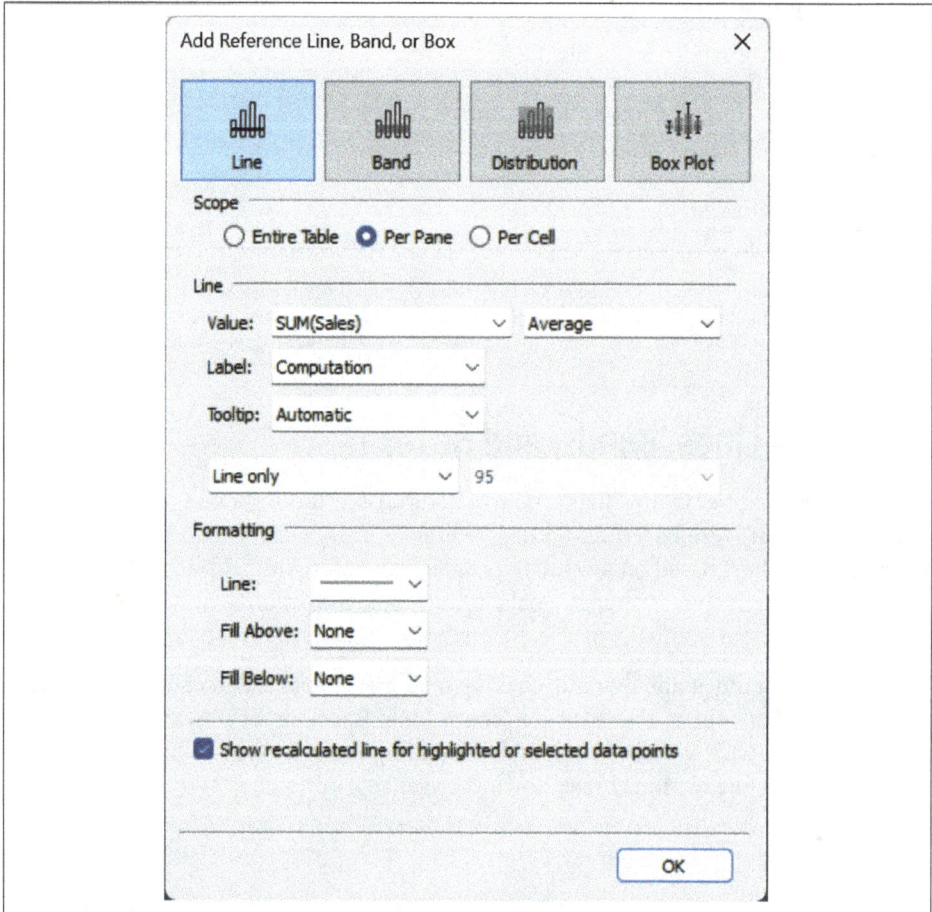

Figure 4-11. The Reference Line window. This screenshot shows the available options when Line is selected at the top.

These formatting options are broken down into three sections:

Scope

This section controls where the line is drawn. The first option, Entire Table, will draw a line across the table based on your indicated value. For a bar chart of sales, you might use this line to indicate the average sales across the entire table.

The next level is pane. A pane is one level of granularity above the most granular detail in the visualization. So, the Per Pane option will take the line and divide it at the second-to-lowest granularity visible in the chart. If the bar chart is divided by one or more dimensions, there will be a line for each value of the second-to-lowest level of granularity. Per Cell will take this division another step deeper and draw an average line for each bar.

As an example, let's say you have a bar chart showing sales by category and sub-category. If you set the line value to Average, you can change the scope option to see what each selection does. Entire Table will show the average sales across the table, Per Pane will show average sales per category, and Per Cell will show average sales per subcategory (see Figure 4-12).

Line

This section controls where the line (or lines) will appear and how it will be labeled. The first option, Value, is the numerical value where the line will be drawn. The second pull-down menu is the aggregation, which controls the choices available in the first pull-down menu. The aggregation can be set to Total, Sum, Median, Average, Minimum, or Maximum. For any of these choices, you can set the first option to the measure value of the chart, a parameter, or a bin. The second pull-down also has an option for Constant. This selection changes the first pull-down menu into a box, which allows you to type a numerical value for where you want the line to appear.

The Label option controls how the reference line is labeled, and there are four options:

- None removes the label.
- Computation shows the aggregation you selected in the second pull-down above.
- Value shows the numerical value of the reference line.
- Custom allows you to type your own custom label and has options to insert the value or computation listed above.

The Tooltip pull-down controls the tooltip that appears when hovering over a reference line. It has only three options: None, Automatic, or Custom. None removes the tooltip, while the Custom option allows you to type your own. The Automatic tooltip is `<aggregation> = <value>`. For example, the entire table reference line in Figure 4-12 might appear as `Average = 136,855`.

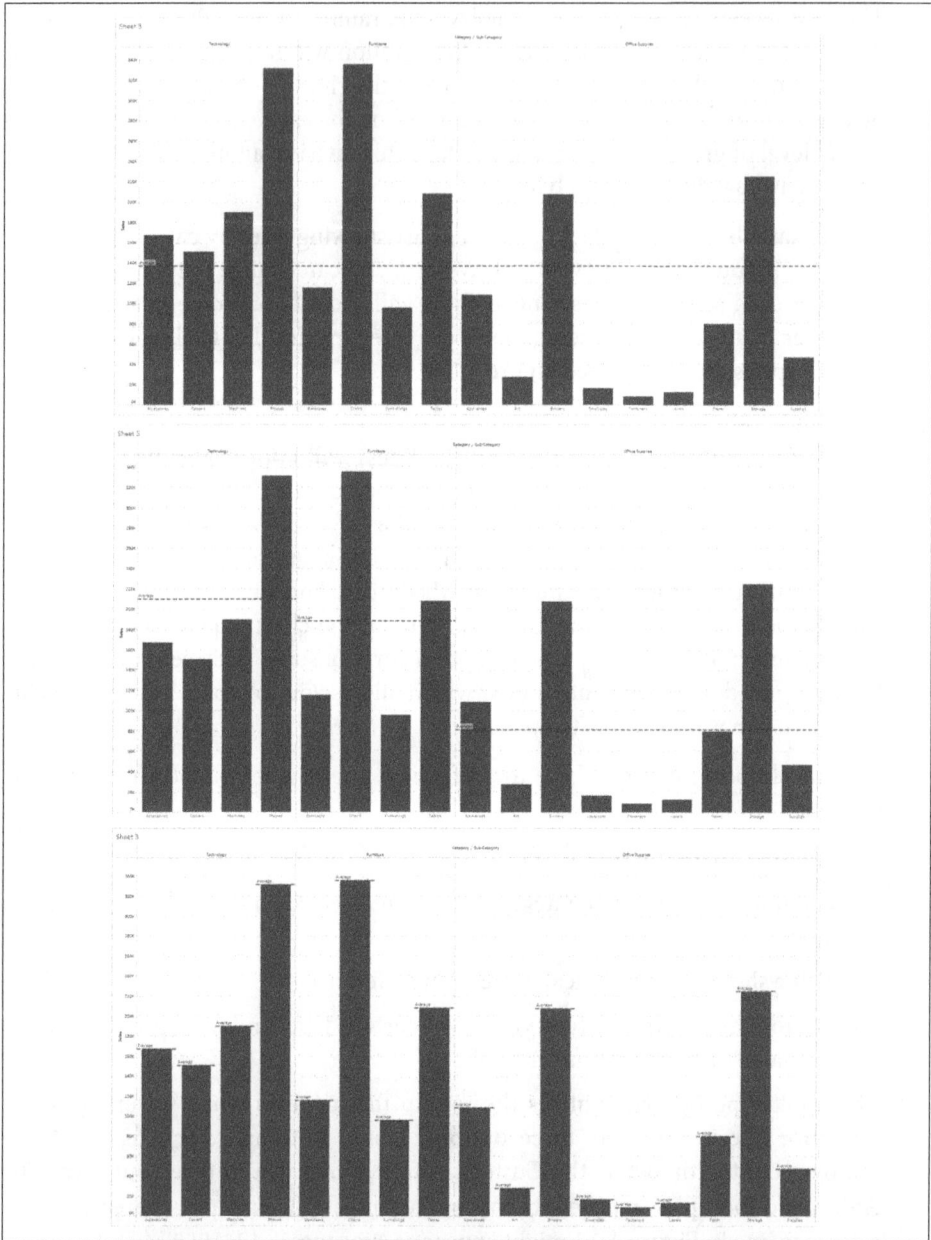

Figure 4-12. Different values of scope on a reference line. The top chart shows an entire table scope, the middle shows the scope per pane, and the bottom illustrates scope set per cell. The reference line has been enlarged and colored red to make it more visible in the screenshots.

Formatting

This section of the window controls the physical appearance of the line. The first pull-down controls the type of line (solid or dashed), and its thickness and color. I used it to change the appearance of the lines in Figure 4-12. The Fill Above and Fill Below pull-downs control shading color above and below the line.

Recalculating the line

The final option in the Reference Line window is a box labeled "Show recalculated line for highlighted or selected data points." This option, if selected, will move the reference line based on a selected dimension. For example, if the reference line is set to the average sales for the entire table, the user can click on one of the values of the Category dimension, and the reference line will redraw to show the average sales for the selected category. The line will still cross the entire table, but will be shown at this new value. A faded version of the original reference line at the overall average for the table will still be displayed (see Figure 4-13).

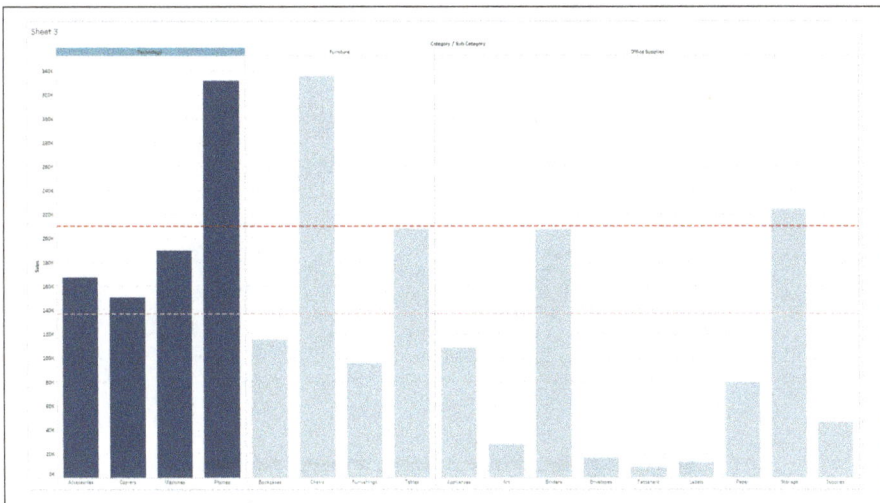

Figure 4-13. The bottom option in the reference line window allows users to select a dimension value to see an adjusted reference line, such as selecting the Technology category. The original line still appears, but it is faded out. The new reference line still crosses the entire table.

> The exam will test you on your ability to create a reference line at an indicated value and label it appropriately. Practice making reference lines at various aggregations of the measure value. Use custom labels that incorporate the type and value of that aggregation. Also, try creating a reference line at a custom numerical value. Experiment with shading everything below or above that value.

Band

Unlike a line, a *reference band* is an area within two values on a chart. This means that there are twice as many options to control its appearance, making this window quite different from the Reference Line window (see Figure 4-14).

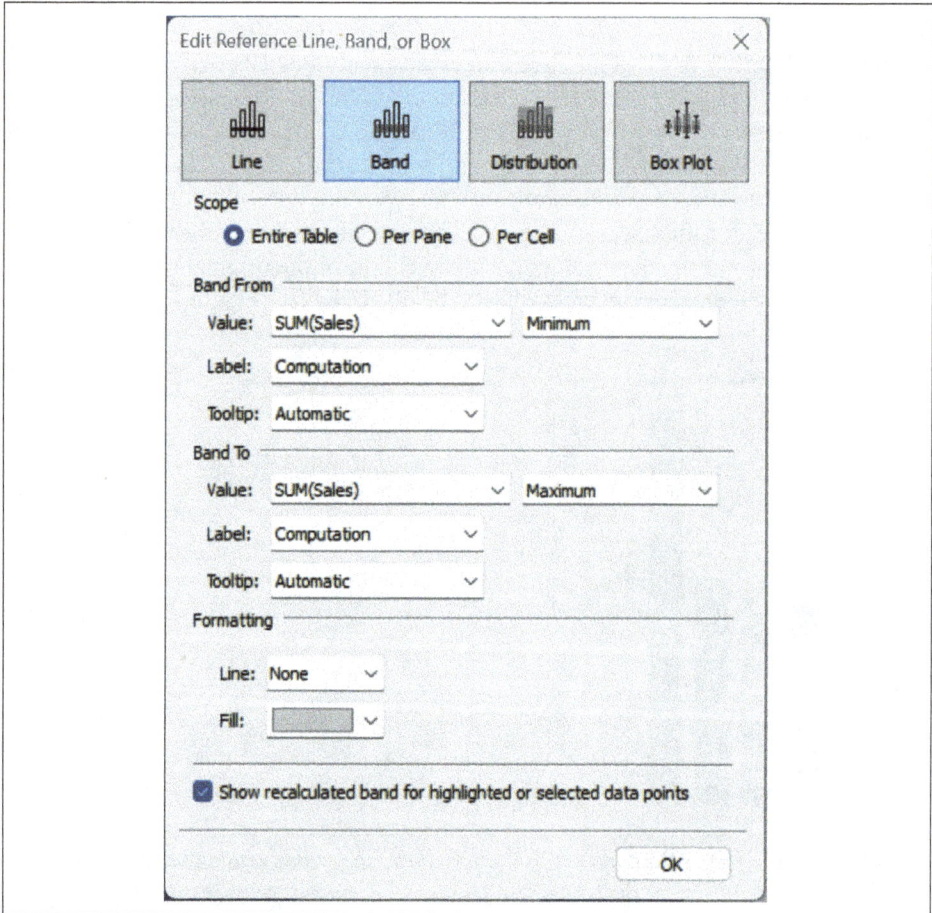

Figure 4-14. The Reference Band window still has Scope options, which now control the space between two lines.

The available options can be broken down by the sections:

Scope
> This controls the granularity of where the band appears.

Band From/Band To
> Since the band is an area on a chart between two lines, you need to indicate to Tableau where to put the upper and lower barriers. In short, these are two reference lines. You can select the aggregation or a constant value for both. You can adjust the label the same way, and you can modify the tooltip for each independently.

Formatting
> There are two options in this section, Line and Fill. The Line pull-down controls the appearance of the upper and lower borders that contain the band. There are no physical lines by default, but you can turn them on and adjust their style, width, and color. The fill is the appearance of the area between the lines. You can adjust it to any color or opacity.

Recalculating the Line
> Just like reference lines, there is an option to shift the band based on dimension values selected in the chart.

Distribution

The Distribution band is based on statistics. Everything in a distribution is based on statistical ranges calculated on the measure value (or any other identified value) in the chart. There is still a wide range of options for controlling the distribution, depending on what you want to measure (see Figure 4-15).

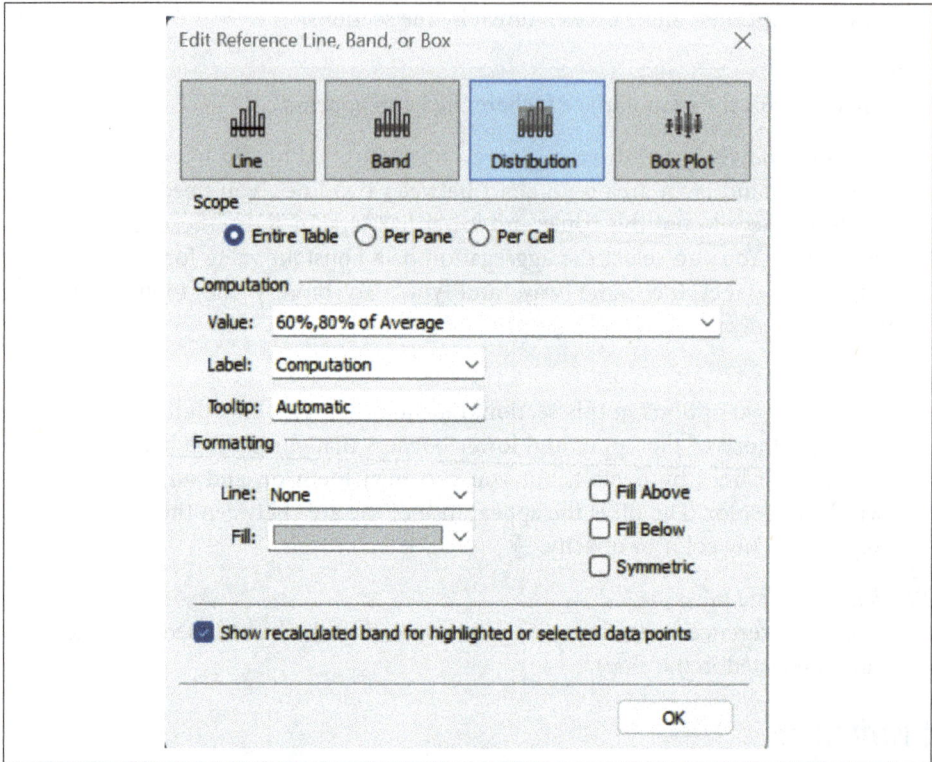

Figure 4-15. The Edit Reference Line, Band, or Box window with options shown for a distribution band.

The distribution options are broken down into Scope, Computation, and Formatting:

Scope
Just like reference lines and reference bands, distribution bands are based on scope.

Computation
The Computation section controls where the distribution band is shown. The first pull-down in this section identifies what is being measured. It has four options, each with secondary options:

Percentages
Calculated based on a measure, a parameter, a bin, or a constant value. You can select the aggregation on that value similar to the way you choose aggregation for a reference line. There is even an option to enter a constant value. You can then change the percentage of that value you wish to include in that band. For example, if the chart shows the sum of sales, you might create a

band that shows 60 to 80% of the average sales. Multiple bands can be created by including additional values separated by commas.

Percentiles

This option provides a single space to select a value or type your own. Where percentages are the percent of the value, percentiles define where portions of the dimension values fall. For example, if you manually type in "50," the line will be added to the chart at the point where 50% of the dimension values have higher sales and 50% have lower. The degree above or below this percentile line is irrelevant. It's simply grouping the dimension values. As with percentages, percentiles can have multiple values.

Quantiles

This option is a combination of multiple percentiles. It draws lines at each and shades between each line. For example, if you set the value to 4, you will get three percentile lines that divide the chart into four sections. Each section will contain 25% of the dimension values, split by the measure. If there are 12 dimension values, three will appear in the first band, three in the second, three in the third, and three in the fourth. Again, it doesn't matter where in the range the sales values for each fall, this simply divides the dimension values based on the measure.

> This option's name changes depending on how many quantiles you create. If you create four, the option name will change to *Quartiles*. For three, it will be *Terciles*.

Standard Deviation

Another statistical measure of your data. In simple terms, it shows which data values fall within a range of the mean. One standard deviation from the mean contains approximately 68% of the data points, while two standard deviations contain about 95%. When you select standard deviation, you can choose how many deviations you go from the mean. You can also choose if your data reflects the entire population or only a sample.

Formatting

The formatting options are similar to those already covered: you can control the lines and the shading between them. There are three additional options worth mentioning: Fill Above, Fill Below, and Symmetric. To understand these options, imagine that you divide your chart by quintiles (into five separate areas). Fill Above and Fill Below will turn the shades of color above or below the minimum and maximum quintiles, respectively, into a gradient. Both options enable a checkbox to reverse the shade gradient. The Symmetric option shades the middle option darkest, then shades each quintile step away a shade lighter.

Recalculating the line

Just like reference lines, there is an option to shift the band based on the dimension values selected in the chart.

Example Question

What are the three scope levels for reference lines and bands?

A. Table

B. Chart

C. Pane

D. Cell

E. Dimension

Answers: A, C, and D—Reference lines apply to the whole table, a portion of the table, or a single cell. Chart and dimension are not available options.

Box Plot

A *box plot*, also known as a *candlestick plot* or a *box-and-whisker* plot, uses statistics to define where a majority of the points appear in relation to the mean value of the data. It is usually used on a scatter plot showing multiple values within a given dimensional value—for instance, a scatter plot of sales by product name within each category.

The box overlays the scatter plot and contains what is called the *interquartile range*. In simple terms, the box identifies the half of the data points closest to the mean. It is expanded by lines that reach out a distance from the box in either direction and are usually referred to as *whiskers*. See Figure 4-16 for box plot specifics.

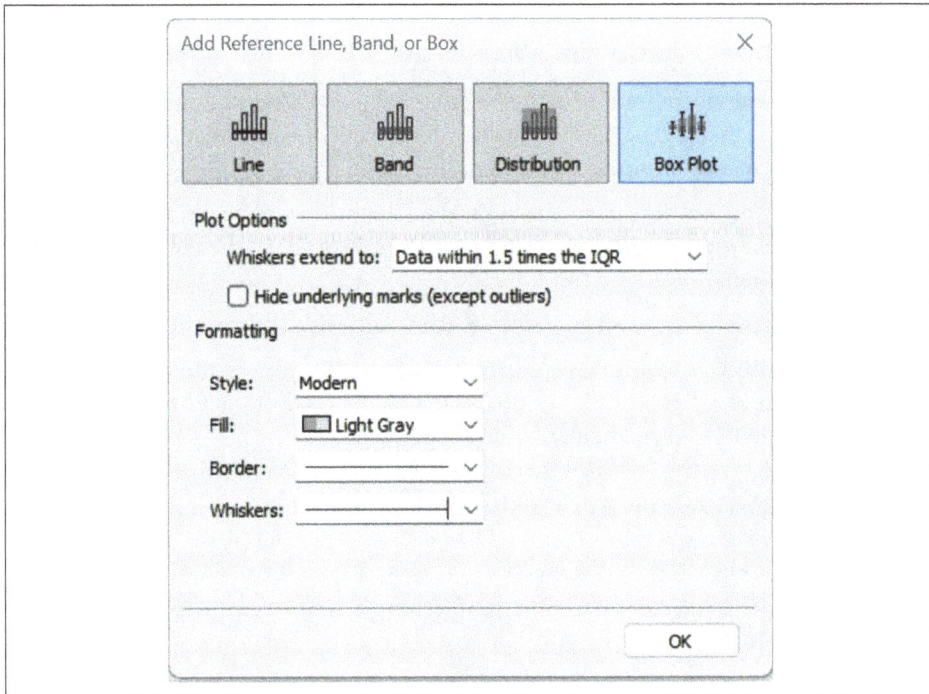

Figure 4-16. The Add Reference Line, Band, or Box window showing options for controlling a Box Plot.

This distance and the formatting of the box plot are controlled by the Box Plot options:

Plot Options
> There are two options listed under Plot Options. The first is a pull-down that controls how far the whiskers reach beyond the box. The default is 1.5 times the IQR (interquartile), but they can also be set to encompass the entire data set. The other option is a checkbox that hides or shows data points where the box appears.

Formatting

The formatting of the box plot is broken down into four pull-downs:

- There are several preformatted versions of a box plot, and those are listed in the Style menu. The options include Modern, Glass, Classic, and Classic with Dual Fill. They control the borders and the fill shade of the box.

- Depending on the Style you select, the Fill option will be a single fill color or options for a two-color fill (one color for values above the mean, one for values below).

- The Border pull-down controls the color and width of the outline of the box.

- The Whiskers pull-down controls the color and width of the whisker lines. It also has an option to change the perpendicular end of the line (short perpendicular, long perpendicular, or no perpendicular).

You can create box plots quickly using the Show Me menu. This option will automatically add a reference line to create the box and whiskers. It can be modified the same way as a manually created reference line: right-click on the axis and choose Edit Reference Line.

Example Question

When creating a reference line, which aspects of the line can be added to its label using the label menu? Select all that apply.

A. The value of the line

B. The interquartile range

C. The slope of the line

D. The number of measure value points that fall exactly on the line

E. The computation being used to generate the line

Answers: A and E—In addition to custom text or displaying no text at all, the label for a reference line can be configured to include the value of the reference line and the computation used to create it (such as AVG, MIN, MAX, etc.).

Parameters

Another way you can grant end users some control is through *parameters*: a user-generated list of one or more strings, numbers, or dates used to alter a visualization. They are created manually, provided a range, or populated with the values from one of the data source fields. Unlike filters, parameters can only have a single value, and they require other parts of Tableau to function. A parameter by itself does nothing—you have to tell Tableau what to do based on its value. Parameters are also beneficial, as they are not data source specific. One parameter can be used to interact with multiple data sources.

Creating a Parameter Manually

There are two ways to create a parameter manually. The first method is by using the pull-down menu at the top of the Data pane. This is the same way you create a calculated field manually, but instead of selecting Create Calculated Field, you select Create Parameter (see Figure 4-17). This brings up the Create Parameter window (see Figure 4-18). The second way to create a parameter manually is to right-click a field from your data and choose Create → Parameter. This method automatically populates the parameter with the values of the field before providing the Create Parameter window.

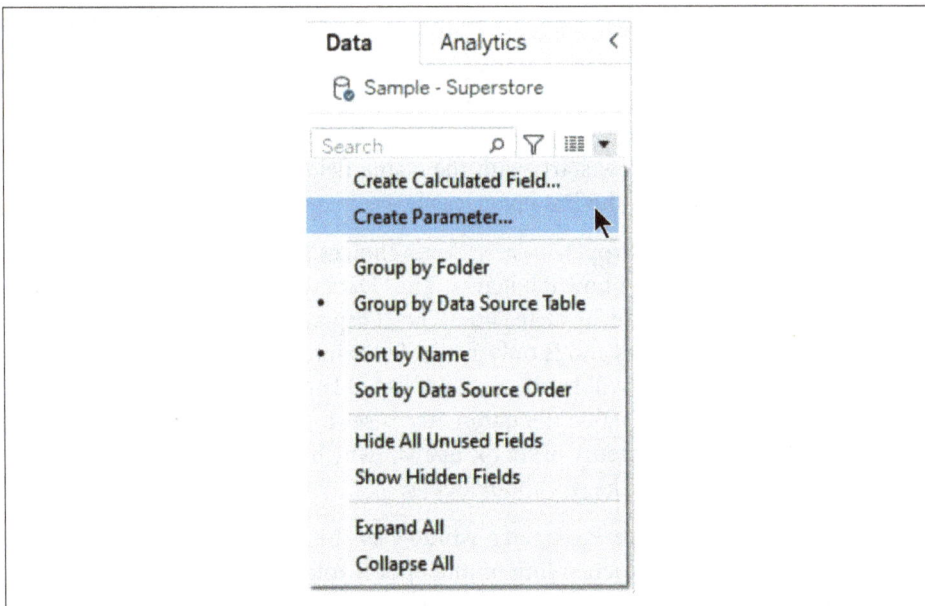

Figure 4-17. Use the pull-down menu at the top of the Data pane to create a parameter manually or right-click on a field in the Data pane.

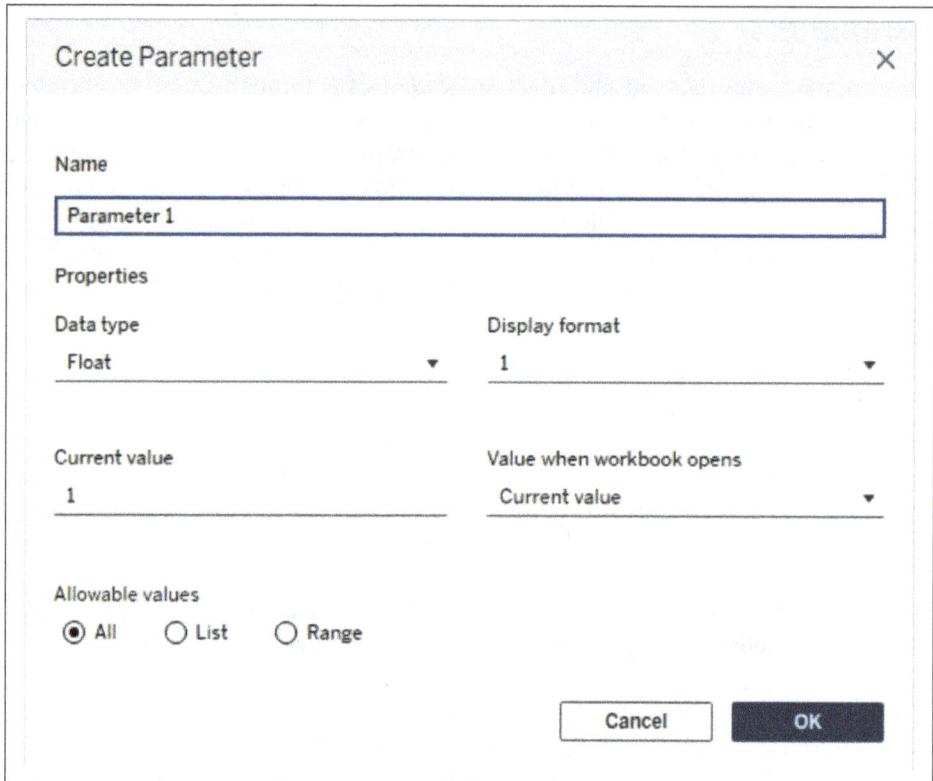

Figure 4-18. The Create Parameter window with base options selected.

The Create Parameter window starts with the Name field. Name it something recognizable, so you can find it in the Data pane easily.

After the Name field is the Properties area. Your choices here determine what type of data the parameter holds and how it behaves. The "Data type" field can be set to Float, Integer, String, Boolean, Date, or DateTime. The "Display format" field controls how the selected data type appears and is only available for integers, floats, dates, and date-times. Field display formats will be discussed in detail later in this chapter. The "Current value" field reflects the value the parameter is set to in its current state. The last properties field is "Value when workbook opens," which lets you set a default value for the parameter each time the workbook opens.

The final area of the Create Parameter window is the "Allowable values" section, which changes dramatically depending on the option you select. The first option, All, allows any and all values of the given data type to be selected as an option using the parameter. For example, if Integer is selected as the data type, any numerical value without a decimal will be a valid option. For this reason, when a parameter with all values is displayed, it will usually appear as a type-in field.

The second option in "Allowable values" is List, which lets you provide a list of options to your end users rather than offering them all values. When you select this option, the space below the "Allowable values" radio buttons will populate with a crosstab grid and additional options (see Figure 4-19). The two columns work together to make the parameter function and appear in a certain way to the end user.

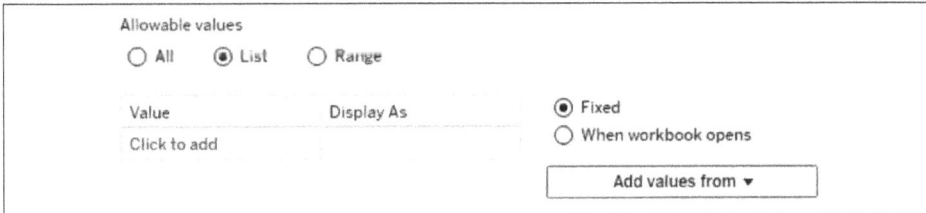

Figure 4-19. The "Allowable values" area changes to a crosstab with options if List is selected.

The Value column is the part of the parameter behind the scenes. It contains the values you can interact with via filters, sets, or calculated fields. The values here are what you utilize to make the parameter do something. The Display As column is what your end user will see. For example, your Value column might show "MI" while the Display As column shows "Michigan." You would use the "MI" value in your calculated fields, but the end user would only see "Michigan."

To the right are two toggles and a pull-down menu. These options control how the list is populated. When Fixed is selected, the crosstab is editable, allowing you to manually enter values for the parameter. Alternatively, the "When workbook opens" option populates the parameter list with values from a field each time the workbook opens.

The pull-down allows you to select which field is used to populate the parameter. This pull-down is dynamic, based on the data type selected above. For example, if you select Float as a data type, you will only see fields in your data that contain a floating decimal value. You can also use the pull-down to prepopulate a parameter with field values while the toggle is set to Fixed. This populates the list, but then allows you to return to the crosstab to modify the values.

The final toggle button under "Allowable values" is Range. This option is only available for the data types Integer, Float, Date, and DateTime. When range is selected, the "Allowable values" area changes depending on the data type. For Float and Integer data types, you are given the option to set a Minimum, Maximum, and "Step size" for the range. For Date and DateTime data types, the "Step size" additionally requires a duration measure, such as minute, hour, day, or week.

The Minimum and Maximum values control the bounds of the range, while the "Step size" indicates how the space between is split up. For example, you could split a range from 1 to 100 into steps of 1, 2, 5, or 10. The resulting parameter would only have options that fall on those intervals.

Finally, the Boolean data type does not have an "Allowable values" section. Instead, it contains an Aliases section, which lets you change the default values of True and False to different names. The "Current value" is also restricted to a toggle between True and False.

Making Parameters Accessible

Once you create a parameter, you need to make it accessible. Created parameters appear in the Data pane at the very bottom of the window. To make a parameter usable, you need to make it visible. Right-click on the parameter and select Show Parameter from the menu that appears. The parameter control appears in the upper right corner of the desktop window, similar to filter controls.

The parameter control, like the filter control, has a pull-down at the top that allows you to change its type and format. Since parameters are single-select only, the options are limited:

Single Value list
> This is a list of options selectable via radio buttons.

Compact list
> This is a pull-down menu allowing the user to select one from a list of items.

Slider
> This parameter control is a bar with a slidable dot. The position of the dot indicates the value selected.

Type In
> This control allows you to enter values manually. This type of control is better suited for numerical values, as text-based values require an exact match.

The pull-down menu also contains options for formatting parameters, including changing the font and alignment of the title and adjusting the font, shading, and border of the parameter-control body.

Alternate Methods for Creating Parameters

Creating a parameter manually allows you to set it up exactly how you want it, but this is not the only way. You can also create one using a dimensional filter or a set. Dimensional filters (Chapter 2) and sets (Chapter 3) both have an option for using Top as a method of creation. The *Top* method filters the data or populates the set based on the top N values. The value of the parameter controls how many products are shown in the chart. The parameter can be created to control what that N value is.

Let's pretend you have a chart showing sales by product, and you want to filter it to only show the top *N* products by sales. You do this by dragging the Product field to the filters. On the Filter window, you select the Top tab as the method for creating the filter, then select the "By field" option to choose Sales (see Figure 4-20). At this point, you can enter a value to dictate the number of products you want to see or use the numerical pull-down to indicate a parameter instead.

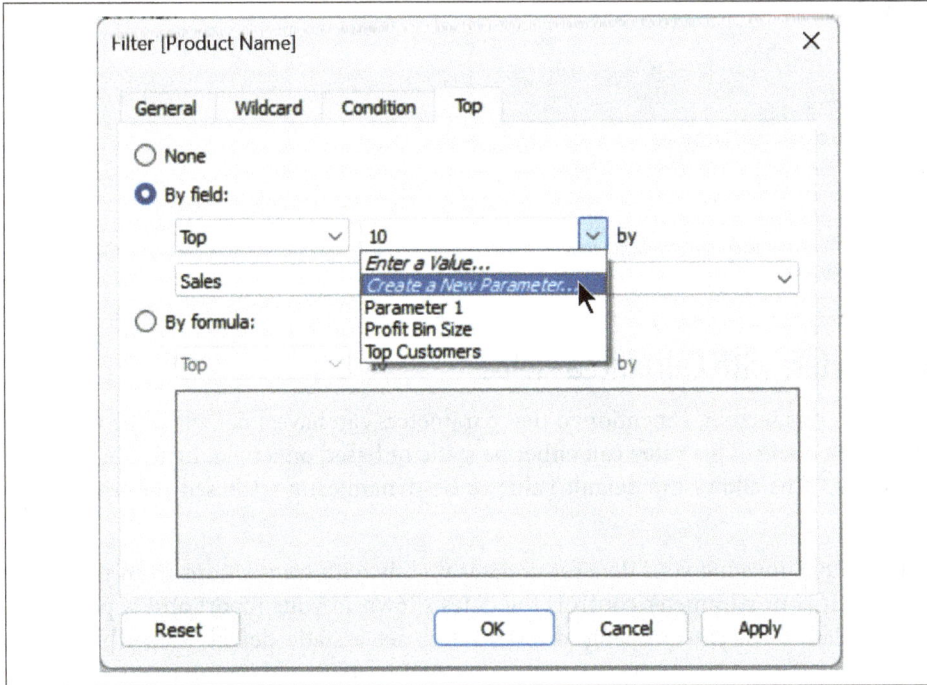

Figure 4-20. The Dimension filter window has a Top method for filtering the dimension. Instead of entering a static value, you can choose to create a parameter instead.

When you select "Create a New Parameter" in the value pull-down, the Create Parameter window opens and defaults to a data type of Integer. From here, you populate the field just as you would if you created a parameter manually. You can also use a prepopulated integer parameter, similar to those shown in Figure 4-20. Once the parameter is created, it is active, and the Value field in the filter is populated with its name.

You can use the parameter to show the top product, top 10, or any number of products by sales. This makes the chart dynamic and more powerful to your end users. (Sets have a similar Top field, and a parameter can be created from Top sets in the same way. The only difference is that the parameter controls set membership rather than filtering a chart.) You can also create a parameter using the Value field in the "Add Reference Line, Band, or Box" window.

Example Question

A parameter can be one of several data types. Which of the following is *not* a valid parameter data type?

A. Integer

B. Boolean

C. Geographic

D. String

E. Date or DateTime

Answer: C—Parameters cannot be geographic fields, but can be based on one. If you use a geographic field to create a parameter, the parameter data type becomes String.

Parameters with Calculated Fields

Earlier in this section, I mentioned that parameters can have a default value when the workbook opens. This value can either be static or based on a field, including calculated fields. This allows the default value to be dynamically set based on criteria you specify.

For example, imagine your data set updates nightly with transactions from the previous day. If your parameter controls the dates shown in your report and is populated from a date field, you probably don't want to set a static default value, because it would become outdated very quickly—your end users would be forced to adjust the parameter before they could see the most recent data. Instead, create a calculated field to set the default value of the parameter to yesterday:

```
DATEADD('day', -1, TODAY())
```

This calculated field returns the date for yesterday. Since the parameter and the calculated field are both dates, you can select the calculated field as the default value of the parameter. The parameter will default to yesterday each time the workbook is opened.

Parameters can also be connected to numerical calculated fields. A *calculated field* uses the value of the parameter to adjust other parts of the visualization. For example, if you want to provide your end user the ability to adjust discount values, you can create a Float data type parameter and populate it with potential discount values (say, 0%, 5%, or 10%). These can then be applied in a calculated field to illustrate the discounts' impact on sales:

```
SUM([Sales]) * [Discount Parameter]
```

One of the more common ways to integrate parameters into workbooks is through *logic* calculated fields. Logic calculations assess the value of the parameter and react accordingly. For example, imagine you have human resources data, such as employee counts and demographic information. You want to create charts that show the population of employees by various demographics. Instead of building multiple charts, you can create a parameter of demographics and a calculated field.

The parameter is populated with the various types of demographics available in your data. The calculated field then uses these values to swap in the demographic fields from your data set:

```
CASE [Demographic Parameter]
    WHEN 'Sex' THEN [Sex Field]
    WHEN 'Race' THEN [Race Field]
    WHEN 'Age' THEN [Age Field]
    ...
    ELSE ''
END
```

This calculation uses the values from the value column of the parameter (Sex, Race, Age) to determine which field from the data to pull in. As the parameter changes, the field used in the visualization is swapped out dynamically. You can create a "no demographic" value in the parameter to default to an unsplit chart—that's what the ELSE clause is for.

The resulting chart is actually multiple charts in one. The user sees employee counts and can divide them by the demographic of their choice. The calculated field is also flexible. You can use it to divide the chart if it is placed on rows or columns, or to add details to the chart if it is placed on the Color, Shape, or Size marks.

Parameters are a flexible tool for adding user interactions to your charts. They are also effective in controlling charts created from disparate data sets. You can use a parameter to change charts even if no relationship has been established between the two sets of data. You can use calculated fields in each data set to react to the value of a single parameter. When the parameter is adjusted, it affects the values in charts from both data sets.

Parameters have two additional features that can be very powerful when used together. First, you can insert them into SQL if your data set permits custom code. When connecting to relational databases, the Custom SQL Code window contains an option to insert parameters. Second, Tableau allows you to set parameter values using dashboard actions (details in Chapter 5). This means you can create a dashboard where the parameter value is set based on something clicked in a visualization. If you combine these two features, you get an effective way of setting parameter values and utilizing them in live custom SQL WHERE clauses to limit large data pulls.

Parameters provide a way for your users to interact with the data in your visualizations. The wide array of data types and parameter options give you a flexible tool for adding interactivity and insight generation. This makes your visualizations more dynamic, responsive, and valuable to end users.

Example Question

Which of the following is *not* a location for creating a parameter?

A. Reference Line window

B. Create Calculated Field window

C. Pull-down menu in the Data pane

D. Set or Filter "Top" tab

E. Right-click menu on a field in the data set

Answer: B—Parameters can be based on a calculated field or referenced by a calculated field, but the Create Calculated Field window does not have an option to create a parameter.

Hierarchies

When I build dashboards for customers, I am often asked to provide ways to "drill down" into the data. My end users want to see the overall values displayed on my charts, but they also want to dig down to the more granular details. Sometimes I can make this possible through additional charts or tooltips, but Tableau also provides another way to get more granular with the data: a hierarchy.

Hierarchies are structures of data stacked upon each other in increasing granularity. Geographic data is a popular place for hierarchies. At the least granular level, you might have countries. As you drill down, you get more and more granular to include states or provinces, counties, cities, and potentially addresses. The underlying idea is that each level of the hierarchy is another level of detail on the chart.

Tableau comes with a type of hierarchy built in: dates and times. Dates are another perfect example of where a hierarchy makes sense. The least granular level is years, but the hierarchy can have any number of sublayers, including quarters, months, weeks, days, hours, minutes, and seconds. The further into the hierarchy you dig, the more detailed the results.

Hierarchies are simple to build. Simply drag one field in your Data pane onto another, less granular field. When you first do this, Tableau prompts you to name your hierarchy; it will default to the names of the two fields used, separated by a comma. Once you enter a name and press OK, the fields in the hierarchy shift within the Data pane. Your hierarchy shows a new icon and contains the two fields you stacked, slightly indented, below it (see Figure 4-21). To add additional fields at any level of the existing hierarchy, drag them above the hierarchy in the Data pane until a line appears, indicating where the new field will fall. Hierarchy order can be changed via this drag-and-drop method as well.

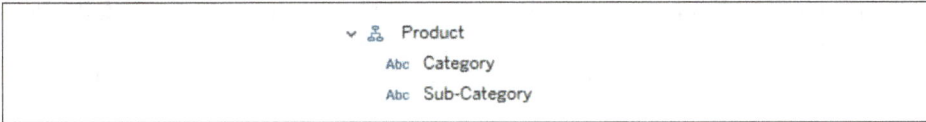

Figure 4-21. A hierarchy named Product with the field Sub-Category nested beneath Category.

Once you settle on a hierarchy, you can use it within your visualization. The hierarchy or any field within it can be added to Rows or Columns. Once the field is placed, it will appear with a "+" symbol on it. This means that this field has a more detailed field nested below it. If you click on it, the sublevel field will appear and the chart will expand to show the sublevels. Once a field is expanded, the "+" symbol will change to a "-" symbol, indicating that it can be collapsed back down (see Figure 4-22).

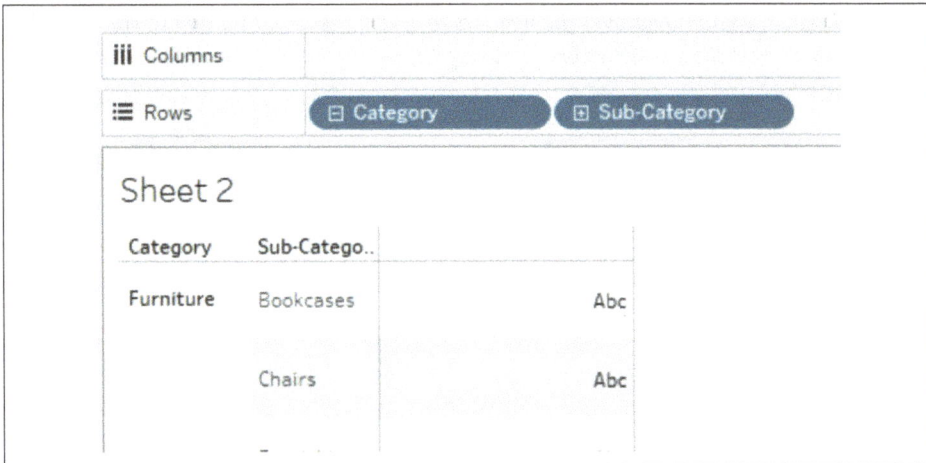

Figure 4-22. The Category field has been drilled into, exposing the Sub-Category field, and the chart below displays this. The Sub-Category has another field nested below it and shows the plus sign. The Category field, since it is already expanded, shows the minus symbol.

You can also use hierarchies in locations such as the Marks card; however, the drill-down capabilities won't be visible to your end users.

Hierarchies pair perfectly with groups (see Chapter 3). Groups use a granular field to populate a less granular set of options. Because of this, you can usually drag the field used to create the group onto the group itself to make an automatic hierarchy. When your users drill into the group field, it reveals the subvalues populating each group.

There is one drawback to using hierarchies in your visualizations: once you publish the chart to a shared location, such as a server or cloud (see Chapter 6), the Columns and Rows shelf won't be visible to end users. The hierarchy icons will be hidden on the column headers. To drill down, end users will need to hover over the headers to reveal the "+" symbol (see Figure 4-23).

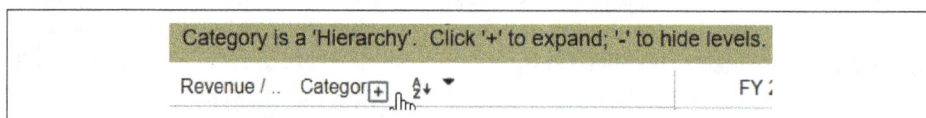

Figure 4-23. The hierarchy controls are hidden in the field headers once the workbook is published. You have to hover over the headers to reveal the icon that allows you to drill down. In this screenshot, instructions for using the hierarchy were included in the title area of the chart.

Example Question

Which data type in Tableau has a natural built-in hierarchy?

A. Number

B. String

C. Date

D. Geographic

E. Boolean

Answer: C—Dates and DateTimes have a natural built-in hierarchy that allows users to drill into the deepest level of granularity on the field.

Add a little instructional text to your chart title to help your users know to look for the controls, as in Figure 4-23. For more information on editing titles, see the section "Formatting Chart Titles" on page 205.

Formatting the Chart

The visualization building blocks give you a huge amount of control over your chart's appearance. You can change the chart type, adjust colors and fonts, and add tooltips to make your chart easier to use and more accessible. But beyond those available in the Marks card, Tableau has a huge variety of other ways to adjust the appearance of a chart.

There are multiple ways to get to these formatting options. The first way is through the Format menu at the top of the application. There are five components in here that will open the Format pane: Font, Alignment, Shading, Borders, and Lines. While each option relates to a different type of formatting, all of them will open the Format pane in place of the Data pane.

You can also open the Format pane by right-clicking on any part of a chart and selecting Format from the menu that appears. It will default to the format options for the part of the chart you used to open the pane. For example, if you opened the format panel by right-clicking on a total, the options available would all apply to totals. The same navigation options appear regardless of what part of the chart you use to open the Format pane.

The Format pane is broken up into sections, identified by icons at the top of the pane (see Figure 4-24). All of these sections have tabs that allow you to apply the format to rows, columns, or the entire chart. If the row or column does not contain text to format, the options within will be grayed out. Additionally, the pull-down menu at the upper right allows you to focus the formatting on specific dimensions or measures within the visualization. These controls work together to help you apply the format you desire where you desire it.

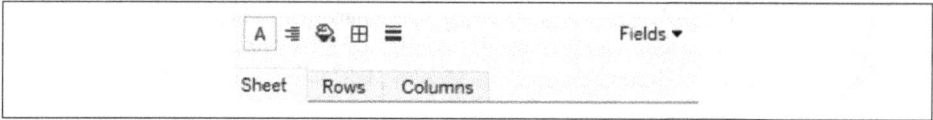

Figure 4-24. The Format pane is divided into five sections, identified by the icons at the top of the pane. The tabs below control what aspect of the chart the formatting applies to. The Fields pull-down lets you get even more granular by applying formatting only to specific fields.

Format Font

The first tab on the Format pane controls font (see Figure 4-25). In the Format Font pane, you can control the default appearance of text throughout your visualization, altering the default font type, color, and size of any text. These options are categorized into three sections, detailed in Table 4-1.

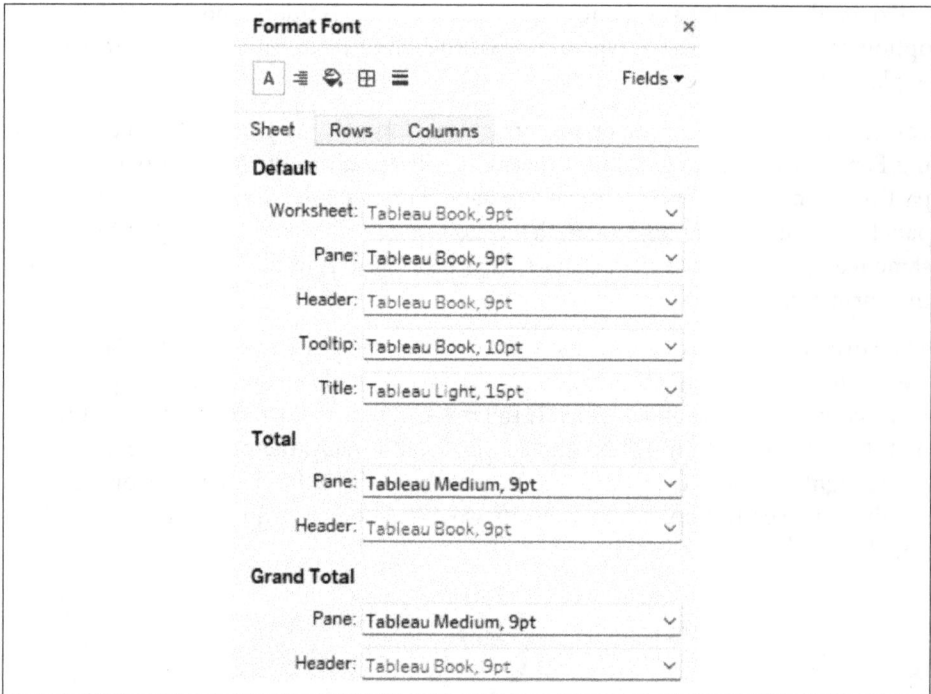

Figure 4-25. The Format Font pane.

Table 4-1. Options available in the Format Font pane to control how text appears throughout a visualization.

Section	Area	What it formats
Default	Worksheet	This controls the overall appearance of text for the entire visualization.
	Pane	This controls the appearance of text in the numerical and visual parts of a chart.
	Header	This controls the appearance of text in the dimensional headers that split up your chart. It is also used to format text that appears on axes.
	Tooltip	This controls the default text appearance in tooltips.
	Title	This controls the default text appearance in the chart title.
Total	Pane	If you have totals enabled, this controls their appearance.
	Header	This controls the appearance of the total label (not the numbers themselves).
Grand Total	Pane	If you have grand totals enabled, this controls their appearance.
	Header	This controls the appearance of the Grand Total label.

You may notice that some of the Format Font options seem to match those of the Marks card. The Format pane controls the defaults, but can be overridden by the font controls in each respective area. If you change the font specifications directly in the title, label, or tooltip, it will override anything set in the Format pane. It's also important to note that the *header* is the label for the dimension, total, or grand total, whereas the *pane* holds the numerical value for each, respectively.

Format Alignment

The Format Alignment options control the vertical and horizontal position of text in a visualization. These options can be set to Top, Middle, or Bottom and Left, Right, or Center. The alignment pull-downs control the text's orientation of the text (normal or oriented 90 degrees to the left or right) as well as how it wraps if it is too long to fit in the designated area (see Figure 4-26). Text wrapping can be enabled or disabled. A full description of all format options is available in Table 4-2.

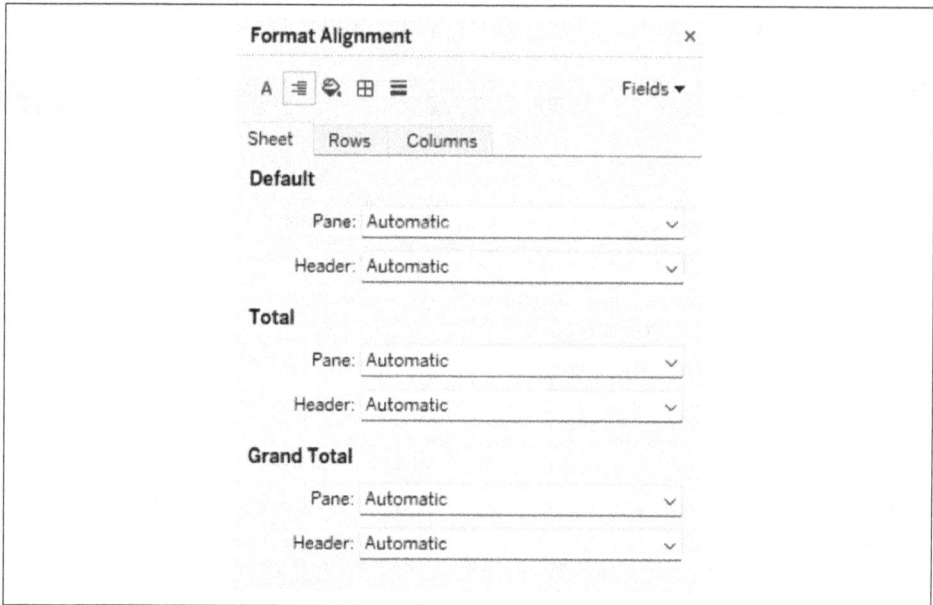

Figure 4-26. The Format Alignment pane.

Table 4-2. Alignment options for text within a visualization.

Section	Area	What it formats
Default	Pane	This controls the alignment of text in the numerical and visual part of a chart.
	Header	This controls the alignment of text in the dimensional headers that split up your chart and in axes.
Total	Pane	If you have totals enabled, this controls their alignment.
	Header	This controls the alignment of the total label (not the numbers themselves).
Grand Total	Pane	If you have grand totals enabled, this controls their alignment.
	Header	This controls the alignment of the Grand Total label.

Format Shading

The Format Shading pane controls shading behind your visualization or portions of it (see Figure 4-27). There are options to control the color and opacity of shading, and the None option renders the background transparent, which can be especially benefi-cial if your dashboard background color needs to shine through the chart. Be sure that the color and opacity of your background don't interfere with the readability of your chart. Table 4-3 lists the Format Shading options.

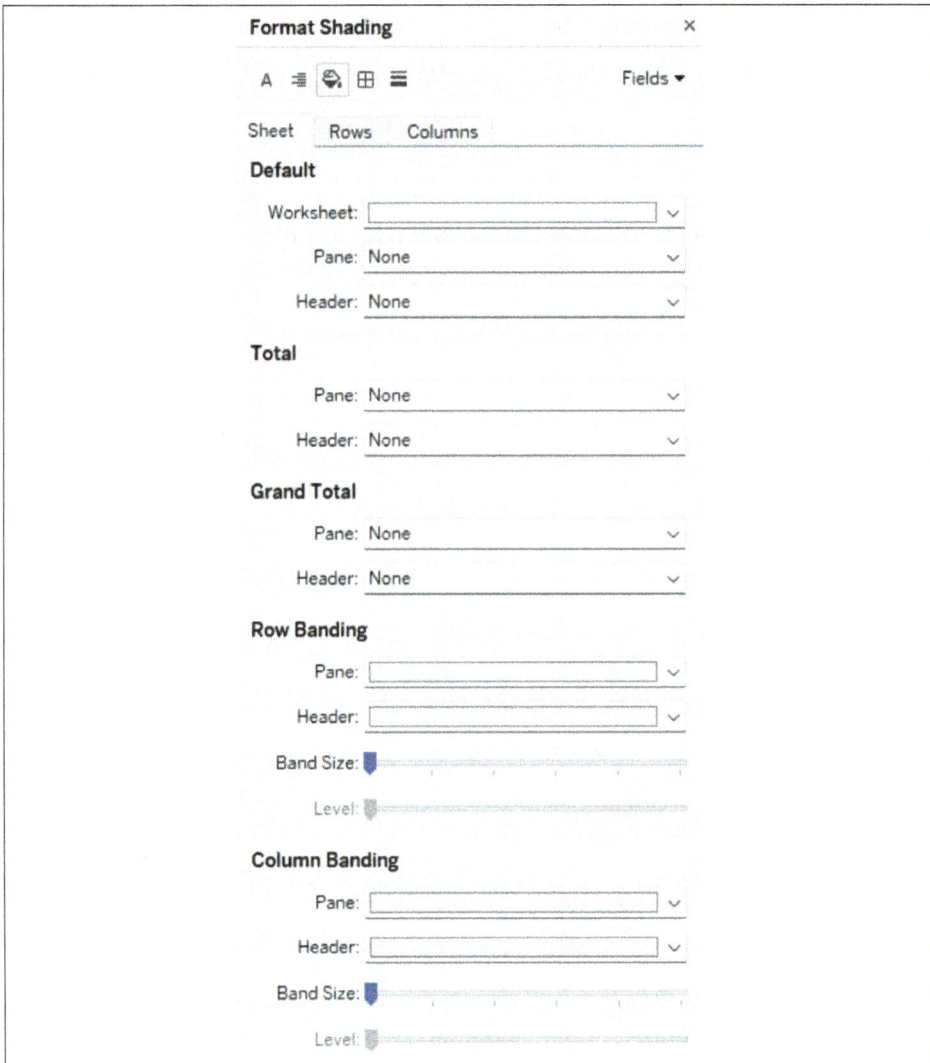

Figure 4-27. The Format Shading pane.

Table 4-3. Shading format options for charts.

Section	Area	What it formats
Default	Worksheet	This pull-down allows you to set the background color of the entire worksheet. It defaults to white, but can be set to any color or removed entirely (None).
	Pane	This controls the background color behind the numeric values or visualization part of the chart.
	Header	This controls the shading behind the dimensional headers that split up your chart and the axes.
Total	Pane	If you have totals enabled, this controls the shading behind them.
	Header	This controls the shading behind the Total label.
Grand Total	Pane	If you have grand totals enabled, this controls the shading behind them.
	Header	This controls the shading behind the Grand Total label.
Row Banding	Pane	This controls the shading behind the data in selected rows, based on the band size and level indicated.
	Header	This controls the shading behind the dimension headers in selected rows, based on the band size and level indicated.
	Band Size	This controls how many rows are shaded per group before shading is switched.
	Level	This controls the dimension level at which the shading bands are applied.
Column Banding	Pane	This controls the shading behind the data in selected columns, based on the band size and level indicated.
	Header	This controls the shading behind the dimension headers in selected columns, based on the band size and level indicated.
	Band Size	This controls how many columns are shaded per group before shading is switched.
	Level	This controls the dimension level at which the shading bands are applied.

The banding options usually apply to crosstabs and control how and where bands are applied on a visualization. *Bands* create alternating rows or columns of shaded fields to help end users follow the divisions of data within the visualization. The level controls the dimensional level where the band applies. For example, imagine you build a crosstab with sales by category, subcategory, and manufacturer. By default, Tableau will add banding at the lowest level of granularity: the manufacturer. The Level option allows you to make the band appear at lower granularities (see Figure 4-28). The number of levels available corresponds to the number of dimensions on the corresponding row or column.

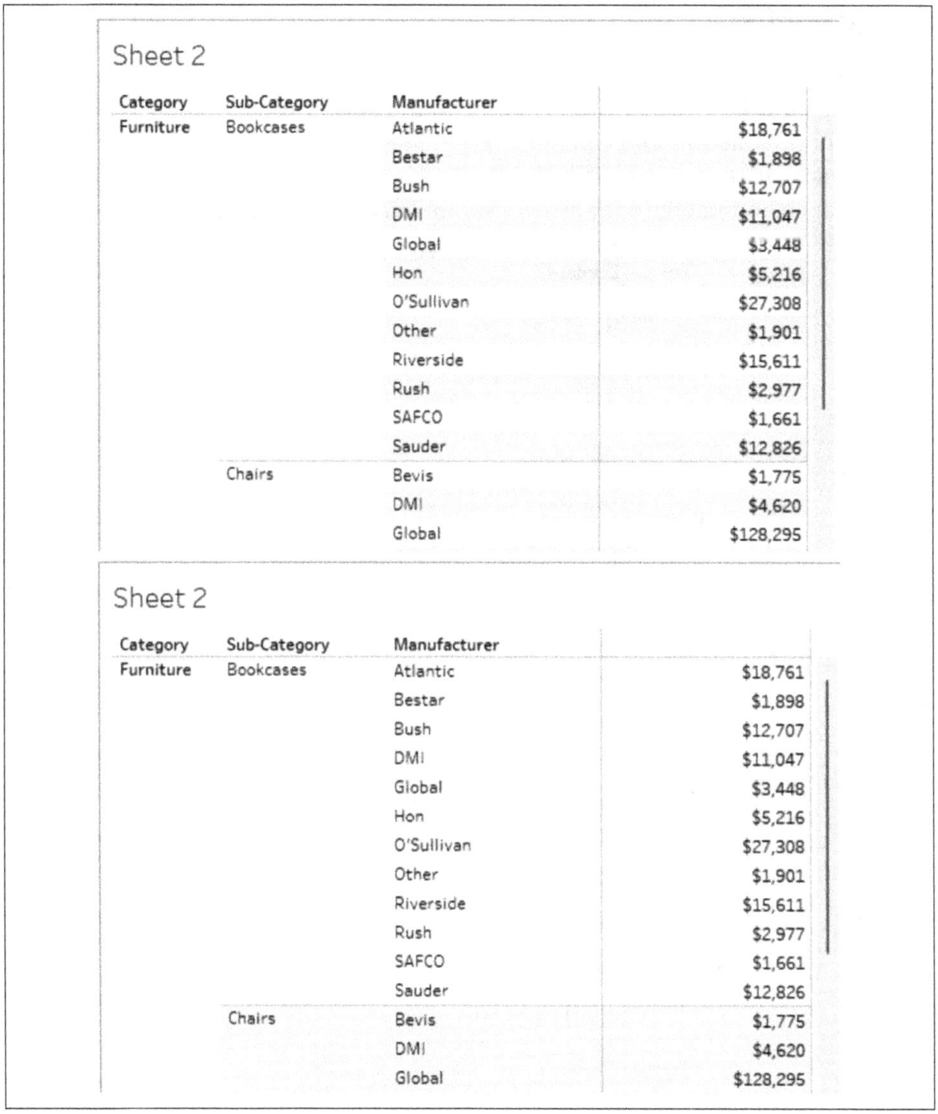

Sheet 2

Category	Sub-Category	Manufacturer	
Furniture	Bookcases	Atlantic	$18,761
		Bestar	$1,898
		Bush	$12,707
		DMI	$11,047
		Global	$3,448
		Hon	$5,216
		O'Sullivan	$27,308
		Other	$1,901
		Riverside	$15,611
		Rush	$2,977
		SAFCO	$1,661
		Sauder	$12,826
	Chairs	Bevis	$1,775
		DMI	$4,620
		Global	$128,295

Sheet 2

Category	Sub-Category	Manufacturer	
Furniture	Bookcases	Atlantic	$18,761
		Bestar	$1,898
		Bush	$12,707
		DMI	$11,047
		Global	$3,448
		Hon	$5,216
		O'Sullivan	$27,308
		Other	$1,901
		Riverside	$15,611
		Rush	$2,977
		SAFCO	$1,661
		Sauder	$12,826
	Chairs	Bevis	$1,775
		DMI	$4,620
		Global	$128,295

Figure 4-28. The top chart has row banding at the most granular level (Manufacturer), while the bottom chart has the banding one level higher (Sub-Category).

Format Borders

The Format Borders pane controls the appearance of border lines within a visualization (see Figure 4-29). These lines are used to divide up the chart at the dimensional level defined by the row and column level settings. Similar to shading, lines between sections of a chart can make it easier for end users to follow a header from left to right or top to bottom; the options are also similar, as described in Table 4-4.

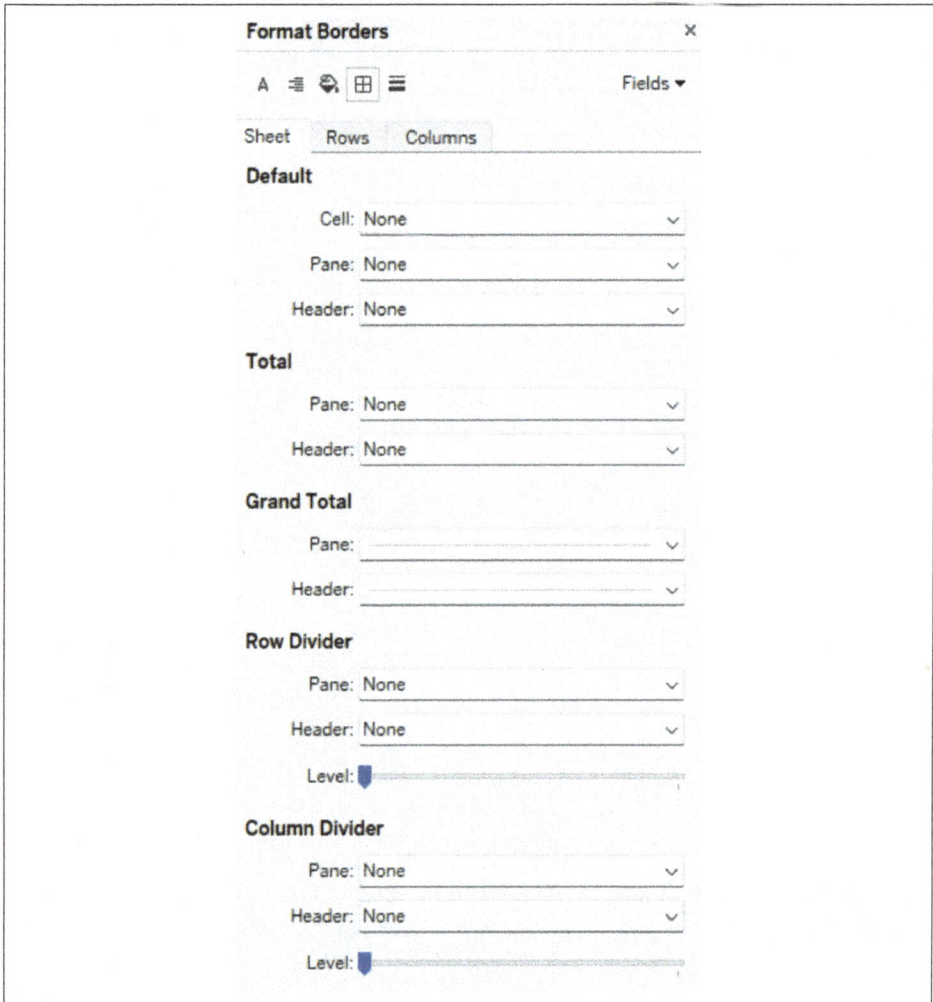

Figure 4-29. The Format Borders pane.

Table 4-4. Dividing line format options for charts.

Section	Area	What it formats
Default	Cell	This pull-down allows you to set the default border color and thickness of data cells at the most granular level.
	Pane	This pull-down allows you to set the default border color and thickness of data cells at one level higher than the most granular level.
	Header	This pull-down allows you to set the default border color and thickness of the dimensional header values on your chart.
Total	Pane	If you have totals enabled, this controls the border around them.
	Header	This controls the border surrounding the Total label.
Grand Total	Pane	If you have grand totals enabled, this controls the border around them.
	Header	This controls the border surrounding the Grand Total label.
Row Divider	Pane	This controls the lines between rows at the level of granularity defined with the level option. These lines override the formatting set in the default section.
	Header	This controls the lines between rows for the headers at the level defined.
	Level	This controls the dimension level at which the lines divide rows within the chart.
Column Divider	Pane	This controls the lines between columns at the level of granularity defined with the level option.
	Header	This controls the lines between columns for the headers at the level defined.
	Level	This controls the dimension level at which the lines divide columns within the chart.

Default settings are overridden by the divider settings. You can also adjust the details about where the lines appear using the Rows tab, Columns tab, and the Fields pull-down. This gives you more detailed control over how and where dividing lines are displayed. Dividing lines also appear in charts with multiple visualizations, such as those with two measures that are not on a dual axis. These format controls also manage dividing lines in visualizations with multiple dimensions, such as bar charts.

Format Lines

While the Format Borders pane focuses on the lines that divide a chart, the Format Lines pane focuses on other lines, such as axes and trend lines (see Figure 4-30) that help clarify values. They can also be used to make lines on a chart easier to see. A list of these options and their use is available in Table 4-5.

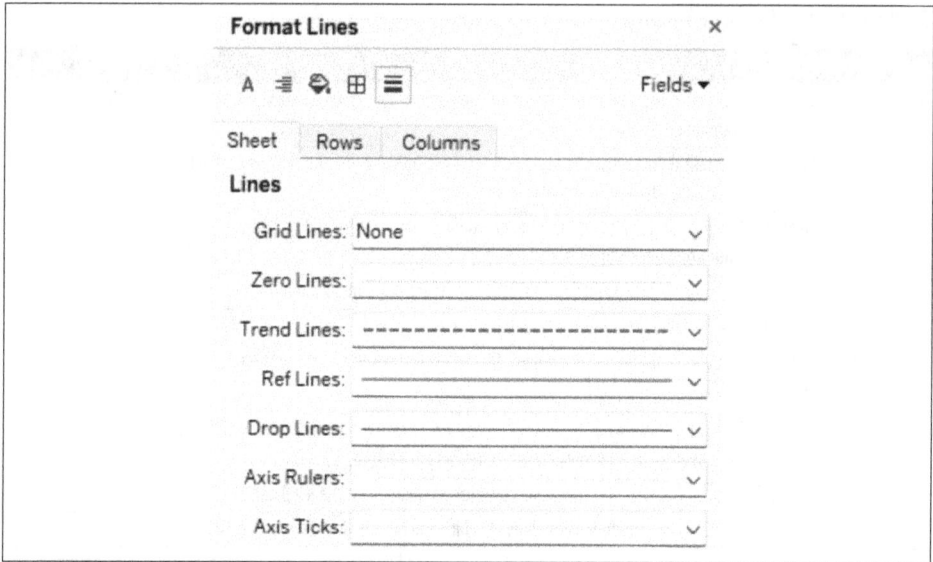

Figure 4-30. The Format Lines pane.

Table 4-5. Options for formatting specific lines within a visualization.

Section	Area	What it formats
Lines	Grid Lines	Grid lines divide up a chart's background area with thin, grayed-out lines. These help you identify chart values by providing landmark lines at key measure levels.
	Zero Lines	This option adds a thin line at 0 on the axis. It is extremely helpful if your data travels between negative and positive values on a chart.
	Trend Lines	Trend lines (see "Analytics Pane" on page 149) control what that line looks like on the visualization.
	Ref Lines	This controls the default appearance of reference lines on a chart.
	Drop Lines	If you right-click on a point in a line or scatter plot visualization, there is an option to add a drop line. *Drop lines* simply connect the point to the corresponding locations on both axes.
	Axis Rulers	This controls the thickness and color of the axes.
	Axis Ticks	This controls the formatting of the thin little lines between the axes values and the axis.

Formatting External Chart Components

How your users interact with a chart is as important as the chart itself. You want the filter and parameter controls to be easy to view and use. Choose a title that is descriptive and easy to read. These are valuable components of how your end users interpret your chart. Tableau provides a wide selection of options to control how these objects are displayed and what they contain.

Chart Controls Formatting

Although you've seen the built-in options for controlling the appearance of filters, parameters, and reference lines, there are additional formatting options you can apply once the object has been built to control things like fonts, colors, alignment, and more (see Figure 4-31).

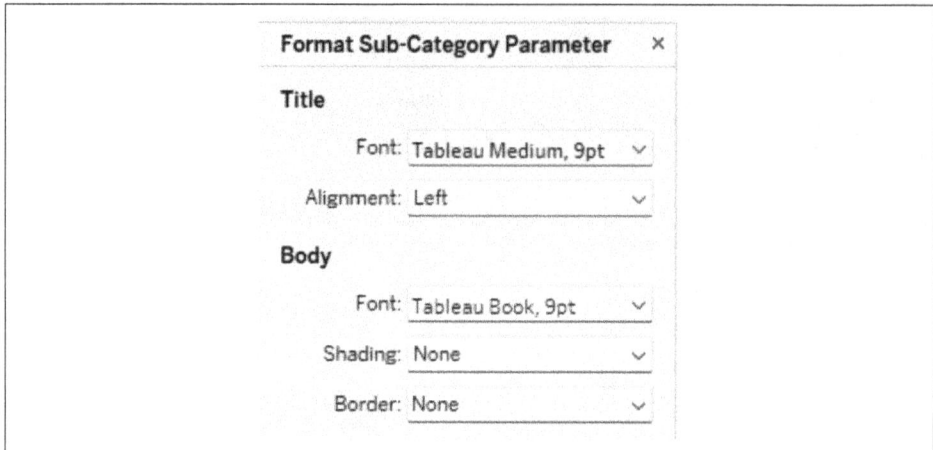

Figure 4-31. The Format pane replaces the Data pane when it is selected from an object menu. This window contains nearly identical options for parameters, filters, and legends.

Most of these options are located in a special window that appears above the Data pane on the left side of the screen:

Filter Control Formatting

For filter controls, click on the menu in the upper right corner and select Format. Within the Format submenu are two options: "This Filter or Set Control" or "All Filter and Set Controls." The first option will change a specific filter control, while the second option allows you to make a global change to all filter controls at once, saving you time. Selecting either option will make a Format window appear in place of the Data pane with options to adjust the title's font, color, and alignment and the font and color of the body text. There are also options to shade or add a border to the control as a whole.

Parameter Control Formatting

Parameter controls have exactly the same menus and options as filters.

Reference Line Formatting

To access the formatting window, right-click on the reference line or band once it appears in your chart and select the Format option. The Format pane replaces the Data pane, with options to change the appearance of the line and the space above and below it. If you are showing any text, you can change font, color, alignment, number formatting, and shading behind the label.

Legend Formatting

When you apply a dimension to the Color, Size, or Shape mark, a legend will appear. This can be formatted just like other user controls. Click the pull-down on the upper right corner of the legend and select Format. You will get an option to change only this legend or all legends in the workbook. The legend formatting options are exactly the same as those for parameters and filters.

Formatting Chart Titles

By default, chart titles are populated with <Sheet Name>, which reflects the label on the tab at the bottom of the screen (see Figure 4-32). If your tab is titled Sheet 1, the title of the chart will be Sheet 1. If the tab name changes, the chart title will change. The sheet name is only the default value for the title.

You can modify a chart's title by double-clicking it. This brings up the Edit Title window, which allows you to change its current value to anything you wish. You can also add predefined text fields from the Insert menu.

The Edit Title window contains a typical menu bar at the top, which gives you control over how the title appears. Different sections of the title can have different appearances. For example, you may want your main title to be a larger font, while your subtitles are a bit smaller. All the text in the Edit Title window can be changed to a different font, color, or alignment. You can also add basic formatting such as italics, bold, and underline.

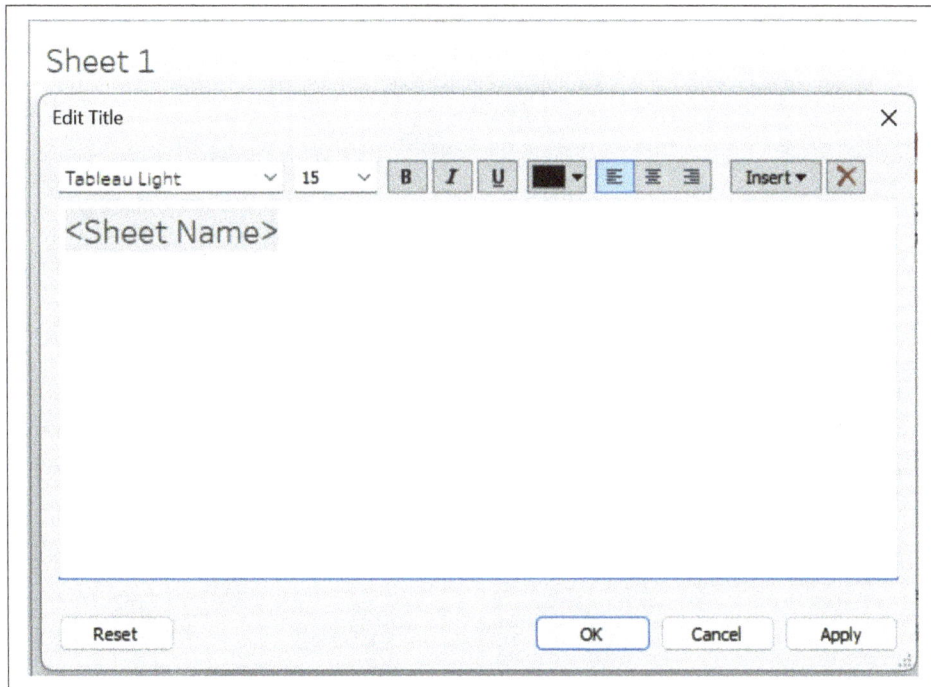

Figure 4-32. The Edit Title window provides options for altering the title and its font, color, and alignment.

The Insert menu offers a list of canned text objects to place into the title (see Figure 4-33), such as the data source name and update time, the workbook title, or the current sheet title. You can also add page information (see the section "Marks, Filters, and Pages" on page 38) or information about the user.

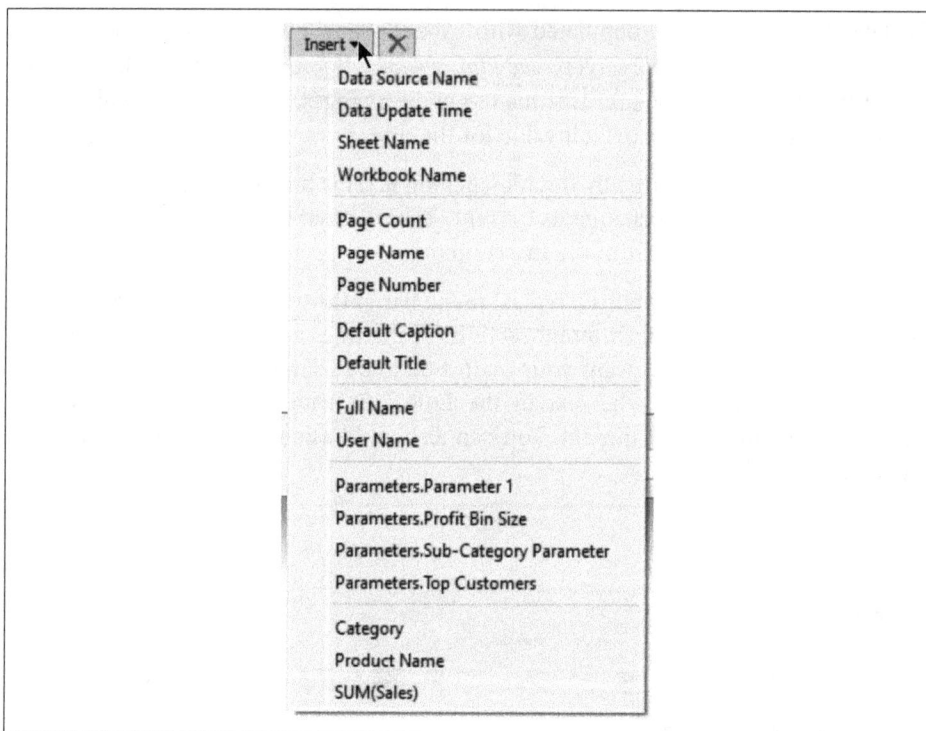

Figure 4-33. The Insert menu in the title window offers options to insert default text.

The most important options within the Insert menu are the parameter and dimension values, which populate the title with information about what parameters are set to as well as what dimension values are contained in the visualization. For example, if you created a parameter to show the top N customers by sales, that parameter value could be added to the title. Dimension values can be an excellent way to identify what is visible in the chart after applying filters (see Figure 4-34).

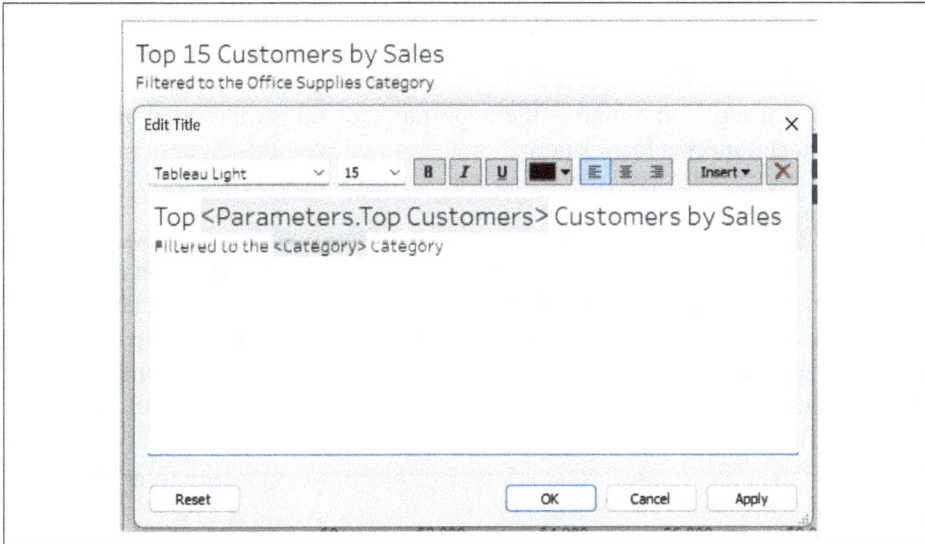

Figure 4-34. A title with an inserted parameter value and dimension. Above the Edit Title window is the title of the chart, reflecting these inserted field values.

The title can also be formatted via a right-click menu. If you right-click on a title and select Format, the Data pane will be replaced with a Format Title and Captions pane that gives you options to modify the background and border of the title (or captions). You can set the title's shading to any color and opacity and modify the border's color, thickness, and appearance.

> *Captions* are pieces of text that appear below a visualization. By default, they populate with information about how the chart is built and what it shows. You can turn captions on using the Worksheet menu at the top of the screen and modify them in a similar way to titles. You should be familiar with where they are and how to change them, but they are not as likely to appear on the exam as other topics.

Additional Formatting Options

Additional ways to format aspects of a visualization are nested within different sections of the interface and control the appearance of things like total aliases, axes information, and specific mark labels.

Totals and Grand Totals

You can rename the labels for totals and grand totals by right-clicking on a chart and specifying which field you are modifying. You can do this by right-clicking directly on the totals and selecting Format or by selecting a specific field in the pull-down at the top of the Format pane. If you open the Format pane with either of these options, two new fields will appear in the pane: Totals Label and Grand Totals Label (see Figure 4-35).

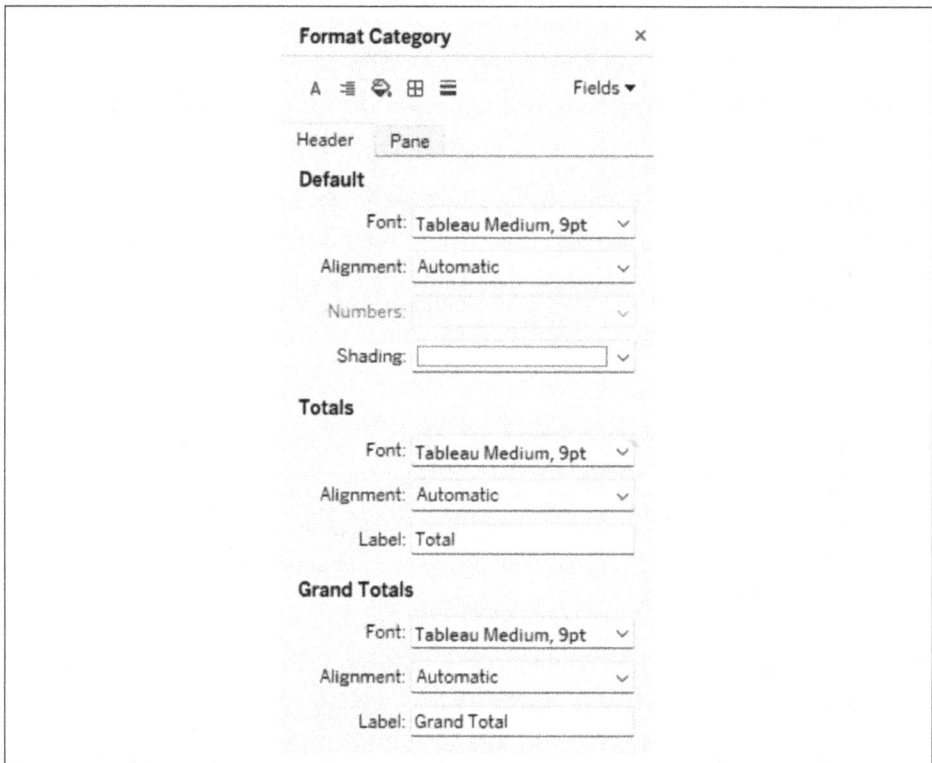

Figure 4-35. Opening the Format pane using a total or grand total in a visualization will provide you with options for renaming those fields.

If your visualization has multiple dimensions and you enable subtotals, Tableau will add a subtotal for each visible dimension. You can decide if you want all the subtotals on or if you want to turn some of them off by right-clicking on the field in the rows or columns and unchecking the Subtotal option. Once you enable Subtotal from the menu, you can enable or disable any subtotal the same way.

Edit Axis

While the visual aspect of the axes is controlled in the Format pane, you can also right-click on any axis and choose Edit Axis to change the range, scale, or title of any axis (see Table 4-6).

Table 4-6. Axis formatting and control options available in the Edit Axis window.

Section	Area	What it formats
General	Range	These radio buttons let you choose if the axis is automatically sized, uniform across multiple axes, independent between multiple axes, or a custom range. The Custom Range option allows you to set the bottom and top of the available values. There is also an option to force the inclusion of zero on the axis.
	Scale	The two options here are Reversed and Logarithmic. The Reversed option switches the direction of the values on the axis (higher to lower instead of lower to higher). Logarithmic changes the axis increments from linear to exponential; so, the axis will go from 1, 10, 100, 1000 instead of 1, 2, 3, 4. You can choose to include only positive values in the logarithm (Positive) or also negative values (Symmetric).
	Axis Titles	This section allows you to change the title of the axis or use the name of one of the dimensional fields. You can include an automatically generated subtitle or enter one yourself. This window is helpful for updating axis titles in dual-axis charts (discussed in Chapter 3).
Tick Marks	Major Tick Marks	This section of the Tick Marks tab controls how frequently the major points along the axis are labeled and where these labeled ticks begin and end.
	Minor Tick Marks	*Minor tick marks* are the small sublines ticks between the major ticks. For example, if major ticks occur where the measure is evenly divisible by five, the minor ticks might mark the four ticks between them. These options control the frequency and beginning and ending points for minor ticks.

Example Question

You have a data set with a few extremely large values that cause the smaller values not to appear in a visualization. What option might you use to make them all visible on the same axis?

A. Logarithmic

B. Reversed

C. Hierarchy

D. Scale

E. Tick Marks

Answer: A—Logarithmic scales increase by an exponential value as they go up, allowing small values and large values to appear with similar size on the same axis. It is important to call this out to end users to avoid confusion, though!

Annotation

Another way you can format charts is through *annotation*. You can right-click anywhere on a visualization to add a note or additional information, such as existing marks or a specific area or point that you want to label or call out (see Figure 4-36). When you create an annotation, Tableau immediately prompts you for text. You can modify this text field exactly the same way as a label or tooltip. Use the Insert menu to add specific fields.

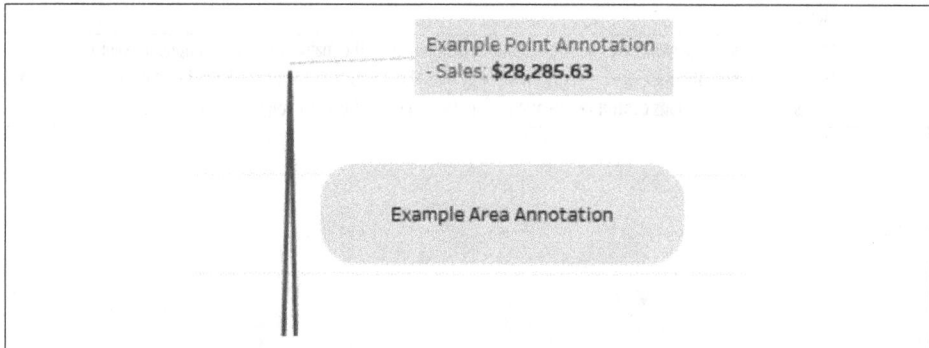

Figure 4-36. Point and area annotations.

You can control where an annotation appears and what it encompasses by clicking on it. This highlights the annotation, along with a line to the point or box being annotated. If you annotate a point, you can use the small square controls on the line to adjust where the point is located. The data in the annotation will adjust with the location. If you annotate an area, the controls manage the corners of the box, which allows you to adjust the included area.

Annotations have their own Format pane (see Figure 4-37), which can be accessed through the right-click menu on the annotation itself. The details of the format options are included in Table 4-7. Annotations can be removed through the same right-click menu.

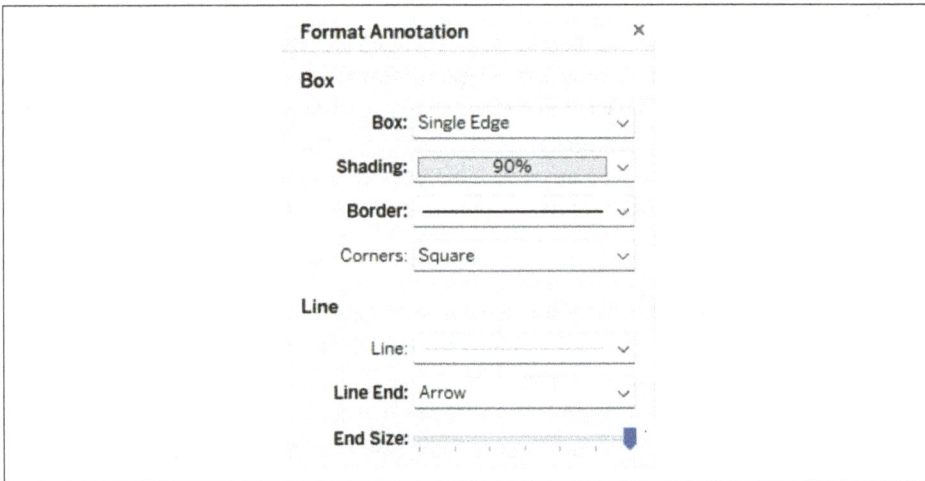

Figure 4-37. The Format Annotation pane.

Table 4-7. Available options in the Format pane for annotations.

Section	Area	What it formats
Box	Box	This controls where the border appears on the annotation box. It can be a full border, a single border side, or no border at all.
	Shading	This option controls the background color and opacity of the annotation label.
	Border	If a border is enabled in the Box menu, this option controls its color, style, and thickness.
	Corners	The annotation label is included in a box; this option allows you to round the corners of that box.
Line	Line	For point annotations, this controls the color, thickness, and style of the line traveling from the label to the indicated point.
	Line End	For point annotations, this option controls if the line end is normal, an arrow, or a dot.
	End Size	This option controls the size of any line end.

Null and Missing Values

Sometimes your data is incomplete. By default, Tableau treats missing measures as null. It will also exclude dimension values, such as dates, if there is no data associated with that date. This can lead to misleading charts: the visualization will display the dates together even though there are gaps in between. These menu options help you restore these missing points to make your chart more accurate.

The first option is the Special Values submenu. It handles fields that have null values, and contains two options: Show and Hide. If Show is selected, Tableau will replace any null with a zero. If Hide is selected, the field is simply not shown.

The second option handles missing dimensional values. There are two ways to access it: through the Table Layout submenu under the Analysis menu, or through the right-click menu on the corresponding axis. This option fills in the blanks on dates and dimensions that might otherwise not show. For example, if your data set is missing data for a specific date in a range (such as a holiday), the missing-values options let you force these dates to appear anyway. This option also works for dimensions that are null when other dimensions are not (such as a row of data with an empty dimension field).

> Missing values will only be shown if context is provided, such as when one dimension is null and the others are not, or when a date is missing between two other dates. Tableau will not add dates before or after the range of dates available in the data.

> The Infer Properties from Missing Values option in the Analysis menu allows you to run calculations on missing values for predictive modeling. For more information, see "Predictive Modelling with Generated Marks" (*https://oreil.ly/D671T*) from Tableau.

Conclusion

When you build a visualization, make sure that it answers the customer's question—but don't stop there. Your visualization should inspire additional questions. A great analyst will provide an interactive visualization that is well formatted, easy to read, and clearly labeled, letting end users dig into the data for answers easily. That's why user interaction and visualization formatting are invaluable to understand—and why they comprise such a large portion of the analyst exam.

CHAPTER 5

Combining Visualizations in Dashboards and Stories

Often, a single visualization is not enough to tell a complete story about the data. In my work at the university, my job is to analyze data and present my findings in a single cohesive structure. For example, I am regularly asked to analyze student admissions data. My base visualization is often student counts by applications, admissions, and matriculations; however, my customer also wants information on residency, demographics, and admission type.

For these types of questions, I build multiple charts. The main chart shows the different counts, and the other charts provide a more detailed breakdown of the demographics. I could leave the charts as they are and provide them in a tabbed view for my end user; however, the charts are far more effective at providing insights if they are combined into a single cohesive unit.

To accomplish this, I turn to dashboards and stories. Tableau delivers multiple ways to structure visualization layouts, improve user experience, and incorporate interactivity. This chapter will dig into these aspects of dashboard building, dashboard actions, and story structures. The goal is to ensure that you understand the two methods of dashboard construction, you can incorporate dashboard actions to improve user interaction, and you can build a story presentation to guide your users to actionable insights based on the data.

Dashboards

A *dashboard* is a single-page structured layout that makes one or more visualizations and corresponding controls accessible to the end user. For example, a single monthly sales chart provides vital information to a retail organization, but a dashboard of charts that break the sales numbers down by region expands those insights. Dashboards combine related charts to provide a better designed, easier to understand, and more detailed look at the data. Built correctly, they can make the user interface cleaner, easier to use, and more intuitive to your end user.

Dashboard Interface

You create a dashboard by clicking the new dashboard icon at the bottom of the screen. Once the dashboard opens, the left side of the screen changes to the Dashboard control pane, while the right side displays the blank dashboard. The pane on the left is divided into two tabs: Dashboard and Layout.

The Dashboard tab is broken down into four separate sections:

Device Area

At the top of the pane is an area that provides options for dashboard design based on the end user's device (see Figure 5-1), with a default layout and options for phone and tablet layouts for specific devices. The Device Preview button shrinks the dashboard view to imitate how it would behave on various devices and screen resolutions. The additional layout options are available in the Dashboard menu at the top of the window.

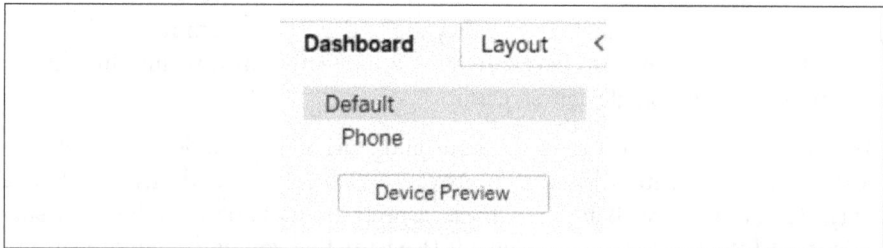

Figure 5-1. The Dashboard pane offers options for dashboard layouts on different devices. The Device Preview button allows you to see how the layout will appear when rendered on a particular device.

Size

The Size section holds a pull-down menu that offers a wide variety of default screen resolutions (see Figure 5-2), including a basic desktop browser, a laptop, and a wide variety of paper sizes. There is also an option to manually dictate the height and width of the dashboard and one to set the dashboard size automatically. These automatic settings give the dashboard flexibility to fit the resolution of the screen on which it is displayed; however, they can also adjust the locations of content, causing your beautiful design to appear broken. Fixed sizes are also better for performance: they allow the server to save a cached version for faster load times.

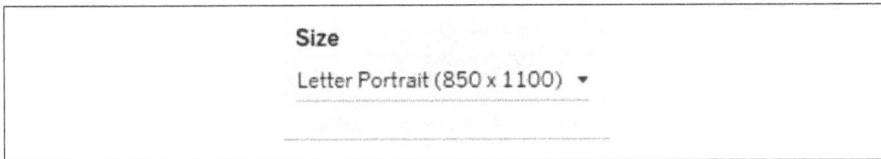

> **Size**
>
> Letter Portrait (850 x 1100) ▾

Figure 5-2. The size area of the Dashboard pane allows you to choose between predefined dashboard sizes or set your own dimensions.

Sheets

The Sheets section lets you drag and drop the visualizations that you have built for that workbook onto the dashboard (see Figure 5-3).

> **Sheets**
>
> Sales & Profit
> Furn
> Office
> Tech
> Orders by ...

Figure 5-3. The Sheets pane lists the visualizations that are available to add to a dashboard.

Objects

The Objects section holds components that can be added to a dashboard (see Figure 5-4). They will be covered separately later in this chapter.

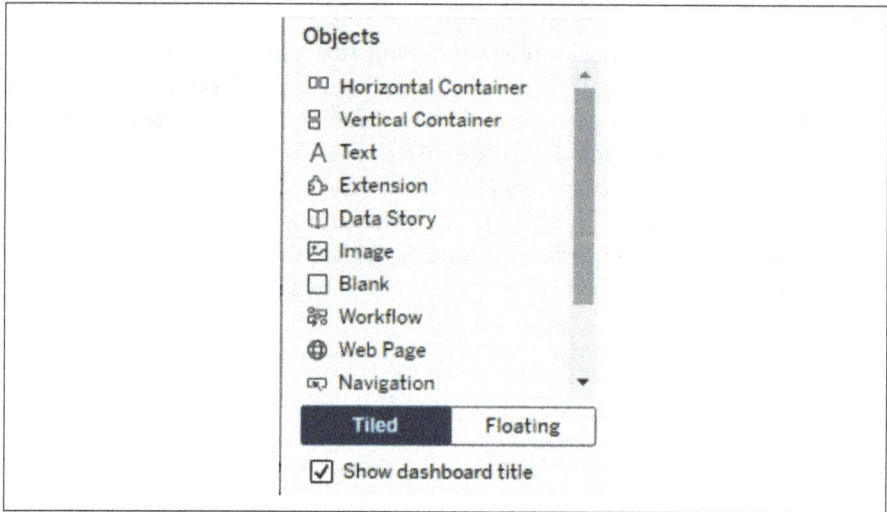

Figure 5-4. The Objects section at the bottom of the Dashboard pane holds items besides visualizations that can be added to improve the layout, design, or functionality of the dashboard.

Example Question

What are the three available device types for designing a dashboard layout? Select three.

A. Desktop

B. Default

C. Web Page

D. Tablet

E. Phone

Answers: B, D, and E—The dashboard starts in the default layout, but you can add phone and tablet layouts.

The other tab on the left pane is the Layout tab, designed to help you manipulate the size, position, border, and background of any item on the dashboard. It also provides a hierarchy section, which is extremely useful when you're building a tiled design (more about that in the next section):

Selected item

This section identifies the object you have selected on the dashboard and provides you with related options (see Figure 5-5). The first option, "Show title," allows you to enable or disable the title on any visualizations you add to the dashboard. Floating enables or disables floating for the object (floating layouts will also be covered in the next section). "Control visibility using value" allows you to hide or show a visualization based on another value in the dashboard or a parameter. When you enable this option, a pull-down menu appears that prompts you to identify the controlling value.

Figure 5-5. The "Selected item" area of the Layout pane provides options like the title and floating or tiled status of the selected object.

Position

The x and y coordinates of a selected object are displayed here. These numbers reflect the upper left corner (see Figure 5-6), where the object begins, and extend to the lower right corner based on the size values in the next section.

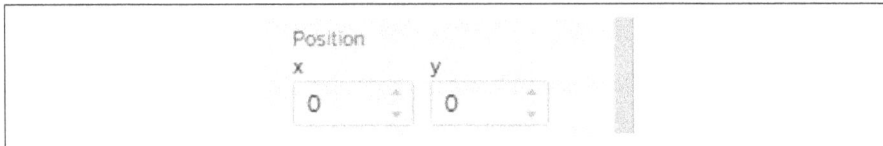

Figure 5-6. The Position area of the Layout pane identifies the upper left corner of the object selected.

Size

The w and h fields reflect the width and height of the object, respectively (see Figure 5-7). The upper left corner is dictated by the position field and the object extends w pixels to the right and h pixels down from that location.

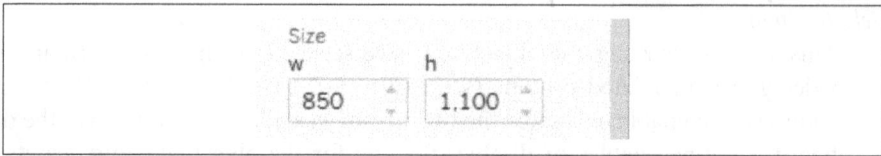

Figure 5-7. The width and height of an object are controlled by the size section of the Layout pane.

Border

You can add a border to any object on the dashboard (see Figure 5-8). The border controls are similar to those elsewhere in Tableau, allowing you to change the border's thickness, color, and style.

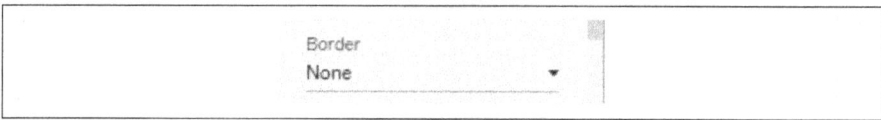

Figure 5-8. The Border section of the Layout pane gives you control of the width, style, and color of the selected object on the dashboard.

Background

This option allows you to change the background color of a selected object on the dashboard (see Figure 5-9). The default background for visualizations is white (not transparent). If you change the background color of your dashboard and then add a visualization, the background of the visualization will be white unless you change it.

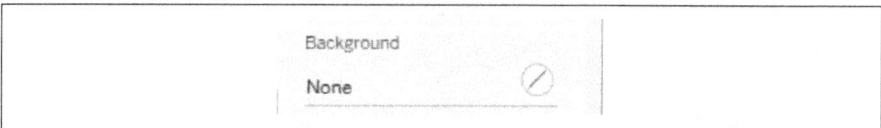

Figure 5-9. The background of a selected object can be any color, including transparent. The Background section of the Layout pane controls this background.

Outer Padding

Outer padding refers to the space outside the edge of the object selected. For example, if your object has a border, the outer padding will go outside of that border. There is a checkbox option within the Outer Padding fields that will force Tableau to keep the padding uniform around the object (see Figure 5-10).

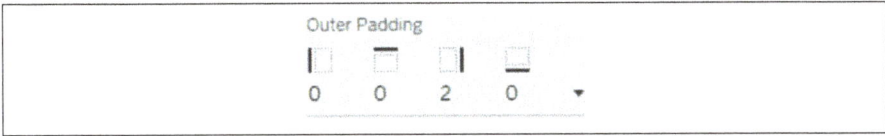

Figure 5-10. Outer Padding controls the space between the selected object and the next adjacent object.

Inner Padding

Inner padding is the distance from the actual object to its border. The Inner Padding area also contains a checkbox that allows for uniform padding (see Figure 5-11).

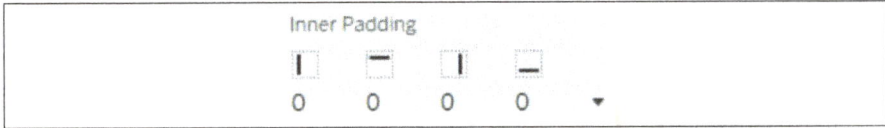

Figure 5-11. Inner Padding controls the space between the content inside the select object and its outer edge.

Item hierarchy

When building a dashboard layout, the *hierarchy* tracks where the object appears on the dashboard (see Figure 5-12). This is especially significant for tiled layouts, which often hold several layers of nested containers to create the desired dashboard structure.

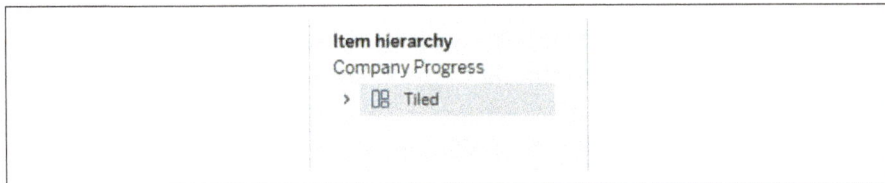

Figure 5-12. The "Item hierarchy" illustrates the nested container structure of a tiled dashboard. Floating objects appear above the hierarchy itself.

Inner and outer padding add space around an object. As a result, they directly affect that object's size. If you build an object that is 50 pixels tall and add 4 pixels of padding to the top and bottom, the resulting object will be 58 pixels tall!

Example Question

What information is *not* available on the Layout tab about a selected object?

A. Size

B. Location

C. Source sheet name

D. Border

E. Padding

Answer: C—The source sheet is not listed on the Layout tab; it is found on the Dashboard tab.

Dashboard Objects

Near the bottom of the Dashboard tab in the left pane, there's a section called Objects (see Figure 5-13). This is where you can add things other than visualizations to a dashboard. Most objects have multiple related options that can be accessed through a right-click menu.

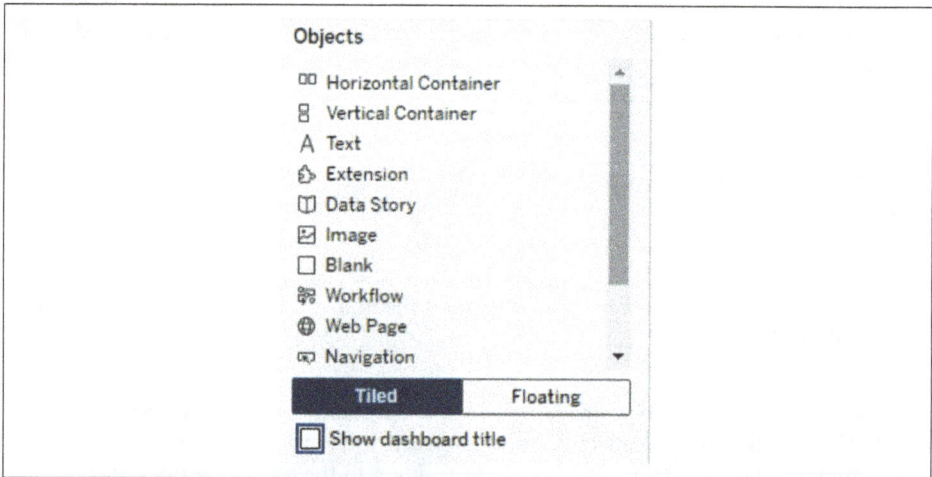

Figure 5-13. Below the list of visualizations on the Dashboard tab are objects that can be added to enhance a dashboard. This section also controls if objects added are tiled or floating and contains an option to show or hide the dashboard title.

The object options are:

Horizontal Container

A *container* is a space used to hold other objects. *Horizontal* containers, specifically, hold objects that are next to each other horizontally. You can specify the width of objects in a horizontal container, but their height is controlled by the container's dimensions.

Vertical Container

A *vertical* container is similar to a horizontal container, except that objects are placed vertically. It allows you to control the height of contained objects, while their width is managed by the container's dimensions.

Text

This object allows you to add a text field to the dashboard. This text can be anything you wish, and the formatting options are very similar to those for labels and tooltips. When you drag a text object to a dashboard, a window appears where you can enter, format, and align your text. The Insert menu allows you to insert parameter values, sheet-specific values, or user-specific variables.

Extension

Some functionality is not built into Tableau. To handle these challenges, Tableau developed *extensions*, which are small chunks of code designed to perform certain actions when triggered. A wide variety of extensions is available to do many different things. Example extensions are available on Tableau Exchange (*https:// oreil.ly/f0Qt-*). Extensions can be created by third parties as well but may not be at the same level of quality or support as those provided by Tableau.

Data Story

Tableau can examine a visualization to provide detailed information about what it shows. When you add a data story, Tableau prompts you to identify the visualization you want to tell a story about, including which field or fields you want to describe or ignore. Tableau then analyzes your selections and provides a written text description of what is taking place. This text can include trend information, high points and low points in the data, and cyclical patterns.

Image

The Image option allows you to bring an image into your dashboard. The Image window prompts you to identify if the image is stored locally or accessible via URL. Once you choose an image, you can fit it to the space, center it, hyperlink it, or provide alternate text for accessibility.

Blank

The Blank object is exactly what it's named: a placeholder that provides blank space on a dashboard. It can also hold open containers as you add visualizations or other objects. It was originally used for spacing before the padding feature was added to Tableau's dashboard design.

Workflow

This option triggers an external Salesforce workflow based on something the end user clicks in a dashboard. These workflows perform actions within your organization's Salesforce instance, such as sending out a prepopulated email.

Web Page

A Tableau dashboard can hold a framed version of a web page; just provide the URL and the web page will render as part of the dashboard.

Navigation

This option provides a button that gives your users a way to traverse multiple dashboards within a workbook. By default, the button is a box with text, but you can right-click it and choose Edit to see more options. In the Options window, you can identify the dashboard to which the button will navigate and change the button's content between text and an image. Image buttons require you to provide an image file, while text buttons give you options for the text and the font. Both styles of buttons allow you to control the border style and background color and provide alternate text.

Download

Similar to a Navigation object, the Download object defaults to a text box when dragged into a dashboard. If you right-click and edit the object, you have exactly the same options as a Navigation button. The only difference is that you can choose a download format rather than a navigation destination.

Add Filters

This built-in extension allows end users to show and hide sections of the dashboard. You can right-click on this object to dictate what portions of the dashboard users can show or hide. This object appears as a button, just like the Navigation and Download objects, and offers all of the same design options.

Einstein Discovery

This extension utilizes Salesforce Einstein Discovery to perform a predictive analysis of your visualization based on the existing values. Along with its predictions, it explains what indicators led to those results.

Below all the objects, you'll see a checkbox that says, "Show dashboard title." This checkbox inserts a title object into the dashboard. The title defaults to the sheet name, but you can easily change it by double-clicking on the title field. Like most text fields in Tableau, there are options for font, size, color, and alignment. You can also add a menu to the title that contains workbook-related and user-specific fields.

Data stories are quite complex. Editing extension preferences lets you control things such as narrative, characteristics, and analytics. It is worth experimenting with this object type to familiarize yourself with it. Even if it doesn't appear in the exam, it will be a useful part of your dashboard-development arsenal.

Example Question

What Dashboard object provides syntax with detailed information about the visualization in the dashboard?

A. Text

B. Extension

C. Workflow

D. Story

E. Navigation

Answer: D—A story will analyze a visualization and provide a text-based description of insights related to the chart.

Building a Floating Layout

There are two different ways to build a dashboard in Tableau: *floating* and *tiled*. The floating dashboard layout uses a visual design method that positions objects where you place them. To enable this, simply toggle the Floating option below the Objects section of the Dashboard tab, and every object you add to the dashboard will be placed as a floating object. Any object you place will appear in the item hierarchy area, but will not be part of the hierarchy.

Many people appreciate the floating method of dashboard building for its simplicity: you drag and drop an object onto the dashboard and it appears at that location. You can then click on it and use the handlebar at the top to move it around. You can also hover over the object's corners to get a double mouse arrow, which you can click and drag to resize the object. The main challenge of a floating layout is that it's sometimes difficult to align objects to improve the user experience. As you initially build your dashboard, it is very unlikely that the objects you place will align perfectly with adjacent objects. This is where the Layout tab comes into play.

The Layout pane provides the coordinates and size of the selected object. So, if your first visualization is just below the title of your dashboard and has a *y* value of 50, you can place another visualization beside it and use the layout tab to ensure that it also starts at a *y* value of 50 (see Figure 5-14). Aligning the items on a dashboard improves its accessibility and readability.

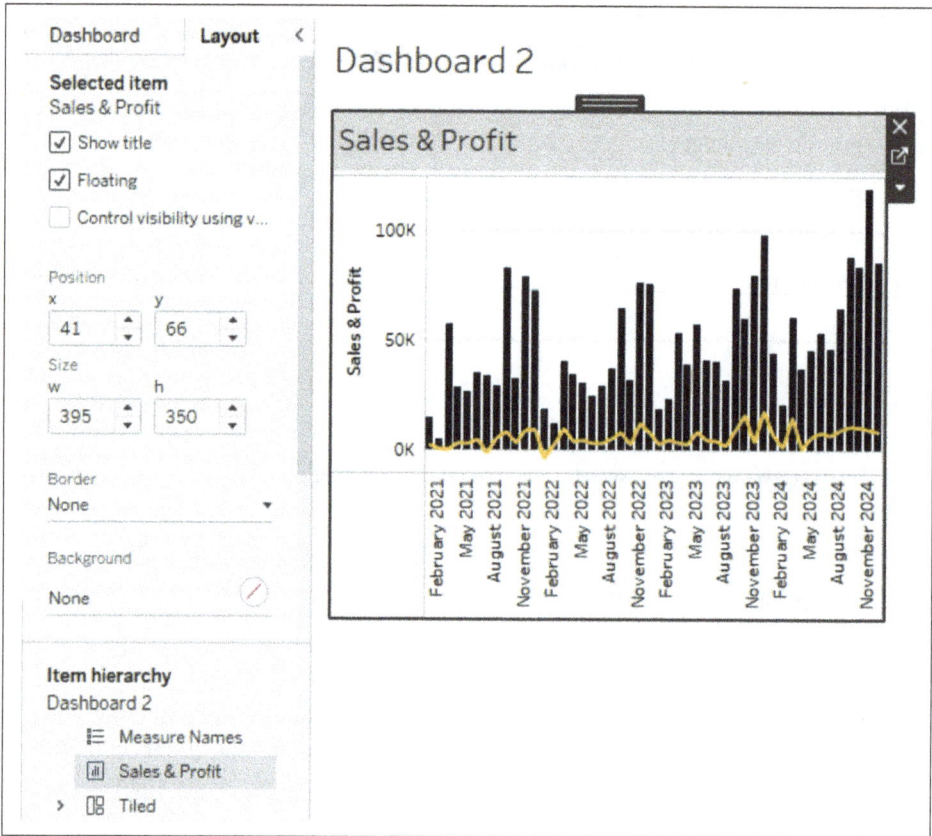

Figure 5-14. If you select an object placed on a dashboard, the Layout tab will provide detailed information about its location, size, border, and background. Floating objects appear in the "Item hierarchy" section, but not as part of the hierarchy.

When you place objects side by side on a dashboard with a floating layout, you will very likely have to do some math. In the previous example, you placed one visualization at the same y level as the previous visualization, aligning their top borders. But let's say you want the left side of the second chart to be adjacent to the first (perhaps with some space). To determine where to place the second visualization, add the width of the first visualization to its own x coordinate. For example, if the first visualization starts at $x = 10$ and is 500 px wide, your second visualization can't start until at least $x = 510$ or it will overlap (see Figure 5-15).

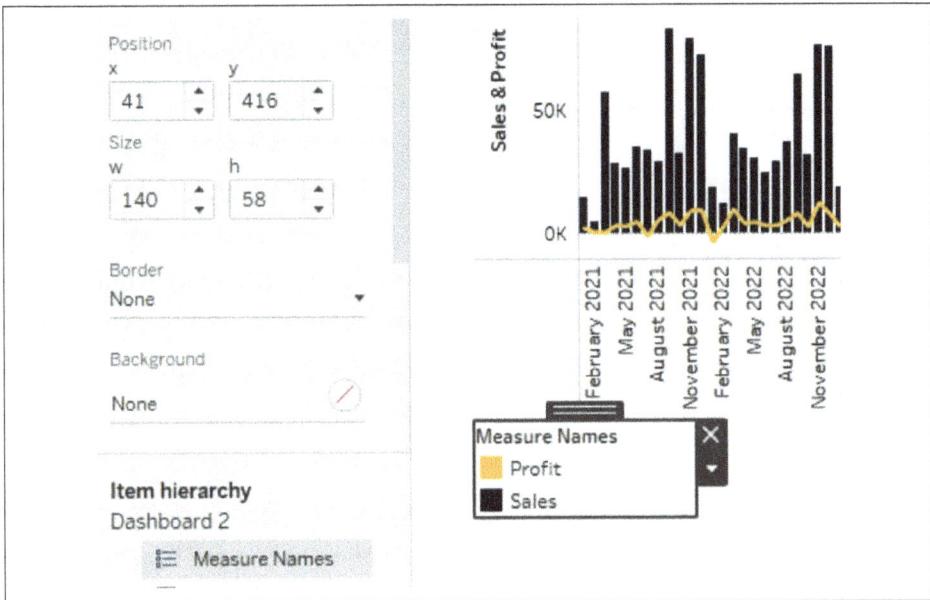

Figure 5-15. To place the legend below the chart and align the left sides properly, you need to do math on the chart's position and height. The chart in this figure is from the previous example. For this legend to line up with the chart in Figure 5-14 and be adjacent to its bottom, the x value needs to be 41 and the y value needs to be 416 (66 position + 350 px tall).

Floating layouts also have the challenge of the third dimension—where objects fall if they overlap. If two objects overlap on a floating dashboard layout, the most recently placed object will appear on top. You can right-click on an object's handlebar or use its pull-down menu to change its Floating Order (see Figure 5-16). The menu that appears contains four options for changing its stack position: Bring to Front, Bring Forward, Send to Back, and Send Backward.

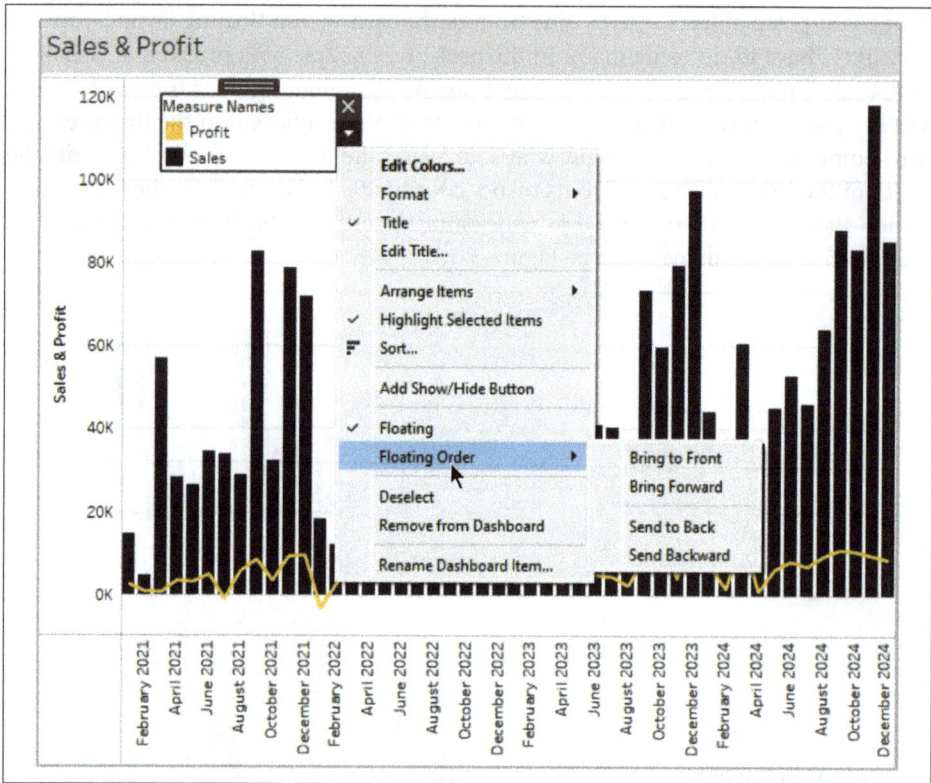

Figure 5-16. You can place a legend on top of its chart in a floating layout. The legend's menu shows the Floating Order options, which change how it is stacked compared to the chart.

Stacking objects can be confusing, but it's beneficial when applying background images to your dashboard. For example, you could add an image object with a custom background, then place a visualization atop it. There are many examples on the Tableau "Viz of the Day" web page (*https://oreil.ly/cNETy*).

In the Dashboard menu, there are two options to help you build your layout strategically: Show Grid and Grid Options. Show Grid places a grid pattern across the dashboard to assist you with placing and aligning objects. Grid Options lets you increase or decrease the size of the grid squares.

Building a Tiled Layout

Tiled dashboard layouts are challenging at first. They rely heavily on nested containers to control objects' height, width, and location. Therefore, these layouts require some advance planning to ensure space for all of the objects you wish to display. Once you get used to them, however, tiled layouts make it very easy to align and distribute objects evenly.

If your dashboard has a title, content, and a footer bar, you'll probably want to start with a vertical container. Containers allow objects to appear adjacent based on type; for example, vertical container allows you to stack objects vertically, which makes sense for this example, since its visualization content is nestled between the title on top and the footer below.

Once you've established the overall container, you need to plan what will appear in each section. For example, if you want a company logo to the left of the title, you may need a horizontal container to hold the title. Will you have more than one visualization? If so, do you want to tile them horizontally or vertically? Ask these questions ahead of time so you can decide what type of container to add and where (see Figure 5-17).

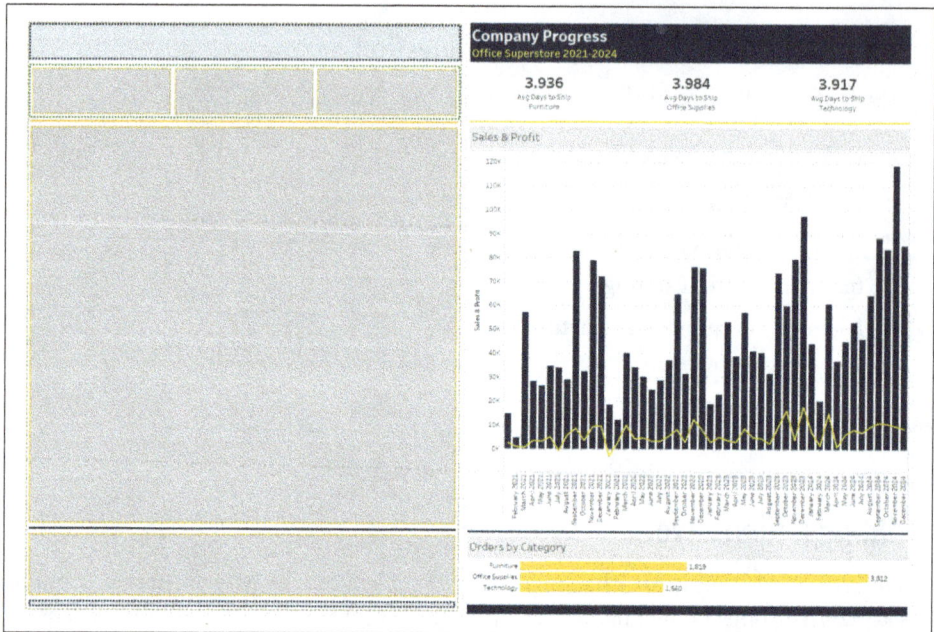

Figure 5-17. Tiled layouts require planning (left) to determine the type of containers needed, where they are nested, and if they are styled in any way. The final result (right) shows how the containers hold the charts and maintain alignment throughout.

When you drag an object such as a visualization onto the dashboard, you hover over the container to indicate where you would like to place it. Tableau creates a shaded area in the container to reflect where the object will be placed (see Figure 5-18). For empty containers, this shade will cover the entire space of the container. For containers with other objects already inside them, the shade will appear to the left, right, above, or below the existing object. The placement of your second object can also change the container type; for example, placing an object to the left or right of another in a vertical container will make the container horizontal.

Figure 5-18. When you drag and drop an object into a container, Tableau shades an area gray to indicate where the object will be placed. The gray area will fill an empty container and appear above, below, to the left, to the right, or in between objects already placed in the container (as shown here).

Remember, you can adjust the height of objects in a vertical container and the width of objects in a horizontal container, but the other dimensional size is controlled by the container itself. So, width is controlled by the vertical container and height is controlled by the horizontal container.

Charts with legends, filters, and parameters also make tiled layouts challenging. When you add a visualization with any of these features, Tableau automatically nests a horizontal container around your visualization to create space. Filters and legends will usually appear in a vertical container to the right of your visualization. This can be quite frustrating if you don't want these objects in this location. Fortunately, it is very easy to drag and drop them to other places of the tiled layout.

When you build a tiled layout, you should rely heavily on the Layout tab in the left pane (see Figure 5-19). At the bottom of this tab is the "Item hierarchy." This shows you which objects are in which nested containers. It also provides a sort of "map" that you can click to select a container or object quickly, without trying to find it on the dashboard itself.

```
Item hierarchy
Company Progress
  ⌄  ⊟⊟  Tiled
        ⌄  ⊟  Vertical Container
                  ⊓⊓  Company Progress Office S...
              ⌄  ⊓⊓  Horizontal Container
                      ⊞  Furn
                      ⊞  Office
                      ⊞  Tech
                  ☐  Blank
                  ⊞  Sales & Profit
                  ☐  Blank
                  ⊞  Orders by Category
                  ☐  Blank
```

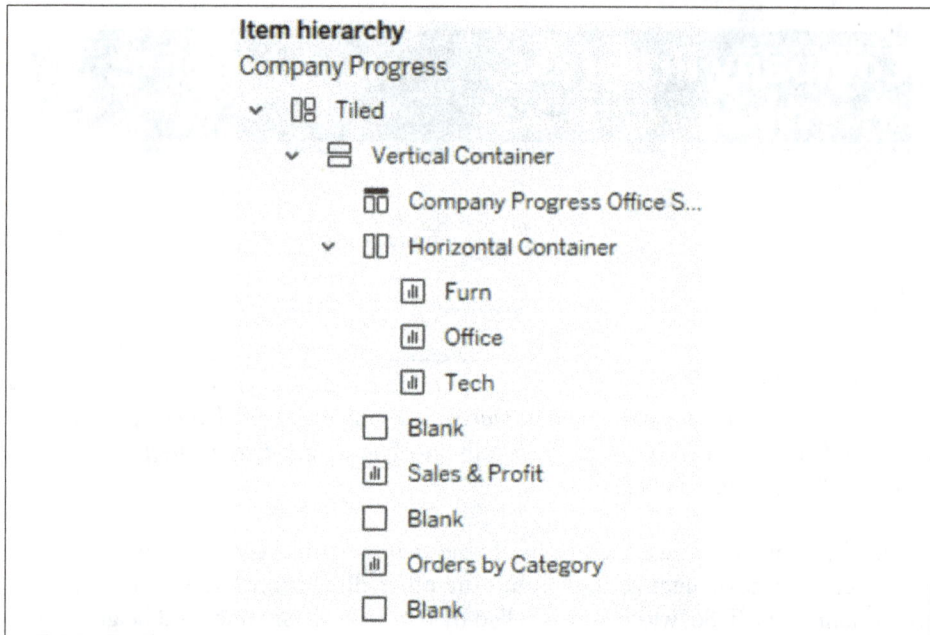

Figure 5-19. An "Item hierarchy" list for the tiled layout shown in Figure 5-17. The additional blank fields between the horizontal container and the other charts are slender blank spaces (11 px tall with 4 px padding on top and bottom) filled with background color to create the lines that divide up the dashboard.

There are other important things to remember about containers:

- Containers have all the same features as other objects on the dashboard, including background color, border, and padding.
- Double-clicking on an object will select the container that holds it.
- Containers have a pull-down menu that allows you to distribute the objects they contain. This is very useful when you want several visualizations to be the same size. Enabling this removes the resizing controls, however!
- You can use containers with floating layouts to provide alignment, structure, and distribution.
- The container menu has two options to remove the container. *Remove Container* will remove the container but leave its contents; *Remove from Dashboard* will delete everything within the container as well.
- You can rename containers, like other objects, via the container pull-down menu or by right-clicking the object in the "Item hierarchy."

By default, tiled layouts are nested in a Tiled container by default, which can hold objects above and below or side by side. When you try to resize an object within a container manually instead of using the height or width fields, Tableau sometimes adds Tiled containers to help align objects in adjacent containers. For example, imagine you have two vertical containers side by side and you resize the height of an object in one to match the height of an object in the other. Tableau will indicate when the two objects are the same size. If you release the mouse at this point, it will dump the objects into separate vertical containers and nest them in a tiled container. If you don't want the additional containers in your dashboard, align the objects using the height controls on the Layout tab instead.

You are not restricted to just one type of layout—you can use floating and tiled objects together to build a dashboard. For example, if you like floating layouts, but want to ensure that several smaller objects (such as filters) align, you can place a floating horizontal container on your dashboard, then switch the layout to tiled and drag the filters into the horizontal container. Even though the container is floating, the objects within it will be tiled, appearing side by side with the same height and alignment. Likewise, you can build a tiled layout and then use float to strategically place a company logo or other object within the dashboard.

Example Question

Tiled layouts place objects above, below, and aside other objects using what feature?

   A. Containers

   B. Coordinate positions

   C. Border

   D. Padding

   E. Blanks

Answer: A—Horizontal containers hold things next to each other side by side and vertical containers hold objects above and below each other.

Additional Dashboard Features

Whether you build your dashboard tiled or floating, there are several things you can do to organize it and make it easier to understand and more accessible to visually impaired users. These features take advantage of the dashboard-building process as well as incorporating aspects of some of the objects available in the Dashboard tab.

First, all objects on the dashboard can be renamed: visualizations, objects, and even containers. While this might seem tedious and unnecessary, you should know that screen readers "see" these names. For example, if you use horizontal and vertical containers in a dashboard, the screen reader will read aloud the default names of those containers: "Horizontal Container" and "Vertical Container," respectively. You should rename the containers to make more sense to the end users who see them, even if most end users never do. "Filter Container" means much more to a visually impaired user than "Horizontal Container."

Next, you can quickly swap visualizations out of dashboards. Imagine that you build a dashboard with several charts, but realize that one of the charts has a mistake. You duplicate the chart and adjust it to correct the error. Now you can swap it with the old one in the dashboard: Click on the old chart in the dashboard, then hover over the new chart's name on the Dashboard tab and click the circular arrow that appears on the right to replace the selected visualization (see Figure 5-20).

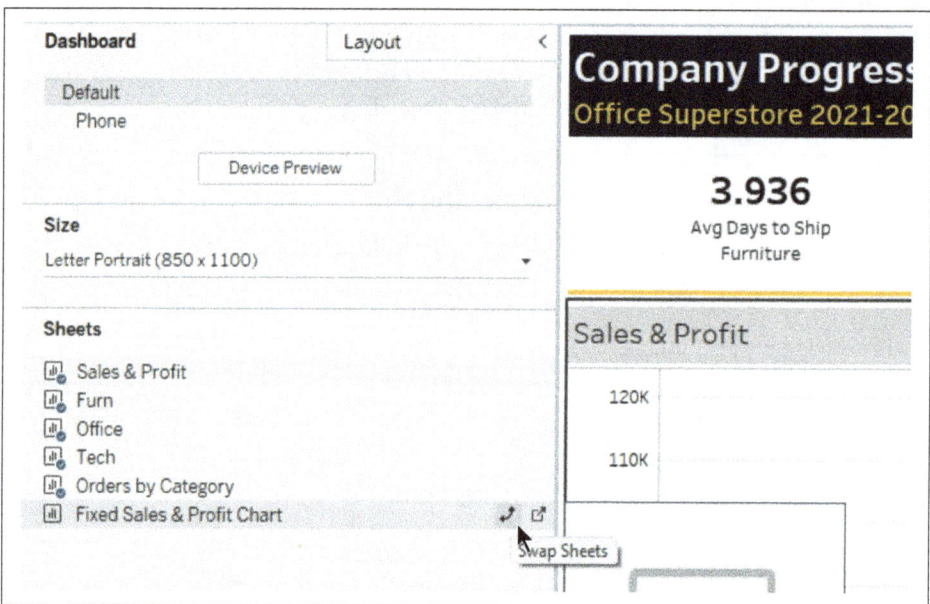

Figure 5-20. When a chart is selected in a dashboard, you can hover over a visualization in the dashboard tab to get a Swap Sheets option. In this figure, the Sales & Profit Chart is selected in the dashboard, and the user wishes to swap in the Fixed Sales & Profit Chart. The originally selected chart has a very light gray highlight in the list.

Another beneficial feature is copy and paste; you can use these keyboard commands (Ctrl-C, Ctrl-V) with most objects within a dashboard. For instance, you can duplicate a layout object that has a certain appearance using copy and paste; Tableau will place it as floating by default to ensure that it appears exactly where the mouse cursor is located. If you are using a tiled layout, you can then disable the float and place the object accordingly.

Every dashboard object has a hidden menu of controls at the top that appears when you select that object (see Figure 5-21). For most objects, it contains an "X" to remove the object, a pushpin to fix its size, and a pull-down menu that allows you to deselect, copy, delete, float/unfloat, select the container object, or rename the selected object.

For visualizations, this menu has two more choices. One button, which appears as a box with an arrow exiting it, navigates from the dashboard to the tab of the visualization you selected. The other appears as a funnel, which will make the chart a filter for the other visualizations on the dashboard. (This will be discussed further in the section "Dashboard Actions" on page 234.) Additional controls on the visualization pull-down include adding legends, filters, parameters, and a text-based description of the chart (for accessibility).

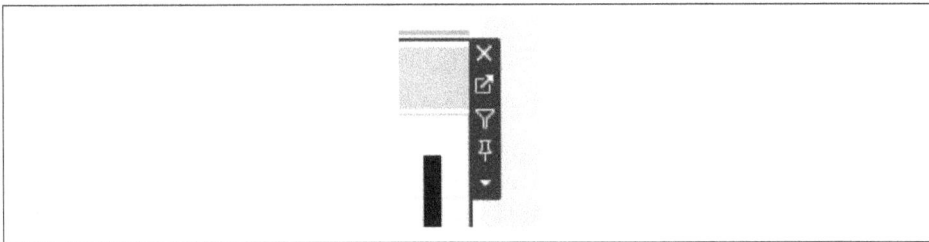

Figure 5-21. Selecting an object in a dashboard will make a menu appear in the upper right corner.

Finally, you can easily duplicate dashboards just like visualizations for consistency throughout the workbook: right-click on the Dashboard tab and select Duplicate. This is an extremely useful feature, which allows you to have multiple dashboards related to multiple topics while keeping the same look and feel throughout. This pairs perfectly with the Swap Sheets feature mentioned earlier: once you duplicate a dashboard, you can simply swap in a different chart.

Dashboard Actions

Tableau provides several ways to incorporate interaction within dashboards, such as controlling the data and navigating within the workbook or to another location entirely. Interactivity can make your dashboard more dynamic, more informative, and easier to use.

The Actions window appears when you select Actions from the Dashboard menu (see Figure 5-22). The window is separated into three parts. The top is a radio-button option that allows you to show actions for the whole workbook or just those related to the current dashboard. Below that is a table listing the actions added to the workbook or dashboard, including the action's name, how it is triggered, what triggers it, and what fields are involved. The last part is a pull-down menu that allows you to add an action. There are six types of actions available for dashboards.

The first action, called a *Filter action*, uses one or more fields in one chart to filter the values of fields in another chart. This type of action is the only one that has a shortcut to creation. If you select any chart in a dashboard, the icon menu that appears in the upper right corner contains a funnel (see Figure 5-23). Select it to enable the chart as a filter for other charts in the dashboard.

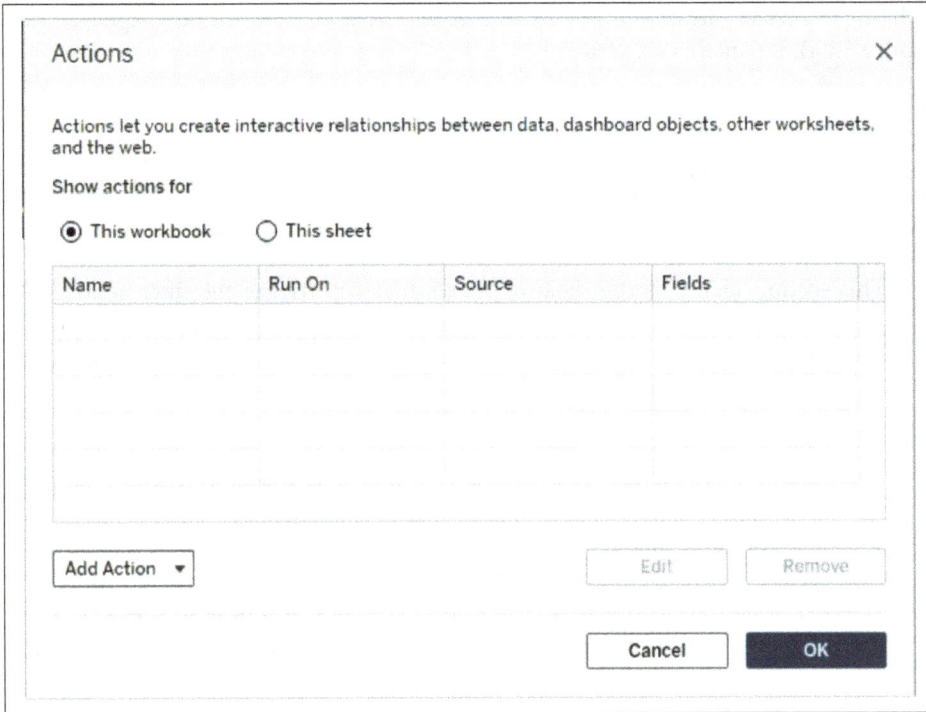

Figure 5-22. *The Actions window is available for any dashboard and contains a list of actions, as well as a pull-down to add more.*

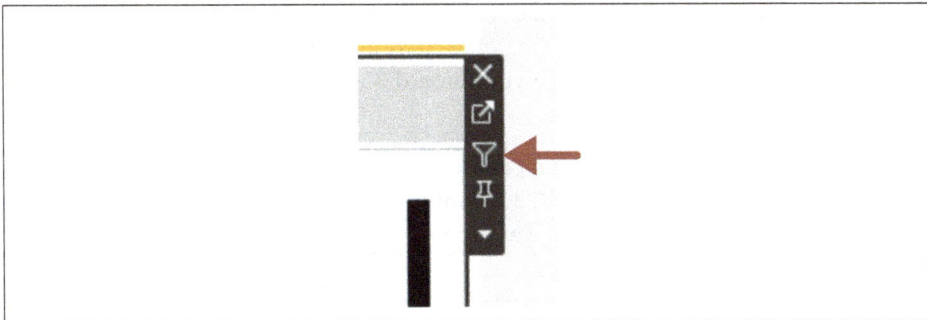

Figure 5-23. *The Filter action is visible as an icon when a chart is selected. This automatically adds a filter action to the chart that impacts the other charts on the dashboard. To edit this action, navigate to the Actions window in the Dashboard menu.*

When you select the Filter action, the Edit Filter Action window appears (see Figure 5-24). It contains six areas:

Name

> This is the name that will appear in the Actions window; label it appropriately so you can easily identify it later. It contains an Insert field that provides field values from the charts in the dashboard.

Source Sheets

> This section identifies the sheet or sheets that will trigger the filter action. The pull-down menu lists the dashboards in the workbook, and the list below that contains the sheets within the selected dashboard. A checkbox on a sheet indicates that it will trigger the filter action.

Run action on

> This indicates what triggers the action: hovering over the chart, clicking on it, or right-clicking on it to pull up a menu. The menu choice adds an option to the object's right-click menu that triggers the filter. The final checkbox indicates whether the user can select multiple parts of a chart or only one at a time. For example, if the box is unchecked, the user can click and drag to select multiple countries on a world map; if it's checked, they can only select one country at a time.

Target Sheets

> This list indicates what charts will filter based on what is selected in the source chart. The target charts do not need to be on the same dashboard as the source. You can have a chart on one dashboard trigger changes on charts in another. When the user clicks on something on a chart in dashboard A, the workbook will navigate to and filter the sheets on dashboard B.

Clearing the selection will

> These options control what happens to the target chart(s) when you deselect them: the values remain filtered, everything is shown again, or nothing is shown at all. This is a great way to hide a visualization until something is selected on a different chart.

Filter

> This table controls what will be filtered based on the selected chart. You can choose to filter everything or specific fields. For example, if the source chart has sales by year and category, you can filter a different chart by the year, the category, or both. The "Selected fields" option lets you choose a field from the source chart and a corresponding field from the target chart. Tableau will indicate if there are field availability issues with adding the filter.

Figure 5-24. The Edit Filter Action window controls what sheets have marks selected in them and which sheets are filtered by that selection.

Highlight actions are very similar to filter actions, except that they highlight target charts instead of filtering values. The Add Highlight Action window is very similar to the Edit Filter Action window (see Figure 5-25):

Name
> The top line is available to name the highlight action.

Source Sheets
> This section identifies the sheet or sheets that will trigger the highlight action.

Run action on
> This indicates how to trigger the action: hovering over the chart, clicking on it, or right-clicking it to pull up a menu. Highlight actions cannot be limited to a single selection like filter actions can.

Target Sheets
> This list indicates what charts will filter based on what is selected in the source chart.

Target Highlighting
> This area indicates which field or fields will be highlighted in the target chart based on what is selected in the source chart: all fields, fields associated with dates, or fields manually selected from an available list.

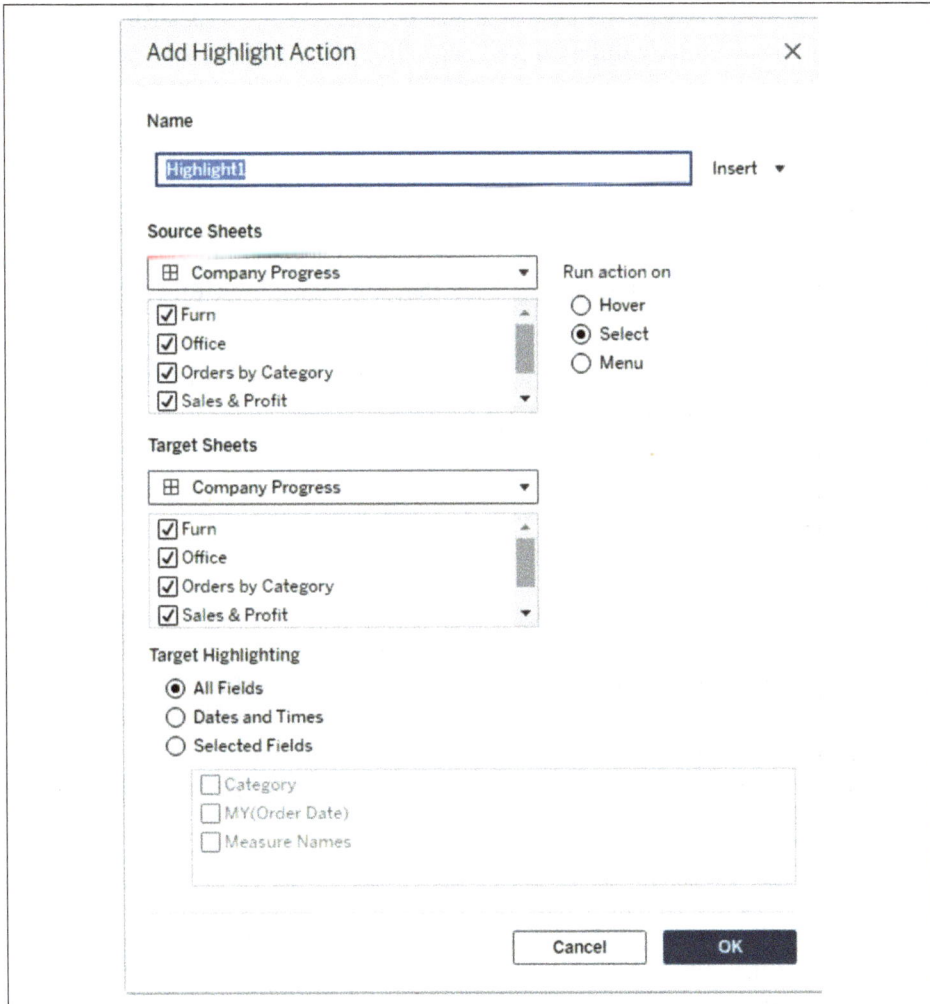

Figure 5-25. The Add Highlight Action window is similar to the filter window.

Go to URL actions navigate the user to a specific place on the web, such as another visualization or an entirely different web page altogether. URL actions can incorporate values from the data to build a dynamic URL. Everything is controlled in the Add URL Action window (see Figure 5-26):

Name

The top line is available to name the URL action.

Source Sheets

This section identifies the sheet or sheets that will trigger the URL action.

Run action on

This indicates how to trigger the action: hovering over the chart, clicking on it, or right-clicking on it to pull up a menu.

URL Target

This option controls whether the targeted URL opens in a new tab or a new browser window.

URL

This is where you enter the URL value. It can be a static web page, such as your company's homepage, or dynamic, based on the values of the data selected. The Insert menu at the end of the URL line allows you to insert fields from the data: for example, in a world map visualization, you might want the URL action to open a URL based on the country selected. You could insert the country field as part of the URL. Keep in mind that this requires the URL's syntax to match that of the values in the data!

Data Values

This section provides options for how to control data that needs encoding (due to special characters or other issues). You can also specify parameters to add to the end of the URL, which may change its destination. For example, you could send the user to a company staff listing and include a URL parameter to automatically navigate to a specific person based on the selected data value: *https:// companydirectory?name=<username>*.

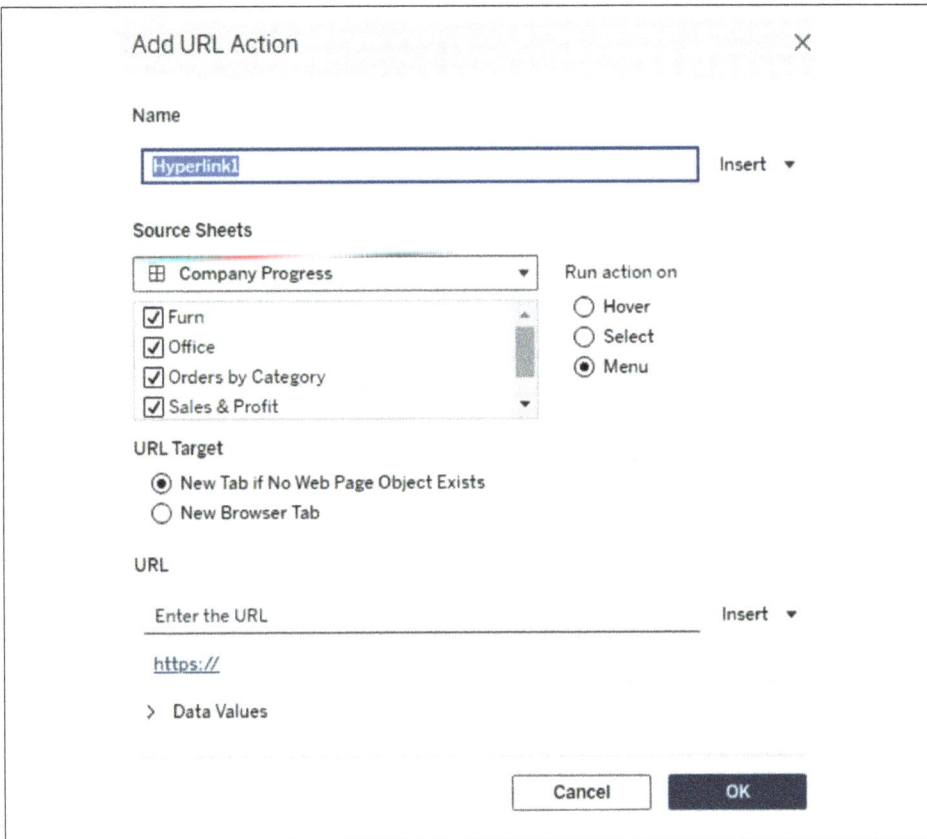

Figure 5-26. The Add URL Action window allows you to create dynamic URLs based on field values.

The next dashboard action is a navigation action that moves the user to another dashboard or visualization within the workbook. This is very similar to a filter action, except the target charts are not filtered. The Add Go to Sheet Action window is almost identical to the top half of the Edit Filter Action window (see Figure 5-27).

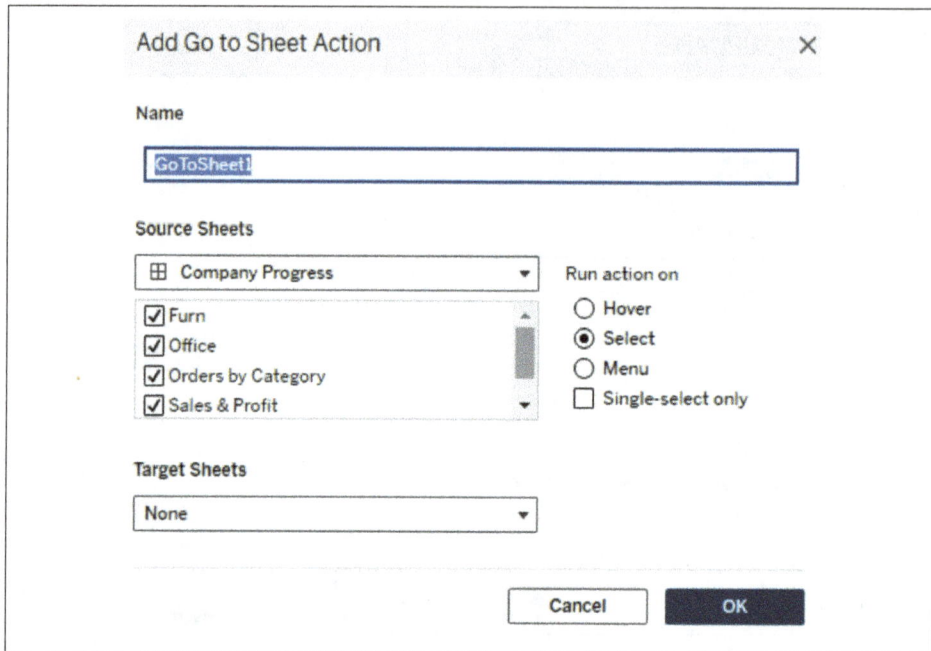

Figure 5-27. The Go to Sheet Action window adds navigation to visualizations. You can use it instead of using a navigation object in the dashboard.

The options are:

Name

    The top line is available to name the action.

Source Sheets

    This section identifies the sheet or sheets that will trigger the action.

Run action on

    This indicates how to trigger the action: hovering over the chart, clicking on it, or right-clicking to pull up a menu. The "Single-select only" option is available here.

Target Sheets

    This pull-down indicates to which dashboard or visualization the action will navigate.

Some actions, called *Parameter actions*, change the value of a parameter. The parameter must be a dynamic field or be populated with values from the selected field. Clicking on the field in the target sheet will set the parameter to this value (see Figure 5-28).

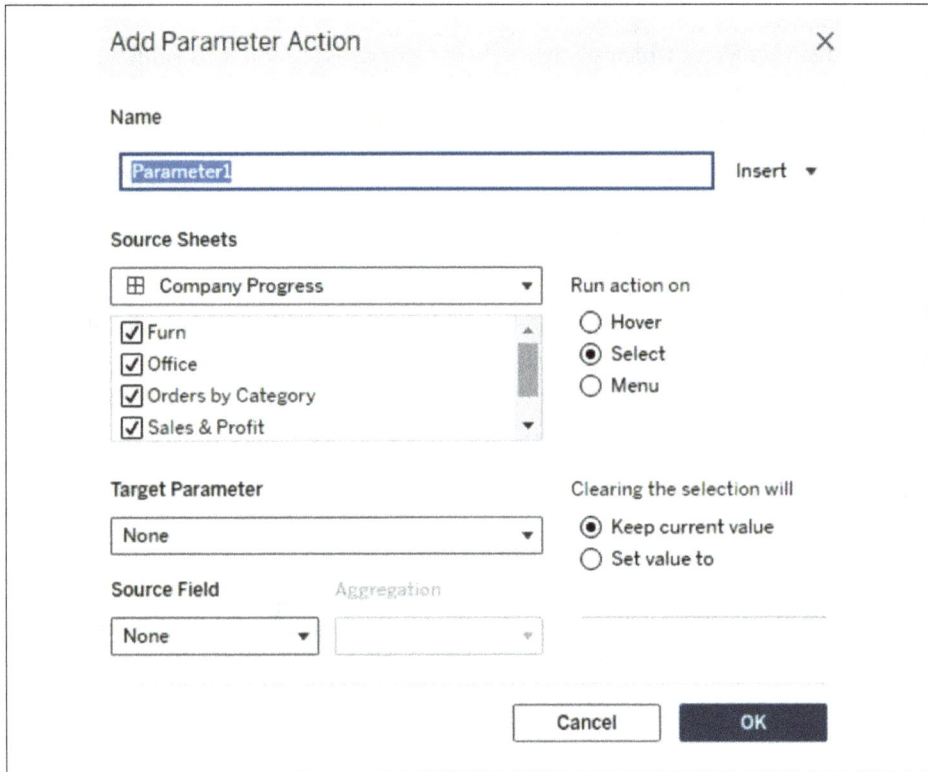

Figure 5-28. The Add Parameter Action window gives you options to change the value of a parameter based on a selected value in a chart.

Add Parameter Action window options include:

Name
> The top line is available to name the action.

Source Sheets
> This section identifies the sheet or sheets that will trigger the action.

Run action on

This indicates how to trigger the action: hovering over the chart, clicking on it, or right-clicking to pull up a menu. By default, the action *must* be single-select, because a parameter can only be one value at a time.

Target Parameter

This field indicates which parameter will be updated to the field value selected in the source chart.

Clearing the selection will

This section indicates what will happen once the source field is unselected. Does the parameter value stay the same or does it revert to a default value? If the latter, you can set the default value.

Source Field and Aggregation

This section indicates to which field in the source chart the parameter will be set. If it's a dimension, the Aggregation field will be grayed out. If it is a measure value, the Aggregation field will let you indicate the appropriate aggregation and set a dynamic integer or float parameter to a value, based on the measure selected in the source chart.

> The Add Parameter action can significantly improve performance on live data pulls. You can insert parameters into custom SQL on the Data pane. If you have an extremely large and detailed data set, you can use a smaller data set to dictate the parameter value. Then insert the parameter into a custom SQL WHERE clause for the larger data set, so it only pulls the data you need. See this Tableau hack article (*https://oreil.ly/LvaP0*) for detailed information.

The final type of dashboard action, setting actions, changes set values. You can use this action to filter or highlight, depending on how the set is implemented in the target visualizations (see Figure 5-29).

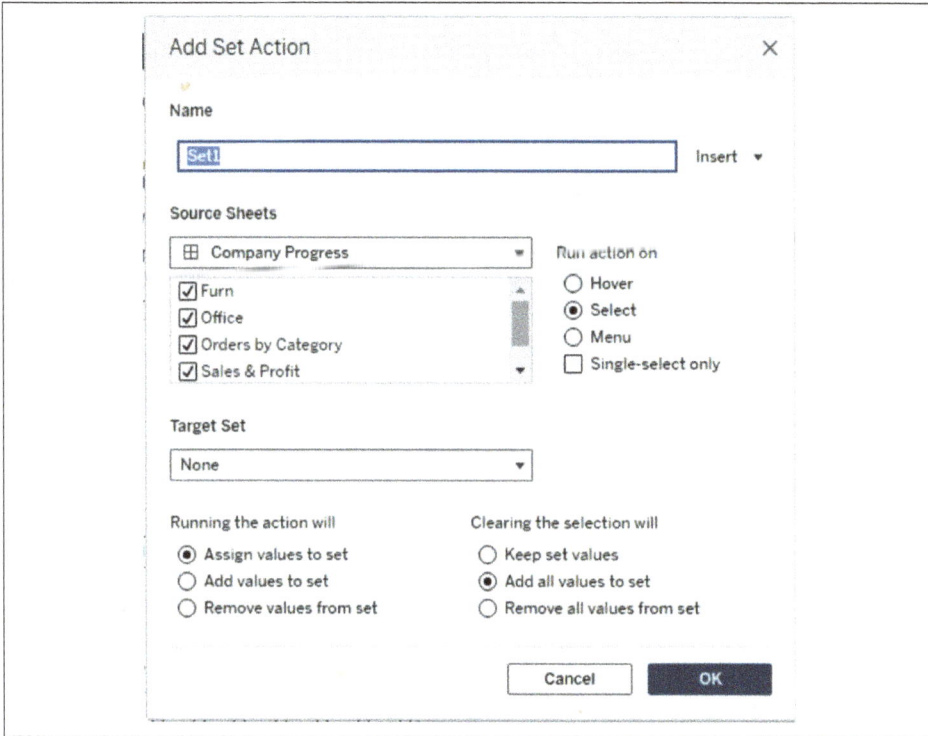

Figure 5-29. The Add Set Action window gives your users control over what values a set includes or excludes, based on what they click in a visualization.

Add Set Action window settings include:

Name
> The top line is available to name the action.

Source Sheets
> This section identifies the sheet or sheets that will trigger the action.

Run action on
> This indicates how to trigger the action: hovering over the chart, clicking on it, or right-clicking to pull up a menu. "Single-select only" is an option for sets.

Target Set
> This field indicates which set will be updated based on the values selected in the source chart.

Running the action will
> This section controls whether the set will assign, add, or remove values to or from the set, based on what is selected in the target sheet.

Clearing the selection will

> This section indicates what will happen once the source field is unselected. The set can keep the values, add them back to the set, or remove everything from the set entirely.

Example Question

What are two ways to provide navigation on a dashboard? Select two.

A. Navigation objects

B. Images

C. Dashboard actions

D. Text

E. User controls

Answers: A and C—Navigation is available via an image or text navigation button. It can also be added to a visualization through dashboard actions.

Tableau provides a wide range of tools and objects to provide end users with insights in a well-aligned, easy to read, accessible format. Dashboard objects provide structure, imagery, and navigation to lay out collections of data visualizations intuitively. Dashboard actions insert interactivity to help users navigate the data and derive additional information. Used together, these features create powerful dashboards that combine multiple visualizations to form a cohesive palette of insights.

> Questions about building a dashboard in Tableau may appear on the exam. There may also be questions about how actions work and how to configure them. Familiarize yourself with building basic layouts and adding interactivity to prepare for the exam.

Stories

In addition to dashboards, Tableau provides another way to display multiple charts: stories. A *story* is a slideshow presentation of dashboards or visualizations used to walk an audience through an analysis, much like a slideshow. When you add visualizations to a story, their legends, filters, and parameters come with them so that each visualization maintains its interactivity. Alternatively, a single chart can be added to multiple pages of a story with different selections. This can be used to highlight key values, explain trends, or further aid in the storytelling process.

To create a story, use the New Story button ( ) at the bottom of the Tableau window. The Story interface provides two main areas: the Story pane on the left and the design interface on the right. The Story pane has two tabs, Story and Layout (see Figure 5-30).

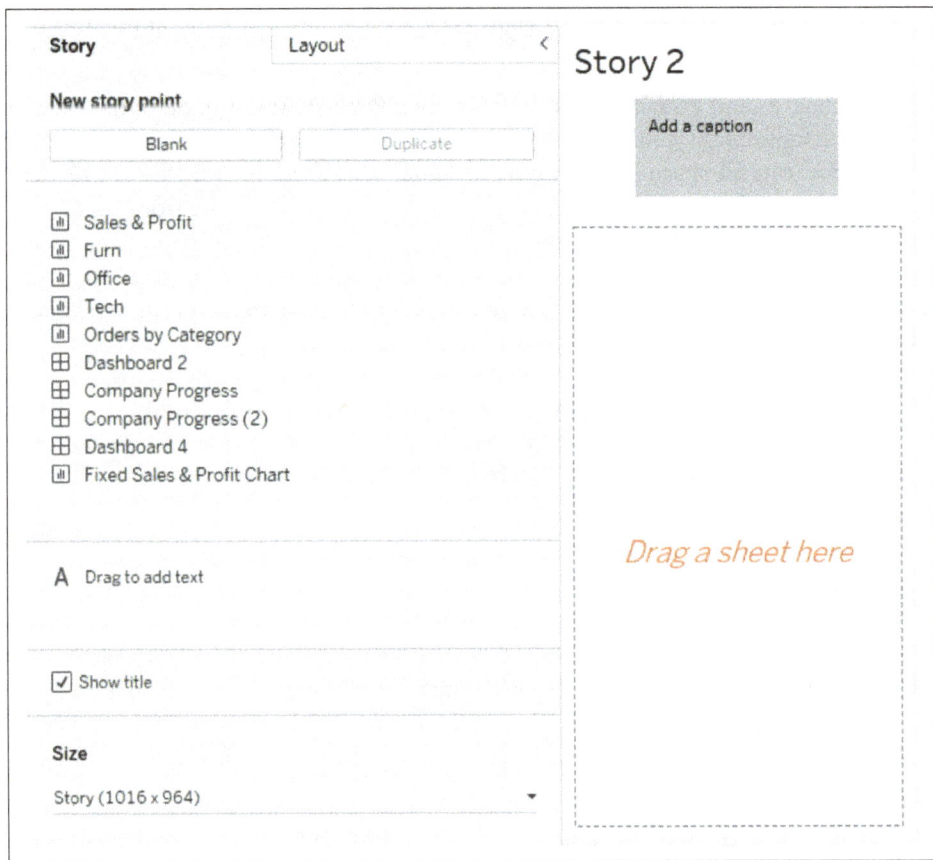

Figure 5-30. The New Story layout contains a control panel to the left and the story to the right.

The options at the top of the Story tab let you add additional slides called *story points*. These can be blank or duplicates of the current page. Below this is a panel that holds all of the workbook's dashboards and visualizations, which you can drag and drop to add to the story just as you'd add them to the dashboard. There is also an option to drag text to the visualization, add a title, and adjust the layout size of the story overall.

The Layout tab is much simpler, with four options to modify the navigation: "Caption boxes," "Numbers," "Dots," and "Arrows only." *Caption boxes* create boxes for a description of each story point at the top of the page. *Numbers* provides a numbered box for each story point. The *Dots* option replaces the numbers with small dots. Each of the previous three choices has an option to include left and right navigation arrows on either end of the page list. The final navigation style is to *only* show these navigation arrows.

Each story page can be interactive, with filters and parameters, or it can highlight a portion of the chart. You can also right-click to add story-specific annotations to charts.

Like dashboards and visualizations, stories have a Format Story option in the Format menu with options to control background color, title, navigation objects, and text objects. You can fill space by setting the original visualization to fit the entire view. Dashboards are shown at their default size—if they don't fit on the story point, you will have to change the size of either the story or the dashboard. However, once a story exists, dashboards created within the same workbook can be sized to fit the dimensions of the story. The option appears under the Size menu on the Dashboard tab when building a dashboard.

> Stories aren't always part of the exam, but it's important to be familiar with them. A story is an excellent way to present insights through a slideshow-like presentation of visualizations.

Conclusion

Dashboards and stories combine your data visualizations to draw insights together or tell a story. Building a dashboard, like building a visualization, is part science and part art. You need to prepare your layout carefully to ensure that users can see everything and feel the full impact of the visualization. Interactions let you provide end users with ways to explore the data on their own.

Most importantly, design with your audience in mind, and include accessible options for those users with vision impairments. Dashboard design and story building are key ways to guide your user from exploring visualizations to reaching an insight, and both are valuable tools for data analysts' tool belts.

CHAPTER 6

Distributing and Sharing Your Visualizations

When I publish workbooks or data sources for my job, I have to keep a great many things in mind. I need to determine where the files will be located on the server, who can access them, and how I'll keep them up to date. I need to ensure that my filters, parameters, and configurations default to appropriate values and that nothing is preselected that might cause confusion. If you plan to publish your Tableau creations, you'll need to think about these key concepts too, and they're likely to appear on the certification exam. This chapter deals with managing published Tableau workbooks and visualizations on servers, including permissions and user-based controls.

Publishing to Server or Cloud

There are multiple things you can publish in Tableau Desktop and Tableau Prep, including workbooks, data sources, and data flows. The available options depend on what you are publishing and to what type of server. This section will help you understand why you would publish each of these, and what options are available when you do.

Tableau provides three places where you can publish a dashboard:

Tableau Public
> Tableau Public is an open online server where thousands of users share visualizations and dashboards, making them publicly available to anyone visiting the site. You cannot publish flows to Tableau Public.

Tableau Cloud

Some organizations elect to have Tableau manage their Tableau server's infrastructure and maintenance, and this service is called Tableau Cloud. To publish to it, select Tableau Cloud as your publish location.

Organizational Tableau server

Many organizations choose to host their own Tableau server, managing and maintaining its build, upgrades, security, and stability. You will need to contact your organization's Tableau server administrator to acquire the server path.

When I refer to *Tableau server* in this chapter, I am referring to both Tableau Cloud (in the cloud) and organizational servers (on prem); Tableau Public is somewhat different because it's publicly accessible.

Whatever and wherever you publish, you need to start in the Server menu. In both Tableau Desktop and Tableau Prep Builder, the Server menu holds settings for connecting to Tableau Cloud or your organization's Tableau server (see Figure 6-1). If you are not currently logged in to a server or cloud, the first option will be Sign In. If you choose it, a window will appear prompting you to enter the server path. Below that field is a hyperlink to connect to Tableau Cloud instead.

If you are already logged into your organization's Tableau server or Tableau Cloud, the first option will be "Signed In to" followed by your server's information, including the site on the specific server. Once you are signed in, a submenu becomes available that allows you to log into a different server, a different site, or log out.

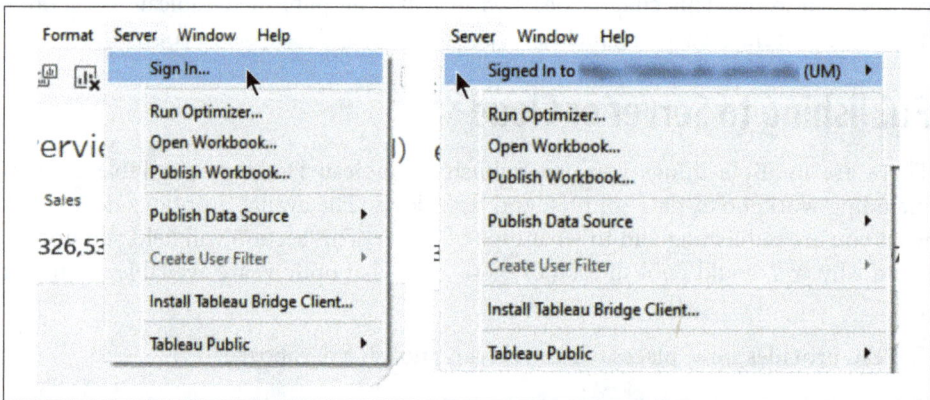

Figure 6-1. The Server menu will show Sign In (left) if you are not authenticated to a server or "Signed In to" (right) if you are already authenticated. If you are authenticated to a server, a submenu allows you to sign in to another server, select a different site on the server, or sign out.

The sign-in process for both cloud and organizational servers can vary greatly, so it's unlikely to appear on the exam. When preparing to publish within your organization, contact your server administrator for assistance with the authentication process.

Once you sign into your Tableau server or Tableau Cloud, you may be prompted to identify the site on which you wish to publish. A *site* in this context is simply a division of a Tableau server; these divisions are designed to work independently from each other. Once you select a site, the server menu and any pop-up windows close. There is no indication that you are connected to the server, so to verify that you are connected, click on the Server menu again to see if the server now appears in the menu shown in Figure 6-1.

Once you are connected to the server, you can publish data flows, data sets, and workbooks. Each item has its own steps and options.

Example Question

Which three locations are potentially available for publishing content? Select three.

A. Tableau Cloud

B. Tableau Web

C. Organizational Tableau server

D. Tableau Share

E. Tableau Public

Answers: A, C, and E

Publishing Data Flows

Once you build a data flow in Tableau Prep Builder and publish it on a Tableau server, you can schedule it to run at regularly scheduled intervals to keep the data accurate and up to date. Keep in mind that you can publish a flow itself or the *output* of a flow. These are two different things, and one is dependent on the other.

When you publish the output of a flow to Tableau server, you are publishing a data set. To do this, you need to add an output step that tells the flow what to do with the data once it is combined and cleaned. At the tail end of any flow, click the plus symbol and choose Output (see Figure 6-2). This will open a side panel to the left of the data preview that contains several options, based on the destination you select (see Figure 6-3).

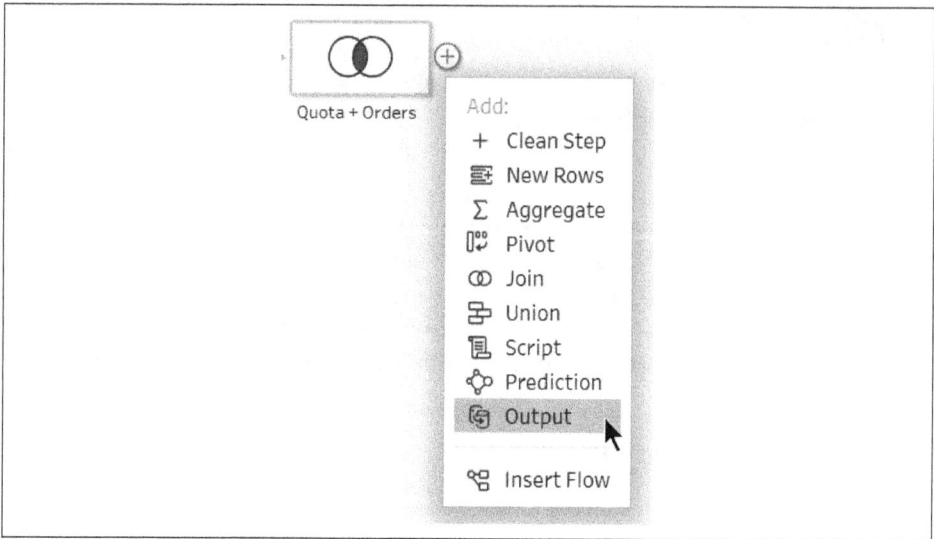

Figure 6-2. Adding an output step to the end of your flow.

Figure 6-3. When you add an output step to a flow, a side panel appears, providing options for how to manage the output.

The "Save output to" pull-down menu allows you to choose where to send the data the flow outputs: a file, a published data source, or a database or data cloud. Several of these choices provide pull-down menus that let you switch between a full refresh and an incremental refresh:

File
> This option will prompt you to provide a location and a filename for the file. You can also choose to save the file in Excel, CSV, or Hyper file format. If you choose this option and wish to publish the flow to your server, make sure the server account can access the destination file location.

Publish data source
> If you choose the "Publish data source" option, Tableau's menu will populate with the server identified in the Server menu at the top. Choose a title and a location for the data set to reside. This is the option you will likely choose if you want your flow to run on the server to create an accessible data source.

Database and Cloud Storage
> This option requires you to provide a database connection (such as an Oracle or MySQL database) to write back to.

CRM Analytics/Salesforce Data Cloud
> The final two options require a Salesforce installation. You will need to work with your Salesforce administrator to determine the correct settings and permissions to enable these options.

To use some of these options, you will need to coordinate with your Tableau server administrator, your database administrator, or other local IT. For the flow to run successfully, the output step must be accessible to the Tableau server. For instance, you cannot publish a flow that saves the output to your desktop, as the Tableau server likely doesn't have access to write to your personal computer. Likewise, you will need permission to write to a database if you choose the Database and Cloud Storage output option.

Once you confirm the output, you are ready to publish the flow. When you click the Publish button at the top right of the application, the Publish Flow to Tableau Server window appears (see Figure 6-4).

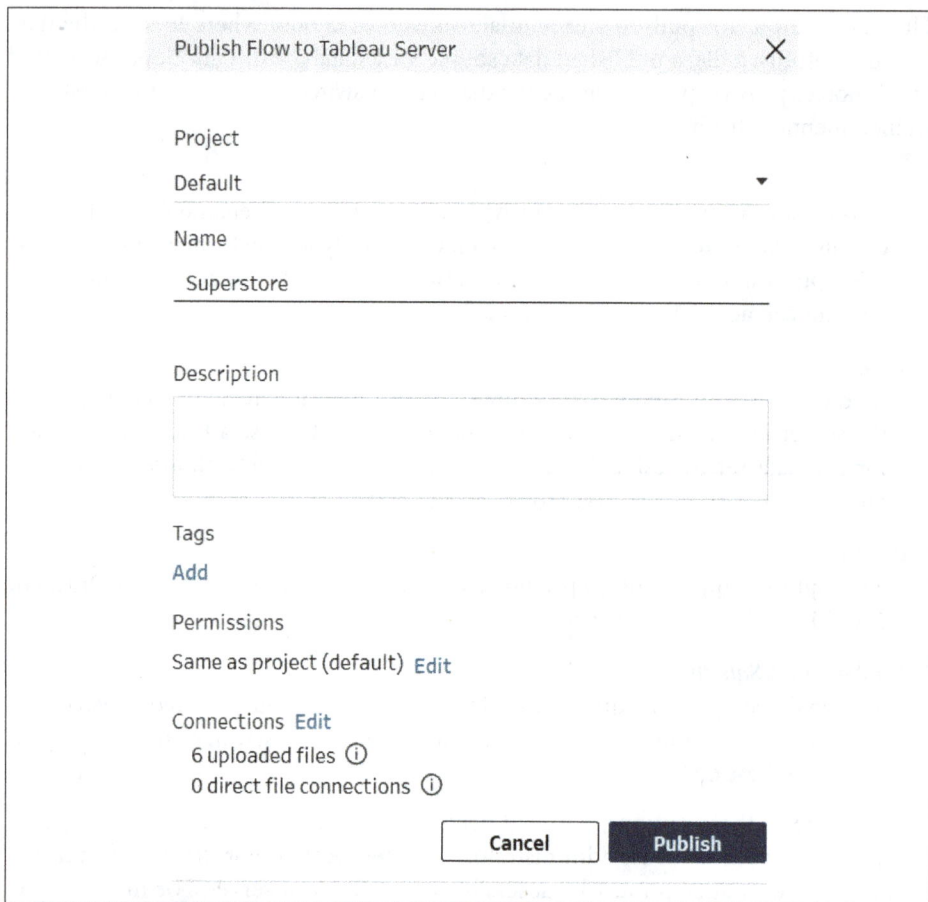

Figure 6-4. The Publish Flow window.

This window has five options:

Project
> This option allows you to choose a project location for your flow. A project on a Tableau server is like a folder: it's a repository for published workbooks, data sources, and flows, and it can contain nested project folders.

Description
> This field holds a description of the flow that will appear once it is published on the server.

Tags
> This field holds keywords to help users search for the data flow.

Permissions

This section allows you to adjust access to the flow on your Tableau server (if applicable). The flow's permissions default to the project permissions, but they can be changed if the project permissions allow for independent grants (see the section "Managing Server Permissions and Access" on page 267).

Connections

The Connections section lists the data sources used to create the data flow—and, more importantly, controls stored permissions for those data sources so the server can authenticate to them during a refresh.

When you click Publish, the flow is copied over to the Tableau server, and a web browser opens and displays the published flow. From here, you can run the flow manually or schedule it to run automatically. You can also update the description, tags, and permissions. You can use a flow Tableau server to pull data in, clean it, and generate a published data source.

Publishing Data Sources

Even if you can't use Prep Builder to make data sets, you can still use Tableau Desktop to publish data sources to the server. Published data sets take a regular data connection in Tableau Desktop and push it to the server. There are many reasons why you would do this, including:

Speed

The Tableau server probably has more processing capacity than your personal desktop, so data refreshes and functions within workbooks faster than with an embedded data source.

Timeliness

You can schedule refreshes for data sources on Tableau server, so each time you connect, the data will already be up to date. Embedded data sources require you to refresh manually.

Sharing

Published data sources can be used in numerous workbooks, not just your own. If you build a data source that has valuable information, others can connect to it and use it to build their own visualizations. The shared data source only needs to be updated once, as opposed to multiple separate embedded data sources (see Figure 6-5).

Familiarity

In Tableau Desktop, you can create calculations and change field names and dimension values to make the data source use recognizable business language. This can help users who are less familiar with the data.

Certified

You can validate data source values prior to publishing. If the pull is structured correctly and updated consistently, you may want to mark it as certified. This indicates to other users that the data contained within is accurate.

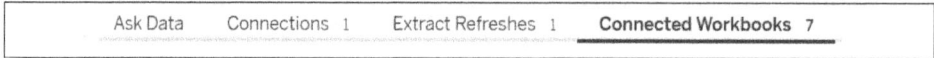

Ask Data	Connections 1	Extract Refreshes 1	**Connected Workbooks 7**

Figure 6-5. You can easily see how many workbooks utilize a data source by navigating to it on Tableau Server.

When you are ready to publish a data set in Tableau Desktop:

1. In the Server menu at the top of the application, verify that you are connected to the correct Tableau server on the correct Tableau site. They should be listed at the very top of the menu.

2. While in the menu, click on Publish Data Source.

3. Click on the name of the data source you wish to publish.

These steps will open the "Publish Data Source to Tableau Server" window (see Figure 6-6), which has seven parts and is similar to the "Publish Flow to Tableau Server" window. Depending on your data source, you may be prompted to authenticate before the window appears:

Location

This option allows you to choose a project location for your data source.

Name

The name field is how your data source will appear to others on Tableau Server. The name should be intuitive and clearly describe the data.

Description

The description field allows you to provide a description to clarify what the published data set contains.

Tags

The fields entered in this area provide keywords that can be used to make searching for the data set easier.

Permissions

This section allows you to adjust access to the data set on Tableau server (if applicable). These permissions default to the project permissions, but can be changed if permissions allow for independent grants.

More Options

There are two checkboxes within this section. "Include external files" will copy files related to the data source across to the server. For example, if you are pulling from Excel, this option will create a replica of the Excel file on the Tableau server. The second option, "Update workbook to use the published data source," will switch your current workbook to use the published data source once it is on the server. Your current connection to the data, regardless of where it is, will be replaced by the version on the Tableau server.

Workbook Optimizer

This tool is included when you publish data sets or dashboards; it looks through the workbook and identifies unused data sources or data fields. It will also suggest ways to improve performance, like replacing a live connection with an extract.

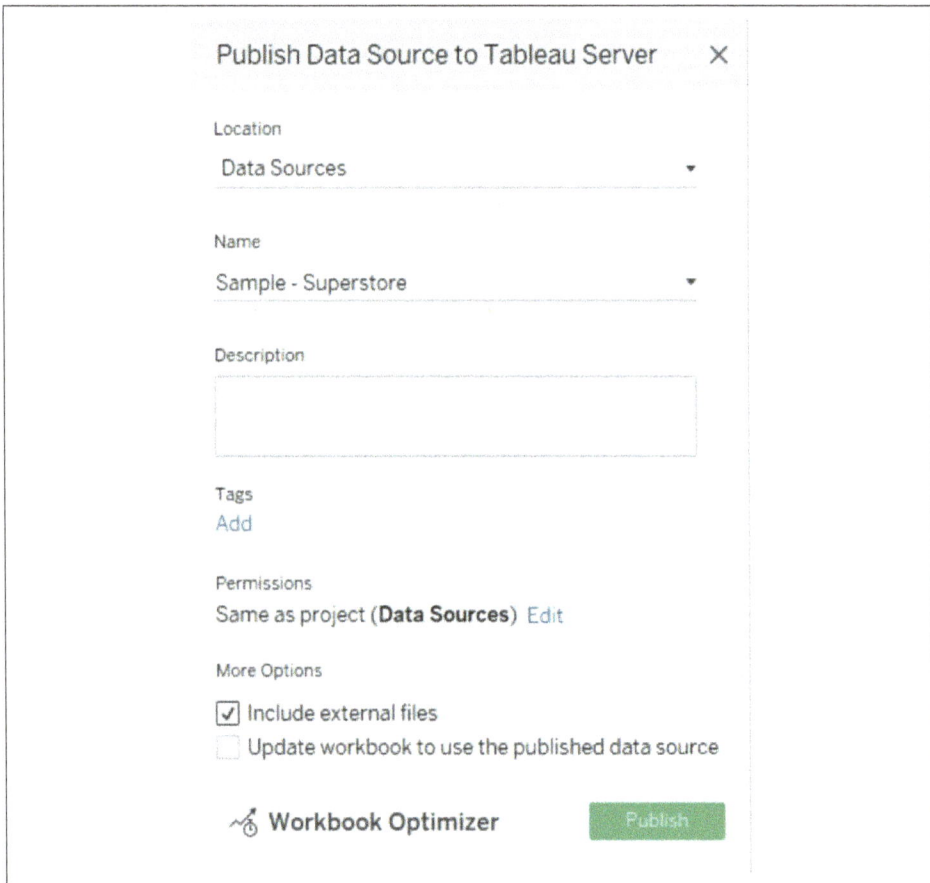

Figure 6-6. The Publish Data Source to Tableau Server window.

Clicking the Publish button copies the data source up to your Tableau server and makes it available for connections, so you can use the data to build visualizations and dashboards.

When you work with published data sets, you have to be careful. Tableau copies *everything*, including calculations and parameters. This can be extremely beneficial if you develop a calculation that others can use, but it can also be confusing if some calculations and fields are specific to your area. The nice thing about published data sets is that users can create calculations on top of them that are specific to that user's workbook and won't show up for other users connecting to that data set.

One caveat: published data sources are *locked*. Once a data set is published, you cannot change its calculations. The only way to update it is to open a workbook connected to the same data, create the new calculation, and republish the data set. For this reason, it is often advisable to keep your source workbook pointing at the original data location to keep it local and editable. You can then build visualizations in a separate workbook connected to the published data source.

If you ever need to edit a published data source, open a workbook and connect to the published data source. Then right-click on the data source and choose Create Local Copy (see Figure 6-7). You may be required to authenticate to the copied data source, because these steps pull down the published data source and extract the connections used to build it.

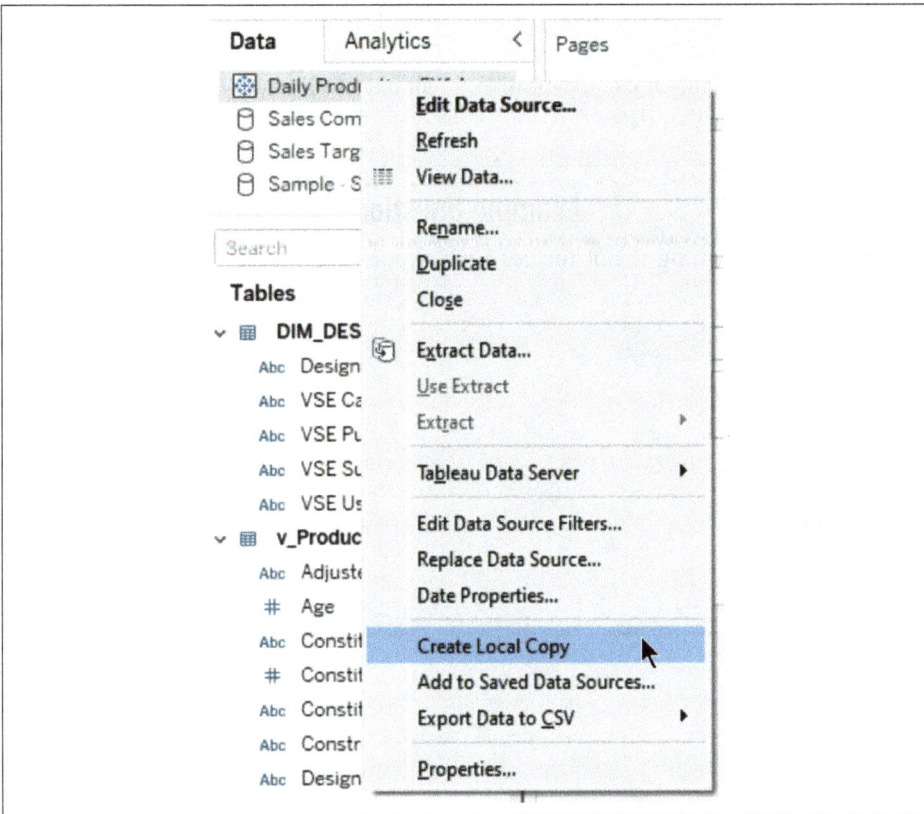

Figure 6-7. You can edit a published data source by creating a local copy, making changes, and republishing the data source.

For example, assume you connect to a published data source that's pulling from Oracle. When you create a local copy in Tableau Desktop, it creates a separate data source pointing at the original Oracle location. You will have to log into Oracle to verify your permission to access that data.

Example Question

Which of the following is not included when publishing a data source to Tableau Server?

A. Fields

B. Calculations

C. Parameters

D. Visualizations

E. Groups/Sets

Answer: D—Published data sets include everything within the data, but not any visualizations created within that workbook.

Publishing Workbooks

Data flows and data sets all support your workbooks, which hold your visualizations and dashboards. These workbooks are the heart of Tableau, and they are the key way to share data insights with your users. Therefore, when you publish a workbook to Tableau server, you want it to be as accurate, secure, and well designed as possible. You will need to verify a wide list of options and settings to ensure that what you publish is what your end users see. In the server menu, verify that you are connected to the correct Tableau server on the correct Tableau site. They should be listed at the very top of the menu. Click on Publish Workbook (see Figure 6-8).

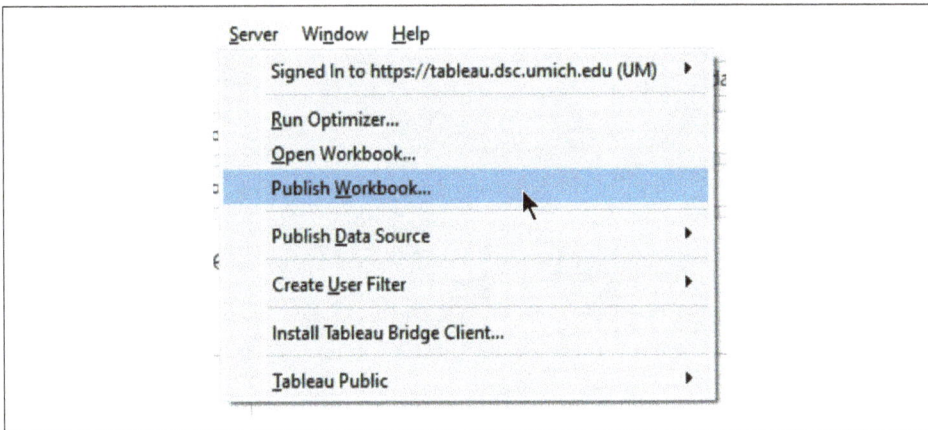

Figure 6-8. When publishing a workbook to the server, verify that you are signed into your server by reviewing the top option in the server menu and then choose Publish Workbook.

The Publish Workbook to Tableau Server window has similar options to data sources, including fields for the name, project, description, tags, and permissions (see Figure 6-9). There are a few new options that you need to verify as well, because workbooks can contain multiple visualizations or data sources, and you need to decide which ones to publish.

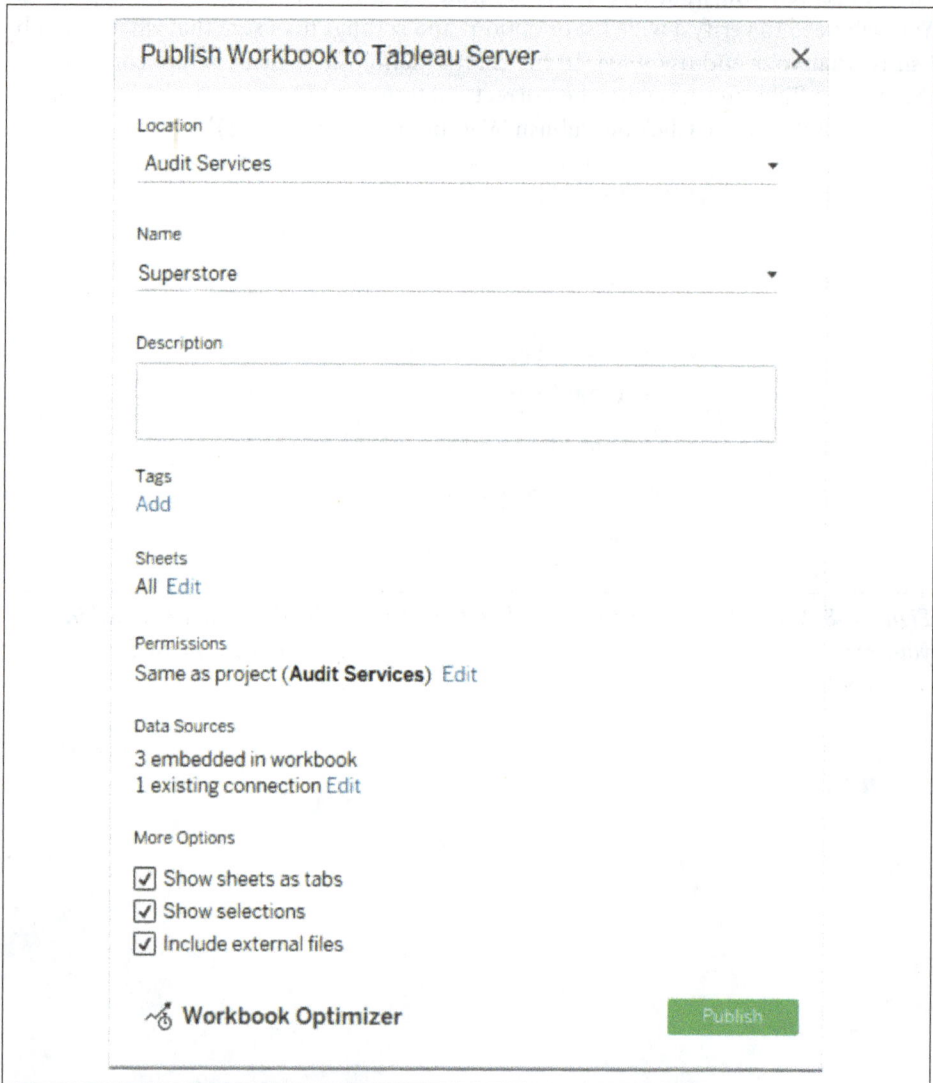

Figure 6-9. *The Publish Workbook window.*

The options include:

Location

This option allows you to choose a project location for your workbook.

Name

The name field is how your workbook will appear to others on Tableau Server; it should be intuitive and clearly describe the visualizations within.

Description

The description field allows you to provide details on the visualizations and information in the workbook.

Tags

The fields entered in this area provide keywords that can be used to make searching for the workbook easier.

Sheets

The Sheets section allows you to pick and choose which visualizations or dashboards to publish. If you publish visualizations outside of dashboards, any filters and legends visible on that tab will also be visible when published.

Permissions

This section allows you to adjust access to the workbook on Tableau Server (if applicable). The permissions are automatically set to the project's default workbook permissions, but can be changed if permissions allow for independent grants.

Data Sources

This section contains pieces of information about your data source(s) that you need to review. First, it gives the number of data sources, split into two categories: published and embedded. When you click the Edit link within this section, you are prompted with options to embed credentials for the data source before publishing. This setting can be slightly different depending on the data source type. If you do not embed credentials, your end users will be prompted to provide their own when they attempt to access your workbook.

More Options

There are three very important checkboxes within this section. "Show sheets as tabs" will make each dashboard or visualization its own tab at the top of the page when published. This allows for easier navigation and rolls up the security to the workbook level. The second option, "Show selections," keeps any highlighted items highlighted when the workbook is published. For example, if you click on a bar in a chart to highlight it, this option will highlight that bar by default whenever anyone visits the visualization. The final option, "Include external files," copies any local files used to build the workbook up to the Tableau server. This includes data source files, like Excel or CSV, as well as any image files.

> If you turn off tabs on a workbook when you publish it, the permissions for the workbook are applied at the view level. Each view will have its own permissions rather than inheriting those of the workbook. Disabling tabs is most commonly used when embedding a visualization in a website.

Workbook Optimizer

The optimizer looks through the workbook and identifies unused data sources or data fields. It will also suggest ways to make it perform better, like replacing a live connection with an extract.

Show thumbnails as

This option only appears if the workbook contains calculations involving the logged-in user. For example, if a visualization's appearance changes depending on who is logged in, you need to identify a default user to generate the thumbnail.

Once you have everything configured, click the Publish button. Tableau Desktop will push the workbook to the Tableau server, open a browser window, and automatically navigate to the newly published dashboard. At this point, you can adjust permissions and add a refresh schedule (these will be covered in more detail later in this chapter).

Example Question

What information is *not* required when connecting to a Tableau server? Select two.

A. Server path

B. Server role

C. Credentials

D. Site

E. Project

Answers: B and E

Managing Workbooks on the Server

Once the workbook is on the server, you can manage several aspects of how it works using that workbook's pull-down menu (see Figure 6-10). There are options to set tags, add a description, or rename the workbook.

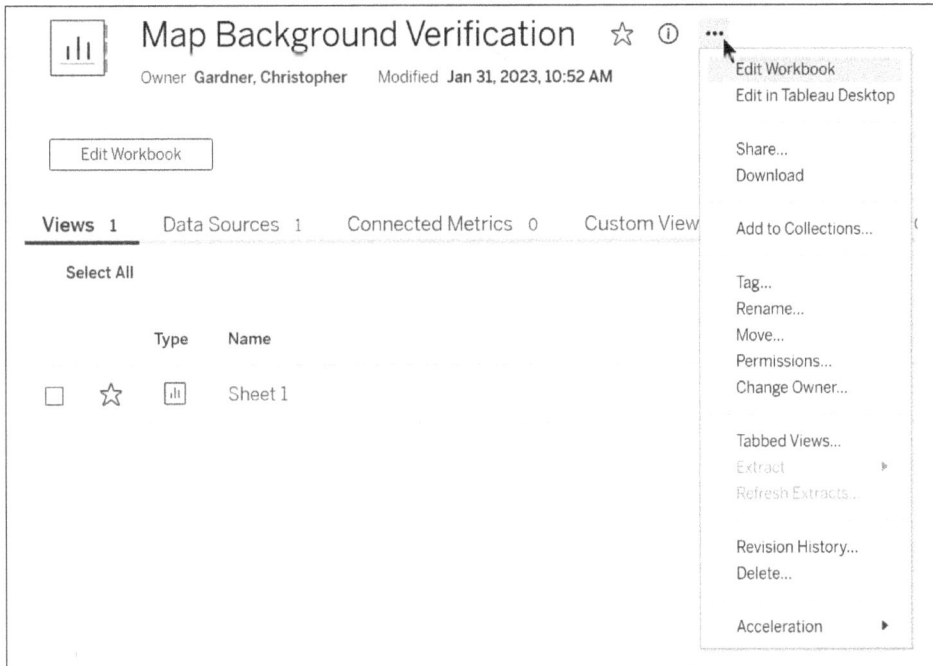

Figure 6-10. The Workbook menu on Tableau Server can be accessed via the ellipsis next to the workbook name while viewing the list of workbooks in a project or next to the title after navigating to the workbook itself.

There are also additional options related to how the workbook is displayed and how data is refreshed:

Edit Workbook/Edit in Tableau Desktop
> The first options in the menu allow you to modify the workbook online or pull the file down locally to modify it in Tableau Desktop. Online workbook editing is very similar in appearance and capabilities to Tableau Desktop.

Share
> The Share option allows you to copy the workbook's URL to share with users via email or chat. It also offers a list of available users on your server, from which you can select someone to share your workbook with. You can include an optional message. When you share in this way, the end user receives an email with a snapshot image of one of the visualizations and a link to the published workbook.

Download

This option allows you to download a copy of the workbook. The workbook is saved as a packaged workbook (*.twbx*) file at the same version as the Tableau server.

Add to Collections

This option allows you to create a collection of workbooks related to you or to a specific topic. Collections shows lists of user-created collections to explore.

Tag/Rename

These two options are the server-based method for applying tags or renaming the workbook, similar to those in the Publish Workbook to Server window.

Move

This option allows you to move the workbook to another project on the same site on the server.

Permissions

This area of the menu controls permissions on the workbook itself (see the section "Managing Server Permissions and Access" on page 267).

Change Owner

When you publish a workbook to your Tableau server, you are its owner by default. The Change Owner option allows you to change the owner of the workbook to another user. Owners have administrative-level permissions to the workbook and must have publisher permission on the server.

Tabbed Views

This option enables or disables tabs. If you enable tabs when you publish a workbook, Tableau creates a tab at the top of the window for each published dashboard and visualization so users can quickly navigate from dashboard to dashboard. You may want to disable tabs if you intend to embed the dashboard or visualization in a webpage.

Refresh Extracts

If your workbook pulls data via an extract, this option provides options for scheduling refreshes. There are also options to run the extract on demand and toggle between a full and incremental refresh.

Revision History

The revision history keeps track of all changes to the workbook and allows you to preview, download or delete older versions. This is a valuable tool if something goes wrong with your local file.

Delete

This option removes the workbook from the server.

The refresh schedule is extremely important if your workbook uses extracted data sources. It gives you options for how often and how much of your data to refresh. Schedules are controlled by the server administrator, and it's easy to add more. Extracts can be set to refresh all rows in the data (a *full refresh*) or only rows where a specific field value has changed (an *incremental refresh*). Incremental refreshes are only available if you configured them as part of the original extract in Tableau Desktop or Tableau Prep (discussed in Chapter 1).

Example Question

When you create a workbook using extracted data and publish it to a server, what server tool is used to keep that data up to date?

A. Extract schedule

B. Refresh permissions

C. Published data sets

D. Virtual connections

E. Data flows

Answer: A—Extract schedules control the frequency that updated data is pulled into data extracts.

Managing Server Permissions and Access

When you have a workbook published to a server, your primary concern should be who has access to it. Tableau applies server security at many levels, and all of them work together to control who has access and to what actions. Tableau server provides an interface where you can check and verify access rights for any given individual. You can also identify access grants based on group memberships.

Understanding Tableau Server Structure

Before we dig into Tableau security, it's important to understand its structure and nomenclature. The components of Tableau security include:

Site

Sites are divisions of the Tableau server. They are designed to create independent, unrelated sections for separate units on a single server. Each site is completely independent of the others. Adding a user or group to one site does *not* add them to any other site.

Project

Projects are subfolders of a site that can be nested within each other. These are owned by a single individual and control some degree of access to the contents within. They can be locked or open (defined later in this section). Projects divide sites into smaller sections. They differ from sites in that they share users and groups with other projects on the same site. They contain content such as published data sources, flows, and workbooks.

Workbook

This is a collection of dashboards (views) published to the Tableau server.

View

A *view* is the collective term for any dashboard or independent visualization published to Tableau Server.

A basic Tableau server is divided into one or more sites, each of which contains any number of projects, which can be considered folders. They are containers for the content within the site. They can also nest within other projects. Within workbooks, there are views, which, as mentioned previously, can be dashboards or independent visualizations.

The server configuration controls how users and groups are added to the Tableau server. For the exam, it's more important to understand that users can be added independently *or* as part of a group or groups. Both groups and users can be granted access to the server.

Finally, Tableau Server has *schedules:* time slots when various actions occur on the server with any degree of frequency, from hourly to monthly. The server administrator sets schedules based on usage and demand. There are three types of outward-facing server schedules:

Data Extract Refresh

This is usually the most common scheduled action on Tableau Server. Any workbook or data source added to an extract schedule will refresh its data at the given time slot.

Data Flow

This schedule controls when flows created in Tableau Prep run.

Subscriptions

If users want to see your visualizations at regularly scheduled intervals, they can subscribe. *Subscriptions* email the user a screenshot and a link to the workbook so they can quickly preview the data in the report and visit the workbook if they have additional questions.

Tableau Server administrators monitor schedules for potential issues. Often, the problems that arise with data source extracts and data flows are related to changes in the permissions, firewall, or underlying data. Content owners are notified if one of their scheduled items fails for any reason.

The Layers of Permissions

Tableau security is complex and sometimes tricky to understand; however, that very complexity is what lets Tableau grant or deny permissions at multiple degrees of granularity. The levels of security are shown in Figure 6-11.

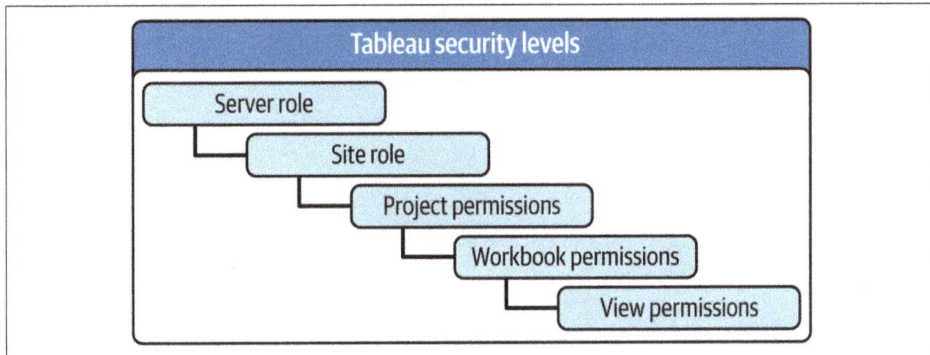

Figure 6-11. The hierarchy of Tableau security roles and permissions.

There are several roles available for granting permissions, and several permission areas that can be granted to those roles. *Roles* dictate what types of permissions a user can have at the project, workbook, and view levels, while the permissions themselves control what the user can do within a project, workbook, or view. For example, a user with the Explorer role can view workbooks and filter and download data, but cannot publish workbooks to the server.

To complicate things, recall that users who publish workbooks to the server are made *owners* of those workbooks—and ownership overrides granted permissions. The same applies to *project owners*. *Site administrators* can interact with any project, workbook, or data source published on their site, and *server administrators* can view everything across all sites and projects.

> Server administrators only apply to Tableau Server, not Tableau Cloud. Tableau Cloud is managed and maintained by Tableau.

For all users, permissions start very broad and get more granular, as seen in Figure 6-11. At the top is the Server Role. Since servers can have multiple sites, the only real role at the server level is the administrator. They are responsible for managing and maintaining all content across all sites and projects.

The next most granular role is at the site level. Site Roles control the top-level access that anyone can have on a Tableau site, and can be granted using the ellipsis next to any username (see Figure 6-12). Clicking this option will open the Site Role window (see Figure 6-13), which has a single pull-down menu that allows you to change the user's role on the site.

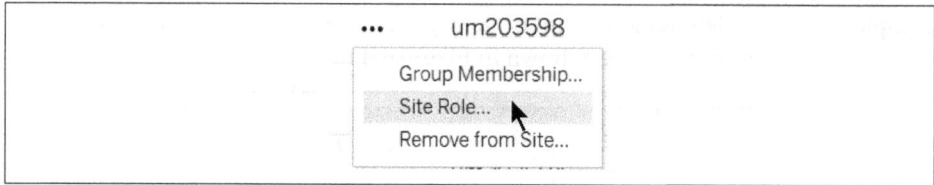

Figure 6-12. The Site Role window can be accessed via the ellipsis menu next to any username on the server.

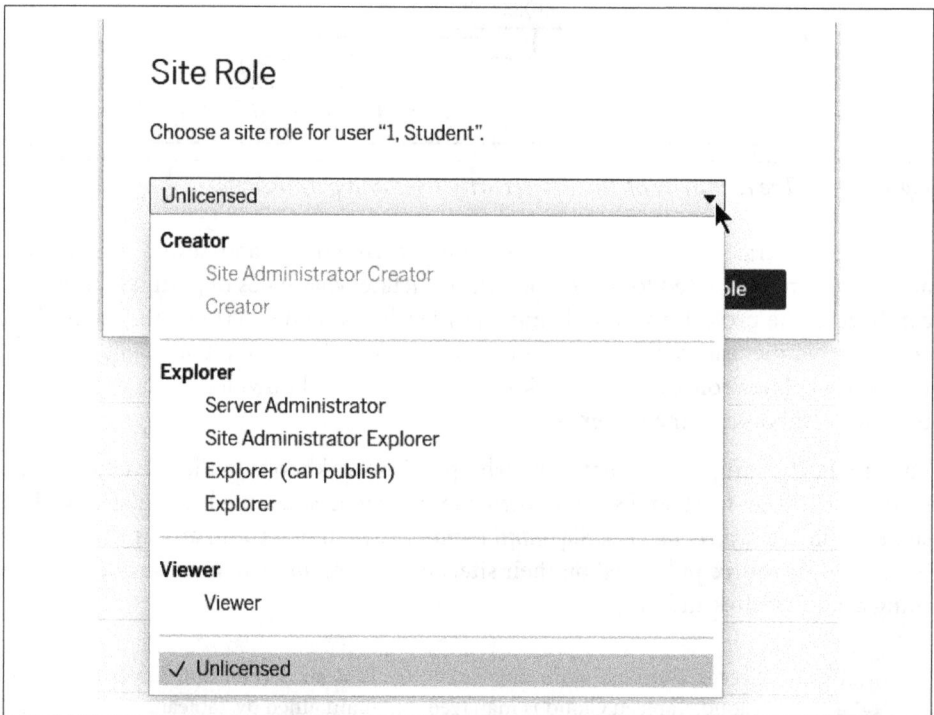

Figure 6-13. The Site Role window has a single pull-down menu that allows you to set a user's individual site role.

These roles have changed as Tableau has grown and depend on whether user licenses are core-based or role-based. The first set of roles uses the Creator role-based license, which allows users to publish and manage content on a server using a local client such as Tableau Desktop or Tableau Prep:

Server Administrator
> While not really a site role, the server administrator role is set at this level.

Site Administrator Creator
> This role grants full administrative access to the specified site on Tableau Server and is the highest level of access on Tableau Cloud. In addition to publishing, this user can control projects, add and remove users, and manage any content on a site.

Creator
> Creators can publish to Tableau Server from a local client, modify content, build new content, and download content from the server.

The next set of roles have an Explorer role-based license:

Server Administrator
> These types of administrators can manage all things on a server and publish from Tableau Desktop; however, they cannot publish Tableau flows.

Site Administrator Explorer
> This role cannot publish Tableau flows, but is otherwise identical to Site Administrator Creator.

Explorer (can publish)
> This role, formerly known as Publisher, can author and publish workbooks and data sources to the server but cannot publish flows or add users or groups.

Explorer
> This role, formerly known as Interactor, can view and interact with workbooks but cannot publish content to the server.

Read Only
> This role, formerly known as Viewer, is only available in one version of Tableau Server (2018.1). It can view workbooks but cannot use any of the interactive features.

The final licensed role utilizes the Viewer user-based license and is far more restrictive than the previous roles:

Viewer
> Viewers can view and interact with workbooks and views on the server but cannot create, publish, or modify any content. These are usually the users who will be opening, viewing, and interacting with your created content.

There is one more role on the server: Unlicensed user. This role is for users who have been removed from the server but still exist as users. This can happen if, for example, the server utilizes Active Directory. If the user is removed from Active Directory but has an account on the server, their account will be set to Unlicensed. Unlicensed users are prohibited from signing into Tableau Server.

Site roles are typically managed by server administrators or site administrators. Even if you are not an administrator in this capacity, knowing these roles can help you troubleshoot users' access to your workbooks.

Example Question

What role can administer only a portion of the projects on a server, but not all?

A. Server Administrator

B. Site Administrator Creator

C. Owner

D. Creator

E. Explorer

Answer: B—Site Administrators can only administer projects on their associated site. Server Administrators can also administer these projects, but they can manage all projects on the server. Owner is not a site role, and Creators only have administrative rights to their own published work. Explorers cannot administer projects.

Project Security

There are two ways to access permissions for all objects on Tableau Server (projects, workbooks, data sources, and data flows). The first way is to navigate to the object itself, open it, and click the ellipsis button next to its title (see Figure 6-14). The second is to navigate into the project containing that object, find the object in the contents list, and click the ellipsis under the Actions column (see Figure 6-15).

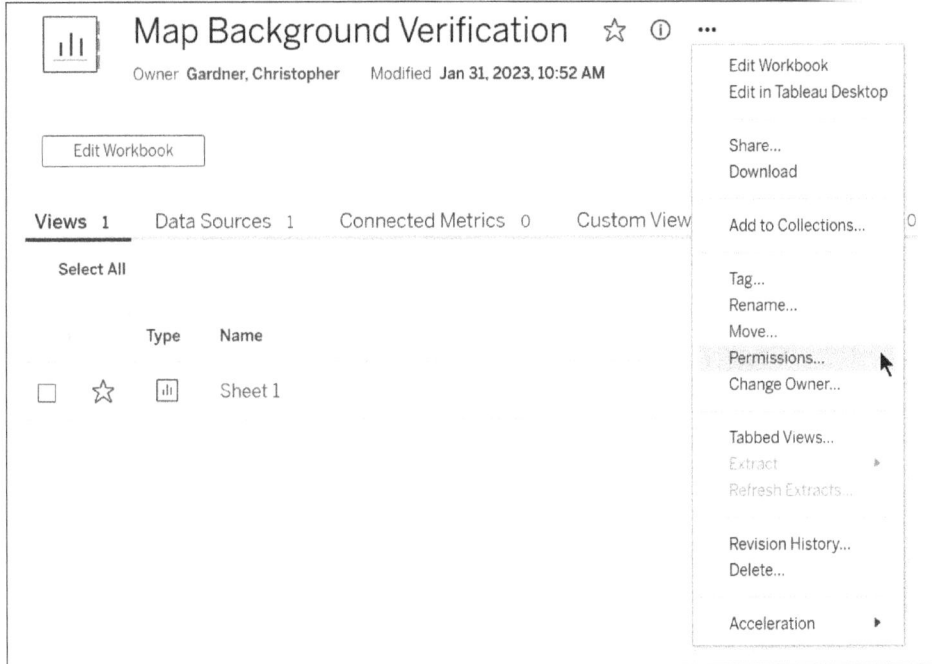

Figure 6-14. To access permissions, navigate to an object and click the ellipsis next to the title.

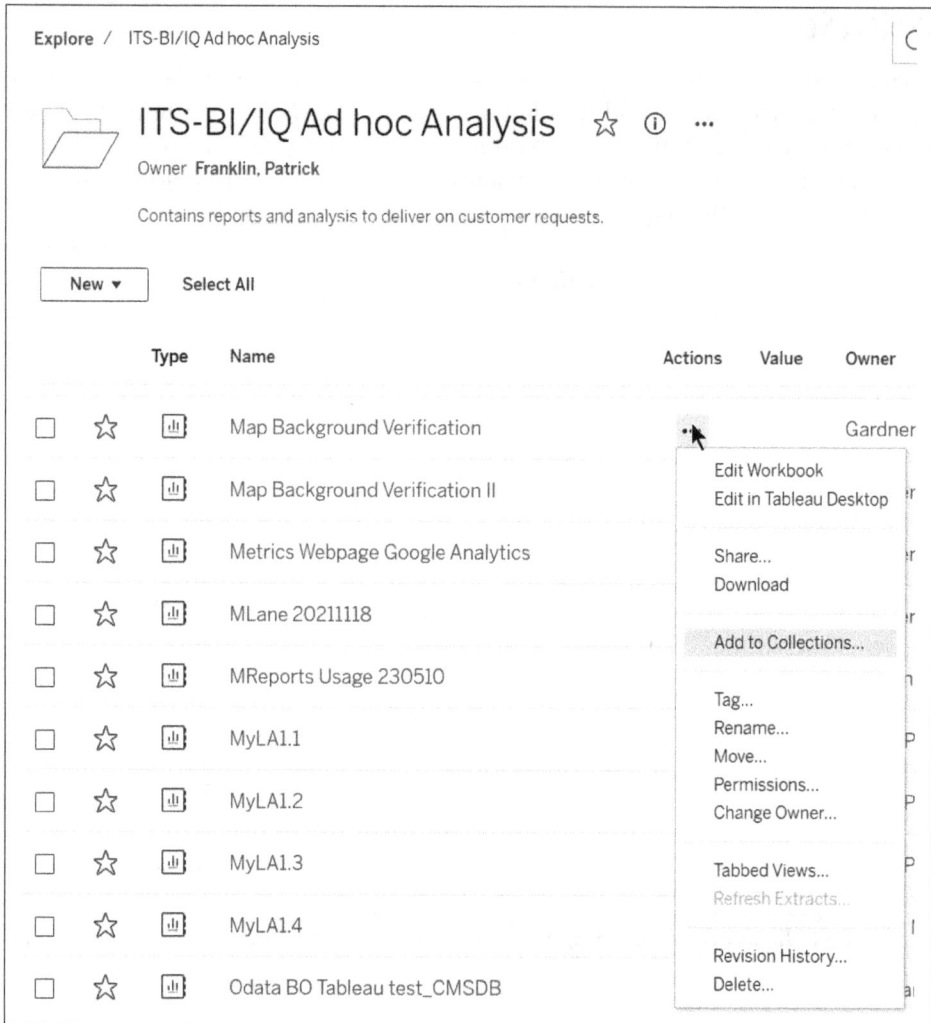

Figure 6-15. Another way to access permissions is to click on the ellipsis in the Action menu next to the object in a project's contents list.

Before you access object permissions, open the Project Permissions window and take a careful look at the project's permissions. A project can be locked or unlocked. *Locked asset* permissions indicate that access to all objects within the project is controlled at the project level. *Unlocked asset* permissions mean that the project manages default permissions, but the objects within can deviate from that.

The locked status can be changed at any time; however, if a project switches from unlocked to locked, all underlying workbook permissions are overwritten with the permissions applied to the locked project. Likewise, if a project is unlocked, the underlying content will retain the project permissions until otherwise changed. You can tell if a project is locked or unlocked by checking the upper left corner of the Project Permissions window (see Table 6-1).

Table 6-1. The text at the upper left corner of the Project Permissions window identifies the project's security type. Clicking the Edit link at the end of the project security description will allow you to change this type.

Image	Meaning
🔓 Asset permissions: Customizable **Edit**	The project has default permissions, but all content within the project (including nested projects) can have permissions applied independent of this project.
🔒 Asset permissions: Locked including nested projects **Edit**	The project has locked permissions. All content within the project (including nested projects) is locked to the permissions applied to this project.

Projects and workbooks also have owners, who are determined when the project is created. Ownership is assigned by the server administrator and can be changed. Workbook ownership is granted to the user who publishes the workbook and provides that user full control over access to their workbook, overriding other permissions.

Permissions to objects can be granted to individuals or via groups. This is incredibly important when determining what access a user has: even if their personal user account has not been granted access to something, they may be a member of a group that *is* granted access, and thus have permission. Conversely, someone could be granted access to a project or workbook, but yet be able to access it due to their site role. For example, a user might be granted publishing rights to a project folder on Tableau Server, but if they do not have a site role such as Creator, they will still be unable to publish to that folder. This is called *layered* permissions, and project administrators need to be careful about it. (Later in this chapter, I'll cover ways to evaluate what permissions a user has.)

The Project Permissions window contains up to nine different tabs, depending on your Tableau Server version. These tabs control the permissions to each of the potential content items within the project, as well as the project itself. Remember, if the project is unlocked, these permissions *only* apply at the project level and as a default for any new content. If you change the permissions on an unlocked project, the changes *will not percolate down to the underlying content!*

Permission Levels

On the Project Permissions window, you can set permissions for the project and its underlying content at three distinct levels, shown in Table 6-2.

Table 6-2. The three levels of permissions.

Level	Name	Description
✓	Granted	The user has access to this permission. This can be overwritten by a Permission Explicitly Denied used elsewhere.
	No Permission Assigned	By default, the user does not have access; however, if the user is assigned this permission via another method, it may still be granted to them. A group may have this permission assigned, but an individual of the group is granted the permission directly, and thus has access.
✕	Permission Explicitly Denied	The user cannot have this permission. This differs from No Permission Assigned in that the user *cannot* receive this permission even if it is granted elsewhere via other methods.

Tableau's default permission level is No Permissions Assigned, indicated by a gray box. A green checkbox indicates the Permission Granted level, meaning that the user or group is granted permission to this action. This can be overwritten by the final level, Permission Explicitly Denied, with a red "X." Even if the user is granted permission to the action via another group or individual access, this level overwrites everything, and they are denied.

Tableau provides a pull-down menu next to each user or group to allow you to quickly apply permissions to a saved preset (see Figure 6-16). This is helpful when applying permissions for multiple users or groups. If you apply permissions using the preset, you can still manually enable, disable, or explicitly deny access. Changing from a default template setting will set the template name to Custom.

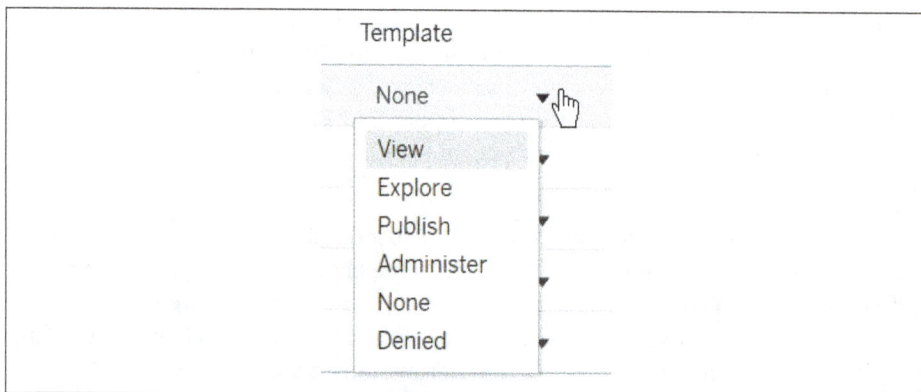

Figure 6-16. Tableau provides predefined permission templates that apply Granted, No Permission, or Denied for each type of access.

Permission grants can come from any group or through individual user grants, which makes checking access difficult. Does a particular user have access? How did this user get access? Why is this other user being denied access? Tableau provides a way to answer these questions.

At the bottom of the Project Permissions window, there is an Effective Permissions section (see Figure 6-17). This section functions in two different ways. First, if you click on a group in the permissions rules above, the Effective Permissions area lists the group's members and details each user's access.

Second, you can use the search box to find a specific user (or group). The user's permissions are displayed to the right. If you click on that user, the top permission rules will gray out, except for any groups of which the user is a member, so you can quickly identify which group granted or denied that user access to specific actions. You can also hover over the level boxes for each action to get a pop-up window explaining why it is granted or denied. This is particularly helpful when the site roles or ownership are overriding the visible permissions.

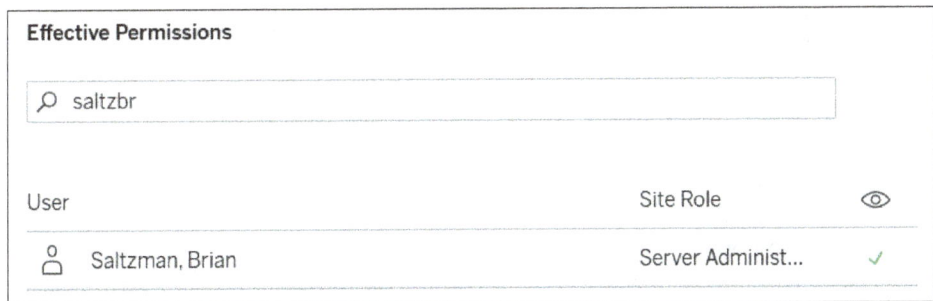

Figure 6-17. The Effective Permissions section of the Permissions window allows you to type in a user's name to see their permissions. If the user is a member of a group that is granted permissions, that group will highlight above.

If you hover over an access level, it will indicate to you if that user is granted or denied access due to a site role or ownership of the project or workbook.

Actions Controlled by Permissions

Next, let's see how these levels apply to the actions available to users on the server. This section breaks down the nine tabs in the Project Permissions window (as seen in Figure 6-17) based on the object(s) to which they apply (see Figure 6-18).

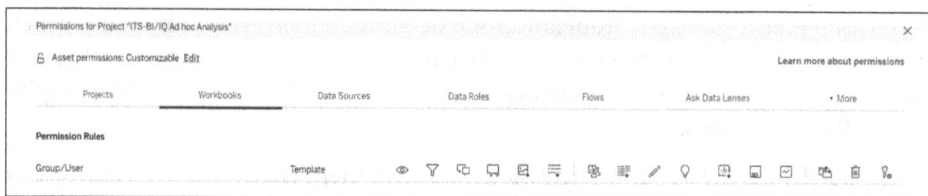

Figure 6-18. A permissions window with the Workbooks tab selected. Since this project is unlocked, the permissions applied will set the defaults for its content. Object permissions can be changed individually for projects or for workbooks, data sources, or data flows within a project.

The first permissions tab applies to project folders (see Table 6-3).

Table 6-3. Project permissions apply to the project folder itself.

Symbol	Access	Permission
◉	View	Users can see the project. This does not mean they can see the contents within; individual workbooks may not have view access granted.
☐	Publish	Users can publish to this project from Tableau Desktop.

The workbooks within a project are managed by two separate permission windows, but the access and permission options are the same (see Table 6-4). The first window appears on the Workbook tab of the Project Permissions. As described in the Project Security section, this tab either controls or sets the default permissions for any workbook, depending on if the project permissions are locked or unlocked. For unlocked projects, a permissions window for the workbook itself, found under the ellipsis menu, controls any permissions that differ from the default ones shown in the Project Permissions window.

Table 6-4. Workbook permissions apply to any workbook in the project. These permissions can also be accessed via the ellipsis next to any workbook on the server.

Symbol	Access	Permission
◉	View	Users can see the workbook.
▽	Filter	Users can interact with filters within the workbook.
⊡	View Comments	Users can view comments others have made about the views in a workbook.
⊡+	Add Comments	Users can add comments about views in a workbook.
⊡	Download Image/PDF	Users can download a static view of the views in a workbook in a *.pdf*, *.png*, or *.ppt* format.
☰	Download Summary Data	Users can download aggregate-level data from a view.
♀	Explain Data	Users can click on a point in a view and ask the server to generate details as to how that point was created.
⊞	Share Customized	Users can customize filters and parameters, then save the view for later use and sharing.

Symbol	Access	Permission
▦	Download Full Data	Users can download the full set of data behind a view as a .*csv* file.
✎	Web Edit	Users can manually edit the workbook online. Only available to users who have been granted an Explorer (can publish) role.
⬇	Download/Save Copy	Users can download a copy of the workbook to edit or view in Tableau Desktop.
⬚	Overwrite	Users can overwrite existing copies of this workbook.
☑	See/Refresh Metrics	Users can create *metrics* from a view—high-level aggregated measures that can be watched—as well as see and refresh any created metrics.
⬔	Move	Users can move the workbook to another project.
⬚	Delete	Users can delete the workbook.
⚿	Set Permissions	Users can control permissions to the workbook (assuming the project permissions are not locked).

Like workbook permissions, data source permissions can be controlled by the containing project or by the data source itself, depending on the locked status of the project. Data set access rights focus primarily on connecting to, altering, or downloading the underlying data (see Table 6-5).

Table 6-5. Data source permissions apply to published data sources.

Symbol	Access	Permission
◉	View	Users can see the data source.
⬒	Connect	Users can connect to the data source to build their own workbooks.
⬓	Download	Users can download the data source for use locally.
⬚	Overwrite	Users can overwrite existing copies of this data source.
⬔	Save As	Users can save a copy of this data source with a new name.
⬔	Move	Users can move the data source to another project.
⬚	Delete	Users can delete the data source.
⚿	Set Permissions	Users can control permissions to the data source (assuming project permissions are not locked).

Beyond workbooks and data sources, projects can also contain objects related to data flows. If your server does not have the data management add-on installed, you may not see these permissions. Since data flows control the path of data from its source to a published location on the server, there are several places where access can be granted: at the database level, the table level of the underlying source, or even the entire flow.

There is a fourth level of access called Data Roles, and it is related to what roles certain fields play. For example, you might identify a field in the data as containing a city name. If this criterion is not met, Tableau will highlight it as a potential error.

This level of access also has a tab in the permissions window called Data Roles. Permission controls for data roles and everything related to data flows all have the same five levels of access (see Table 6-6), found as separate tabs on the Project Permissions window or by right-clicking on the flow object.

Table 6-6. Permissions for data roles, data flows, databases, and tables are specific to the Data Management add-on and may not be present on your server.

Symbol	Access	Permission
👁	View	Users can see the data source and the underlying roles.
🖼	Overwrite	Users can overwrite existing copies of this data source.
🗂	Move	Users can move the data source to another project.
🗑	Delete	Users can delete the data source.
🔑	Set Permissions	Users can control permissions to the data source (assuming project permissions are not locked).

The Data Management add-on for Tableau Server allows you to set up virtual connections. Unlike workbooks or data sources, access levels on these happen at the connection point, so row-level security on the database can be enforced using a virtual connection. A virtual connection can pull from many tables and databases, but it acts as a single connection point used by multiple workbooks or published data sources. Virtual connections have permissions specific to them (see Table 6-7).

Table 6-7. Virtual connections' permissions are specific to the Data Management add-on and may not be present on your server.

Symbol	Access	Permission
👁	View	Users can see the data source.
🔌	Connect	Users can connect to the data source to build their own workbooks.
🖼	Overwrite	Users can overwrite existing copies of this data source.
🗂	Move	Users can move the data source to another project.
🗑	Delete	Users can delete the data source.
🔑	Set Permissions	Users can control permissions to the data source (assuming permissions are not locked to the project).

The final set of permissions that you need to understand relate to metadata. Tableau Server can track usage information over extended periods of time, depending on how the server is configured, such as who has accessed the object, how many times they have accessed it, and when they most recently accessed it. These permissions, found in the Metrics Permissions window (see Table 6-8), control who can access a workbook or data source's usage information.

Table 6-8. Metrics permissions control access to usage metrics on workbooks or data sources.

Symbol	Access	Permission
👁	View	Users can see the metrics.
🖫	Overwrite	Users can overwrite the metrics when publishing new content.
📑	Move	Users can move the metrics with the object if it is moved.
🗑	Delete	Users can delete the metrics.
🗝	Set Permissions	Users can control permissions to the metrics (assuming project permissions are not locked).

> Some of the permissions listed above can be accessed through the project permissions or through the object itself, such as workbooks, data sources, and data flows. Other permissions, like those related to data management and metrics, are specific to the project itself and are only available in the Project Permissions window.

If a project is unlocked, you can change the permissions on individual objects within it. Each object permissions window has access options matching those shown at the project level. For example, if you open a Workbook Permissions window, it will have the same access options as the Workbook tab on the Project Permissions window. The difference is that this Workbook Permissions window controls the *actual permissions*, whereas the Workbook tab in the Project Permissions window only controls the *default permissions* for workbooks published to this project.

Example Question

Which setting ensures that permissions set at the project level apply to all objects contained within?

A. Ownership

B. Locked project permissions

C. Customizable permissions

D. Dashboard permissions

E. Site role

Answer: B—Projects with locked permissions dictate the permissions for all objects within them.

One other piece of security: if a workbook is published without tabs enabled, its security will "roll down" to the view level. That is, each dashboard within the workbook will have its own permissions. The permissions on a view are almost identical to those of a workbook. If you choose to publish without tabs, be sure you check the individual view permissions rather than the workbook permissions!

Example Question

You grant access to a project for your executive team. A few days later, one of your executives calls you and explains that she still cannot open a workbook within the project. What might be the issue? Select three.

A. The executive's site role does not permit it.

B. She's not an owner on the project.

C. Tabs were disabled, so security is at the view level.

D. Permissions were locked to the project.

E. Permissions are incorrect on the workbook.

Answers: A, C, and E—A is a possible answer because the site role dictates the highest level of permissions a user can have on objects within a site, and it could be restricting access. C is potentially an issue because workbooks with tabs disabled often shift permission levels down to the individual views. E is obviously a potential issue if permissions were not granted correctly.

User-Based Workbook Controls

The final portion of this book focuses on additional functionality specific to your end users. The workbooks you publish have features such as parameters and filters that let users manipulate the data while searching for insights. Tableau Server provides additional features that expand on these features, making it easier for your users to track and manage the information you provide. While these features are on the user side of the server, you should get familiar with them so you can encourage users to try them and drive utilization of your workbooks.

Custom Views

Many dashboards go beyond just *showing* the data to implement filters, parameters, and other means of *interacting* with it. As your users browse through visualizations and try these controls, they'll probably focus the data on the area they are most interested in. For example, your regional teams will likely filter to their specific region each time they visit your workbook. Tableau Server provides a tool that assists with these navigation and control settings. *Custom views* are snapshots of dashboards or visualizations with different filters, parameters, highlights, or selections than the default view stored on the server.

You can see how this might be valuable based on the regional team example: a user in Canada, for instance, will most likely want to filter the data in your dashboards to the Canada region each time they visit the page. They can use custom views to skip this step, so that the workbook automatically filters to Canada each time they visit.

To create a custom view, open the Custom Views window, give the view a name, and save it. The Custom Views window can be accessed at the top of the dashboard by clicking on the View: Original link (see Figure 6-19). The name of this link changes if you change default views. Before you add any custom views, the default name will always be View: Original because you are viewing the dashboard as it appeared when it was published.

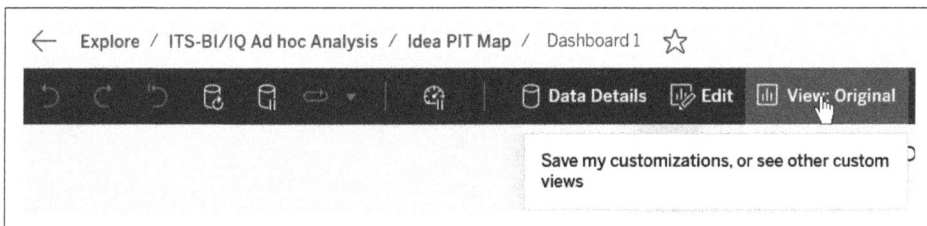

Figure 6-19. The Custom Views menu is available in the top bar above the dashboard. The menu name changes depending on if the current view is the default or something saved by a user.

The Custom Views window is composed of three sections (see Figure 6-20). You can use Save Custom View to create and store custom views. There is a place to give your view a name and two configuration options: "Make it my default" takes your newly created view and saves it as the default shown every time you visit this dashboard or visualization. The second option, "Make visible to others," shares your view with all other users of the dashboard.

Once a view is saved, you can apply it to the dashboard any time you visit by opening the Custom Views window and selecting a view to apply. The bottom two sections of the Custom Views window hold views that you and others have saved: My Views and Other Views. You can click on any of these views to apply their filter and parameter settings.

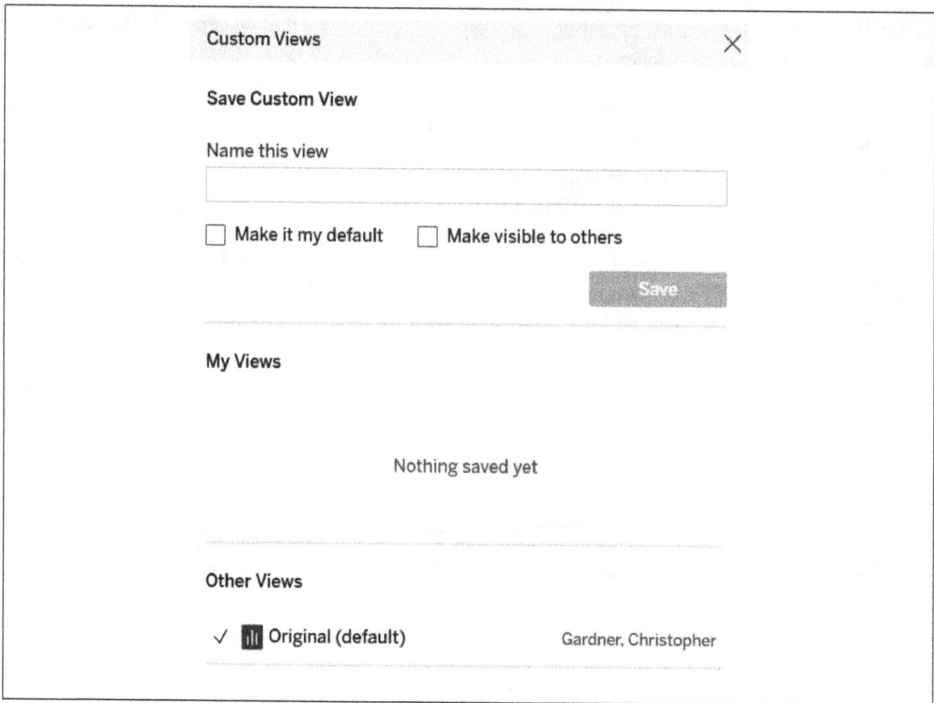

Figure 6-20. The Custom Views window allows you to create, share, and apply sets of filter and parameter settings to a dashboard.

Subscriptions

Users often want regular updates on the information a dashboard provides. Instead of forcing them to visit the dashboard every morning, Tableau Server offers *subscriptions*, which email the user a copy of the dashboard in a PDF or image format, a link to the dashboard, and a link to manage their personal subscriptions to any and all workbooks on the server.

To add a subscription, open the Watch menu in the upper right area of the dashboard (see Figure 6-21) and select the Subscriptions option.

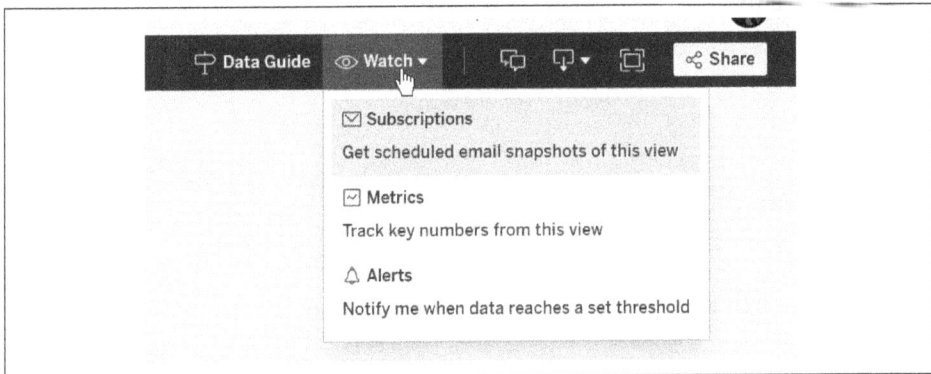

Figure 6-21. The Watch menu contains options for Subscriptions, Metrics, and Alerts.

This opens the Subscribe window (see Figure 6-22).

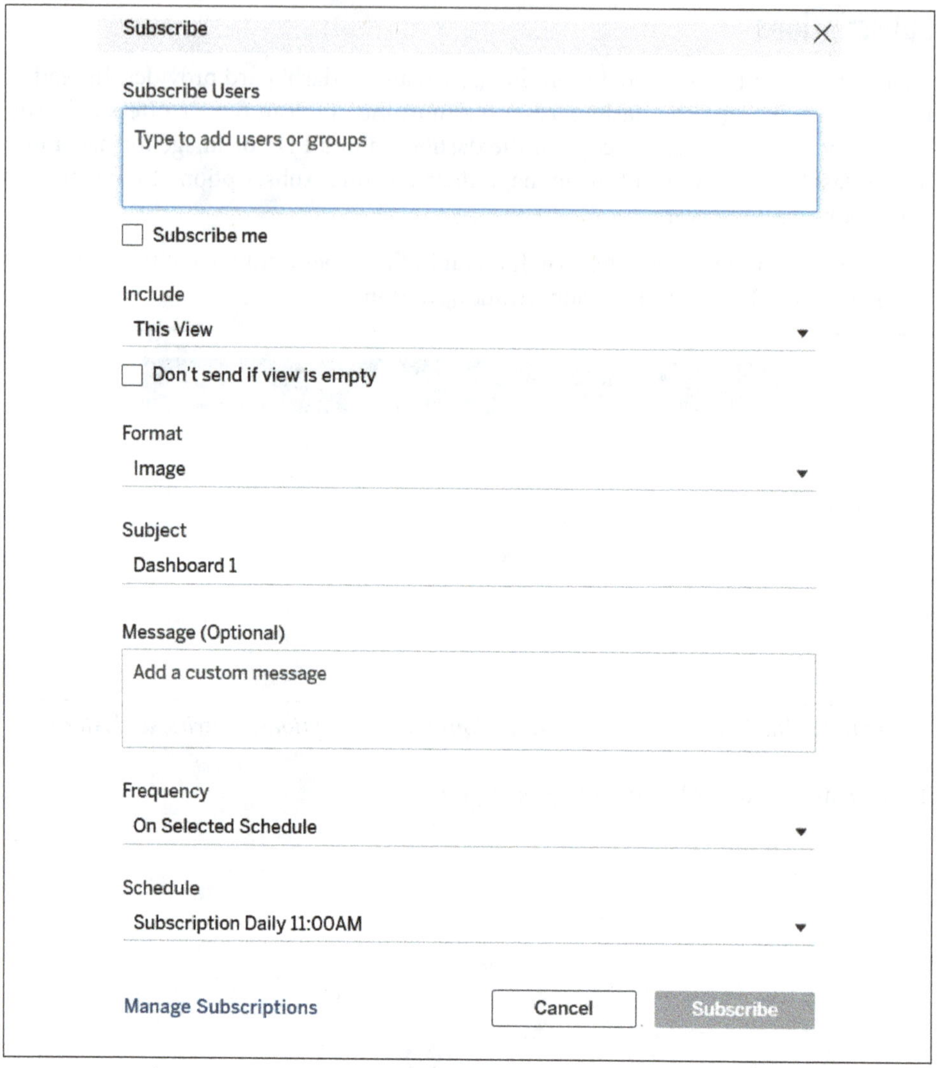

Subscribe	✕

Subscribe Users

Type to add users or groups

☐ Subscribe me

Include

This View ▾

☐ Don't send if view is empty

Format

Image ▾

Subject

Dashboard 1

Message (Optional)

Add a custom message

Frequency

On Selected Schedule ▾

Schedule

Subscription Daily 11:00AM ▾

Manage Subscriptions   Cancel   Subscribe

Figure 6-22. The Subscribe window allows you to control aspects of a subscription.

This window has eight areas:

Subscribe Users

In this section, you can enter the name of any other user on the server to subscribe them to emails. There is also a checkbox to add yourself to the subscription.

Include

This section allows you to include either a singular view/dashboard or the entire workbook in the email. There is also a checkbox that will cancel the subscription email if the view is empty for some reason.

Format

This section controls what is sent in the email: an image, a PDF, or both.

Subject

You can enter a subject for the subscription email here.

Message (Optional)

You can enter an optional text message here to be included with the email.

Frequency

Here, you can choose whether to send emails whenever the workbook data refreshes, or on a preprogrammed schedule on Tableau Server. As with data extract refreshes, the server administrator can add schedules.

Schedule

If the user selects to use a subscription schedule, this option lets them choose from those available on the server.

Manage Subscriptions

This link takes you to the Subscription tab on the current workbook, where you can see the full list of subscribers and add or remove subscriptions.

In the subscription email, there is a similar link to manage subscriptions. The difference between the Subscribe window and the Manage Subscriptions link in the email is that the email link takes you to your own personal subscriptions, whereas the Subscribe window controls options for all subscriptions.

Watch Data/Data Alerts

If your visualization has a chart with a numeric axis, your users can configure a *data alert that will email them* when the values on a chart go above or below a designated threshold, along with a link back to the workbook that generated the alert. It is very useful when tracking vital information in Tableau.

From the Watch menu at the top of any dashboard, select Alerts to open the Alert pane on the right-hand side of the page. To create an alert, select a continuous axis on the chart that you wish to monitor, then click on the Create button in the Alerts pane to open the Create Alert window (see Figure 6-23).

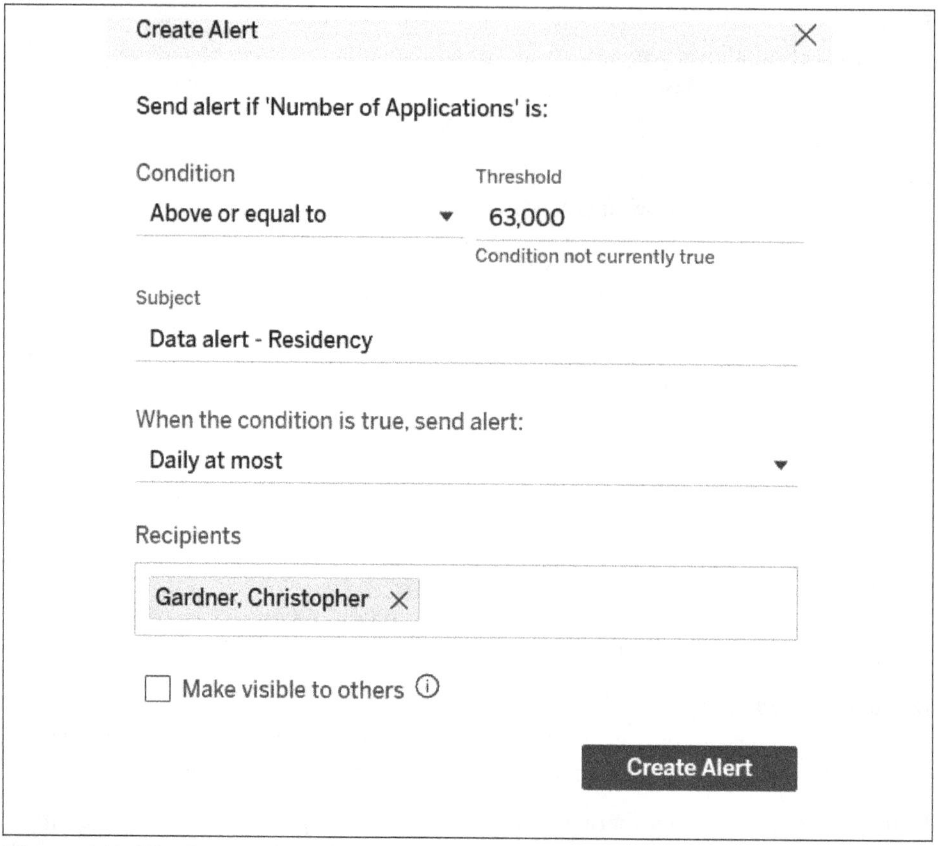

> **Create Alert**   ✕
>
> Send alert if 'Number of Applications' is:
>
> Condition   Threshold
> Above or equal to   ▼   63,000
>   Condition not currently true
>
> Subject
> Data alert - Residency
>
> When the condition is true, send alert:
> Daily at most   ▼
>
> Recipients
> ┌──────────────────────────────────┐
> │ Gardner, Christopher ✕   │
> └──────────────────────────────────┘
>
> ☐ Make visible to others ⓘ
>
>   **Create Alert**

Figure 6-23. The Create Alert window sets the values that trigger email alert messages to users.

There are six configuration sections:

Condition
These criteria determine when an alert should be sent: "Above or equal to," Above, "Below or equal to," Below, or "Equal to."

Threshold
Here, you enter a numerical value that corresponds to the condition. If you read the condition together with the threshold like a sentence, from left to right, you will get the criteria for sending an alert. For example, if you clicked on a Sales axis to create an alert, the alert could read "Sales below or equal to $100,000."

Subject
This box provides the subject line for the alert email.

When the condition is true, send alert

This pull-down controls how often an alert can be sent. You can configure it to avoid multiple emails if the condition and threshold are met for an extended period. There are five options: "Once - the first time it's true," "As frequently as possible," "Hourly at most," "Daily at most," or "Weekly at most."

Recipients

This is the person who receives the alert email if it is triggered.

Make visible to others

This makes the alert visible to other users. If a specific alert already exists and a new user tries to add it, it will appear in the Alerts pane. If they select the existing alert, they can receive it by clicking the Add Me link.

> The axis you use to create an alert must be continuous. You cannot create alerts on charts with a discrete axis or no axis.

Alerts can occasionally break due to data source changes, missing emails, expired credentials, and the like. When this happens, the alert is suspended and a notification is sent to the alert owner. Once the issue is resolved, the alert will send an email to recipients indicating that the issue has been resolved and the alert is active once again.

Additional User Controls

Some user actions are available only if the correct permissions are granted. These actions can be about the data, the visualizations, or sharing content. They are available as icons in the bar above the dashboard, as shown in Table 6-9.

Table 6-9. Additional options available to end users via the menu bar above the dashboard. This menu may not be visible on embedded dashboards and may not contain all the options listed, depending on the server.

Icon	Action	Description
	Undo	Undoes the user's most recent action.
	Redo	Reapplies the most recent change undone.
	Revert to Saved	Sets the dashboard back to its original published state.
	Data Refresh	Refreshes the data in the visualizations. If the data is extracted, this will simply refresh the workbooks with the most recently extracted data; it will not refresh extracts.

Icon	Action	Description
	Pause Auto Updates/Resume Auto Updates	Pauses changes in the visualization as filters and parameters are applied. When clicked, the icon changes to a cylinder with a triangle, which will resume changes if clicked.
	Pause/Continue Acceleration	Forces acceleration to run/pause (acceleration can improve load times for large queries).
Data Details	Data Details	Gives detailed information about the underlying data; only available with the Data Management add-on.
Edit	Edit	Allows users with correct permissions to edit the workbook online. The Tableau Server editing tool's capabilities are nearly equal to those of Tableau Desktop.
Data Guide	Data Guide	Gives information about the visualizations, including data used, filters applied, and insights related to outliers and trends.
	Comment	If enabled, allows users to make comments on the dashboard and visualizations.
	Download	If enabled, allows users to download the workbook, dashboard, or underlying data in several formats: image, PDF, PowerPoint, CSV (for data), crosstab (for data), or a Tableau Desktop file (for workbooks).
	Full Screen	Hides menus and borders, displaying the dashboard full screen.
Share	Share	Allows users to share the workbook with another user on the server, copy the workbook URL, or embed code from this location.

Example Question

Which of the following is not available in the download menu for a workbook on Tableau Server?

A. Excel

B. CSV

C. Image

D. PDF

E. Web page

Answer: E—Web page is not an option in the download menu for users in Tableau.

Conclusion

Tableau Servers provide a stage for sharing dashboards and visualizations. For this reason, it is important to understand not only how to publish a workbook to a server, but also how to control access once it is there. The Tableau exam will touch on how to publish, what the publish settings do, and how to control access to your published work. The exam may also have a question or two on consumer interactions with Tableau Server, so it is beneficial to review these options as well.

At this point, you can test your knowledge using the mid-chapter questions and the full example exam at the end of this book. As you continue forward with your Tableau journey, please return to this book for review to refresh your memory and for reference. Most importantly, good luck with your certification!

Practice Exam

Please refer to Appendix B for answers to the practice exam questions.

1. What type of transformation should you use in Tableau Prep or Tableau Desktop to alter the data shown in the image below?

Dimension	A	B	C	D
Red	4	6	2	1
Blue	7	5	4	3
Yellow	9	2	8	7
Green	3	9	4	8
Orange	8	6	7	5
Purple	3	0	9	2
White	2	2	1	2

→

Dimension	Letter	Value
Red	A	4
Red	B	6
Red	C	2
Red	D	1
Blue	A	7
Blue	B	5
...	...	...

A. Join

B. Pivot

C. Data Interpreter

D. Union

E. Relationship

2. What type of step would you use in Tableau Prep Builder to remove duplicate values?

A. Aggregate

B. Pivot

C. Clean data

D. Output

E. Insert flow

3. Which filter type is performed before data is pulled into Tableau?

A. Context filter

B. Data source filter

C. Relevant values filter

D. The first filter in the Filter pane

E. Extract filter

4. You have published a data source to Tableau Server, but now you need to make some changes to one of the tables. You've connected to the published data source using Tableau Desktop. What step should you take next to make the data source editable again?

A. Right-click the data source and choose Create Local Copy.

B. Right-click on the data source and choose Edit Data Source Filters.

C. Right-click on the data source and choose Extract Data.

D. Right-click on the data source and choose Add to Saved Data Sources.

E. Right-click on the data source and choose View Data.

5. You are working on a workbook with monthly sales data sets. The data tables are exactly the same except that they come from different months. What is the best way to combine these data sets in Tableau Prep Builder or Tableau Desktop?

A. Blend the data tables.

B. Join the data tables.

C. Create a relationship between the tables.

D. Extract the data sources.

E. Union the tables.

6. Relational databases come with tables that often contain large amounts of data. Which of the following options could you use to improve the performance of data pulled from relational databases into your workbook? Select all that apply.

A. Extract filters

B. Left joins

C. Custom SQL

D. Extracts

E. Data filters

7. Imagine you have two data sources that need to be joined in Tableau Desktop; however, the field on which you wish to join them has extra characters that the first data set does not contain. Which one of the following tools is available to help overcome this challenge?

A. Extract filters

B. Blend

C. Relationship calculation

D. Union

E. Outer join

8. Tableau Prep offers a variety of ways to manipulate and clean your data. Which one of these options is *not* available in a clean step in Tableau Prep?

A. Combine fields

B. Repair typos

C. Change data types

D. Data Interpreter

E. Alias field values

9. Tableau Desktop includes a way to remove a field that is not needed for visualization. What is that option called?

A. Filter

B. Hide

C. Remove

D. Exclude

E. Pivot

10. What step type is added to a Tableau Prep flow to save the resulting data set once it is joined, cleaned, and manipulated?

    A. Publish

    B. Output

    C. End

    D. Save

    E. Display

11. When you use Tableau Desktop to build a visualization, your data fields are listed on the left in the Data pane. One of your fields is in the top half of the pane and has a blue "Abc" icon next to it. What type of field does this indicate?

    A. Discrete string dimension

    B. Continuous string dimension

    C. Discrete string measure

    D. Continuous string measure

    E. String parameter

12. Which one of the following is *not* a dynamic field automatically created by Tableau Desktop?

    A. Measure Names

    B. Measure Values

    C. Longitude

    D. [Distinct Field] *(Count)*

    E. Row Number

13. The following crosstab was generated in Tableau Desktop using the following fields: Order Date, Category, Sub-Category, and Sales. Where was the SUM([Sales]) field placed in the interface to create this visualization?

Category	Sub-Category	Order Date 2018	2019	2020	2021
Furniture	Bookcases	$20,037	$38,544	$26,275	$30,024
	Chairs	$77,242	$71,735	$83,919	$95,554
	Furnishings	$13,826	$21,090	$27,874	$28,915
	Tables	$46,088	$39,150	$60,833	$60,894
Office Supplies	Appliances	$15,314	$23,241	$26,050	$42,927
	Art	$6,058	$6,237	$5,961	$8,863
	Binders	$43,488	$37,453	$49,683	$72,788
	Envelopes	$3,856	$4,512	$4,730	$3,379
	Fasteners	$661	$545	$960	$858
	Labels	$2,841	$2,956	$2,827	$3,861
	Paper	$14,835	$15,288	$20,662	$27,695
	Storage	$50,329	$45,048	$58,789	$69,678
	Supplies	$14,394	$1,952	$14,278	$16,049
Technology	Accessories	$25,014	$40,524	$41,896	$59,946
	Copiers	$10,850	$26,179	$49,599	$62,899
	Machines	$62,023	$27,764	$55,907	$43,545
	Phones	$77,391	$68,314	$78,962	$105,341

A. Rows

B. Columns

C. Detail mark

D. Text mark

E. Filters

14. Which *three* filter types require fields to be placed on the Filter pane? Select three.

   A. Data source filters

   B. Measure filters

   C. Dimension filters

   D. Level of Detail

   E. Context filters

15. Which one of the following marks does *not* contain a submenu or window?

   A. Color

   B. Text/Label

   C. Detail

   D. Size

   E. Tooltip

16. The ⬚ icon is available in the icon bar at the top of Tableau Desktop. What does it do?

   A. Sorts the fields in ascending order

   B. Swaps the fields in the rows with those in the columns

   C. Sorts the fields in descending order

   D. Reverses the order of the sort

   E. Changes the sort from alphabetical to measure based

17. The following chart was built in Tableau. What setting was applied to the Label to make it only show on two of the points?

Pages

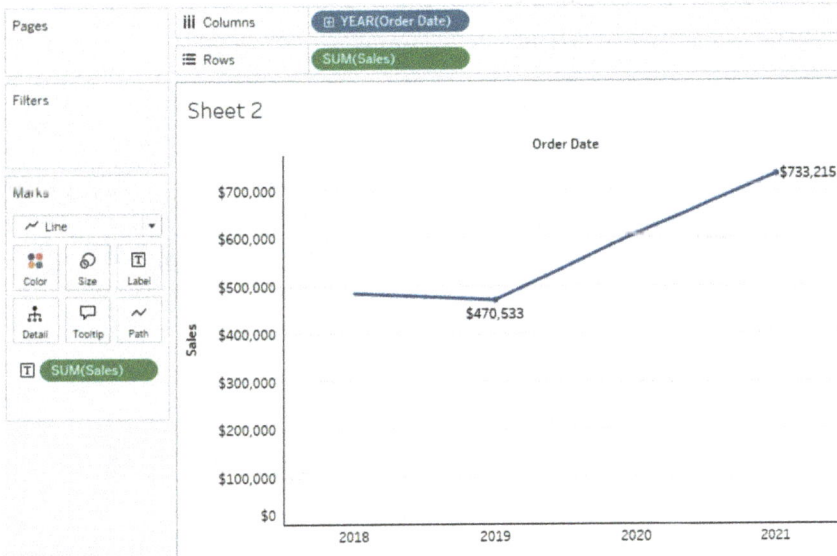

A. "Marks to Label" Selected

B. "Marks to Label" Most Recent

C. "Marks to Label" Highlighted

D. "Marks to Label" Min/Max

E. "Marks to Label" Line Ends

18. Your data set contains information on sales by country. Which one of the following actions will generate a map in Tableau using this data?

A. Dragging the Country field to Rows

B. Dragging the Country field to Columns

C. Dragging the Country field to Detail

D. Dragging Longitude to Rows and Latitude to Columns

E. Dragging Latitude to Rows and Longitude to Columns

19. You have created a map using your data containing cities. Many of the cities are not appearing, and at the bottom of the map is a warning that you have "353 unknown." What is causing this warning, and where are your cities?

A. Your cities have ambiguous names and need context.

B. There are errors in your data.

C. The same city is listed in your data multiple times.

D. The Tableau city database is missing some of your cities.

E. The cities field contains null values.

20. Measure names and measure values are used to show multiple measures at the same time. Which one of the following steps is the *best* way to ensure that only the measures you are interested in appear on your chart when using these fields?

A. Filter Measure Values.

B. Filter Measure Names.

C. Filter the measure fields themselves.

D. Write a calculation that only pulls the appropriate measures.

E. Use Tableau groups to isolate the needed measures.

21. The following chart shows sales by year for each product category. It also shows the difference in sales from year to year using a Difference table calculation. Which *two* of the following are possible ways to apply the table calculation? Select two.

Category		Order Date 2018	2019	2020	2021
Furniture	Sales	$157,193	$170,518	$198,901	$215,387
	Difference		$13,325	$28,383	$16,486
Office Supplies	Sales	$151,776	$137,233	$183,040	$246,097
	Difference		($14,543)	$46,707	$62,157
Technology	Sales	$175,278	$162,781	$226,364	$271,731
	Difference		($12,497)	$63,583	$45,367

A. Table (down)

B. Table (across)

C. Specific values - Category

D. Specific values - Year of Order Date

E. Table (across then down)

22. You've built a crosstab ranking runners in a race. You use a table calculation to apply that rank. You'd like the rank to show ties as the same value, with the next number following appropriately. For example, a tie in second place would result in the ranks appearing as 1, 2, 2, and 3. Which type of rank calculation should you apply?

A. Competition

B. Modified competition

C. Unique

D. Default

E. Dense

23. What character or characters are used to proceed between comments in a calculated field?

A. A hyphen (-)

B. Two hyphens (–)

C. Two backslashes (\)

D. Two forward slashes** (**//)

E. Two greater-than symbols (>>)

24. You want to calculate your company's overall profit-to-sales ratio using a data set
with one row for each sales transaction. Which one of the following calculations
should you use to calculate an accurate overall profit-to-sales ratio?

A. `SUM([Profit]) / SUM([Sales])`

B. `SUM([Profit]) / [Sales]`

C. `[Profit] / [Sales]`

D. `SUM([Profit] / [Sales])`

E. `[Profit] / SUM([Sales])`

25. You want to split a field containing email addresses. You want to separate out the
part of the email address after the "@" symbol into a separate column. Which one
of the following calculations would accomplish this task?

A. `RIGHT([Email],FIND([Email],'@')-1)`

B. `RIGHT([Email],LEN([Email])-FIND([Email],"@"))`

C. `RIGHT([Email],FIND([Email],'@'))`

D. `RIGHT([Email],FIND([Email],'@')+1)`

E. `RIGHT([Email],LEN([Email])-FIND([Email],"@")+1)`

26. What will this calculation return?

`DATENAME('weekday',#07-04-1776#)`

A. 5

B. 4

C. 1

D. Thursday

E. July

27. The chart that follows was generated using the Level of Detail (LoD) calculation FIXED. What fields should appear in the spaces of this LoD calculation?

{FIXED _____ , _____ :SUM([Sales])}

Pages		iii Columns	⊕ YEAR(Order Date)		
		☰ Rows	⊟ Category	⊞ Sub-Category	

Filters

Sheet 1

Category	Sub-Category	Order Date			
		2021	2022	2023	2024
Furniture	Bookcases	162,125	172,330	200,980	219,313
	Chairs	162,125	172,330	200,980	219,313
	Furnishings	162,125	172,330	200,980	219,313
	Tables	162,125	172,330	200,980	219,313
Office Supplies	Appliances	154,014	137,670	186,374	253,835
	Art	154,014	137,670	186,374	253,835
	Binders	154,014	137,670	186,374	253,835
	Envelopes	154,014	137,670	186,374	253,835
	Fasteners	154,014	137,670	186,374	253,835
	Labels	154,014	137,670	186,374	253,835
	Paper	154,014	137,670	186,374	253,835
	Storage	154,014	137,670	186,374	253,835
	Supplies	154,014	137,670	186,374	253,835
Technology	Accessories	177,901	162,993	226,580	272,419
	Copiers	177,901	162,993	226,580	272,419
	Machines	177,901	162,993	226,580	272,419
	Phones	177,901	162,993	226,580	272,419

Marks

Automatic ▼

Color Size Text
Detail Tooltip

T SUM(FIXED LoD)

A. Category, Sub-Category

B. Category, Order Date

C. Sub-Category, Order Date

D. Sub-Category, YEAR([Order Date])

E. Category, YEAR([Order Date])

28. Which *two* of the following are possible ways to do logical calculations in Tableau Desktop? Select two.

A. IF, THEN, ELSE

B. IF, WHEN, ELSE

C. CASE, THEN, ELSE

D. CASE, WHEN, ELSE

E. CASE, IF, ELSE

29. Which *three* filters are applied *before* calculating a FIXED LoD calculation? Select three.

  A. Dimension filters

  B. Context filters

  C. Measure filters

  D. Data source filters

  E. Extract filters

30. Suppose you have a line chart showing average profit across three categories for four years. You want to use a dashed line for the overall average (not split by category), as shown in the following image. Which one of the options is the correct way to format this calculation, assuming its aggregation is SUM when added to the chart?

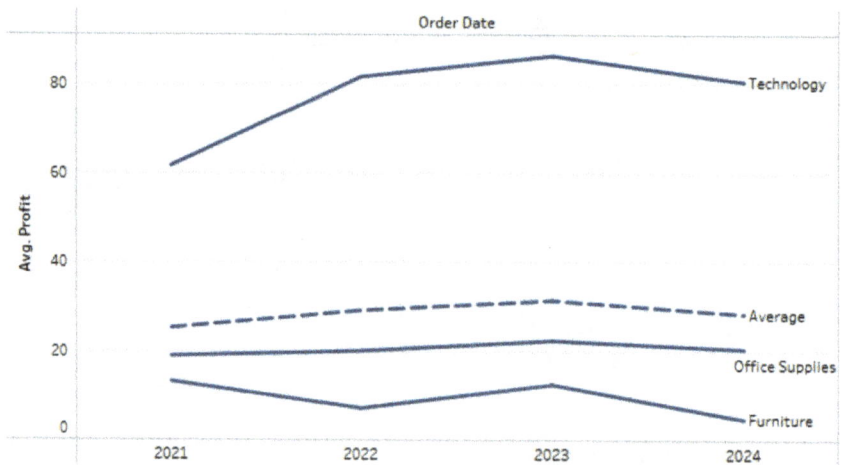

  A. {FIXED [Category]: AVG([Profit])}

  B. {INCLUDE [Category]: AVG([Profit])}

  C. {EXCLUDE [Category]: AVG([Profit])}

  D. {FIXED YEAR([Order Date]), [Category]: AVG([Profit])}

  E. [Profit]/{EXCLUDE [Category]: AVG([Profit])}

31. Imagine you work for a consulting company. You need to track the businesses you support by region. Your company has twelve regions, but there is no Region field in your data set. What is the most effective way to pull the businesses together?

    A. Create a group.

    B. Create a set.

    C. Use bins.

    D. Create an LoD calculation.

    E. Utilize a parameter with a calculation.

32. What *three* methods exist for defining a set? Select three.

    A. Manual selection

    B. Wildcard match

    C. Conditional logic

    D. Top *n* by field or formula

    E. Calculated field

33. The following chart shows the sum of sales by subcategory by the year of order date. Assuming the default box-and-whisker plot has been applied without any changes, what do the middle gray areas represent in each year?

Sales by Sub-Category by Year of Order Date

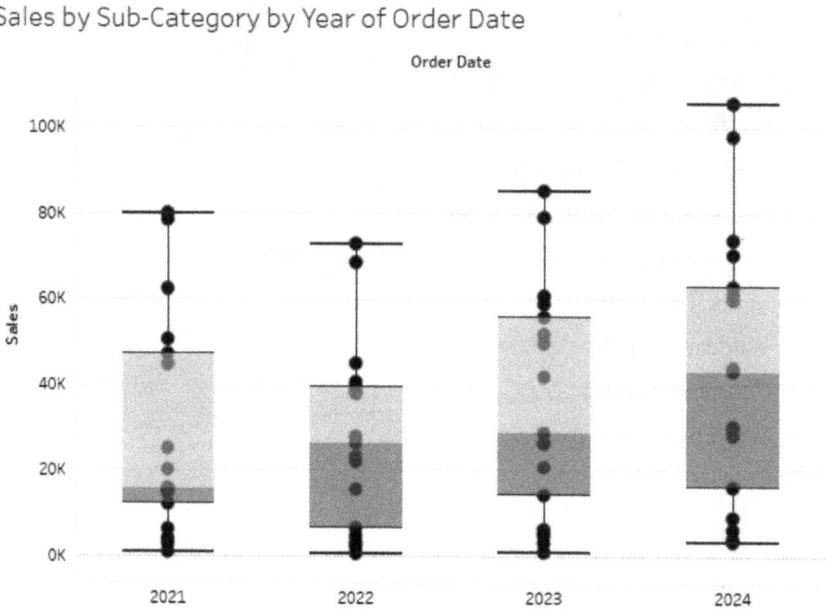

A. The average sales values of the overall data set

B. The subcategories with the lowest sales amount per number of sales

C. The subcategories with the highest sales amount per number of sales

D. The subcategories falling in the median range of sales values for the data set

E. The middle 50% of values when the subcategories are sorted lowest to highest

34. The following chart shows the sum of sales by subcategory by the year of order date. You use a forecast analytics tool on the chart, without changing any settings. The resulting line shows a predicted sales value for the next year. What does the shaded area around the line mean?

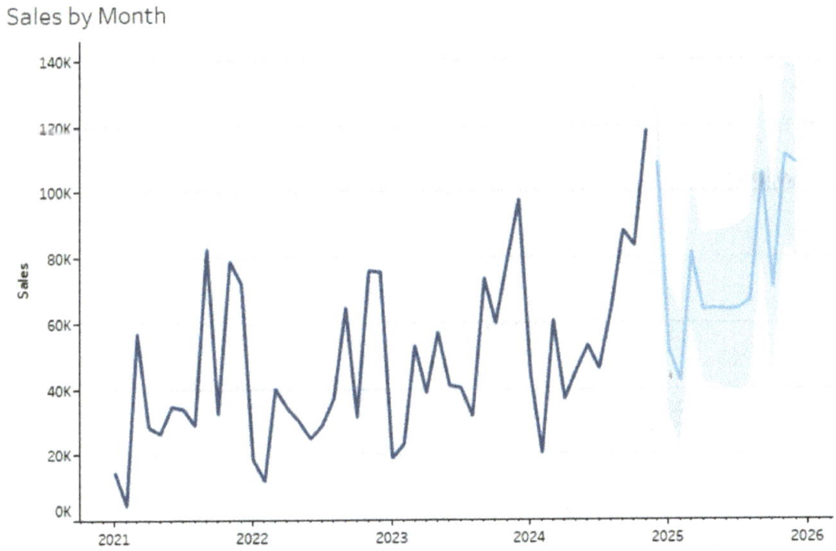

Sales by Month

A. It represents other potential values of the line based on earlier months.

B. It represents the middle 50% of values for all products.

C. It denotes a 10% buffer zone where the line could fall.

D. It represents the min and max margins of error, based on earlier fluctuations.

E. There is a 95% chance the line will fall within this area, based on the other data in the chart.

35. Tableau offers five different modeling options for applying lines to data. Which one of its trend lines offers options to control the degrees of change in the line (curves) to best make it fit?

A. Linear

B. Logarithmic

C. Exponential

D. Polynomial

E. Power

36. What was the reference line label set to in the chart below?

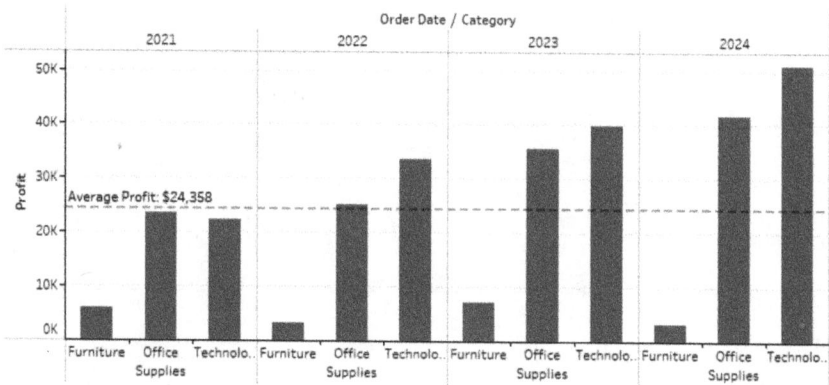

A. Computation

B. Field name

C. Value

D. Custom:Calculation Field Name

E. Custom:Calculation Field Name: Value

37. What was the reference line scope set to in the following chart?

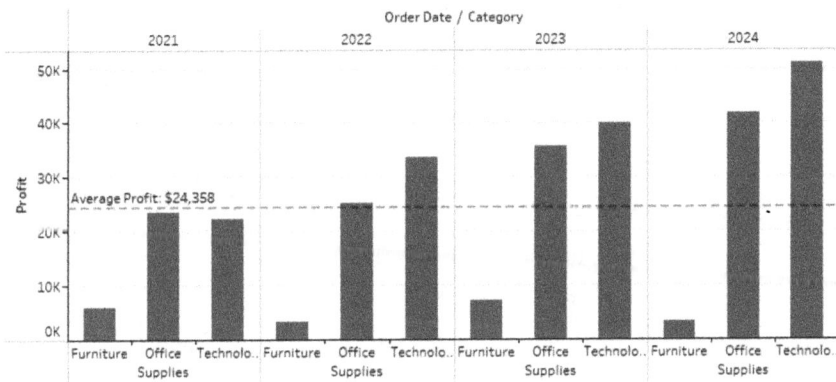

A. Pane

B. Table

C. Range

D. Cell

E. Field

38. What does the following calculation represent?

```
DATEDIFF('day',[Order Date],{FIXED : MIN([Order Date])})
```

A. The first date in the data set

B. The earliest date for each category

C. The day of the week of the first date in the data set

D. The difference in days between today and the first date in the data set

E. The difference in days between the first date in the data set and the date of the given row

39. One data field in the Data pane is represented by a Venn diagram icon. What data *type* does this icon represent?

    A. A continuous number

    B. A group

    C. A hierarchy

    D. A set

    E. A discrete date

40. The following calculation is applied to the Customer field in your workbook:

    ```
    IIF([Customer] = 'Brian','RADAR','Lisa','Unlisted')
    ```

    What will the calculation return if the Customer field value is 'Brian'?

    A. Brian

    B. RADAR

    C. Lisa

    D. Unknown

    E. True

41. What type of filter has values that are dependent on other filters in a visualization?

    A. A multiple-value filter

    B. A relevant values filter

    C. A single-select filter

    D. A context filter

    E. A dimensional filter

42. The following chart shows sales by category and date. How is this visualization sorted?

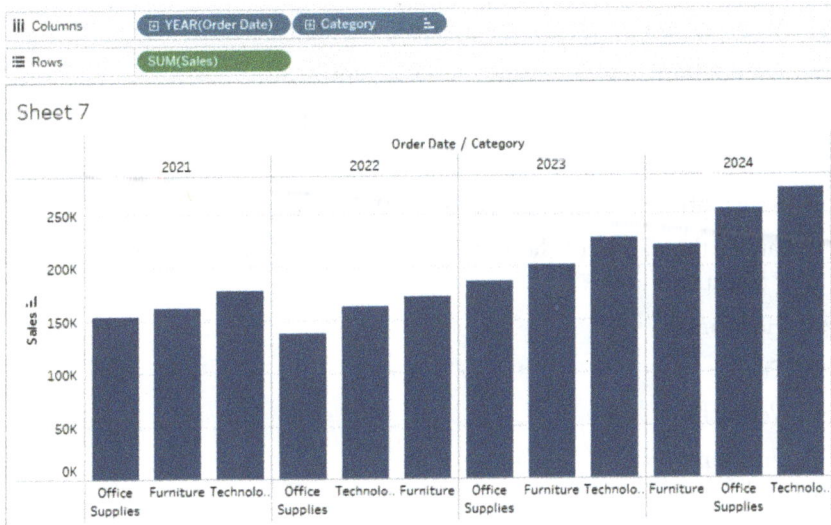

Columns YEAR(Order Date) Category

Rows SUM(Sales)

Sheet 7

A. Nested on Category by Sales, ascending

B. On Category by Sales, ascending

C. Ascending on the year of the Order Date

D. Ascending on the year of the Order Date and Category

E. Manual sort on Category

43. There are four distinct types of filter controls for displaying a dimensional filter. Which one of the following is *not* a filter type available in Tableau?

A. Nested filter control

B. Slider filter control

C. Single-select filter control

D. Multiple-value filter control

E. Typed-in field filter control

44. When manually creating a parameter, you can provide a list of allowable values. When you do, a table appears with two columns. What are the columns and what do they do? Select two.

A. Value: gives the value of the parameter used in calculations.

B. Description: describes what the value represents.

C. Return: indicates what a calculation will return if that value is selected.

D. Display As: presents values for the end user to select from.

E. Select: presents displayed names for the end user to select from.

45. What are the names of the *two* methods for placing objects in a dashboard layout? Select two.

A. Horizontal

B. Tiled

C. Vertical

D. Free form

E. Floating

46. What Tableau tool lets you preview a dashboard's appearance when rendered on a phone or tablet?

A. Layout tab

B. Format menu

C. Device Preview

D. Window menu

E. Size pull-down

47. Which one of the following types of items does Tableau *not* allow on a dashboard?

   A. Navigation button

   B. Blank

   C. Web page

   D. Animation

   E. Container

48. Containers are used to hold objects on the dashboard, especially in tiled layouts. Which one of the following options is *not* available for objects inside horizontal containers?

   A. Height

   B. Width

   C. Distribute contents evenly

   D. Outer padding

   E. Inner padding

49. What type of dashboard action would you most likely use to navigate to another dashboard within the same workbook?

   A. Filter

   B. Go to URL

   C. Go to sheet

   D. Go to dashboard

   E. Navigate

50. The following country-level dashboard was created to show profit by state and city. When a user clicks on a state, the bottom two charts show details on that state (as shown). When the state is deselected, the bottom two charts go blank. What dashboard action settings were populated to make this happen?

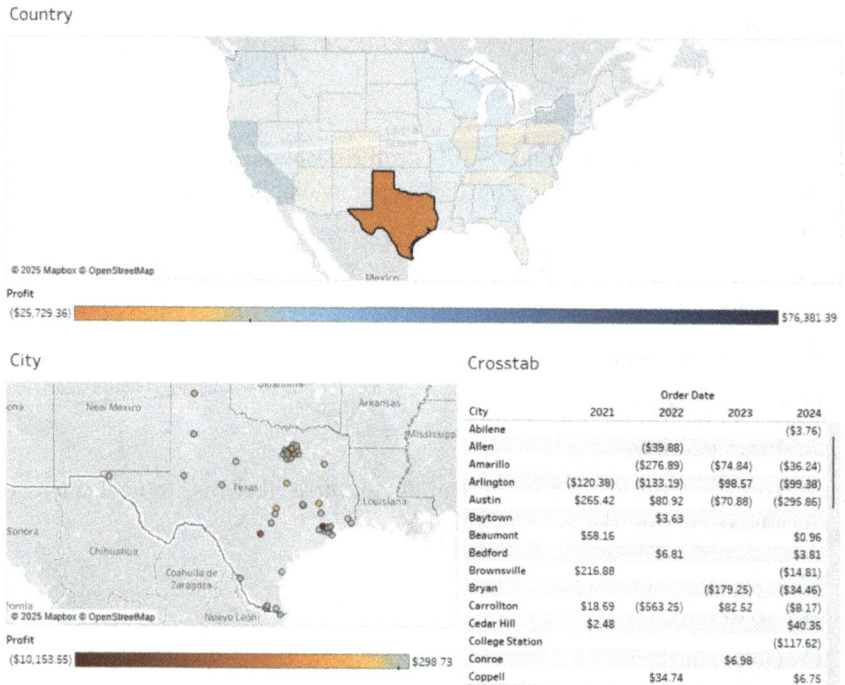

Country

© 2025 Mapbox © OpenStreetMap

Profit
($25,729.36) — $76,381.39

City

© 2025 Mapbox © OpenStreetMap

Profit
($10,153.55) — $298.73

Crosstab

City	2021	2022	2023	2024
		Order Date		
Abilene				($3.76)
Allen		($39.88)		
Amarillo		($276.89)	($74.84)	($36.24)
Arlington	($120.38)	($133.19)	$98.57	($99.38)
Austin	$265.42	$80.92	($70.88)	($295.86)
Baytown		$3.63		
Beaumont	$58.16			$0.96
Bedford		$6.81		$3.81
Brownsville	$216.88			($14.81)
Bryan			($179.25)	($34.46)
Carrollton	$18.69	($563.25)	$82.52	($8.17)
Cedar Hill	$2.48			$40.35
College Station				($117.62)
Conroe			$6.98	
Coppell		$34.74		$6.75

A. Source Sheets: Country, Target Sheets: City & Crosstab, Run action on: Select, Clearing the selection will: Exclude all values

B. Source Sheets: City & Crosstab, Target Sheets: Country, Run action on: Select, Clearing the selection will: Exclude all values

C. Source Sheets: City & Crosstab, Target Sheets: Country, Run action on: Hover, Clearing the selection will: Exclude all values

D. Source Sheets: Country, Target Sheets: City & Crosstab, Run action on: Hover, Clearing the selection will: Keep filtered values

E. Source Sheets: Country, Target Sheets: City & Crosstab, Run action on: Select, Clearing the selection will: Keep filtered values

51. Stories are used to walk a user through the analysis of data. Which one of the following *cannot* be added to stories?

    A. Dashboards

    B. Visualizations

    C. Navigation

    D. Text

    E. Images

52. On which *three* of the following locations can workbooks be published? Select three.

    A. Tableau Server

    B. Tableau Cloud

    C. Tableau Prep Builder

    D. Tableau Public

    E. Tableau Community

53. Which one of the following objects *cannot* be published to a server?

    A. Tableau Prep flow

    B. Workbook

    C. Data source

    D. Tableau Prep flow output

    E. Project folder

54. What are *two* ways of updating a published data source? Select two.

    A. Navigate to the data source on Tableau Server and use the ellipses menu to select Edit.

    B. Connect to the data source in Tableau Desktop, then right-click on it and select Create Local Copy. Once you've made your changes, republish it.

    C. Open the original workbook containing the data source, make your changes, and republish it.

    D. Open a connection using Tableau Prep Builder and modify the calculations and SQL as applicable.

    E. Right-click on the connected workbooks on the server and select Modify Underlying Data Source.

55. Tableau Server utilizes a hierarchy to manage what users can do with workbooks, data sources, and visualizations. Which one of the following is *not* part of that hierarchy?

A. Manager role

B. Site role

C. Project permissions

D. Workbook permissions

E. View permissions

56. Schedules on Tableau Server control which *three* of the following? Select three.

A. Extract refresh times

B. Workbook access times

C. Maintenance windows

D. Subscription delivery times

E. Tableau Prep flow runtimes

57. On Tableau Server, you can lock project permissions. What does this do?

A. Makes it impossible to edit the permissions on the project.

B. Makes the project controllable by the site admin only.

C. Makes the project controllable by the server admin only.

D. Sets permissions on the objects within the project to be controlled by the permissions on the project itself.

E. Filters the permissions on contained workbooks down to the view level.

58. What permission level overrides all other permission levels granted to an object?

A. Allowed

B. Undefined

C. Permission Explicitly Denied

D. Inherited

E. Explicit Allow

59. Where can an end user save default filter values and selections to appear the same way each time they visit a dashboard?

    A. Watch menu

    B. Custom Views → Make it my default (in the View menu)

    C. Data Guide

    D. Pause and Resume Auto Updates icons

    E. Share menu

60. Someone contacts you and asks you to remove a specific user's access to a workbook. When you visit the workbook, you find dozens of separate groups that can all grant users access. What is the most efficient way to find which group is granting that user's access so you can remove it?

    A. Search for the user on Tableau Server and check the Group Memberships tab.

    B. Search for the user in the workbook's Permissions window. Click the user and see which groups are highlighted.

    C. Search through the groups on Tableau Server until you find the user.

    D. Navigate to the project permissions and see where the user appears.

    E. Contact the workbook owner and have them change permissions when they republish the workbook.

Answer Key for the Practice Exam

1. B. A pivot (option B) is the correct transformation to use when needing to convert crosstab data into a columnar format, facilitating easier manipulation and analysis in Tableau. A join (option A) would not be suitable as it is used for connecting two separate data tables based on related fields, not altering the structure of data within a single table. The Data Interpreter (option C) is intended for cleaning up messy data sources and wouldn't serve to restructure the data layout. A union (option D) is used to append similar structured tables together vertically, which does not apply to transforming the layout of data within a single table. Lastly, a relationship (option E) establishes a flexible connection between tables for dynamic data exploration and is unrelated to transforming the structure of data presentation.

2. C. In Tableau Prep Builder, the clean data step (option C) is specifically designed to manipulate data, including the removal of duplicate values, by adjusting or removing entries as needed. Conversely, the aggregate step (option A) focuses on summarizing data, such as summing or averaging, rather than removing duplicates. The pivot step (option B) reorganizes data from a crosstab to a columnar format and does not address duplicate removal. The output step (option D) is merely for exporting the final data product from a flow and does not involve data manipulation such as deduplication. Lastly, the insert flow step (option E) is used to add an existing flow into the current project and does not inherently remove duplicates unless the inserted flow specifically includes such a step.

3. E. Extract filters (option E) are applied before data is pulled into Tableau, optimizing the data extraction process by limiting the data size and enhancing performance. Context filters (option A), although important in the visualization stage, are applied after the data has been extracted and do not influence the initial data pull. Data source filters (option B) are used post-extraction but

pre-visualization, thereby not affecting the initial data extraction phase. Relevant values filters (option C) are utilized during the visualization process to dynamically adjust the values of one filter based on another, occurring well after data extraction. Finally, filters listed in the Filter pane (option D), including the first filter, are applied during the visualization stage and are dependent on the data already being imported into Tableau, which means they do not influence the initial data extraction.

4. A. To make changes to a published data source in Tableau Desktop, the correct approach is to right-click the data source and choose Create Local Copy, as this action converts the published data source into a local copy that can be edited and republished (option A). Choosing Edit Data Source Filters merely allows switching between different published data sources without providing editing capabilities (option B). Selecting Extract Data creates a static extract file from the published data source, which does not facilitate direct editing of the data source itself (option C). Opting for Add to Saved Data Sources saves the data source locally but still connects back to the original published source when opened, thus not enabling editing (option D). Finally, choosing View Data only allows for a preview of the data contained in the data source and does not permit any modifications (option E).

5. E. Unioning the tables (option E) is the best method as it stacks the tables vertically, aligning columns and merging the data under consistent field headers, which is optimal for handling data sets that are structurally similar but temporally distinct. Blending data tables (option A) involves creating on-the-fly joins for visualization purposes rather than fully integrating the tables, making it less suitable for combining complete data sets. Joining the data tables (option B) creates a horizontal layout where each field is treated independently, potentially leading to duplicate field names and complicating data alignment. Creating a relationship between the tables (option C) establishes dynamic joins that do not inherently align data under the same field headers, which is not ideal for seamless data integration. Extracting the data sources (option D) merely creates a local copy to enhance performance and does not combine the tables.

6. A, C, D. Extract filters (option A) improve performance by filtering data prior to extraction, thus reducing the volume of data processed. Custom SQL (option C) enhances efficiency by allowing specific data criteria to be defined, limiting the data that is pulled. Extracts (option D) boost performance by storing data locally after pulling it from the source, optimizing it for faster access. Left joins (option B) do not enhance performance as they merge tables based on shared values, potentially increasing the amount of data retrieved. Data filters (option E) are applied after data extraction and do not influence the initial performance of data retrieval, as all data is still pulled from the database.

7. C. Relationship calculation (option C) is the correct tool as it allows for modifications to the fields being joined, such as removing or altering extra characters to ensure a match. Extract filters (option A) do not address the issue of joining fields with mismatched characters, as they are primarily used for filtering data rather than modifying join conditions. Blending (option B) is not suitable for fields with extra characters as it requires exact field matching and does not allow for field manipulation within the blend itself. Unions (option D) stack similar data tables but do not modify field data for joining purposes, making them ineffective for this scenario. An outer join (option E) would still require exact matching fields to avoid producing null values, which does not solve the problem of extra characters in one of the fields.

8. D. Data Interpreter (option D) is available as an option in Tableau Prep; however, it is part of adding data to the application, not one of the options within a clean step. In Tableau Prep, combining fields (option A) helps consolidate data effectively, and changing data types (option C) allows for appropriate categorization and use of data, such as retaining leading zeros in strings like employee IDs. Additionally, repairing typos (option B) and aliasing field values (option E) are supported features, aiding in the correction of data errors and inconsistencies.

9. B. In Tableau Desktop, the Hide option (option B) is used to keep a field from view during the data visualization process, effectively removing its visibility without deleting the data itself. Filtering (option A), on the other hand, does not remove a field but rather excludes rows based on specific field values. The Remove option (option C) does not exist in Tableau Desktop. Similarly, the Exclude option (option D) is used within the context of filtering to omit data based on criteria but does not serve to remove fields entirely. Lastly, Pivoting (option E) is a method to reorganize data by converting columns into rows, which alters the structure of the data rather than hiding or removing a field.

10. B. In Tableau Prep, the correct step to save the resulting data set after it has been processed is the Output step (option B), as it allows for saving the output into a file or publishing it to a server. The Publish step (option A) is not available in Tableau Prep; instead, publishing functionalities are included within the Output step. The End step (option C) does not exist; the process is concluded by using an Output step. Similarly, the Save step (option D) is not a designated step in Tableau Prep; saving the data is achieved through the Output step. Lastly, the Display step (option E) is also non-existent for finalizing flows in Tableau Prep; while data can be viewed at any step, saving requires the Output step.

11. A. In Tableau Desktop, the blue "Abc" icon next to a field located in the top half of the Data pane indicates it is a discrete string dimension (option A) because dimensions are positioned above the line, and the blue color signifies discreteness, while the "Abc" icon specifically denotes a string type. Continuous string dimension (option B) is incorrect as continuous fields are represented by green

icons, not blue. Discrete string measure (option C) and continuous string measure (option D) are both incorrect because measures are located below the dividing line in the Data pane, and continuous fields would also be green. A string parameter (option E) is also incorrect as parameters are found at the bottom of the pane and have their own distinct section, separate from dimensions and measures.

12. E. Row Number (option E) is not automatically created by Tableau; instead, users must manually create or define this type of field to number rows sequentially in their data visualizations. Measure Names (option A) and Measure Values (option B) are both automatically generated by Tableau Desktop to facilitate data analysis, listing respectively the names and numeric values of all measures in a dataset. Longitude (option C) is similarly auto-generated when geographic data is present, providing necessary geographic coordinates for mapping. The [Distinct Field] (Count) (option D) is a derived field that Tableau creates to count unique data points, automatically generated based on the data's unique identifiers.

13. D. The correct placement for SUM([Sales]) in a crosstab is on the Text mark (option D), as this allows the sales values to be displayed directly within the cells of the crosstab. In Tableau Desktop, the Rows pane (option A) is used for vertical division of the chart, and in this visualization, Category and Sub-Category, not SUM([Sales]), are placed there. The Columns pane (option B) is responsible for the horizontal structuring of the chart, with YEAR(Order Date) placed here, indicating that SUM([Sales]) is not used in this section. The Detail mark (option C) is utilized for adding granularity to the visualization without affecting its visual attributes, and it does not host any measure like SUM([Sales]) for this specific chart. Lastly, while filters (option E) can control which data appears in a visualization, they do not typically display data like SUM([Sales]) directly and are not used to recreate the visual representation of the sales data in this scenario.

14. B, C, E. Measure filters (option B) and dimension filters (option C) require placing respective fields directly on the Filter pane to filter data based on specific measure values or dimension categories. Context filters (option E) involve placing either dimension or measure fields on the Filter pane and setting them to apply before other filters, thereby affecting the processing order of subsequent filters. Data source filters and extract filters (option A) operate before visualization and are not placed on the Filter pane, as they handle data pre-processing. Level of Detail (option D) calculations adjust the granularity of data calculations rather than filtering through placement on the Filter pane.

15. C. Detail (option C) does not open a submenu or window but rather segments data within a visualization without additional interactive settings, distinguishing it from the other options. Color (option A) and Text/Label (option B) both typically involve submenus or windows for selecting attributes like hues or font settings, respectively. Size (option D) and Tooltip (option E) also feature interac-

tive elements, such as sliders for adjusting size and fields for customizing tooltip text.

16. B. The correct functionality of this icon in Tableau Desktop is to swap the fields in the rows with those in the columns, as it is specifically designed for this purpose and not for sorting functions (option B). Sorting fields either in ascending or descending order, or changing the nature of the sort from alphabetical to measure-based (options A, C, E), are functions typically associated with different icons or settings within Tableau, which are located adjacent to the swap functionality but are distinct in their operation. Additionally, reversing the order of an existing sort (option D) is another specific function not served by this icon, which is solely for swapping row and column placements.

17. D. The "Marks to Label" Min/Max setting (option D) correctly labels only the minimum and maximum points in a data set, which explains why only two labels appear on the chart. The "Marks to Label" Selected (option A) and "Marks to Label" Highlighted (option C) both require specific points to be actively selected or highlighted to show labels, which is not indicated in the scenario provided. The "Marks to Label" Most Recent (option B) would label only the latest point in a data sequence, not necessarily the minimum or maximum values. Lastly, "Marks to Label" Line Ends (option E) would typically label the beginning and end points of a line, which does not align with the labeling described in the question, where one label appears midline.

18. C. Dragging the Country field to Detail (option C) utilizes Tableau's built-in geocoding to automatically generate a map by placing each country at its corresponding geographic coordinates. Dragging the Country field to Rows (option A) or to Columns (option B) will merely list the countries linearly in rows or columns, respectively, which is useful for creating tables but not maps. Dragging Longitude to Rows and Latitude to Columns (option D), or vice versa (option E), will not create a map unless a geographic field like Country is correctly assigned, and these fields should be placed in the opposite manner specified to align correctly with Tableau's mapping functionality.

19. A. Cities with ambiguous names can cause confusion in Tableau as it requires additional context like state or country to accurately place them on a map (option A). While errors in your data could exist, they do not directly lead to the issue of cities not appearing on the map (option B). The repetition of city names in the dataset is common and does not contribute to the "unknown" warning in Tableau (option C). Tableau's city database is comprehensive enough to include cities with small populations, making it unlikely that the missing cities are due to gaps in Tableau's database (option D). Lastly, having null values in the cities field would result in a significantly lower count of unknowns, indicating that null values are not the main issue here (option E).

20. B. Filtering Measure Names (option B) is the most effective method as it directly allows the selection of desired measures to display in the chart. Filtering Measure Values (option A) directly is not possible because Tableau converts Measure Values to Measure Names when they are used in the Filter pane, making this approach ineffective for isolating specific measures. Filtering the measure fields themselves (option C) only controls the visibility of values within those measures and does not limit which measures appear. Writing a calculation (option D) to pull specific measures is not feasible because Measure Names or Measure Values cannot be used in calculations. Similarly, using Tableau groups (option E) to isolate measures is not an option because Measure Names or Measure Values cannot be grouped.

21. B, D. "Table (across)" (option B) correctly calculates the difference across years, aligning with the data presentation in the chart, and "Specific values - Year of Order Date" (option D) accurately targets the calculation across different years, making it suitable for analyzing annual sales changes. Applying the Difference table calculation "Table (down)" (option A) would incorrectly compute differences between product categories rather than across years, which does not match the described use in the question. The "Specific values - Category" (option C) approach would inaccurately focus on differences between categories, not reflecting the year-to-year comparison needed. Lastly, "Table (across then down)" (option E) would unnecessarily complicate the calculation by mixing category and year differences, which is not required in this context.

22. E. In the context of ranking runners in a race where ties should reflect the same rank and the subsequent rank should continue sequentially, the Dense ranking method (option E) is the most suitable as it assigns the same rank to tied participants and the next rank follows immediately without skipping any numbers, resulting in ranks like 1, 2, 2, 3. Conversely, the Competition ranking method (option A and option D) assigns the same rank for ties but skips the subsequent rank, leading to a sequence such as 1, 2, 2, 4, which does not meet the requirement. The Modified competition method (option B) incorrectly adjusts the ranks by skipping the rank before the tie and repeating the next, resulting in ranks like 1, 3, 3, 4, which also fails to satisfy the given criteria. Lastly, the Unique method (option C) assigns a distinct rank to each participant, eliminating the possibility of ties altogether, with ranks displayed as 1, 2, 3, 4, which clearly does not address the need for equal ranking in the event of a tie.

23. D. In Tableau calculated fields, comments are correctly denoted by two forward slashes (option D), as they indicate the beginning of a comment line. A single hyphen (option A) is typically used for subtraction in mathematical operations, not for comments. Two hyphens (option B) and two greater-than symbols (option E) are not recognized by Tableau for any specific function including commenting. Lastly, two backslashes (option C) are also incorrect; they are

generally used for different purposes in programming, such as escape sequences, but not for commenting in Tableau.

24. A. To accurately calculate the overall profit-to-sales ratio for a company, using SUM([Profit]) / SUM([Sales]) (option A) is correct because it aggregates total profit and total sales before calculating the ratio, ensuring a comprehensive measure across all transactions. The option SUM([Profit]) / [Sales] (option B) and [Profit] / SUM([Sales]) (option E) will create errors due to mismatched levels of aggregation between profit and sales. Calculating [Profit] / [Sales] for each row (option C) and then summing these individual ratios using SUM([Profit] / [Sales]) (option D) would inaccurately sum the individual transaction ratios instead of reflecting the overall business performance.

25. B. The correct calculation to extract the part of the email after the "@" symbol is RIGHT([Email],LEN([Email])-FIND([Email],"@")) (option B) because it correctly computes the number of characters from the "@" symbol to the end of the string by subtracting the position of the "@" from the total length of the email address. The option RIGHT([Email],FIND([Email],'@')-1) (option A) incorrectly attempts to return characters from the right starting before the "@" symbol, thus including part of the user name. The option RIGHT([Email], FIND([Email],'@')) (option C) erroneously counts characters from the start of the email to the "@" and returns that many characters from the end, which does not isolate the domain. Similarly, RIGHT([Email], FIND([Email],'@')+1) (option D) also miscounts by including the "@" itself in the output. Lastly, RIGHT([Email],LEN([Email])-FIND([Email],"@")+1) (option E) makes a similar error by including the "@" in the results, which is not required for isolating the domain part of the email.

26. D. The DATENAME function is designed to return the name of the specified date part, not a numerical value, making Thursday (option D) the correct answer as it identifies the day of the week for July 4, 1776. Options A, B, and C are incorrect because they represent numerical values, which DATENAME does not provide; for example, DATENAME('weekday',#07-04-1776#) would yield a numerical day of the week (5 for Thursday), and DATENAME('day',#07-04-1776#) would return 4, the day of the month. Option E is incorrect as the calculation specifies 'week day', not 'month', hence returning the day name rather than the month name.

27. E. The correct configuration, Category and YEAR([Order Date]) (option E), appropriately aggregates sales data at the category level annually, matching the chart's presentation and supporting uniformity across years within each category. Including both Category and Sub-Category (option A) would result in identical sales numbers across each date for every sub-category, which does not match the chart's display of varying totals by year. Using Category and Order Date (option B) would inaccurately sum sales for each day rather than annually, leading to

overly granular data that does not align with the yearly aggregation shown. Including Sub-Category and Order Date (option C) would show differing values for each subcategory, contradicting the uniform category-level data depicted in the chart. Similarly, including Sub-Category with YEAR([Order Date]) (option D) would still differentiate data by subcategory, which is inconsistent with the chart's category-focused aggregation.

28. A, D. In Tableau Desktop, IF, THEN, ELSE (option A) and CASE, WHEN, ELSE (option D) are both valid syntax for performing logical operations, with the former being useful for simpler decision structures and the latter better suited for handling multiple conditions efficiently. However, IF, WHEN, ELSE (option B), CASE, THEN, ELSE (option C), and CASE, IF, ELSE (option E) are not recognized logical structures within Tableau, as the correct syntax does not include combinations such as IF WHEN, CASE THEN, or CASE IF.

29. B, D, E. Context filters (option B) are applied before FIXED LoD calculations as they specifically alter the data that is available for processing. Data source filters (option D) and extract filters (option E) are also applied before FIXED LoD calculations because they limit the data at the source or during the extract creation, which precedes any calculations. Conversely, dimension filters (option A) and measure filters (option C) are applied after FIXED LoD calculations, and thus do not influence the initial computation unless they are incorporated into the context.

30. C. {EXCLUDE [Category]: AVG([Profit])} (option C) correctly excludes Category from the calculation, allowing the computation of a single average profit across all categories for each year, suitable for the overall average line. The {FIXED [Category]: AVG([Profit])} calculation (option A) incorrectly locks the average profit to each category, ignoring variations across years, and does not provide a single overall average. {INCLUDE [Category]: AVG([Profit])} (option B) is ineffective because including Category, which is already part of the visualization, does not alter the calculation for the desired overall average. {FIXED YEAR([Order Date]), [Category]: AVG([Profit])} (option D) unnecessarily fixes the calculation to each category per year, which would not yield a single overall average but a sum of category averages per year. Finally, [Profit]/ {EXCLUDE [Category]: AVG([Profit])} (option E) incorrectly attempts to divide each individual profit by the excluded category average, which results in a ratio, not an overall average profit.

31. A. Creating a group (option A) is the most suitable method for organizing businesses into twelve regions as it allows for the consolidation of field values into larger, manageable collections, which is ideal for regional categorization. On the other hand, creating a set (option B) would not effectively handle twelve distinct regions since sets only categorize data into two states: included or not included.

Using bins (option C) is inappropriate for this task because bins are designed for grouping numerical data into ranges, not for categorizing discrete regions. Creating a Level of Detail (LoD) calculation (option D) would unnecessarily complicate the process as LoD calculations are meant to adjust how dimensions impact measures rather than simply grouping data. Lastly, utilizing a parameter with a calculation (option E) would involve cumbersome calculations and is not practical for managing multiple regions and numerous businesses, making groups a more straightforward choice.

32. A, C, D. Manual selection, conditional logic, and top *n* by field or formula (options A, C, and D) are valid methods for defining sets, as they directly allow for the specification and grouping of data points based on specific criteria or rankings. Wildcard match (option B), while useful for filtering data, does not provide a mechanism for creating sets, as it lacks the ability to specify discrete groupings or conditions. Calculated fields (option E) are primarily used for creating new data values or modifying existing ones and do not directly facilitate the creation of sets, though they can incorporate set information for further data manipulation.

33. E. In a box-and-whisker plot, the middle gray areas encompass the middle 50% of values when subcategories are ordered from lowest to highest sales (option E), effectively marking the interquartile range. This range helps in understanding the spread and central tendency of the data without being influenced by outliers. The middle gray areas do not represent the average sales values of the overall dataset (option A), as they specifically illustrate the interquartile range, not the mean. They also do not indicate the subcategories with either the lowest (option B) or highest (option C) sales amount per number of sales, as the plot segments data based on quartiles rather than performance metrics. While these areas do involve median values, they do not exclusively represent the subcategories falling in the median range (option D).

34. E. The shaded area around the forecast line in the chart represents a 95% confidence interval, indicating there is a 95% chance that future sales values will fall within this range based on historical data (option E). It does not simply represent other potential values based on earlier months without a probabilistic context (option A), nor is it restricted to representing the middle 50% of values for all products, which would typically be a description of an interquartile range rather than a confidence interval (option B). The shaded area is also not a generic 10% buffer zone, which lacks a statistical basis (option C), and it specifically indicates the range of likely future values, not just the minimum and maximum margins of error (option D).

35. D. Polynomial trend lines (option D) allow for adjustments in the degrees of the polynomial, which effectively controls the curvature of the trend line to better fit the data, making it the most flexible for modeling non-linear patterns. Linear

trend lines (option A) simply apply a straight line that attempts to capture the overall direction of the data, without flexibility in curve adjustment. Logarithmic trend lines (option B) are useful for data that scales exponentially, where initial changes are rapid and later changes are more gradual, but do not offer control over the degree of curve. Exponential trend lines (option C) are characterized by a consistent multiplicative rate of change, creating a U-shaped curve, which does not allow for adjusting the curve's degree. Power trend lines (option E) model data with a fixed exponent that determines the curve's steepness, but unlike polynomial, they do not permit varying degrees of curvature.

36. E. The correct label 'Custom: Calculation Field Name: Value' (option E) fully matches the chart's label by incorporating both the type of calculation, the field name, and the numerical value, precisely reflecting the detailed format shown. The label 'Computation' (option A) refers to the type of calculation, such as Average, not to the specific labeling format used in the chart. 'Field name' (option B) alone would only display the name of the data field, like Profit, which is insufficient for the detailed label in the chart. 'Value' (option C) indicates the numerical outcome of the computation, which is $24,358, but does not include any descriptive text about the calculation or field. The 'Custom: Calculation Field Name' (option D) would show a label like Average Profit, but it lacks the specific value, making it incomplete compared to the chart's label.

37. B. The correct setting for the reference line in the chart is Table (option B) because it applies to the entire table, indicating a line that spans all the data presented. Pane (option A) is incorrect as it refers to a subsection of the table, not covering the full extent of the data shown. Range (option C) and Field (option E) are not valid scope options for reference lines in this context, hence their inapplicability. Cell (option D) would incorrectly apply a reference line to each individual data point or bar within the chart, making it too granular for the described scenario.

38. E. The calculation DATEDIFF('day',[Order Date],{FIXED : MIN([Order Date])}) specifically computes the difference in days between the first date in the entire data set ({FIXED : MIN([Order Date])}) and the date of each individual order ([Order Date]) (option E), thereby indicating how many days each order occurred after the first date in the dataset. It does not merely identify the first date in the data set (option A), as that would be represented solely by {FIXED : MIN([Order Date])} . It cannot represent the earliest date for each category (option B), which would require fixing the calculation by category, such as {FIXED [Category]: MIN([Order Date])}. The calculation also does not return the day of the week (option C), which would involve using DATE NAME('weekday',...) instead of DATEDIFF. Finally, it does not calculate the difference in days from today (option D), which would use TODAY() in place of [Order Date] in the function.

39. D. In Tableau Desktop, a set is correctly identified by a Venn diagram icon, aligning with the representation of logical combinations of data elements (option D). A continuous number, however, is denoted by a green number sign "#," reflecting its quantitative, non-categorical nature (option A). Groups, which organize categorical data, are symbolized by a paper clip icon, not a Venn diagram (option B). Hierarchies, used to represent nested data, are indicated by a tree-like icon, emphasizing their structured format (option C). Lastly, a discrete date is marked by a blue calendar icon, distinguishing it from the continuous or logical data types (option E).

40. B. The IIF function in Tableau returns a value based on a condition: if the condition is true, the second value is returned, and if it is false, the third value is returned. Therefore, since the condition checks if the Customer field equals 'Brian', and it does, the function returns RADAR (option B), not Brian (option A), which is merely the condition being tested. Lisa (option C) is incorrectly placed as a return value for a false condition in the provided syntax and would not be returned for the condition being true. Unknown (option D) is not a specified return value in this IIF function, and True (option E) is not relevant as the function returns string values specified in the function, not Boolean values.

41. B. A relevant values filter (option B) dynamically adjusts its options based on selections made in other filters, ensuring that only applicable choices are displayed. In contrast, a multiple-value filter (option A) allows multiple selections but its choices are not contingent on other filters. A single-select filter (option C) restricts users to one choice without dependence on other filter settings. A context filter (option D) sets the overarching filtering conditions for a dashboard but does not adapt based on other filters' settings. Lastly, a dimensional filter (option E) simply restricts data based on dimension values and does not interact with or adjust due to other filters.

42. A. The correct sorting method is a nested sort on Category by Sales, ascending (option A), as categories are reordered within each year to maintain the ascending sales pattern, which wouldn't occur in a simple sort. Sorting directly on Category by Sales, ascending (option B) would keep the same order of categories across all years, based on total sales, which is not observed here. Sorting based on the ascending order of the year of the Order Date (option C) does not apply, as the primary sorting focus is on category sales within each year, not merely the date. Similarly, sorting by both year of the Order Date and Category (option D) would maintain a consistent category order across years, which contradicts the observed shifting category order. Finally, a manual sort on Category (option E) would imply a fixed category order across all years, which is inconsistent with the dynamic reordering seen in the chart.

43. A. Nested filter control (option A) is not available in Tableau; while filters can be dependent on one another, a specific nested filter control type does not exist.

Slider filter control (option B) is used in Tableau, allowing users to select values via a sliding bar mechanism. Single-select filter control (option C) exists in Tableau and can be implemented using radio buttons, pull-downs, or value slider bars. Multiple-value filter control (option D) is also available, enabling the selection of multiple items via checkboxes, pull-down checkboxes, or comma-separated fields. Typed-in field filter control (option E) allows users to directly type in a value to filter data, which is a supported feature in Tableau.

44. A, D. The "Value" column (option A) is correct as it holds the underlying value used in calculations, ensuring that the parameter functions accurately within the system's logic. The "Display As" column (option D) is also correct because it specifies how these values are presented to the end user, enhancing usability by allowing users to select from understandable options rather than raw data values. Conversely, the "Description" option (option B) is incorrect because it suggests an explanatory role not aligned with the functional purpose of columns in parameter settings, which are focused on value input and user interaction. The "Return" option (option C) inaccurately implies a direct influence on output calculations, which is not the purpose of a parameter's input columns. Lastly, the "Select" option (option E) is incorrect as it redundantly describes a function already served by the "Display As" column, which is to present user-friendly names for selection.

45. B, E. Tiled (option B) and Floating (option E) are indeed the two methods used for arranging objects in a dashboard, allowing for structured and overlapping placements, respectively. Horizontal (option A) and Vertical (option C) are types of containers used within dashboard layouts but are not methods for placing objects themselves. Free form (option D), while a design style, does not specifically refer to a method for placing objects in dashboards.

46. C. Device Preview (option C) is specifically designed to show how a dashboard will appear on various devices such as phones and tablets, making it the correct tool for this purpose. The Layout tab (option A) is designed for arranging dashboard elements and does not provide rendering previews for different devices. The Format menu (option B) focuses on visual adjustments like font and borders rather than device-specific dashboard previews. The Window menu (option D) manages aspects of the Tableau user interface but does not offer a preview of dashboards on different devices. Lastly, the Size pull-down (option E) allows selection of dashboard dimensions but does not simulate how these dimensions appear on different devices.

47. D. Tableau does not support the inclusion of animation objects (option D) directly on dashboards, which distinguishes the option 'Animation' as the correct answer for this question. Tableau dashboards support navigation buttons (option A) for moving between dashboards, blank objects to manage space and visual layout (option B), and containers (option E) to organize dashboard elements

either vertically or horizontally, as well as the ability to embed web pages (option C) directly within a dashboard.

48. A. In horizontal containers, objects are aligned side by side, allowing for control over their width but not their height (option A), as height adjustments are not feasible due to the fixed vertical alignment. Width (option B) is adjustable to accommodate the horizontal placement of multiple objects within the container. The feature to distribute contents evenly (option C) is available and ensures that all objects within the container are sized proportionally, facilitating a uniform appearance. Both outer padding (option D) and inner padding (option E) are configurable for objects in horizontal containers, providing flexibility in spacing and layout aesthetics.

49. C. The "Go to sheet" action (option C) is specifically designed for navigating directly to another sheet within the same workbook, making it the most appropriate choice for this purpose. Filter actions (option A) are used to modify the displayed data within the same dashboard based on user interactions, not for navigating to different dashboards or sheets. The Go to URL action (option B) is generally used for external web navigation and is not the ideal choice for internal navigation within a workbook, as it is less direct compared to using the "Go to sheet" action. "Go to dashboard" (option D) and Navigate (option E) are not recognized actions in Tableau for internal navigation, rendering them incorrect choices for the task of moving between dashboards or sheets within a workbook.

50. A. The correct dashboard action setting (option A) involves selecting a state on the Country visualization, which triggers updates in the City and Crosstab visualizations; deselecting the state clears these visualizations by excluding all values. Option B and C incorrectly identify the source sheets as City & Crosstab, whereas the action is initiated from the Country visualization. Option D and E incorrectly set the action to run on hover or to keep filtered values upon clearing the selection, neither of which matches the described behavior of the dashboard where clicking (not hovering) on a state updates the visualizations and clearing the selection causes them to go blank.

51. E. Images cannot be directly added to stories in Tableau unless they are part of a dashboard, restricting their standalone use within the storytelling tool (option E). In stories, dashboards and visualizations are integral components, facilitating a structured walkthrough of the analysis (options A and B). Navigation is essential as it allows users to move seamlessly between different parts of the story, such as various dashboards or visualizations (option C). Text can be incorporated within story pages to provide additional context or explanations (option D).

52. A, B, D. Tableau Server (option A) and Tableau Cloud (option B) both serve as secure platforms where organizations can publish and manage access to their workbooks, with the main difference being that Tableau manages the infrastructure for Tableau Cloud. Tableau Public (option D) is an open platform where

users can publish their workbooks for public viewing and sharing. Tableau Prep Builder (option C), however, is used for preparing data and managing Tableau Prep flows rather than for publishing workbooks. Tableau Community (option E) is a forum for discussion and sharing ideas among Tableau users, not a platform for workbook publication.

53. E. Project folders (option E) are organizational structures created directly on the server rather than being publishable items from Tableau Desktop or Tableau Prep, distinguishing them as the only option that cannot be published. Tableau Prep flows (option A) and their outputs (option D) can both be published to a server, allowing for automated scheduling and data management. Workbooks (option B) are commonly published to servers as they are central to sharing and distributing visualizations. Data sources (option C) can also be published to enable live connections or scheduled extractions, facilitating centralized data management.

54. B, C. Creating a local copy of the data source in Tableau Desktop and then republishing after modifications (option B) is a valid method because it allows for local edits before updating the server version. Similarly, opening the original workbook that contains the data source, making changes, and republishing it (option C) is a straightforward way to update the published data source, ensuring all changes are carried over. Navigating to the data source on Tableau Server and using the ellipses menu to select Edit (option A) does not allow for editing the data source itself, only connection settings like credentials. Using Tableau Prep Builder to open a connection and modify calculations or SQL (option D) does not apply to already published data sources, as Tableau Prep is not designed for this purpose. Lastly, right-clicking on connected workbooks on the server to modify the underlying data source (option E) is not a feature supported by Tableau Server, which focuses on local edits before republishing.

55. A. The "Manager role" (option A) is not a recognized part of Tableau Server's hierarchy for managing access to workbooks, data sources, and visualizations, making it the incorrect option. "Site roles" (option B) are integral to defining user capabilities within a specific site on Tableau Server. "Project permissions" (option C) allow for control at the project level, which can be set to either locked or unlocked, affecting the default permissions for published content. "Workbook permissions" (option D) enable specific access controls for individual workbooks, provided the project settings allow for such customization. Finally, "View permissions" (option E) are applicable when managing access to individual views or dashboards within a workbook, particularly when tabbed views are disabled.

56. A, D, E. Schedules on Tableau Server are utilized to determine the timing for extract refreshes, ensuring data remains current (option A). Subscription delivery times are also managed through schedules, allowing users to receive updated workbook content at specified intervals (option D). Schedules are furthermore

used to run Tableau Prep flows at designated times, automating the data preparation process (option E). Schedules do not restrict when workbooks can be accessed, as access is available any time (option B). Maintenance windows are not controlled by these schedules but are instead set by server administrators (option C).

57. D. Locking project permissions sets a standard where all objects within the project inherit their permissions directly from the project itself, ensuring a uniform security protocol across all contained elements (option D). Locking project permissions on Tableau Server does not make it impossible to edit permissions on the project (option A); rather, modifications can still be made at the project level. The control of locked projects is not limited to site or server administrators (options B and C) alone, as other designated individuals can also manage these settings. Lastly, this feature does not extend to filtering permissions down to the view level within workbooks (option E); this is managed differently depending on workbook settings.

58. C. Permission Explicitly Denied (option C) is the highest priority permission because it overrides all other permissions, ensuring that if it is set, no other permission can allow access. Allowed permissions (option A) can be negated by a Permission Explicitly Denied, indicating that even if access is generally permitted, it can be specifically revoked. Undefined permissions (option B) typically mean that default or inherited permissions apply, but these too are overridden if a Permission Explicitly Denied is set. Inherited permissions (option D) are default permissions that a user or group receives from a parent object, but they do not have precedence over an explicit denial. Finally, the Explicit Allow (option E) does not exist in Tableau, reinforcing that it cannot be a correct answer.

59. B. Custom Views → Make it my default (option B) directly allows users to save their personalized filter settings and selections as defaults for subsequent visits, aligning perfectly with the question's requirement. The Watch menu (option A) is used for subscribing to dashboard updates or tracking visualization values, not for setting default viewing preferences. The Data Guide (option C) provides insights about the data rather than saving user-specific dashboard settings. Pause and Resume Auto Updates icons (option D) control the real-time data update behavior and do not save any filter or view settings. Lastly, the Share menu (option E) is intended for distributing dashboard links to other users and does not involve personal default setting functionalities.

60. B. The most efficient method involves searching for the user directly in the workbook's Permissions window (option B), where selecting the user will highlight the groups they belong to, clearly showing which group's access needs to be removed. Searching for the user on Tableau Server and checking the Group Memberships tab (option A) is not practical because there is no such tab in the user profile. Searching through each group on Tableau Server (option C) is highly inefficient

and time-consuming due to the large number of groups. Navigating to the project permissions (option D) does not provide detailed information about specific user access within groups, especially if permissions are unlocked. Finally, contacting the workbook owner to change permissions upon republishing the workbook (option E) does not directly address identifying the specific group granting access to the user.

Index

Symbols

+ symbol, 191
.hyper file extension, 10
.tde file extension, 10
.tds file extension, 10
.tdsx file extension, 10
.tfl file extension, 10
.tflx file extension, 10
.twb file extension, 10
.twbx file extension, 10
// (two forward slashes), 109
{} curly brackets, 124

A

accessibility enhancements, 80, 160, 231-233
Actions window
    actions available, 234-246
    opening, 234
    overview of, 234
Add Filters extension (dashboards), 222
Add Set action (dashboards), 244
Add Table Calculation option, 97
Add to Context option, 41
Advanced menu (color control), 58
aggregation (calculated fields), 112
Aggregation option, 9, 19
aggregation window (measure filters), 44
alerts, 287
Aliases option, 22, 32
Alignment menu, 62
alignment options, 195
Allow selection by category (Edit Tooltip window), 69
Analytics pane

accessing, 149
    modeling tools, 151-153
    reference lines, 154
    sections of, 150
    summarization tools, 150
Angle shelf, 73
annotations, 210-211
Apply button (filter controls), 160
area charts, 52, 77
Attribute option, 49
autocomplete, 110
automatic charts, 52
average line tool, 150
axis formatting, 209

B

Background Images menu, 84
Background Layers option, 85
Background Maps menu, 83
backgrounds, transparent, 196
bands, 198
bar charts, 52, 76-77
bins, 145-148
Blank object (dashboards), 221
blends, 6, 16
borders
    adding to marks, 54
    dashboard content, 218, 225
    formatting, 200-201
box plots, 150, 154, 180-182
box-and-whisker plots, 150, 180
bubble charts, 89
bullet graphs, 76

forward slashes, two (//), 109
Full Outer join, 13
funnel icon, 234

G

Gantt charts, 53, 77
General tab (Create Set window), 144
General tab (Dimension filter window), 43
geocoding, 84
geographic fields, 31, 81
Geographic Role option, 33
globe icon, 31, 81
Go To Sheet action (dashboards), 241
Go to URL actions (dashboards), 240
grand totals, 208
granularity, 124
Group By option, 33
groups, 140, 192

H

Hide All Unused Fields option, 9
Hide Card (filter controls), 161
Hide option, 22, 32
hierarchies, 33, 190-193
Highlight actions (dashboards), 238
highlight tables, 80
Highlighted option (Label shelf), 63
histograms, 76
History option, 9
horizontal bar charts, 76
horizontal containers, 221
.hyper file extension, 10

I

icons
    + (drilldown) symbol, 191
    arrow exiting box, 233
    chain-like symbol, 16
    color indicators, 31
    cylinders, single versus double, 9
    dashboard icons, 214
    data roles, data flows, databases, 280
    data source permissions, 279
    in Format pane, 193
    funnel icon, 233, 234
    globe icon, 31, 81
    indicating data type, 22, 30
    New Story button, 247

quick action icons, 36
    Sort Ascending/Descending icons, 36, 162
    Swap Rows and Columns icon, 36
    user controls, 289
    workbook permissions, 278
if/then function, 121
Image option (dashboards), 221
Image Role option, 33
Include command buttons (Edit Tooltip window), 69
INCLUDE function, 129-132
Include Totals option, 58
Include/Exclude option (filter controls), 160
Inner join, 13
Insert Flow, cleaning data in, 20
Insert menu (Edit Tooltip window), 69
INT calculation, 116
interquartile range, 180
INTERSECTS calculation, 116
ISO (International Organization for Standardization) format, 117

J

joins
    cleaning data in, 19
    compared to relationships, 14
    dynamic joins, 14
    purpose of, 12
    types of, 12

L

Label shelf, 61-65
Layout tab, 216-219
layouts
    floating, 223-226
    tiled, 227-231
Left join, 13, 16
Left Only join, 13
legends, formatting, 204
Level of Detail (LoD) calculation
    EXCLUDE function, 132-136
    FIXED function, 126-129
    function syntax, 124
    INCLUDE function, 129-132
    nesting LoD functions, 137-139
    purpose of, 124
line charts, 52, 77
Line Ends option (Label shelf), 63
lines, formatting, 201

typed-in field filter control, 159

U
unions, 17, 19
unlocked asset permissions, 274
UPPER() function, 13
usage information, 280
Use Full Color Range option, 58
user interactions
    annotations, 210-211
    axis editing options, 209
    box plots, 180-182
    distribution bands, 177-180
    filter controls, 157-161
    formatting chart controls, 203
    formatting chart titles, 205-207
    formatting charts, 193-202
    hierarchies, 190-193
    null and missing values, 212
    parameters, 183-190
    reference bands, 176-177
    reference lines, 171-175
    sorts, 162-170
    totals and grand totals, 208

user-based workbook controls, 282-291

V
vertical bar charts, 76
vertical containers, 221
views, 268, 282
visualization area (view), 34-37

W
watch data, 287
WHEN statements , 123
whiskers, 180
Wildcard tab (Dimensions filter window), 43
wildcard unions, 18
workbooks
    managing on servers, 265-267
    owners, 269
    publishing, 261-264
    user-based controls for, 282-291
    workbook permissions, 278
workbooks, definition of term, 268
Workflow option (dashboards), 222

About the Author

Christopher Gardner is a business intelligence analyst and lead Tableau developer for the University of Michigan. He has over 24 years of experience with the university and has served as a data analyst and Tableau expert for the campus since 2013. Within his role for the university and through O'Reilly boot camps and classes, he has taught thousands of users how to develop data visualizations and dashboards within Tableau. In addition, Christopher is a tech editor and writer for O'Reilly, participating in various Tableau and data-related articles and books. He is a Tableau Certified Data Analyst and has maintained an equivalent of that since 2016. He holds a degree in Actuarial Mathematics from the University of Michigan.

Colophon

The animal on the cover of *Tableau Certified Data Analyst Study Guide* is the green-tailed jacamar (*Galbula galbula*).

An elegant bird with glossy feathers and a long bill and tail, the green-tailed jacamar inhabits woodlands, savannas, and shrublands of north-central South America, where it hunts for insects from its forest perches. It makes its nests from excavated burrows in the earth, or sometimes in termite nests, and is one of many lovely birds to have been memorialized in a postage stamp from Suriname.

The International Union for Conservation of Nature categorizes the green-tailed jacamar as being of Least Concern, from a conservation standpoint. Many of the animals on O'Reilly covers are endangered; all of them are important to the world.

The cover illustration is by Karen Montgomery, based on an antique line engraving from Lydekker's *Royal Natural History*. The series design is by Edie Freedman, Ellie Volckhausen, and Karen Montgomery. The cover fonts are Gilroy Semibold and Guardian Sans. The text font is Adobe Minion Pro; the heading font is Adobe Myriad Condensed; and the code font is Dalton Maag's Ubuntu Mono.

O'REILLY®

Learn from experts.
Become one yourself.

60,000+ titles | Live events with experts | Role-based courses
Interactive learning | Certification preparation

**Try the O'Reilly learning platform
free for 10 days.**

www.ingramcontent.com/pod-product-compliance
Lightning Source LLC
Chambersburg PA
CBHW080716220326
41598CB00033B/5436